Worship Him Who Made . . .

A Daily Devotional

By David A. Steen

TEACH Services, Inc.
P U B L I S H I N G
www.TEACHServices.com • (800) 367-1844

Copyright© 2023 David A. Steen
Copyright© 2023 TEACH Services, Inc.
ISBN-13: 978-1-4796-1563-6 (Paperback)
ISBN-13: 978-1-4796-1564-3 (ePub)
Library of Congress Control Number: 2023900159

Published by

TEACH Services, Inc.
PUBLISHING
www.TEACHServices.com ● (800) 367-1844

Dedication

To Lynn, my high-fidelity lover, wife of 55 years—and joyfully counting. Her life of total commitment to altruistic service, both to me and others within her sphere of sweet influence, is a powerful testimony to her close daily walk with the God of love, truth, and freedom. Her inspiration, encouragement, and unfailing support have given me strength through the long lonely weeks and months of research and writing. I am, of all men, most blessed. She is truly a Proverbs 31 woman, for "many daughters have done well, but you [my love] excel them all" (verse 29, NKJV).

Author's Note
June, 2022

About 15 years ago, I was asked to write a daily devotional to be published by the Review and Herald Publishing Association. Appearing in late 2012, it was entitled *"God of Wonders: A Daily Devotional"* which sold out but was never reprinted. After extensive correcting, editing, and updating of the original text, this book is now being republished under a new title *"Worship Him Who Made..."*

Whether we realize it or not, we all worship–something or someone. And the reality is that we change, we become like what we worship and admire. As a result, we are changed either for good (2 Corinthians 3:18), or for bad (Psalm 115:4-8).

The crucially important end-time message of the three angels of Revelation 14 includes the injunction to worship the Creator who made heaven, earth, the sea, and the fountains of water–a sequence of words closely mirroring the wording of the creation based Sabbath command in Exodus 20:11 as well as other Biblical statements to worship, to praise, to recognize Him who made it all (Nehemiah 9:6, Psalm 69:34, 96:11, 135:6, 146:5-6, Acts 4:24, 14:15, and Revelation 10:6). I especially like the positive and negative, bullet proof, wording in John 1:3, "All things were made by him; and without him was not any thing made that was made."

So this daily devotional *"Worship Him Who Made..."* focuses on God's creation. What can we learn about the unfathomable beauty of the character of God from studying what He made? What can we learn from stories about how His creation affects the lives of His trusting children? How can we grow and mature in our personal friendship with the One who made us and whose greatest desire is for us to know, love, and trust Him?

The promise is, that when we see Jesus as He really is, we will be drawn to Him and we will be changed.

"But we all, with open face beholding as in a glass (mirror) the glory of the Lord, are changed into the same image from glory to glory, even as by the Spirit of the Lord." 2 Corinthians 3:18, KJV.

Beginnings

> In the beginning was the Word, and the Word was with God, and the Word was God. He was in the beginning with God. All things were made through Him, and without Him nothing was made that was made. In Him was life, and the life was the light of men. And the light shines in the darkness, and the darkness did not comprehend it. John 1:1-5, NKJV.

My guess is that you enjoy new beginnings about as much as I do. Plowing the garden in spring, taking out a clean piece of paper to write down a new idea or sketch a new plan, organizing a new semester of lesson plans, or (like today) standing on the threshold of a new year—all are examples of new beginnings that give hope, stir anticipation, and bring on excitement and expectations of the new and the better.

Since we are made in the image of God, He must enjoy new beginnings too. I can only imagine the excitement and expectation that thrilled through His mind as He planned and then created the heavens and the earth and all that in them is—making something from nothing as only God can do. He created all of this for His own pleasure (Rev. 4:11). And being in His image, we get great pleasure too by exploring and studying what He made. It will be our endless delight throughout eternity. Each daily devotional that follows is to give God glory by reveling in short stories and interesting discoveries about a few of God's creations and their surroundings. As I study and write, I can't help standing in awe of my Creator-God. I invite you to join me in exploring the mysteries and wonders of His created handiwork. In Colossians 1:15, 16 the apostle Paul described Jesus as the "image of the invisible God, the firstborn over all creation. For by Him all things were created that are in heaven and that are on earth, visible and invisible, whether thrones or dominions or principalities or powers. All things were created through Him and for Him" (NKJV). Then in the same breath (verses 19 and 20) Paul links the creation to reconciliation between humanity and God: "For it pleased the Father that in Him all the fullness should dwell, and by Him to reconcile all things to Himself, by Him, whether things on earth or things in heaven, having made peace through the blood of His cross" (NKJV).

I pray that as we explore details of the physical creation, we will worship Him who made, Him who paid the ultimate price, and Him who is altogether lovely and wondrous.

Lord Jesus, thank You for the blessing of new beginnings. I ask You to create in me a clean heart and renew a right spirit within me as I begin this new year.

January 2

One Empty Hummer

The Lord shall preserve your going out and your coming in from this time forth, and even forevermore. Ps. 121:8, NKJV.

As a biology teacher I often have people bring dead or dying animals to me. But I'll never forget the tearful student who brought a dead hummingbird into my office one bright, frosty spring morning. She said that she had found the tiny dead bird lying on the sidewalk.

As she laid the miniature body in my hand, I wondered, *Is it really dead*? Could it be that this little guy simply ran out of "gas" during his spring migration? It was early on a chilly morning, and many of the spring flowers had not opened yet. Well now, there was one way to find out.

So with hope in my heart I handed the little bird back to the student and asked her to come with me to the lab. We found a bag of white cane sugar and quickly mixed one teaspoon of sugar with four teaspoons of water. Then while cupping the bird in a warm hand we put its bill into the little pool of dissolved sugar water. For more than a few minutes we held it like that, the dead bird's long saber-like bill immersed in the pool of freshly made artificial nectar.

Then it happened. I saw it with my own eyes. The bill opened just a crack, and a thin dark tongue appeared momentarily. Then the tongue snaked out a few more times. With its eyes still closed and lying on its side in the girl's warm hand, the little hummer's tongue began to flick rapidly in and out as it drank in the life-giving nectar.

Before long it opened its eyes and sat upright, perched on her finger. We let the little bird tank up all it wanted before taking it back outside, where it flew off to continue its spring-day activities.

With a big grin on her face the young student went on her way, knowing that she had been God's fingers to aid one of His tiny creatures. She could so easily have tossed the "dead" little bird into the bushes. From all appearances the feebly flickering flame of life had been extinguished. But she cared for the tiny life and did what she could to find help and revive the flame. For that little bird, her caring made all the difference between life and death.

Lord, help me to remember that in all my comings and goings You watch over me every moment of every day. No matter what I do, You are there beside me. You know what I need and bring people into my life to supply it. Do You really care that much for me?

January 3

The Right Stuff

These all wait for You, that You may give them their food in due season. Ps. 104:27, NKJV.

Attracting colorful hummingbirds to back yard nectar feeders can become an all-consuming passion, especially if you live in the West, which has dozens of different iridescent hummers to observe. With just the ruby-throated hummer and an occasional rufus, easterners don't have the variety of hummingbird species, but attracting and feeding them can be just as fun. The big question is what to put in your nectar feeders.

It is really quite simple. Why not mimic the flowers that nectar feeders frequent most often? Sample some nectar yourself to see what it tastes like. It is a rather dilute solution ranging between 8 and 43 percent sucrose, with only traces of some minerals and amino acids. The wide difference in sucrose depends on the species of flower, the season, and even the time of day. One study of hummingbird-pollinated plants measured their sucrose composition as ranging between 16 and 28 percent, which is why most hummingbird nectar recipes call for one part regular granulated sugar to four parts of clean water, giving approximately a 20 percent sucrose solution. Like children, when given a choice, rufus hummers will choose the sweeter solutions of up to about 50 percent sucrose.

Do not use honey, which consists of fructose and glucose. Avoid using molasses or artificial sweeteners. The hummingbirds need sucrose and water. The four-to-one recipe is the right stuff for them, providing the water that they need along with the energy-giving calories. Their digestive system is set up to metabolize sucrose. Artificial sweeteners don't provide the calories. Honey isn't as digestible, and it promotes the growth of fungus, which can cause fatal tongue infections. You do not need to add artificial colors, which can even be harmful to them.

Some recipes call for boiling the sugar-water mixture to kill fungi and to dissolve the sugar. (Make sure to let it cool before putting it out.) Thoroughly clean your feeder every few days to prevent the growth of bacteria and fungi. But it is not necessary to boil. The first hummer tongue that flicks into your freshly boiled solution will contaminate it anyway. Why bother? Just start with clean drinking water.

Just as fruits and vegetables provide the perfect nutrients for us, hummers with their long bills and feathery tongues are perfectly suited to gather and process nectars. What a Creator!

Lord, Your provisions are perfect. I worship You as my wondrous Creator and constant provider.

A Fine-tuned Universe

For I am the Lord, I do not change; therefore you are not consumed. Mal. 3:6, NKJV.

Have you tried to imagine what getting ready for Sabbath would be like if gravity did not exist? Everything in the house would be drifting chaotically. Dust wouldn't settle to the floor where you could vacuum it up. Casserole ingredients wouldn't stay in the casserole pan. Even the water that you washed your hands with would hover around the room in soapy wet blobs. What a mess! Thank You, Lord, for gravity. The fact is that we can be thankful for many more physical laws or constants. I understand that scientists recognize at least two dozen dimensionless constants that are finely tuned in order for life to exist. For example, the size of the charge on the electron must be just so, and the proton-to-electron mass ratio has to be just right. Those are a couple constants that most of us don't ever bother with. We take it for granted that things will work. But if these constants were different than they are by just a tiny fraction, life would not exist in our universe. That means we wouldn't be here getting ready for Sabbath. Can you handle hearing about just two more constants? There is a fine structure constant, a strong coupling constant, and a cosmological constant. (OK, make that three.) As I understand it, the fine structure constant describes the strength of electromagnetic interactions between particles. The strong coupling constant depicts the intensity of interactions between two or more objects. The cosmological constant is an important factor in understanding gravity, which keeps water flowing down your drain instead of floating around the room. I could cite several more, but you get the idea.

The concept here is that physicists have discovered a whole lot of factors that strongly suggest that the universe is "designed" to support life as we know it. If any one of those factors goes out of whack, life itself would cease to exist. Such knowledge is just too wonderful for me. God, in His infinite love and wisdom, created a place for us that is "very good" operating on laws that don't change. Though we can't see such laws and constants, they are vital to everything that we do see and enjoy. And then He gave us the Sabbath to celebrate the Creator and the freedom to live and to choose who we worship. What a God.

Lord, thank You for Your creative word and for Your finely tuned creation. As we prepare for and enter the Sabbath rest, we do so with profound praise and thanksgiving.

Sabbath Praise

You are worthy, O Lord, to receive glory and honor and power; for You created all things, and by Your will they exist and were created. Rev. 4:11, NKJV.

T he Sabbath is a precious temple in time for us who believe in, know about, and honor the Creator of all. Just think, could there be a better way to "remember now thy Creator" than a special day each week? When I think of what our Creator has done, my heart bursts with gratitude and awe. Like Moses, David, and John, I can't restrain myself from singing His praise "for you make me glad by your deeds, Lord; I sing for joy at what your hands have done. How great are your works, Lord, how profound your thoughts!" (Ps. 92:4, 5, NIV). Lord, I marvel at this round ball of rock, dirt, and water that I live on. Whether I walk, drive, or fly from place to place on this globe, it seems so big, so solid, and so secure. But when I see it from space clothed in its coverings of green plants, blue waters, tan-and-brown rocks, it looks much smaller. And those who study such things tell me that earth is but a mere speck of dust compared to the galaxy that You have placed us in. They go on to describe untold billions and trillions of galaxies as far out as we can see. There seems to be no end of it. Lord, my mind simply can't possibly fathom the dimensions of space, time, and energy in which You reign supreme. Yet the Bible writers tell us that You know each entity of Your creation and call them all by name. You even number the hairs of my head!

Lord, there is nobody or nothing that I can compare You with. You are my incomparable God. For Your dominion includes not only the unimaginably large but also the whirling solar system-like domain of the minuscule atom with its orbiting electrons and all of the component parts of the atomic nucleus. I stand in awe of the symmetry of the very large and the very small.

The Sabbath is a precious temple in time for us who believe in, know about, and honor the Creator of all.

There is nowhere I can go where Your creative powers are not on display. "Do you not know? Have you not heard? The Lord is the everlasting God, the Creator of the ends of the earth. He will not grow tired or weary, and his understanding no one can fathom. He gives strength to the weary and increases the power of the weak" (Isa. 40:28, 29, NIV). "So do not fear, for I am with you; do not be dismayed, for I am your God. I will strengthen you and help you; I will uphold you with my righteous right hand" (Isa. 41:10, NIV). "Turn to me and be saved, all you ends of the earth; for I am God, and there is no other" (Isa. 45:22, NIV).

O Lord, I worship You on Your holy day because You asked me to be here to honor You as my Creator. Because I love You, Your wish is my command.

Super Diffuser

I will also make you a light for the Gentiles, that my salvation may reach to the ends of the earth. Isa. 49:6, NIV.

I am not sure why, but I think that we all have a fascination with things that glow in the dark. I remember that, as a child growing up, I had a nightlight inside a mollusk shell. The soft dim glow of that shell kept nighttime monsters at bay. For biologists, critters that make their own light hold great interest. Most creatures that produce light have translucent skin or transparent membranes that let the light shine out to help find food, attract mates, scare away predators, etc.

Marine biologists Dimitri Deheyn and Nerida Wilson, from the Scripps Institute of Oceanography, recently studied *Hinea brasiliana*, a bioluminescent snail that they collected from rocks of the intertidal zone in Australia. A rather smallish snail, the clusterwink snail perhaps acquired its name because it gathers in clusters and winks its light on and off. With its light on, what one sees is a whole snail shell lit up with a radiant fluorescent green. It can rapidly turn the light on and off, much like the new LED taillights in modern autos. When Deheyn and Wilson checked it out, they found that the snails produced light from a small region of their tiny body always kept buried deeply inside the opaque and light-yellow pigmented shell. What made them turn their light on? And how did it shine so brightly through that hard protective shell?

Various experiments showed that the snails lit up best when other critters bumped into them or otherwise touched them—a surprise because this type of light switch mechanism is fairly rare in other bioluminescent organisms. Could it be the snail's way of calling for help, signaling for predators to come eat what's bugging them?

The biggest mystery, however, was learning how that tiny light source could illuminate the entire shell. By shining different colors of light on the shell, Deheyn and Wilson learned that, with the one exception of the blue-green color, the hard snail shell would let all other colors pass right on through. The blue-green color, however, diffused throughout the entire shell, giving it a remarkably bright glow. The researchers learned, too, that the yellowish shell did not change or color-shift the blue-green color in any way. It diffuses that particular light frequency eight times better than any commercially available diffuser and spreads it to an area 10 times larger. You can bet that scientists are closely studying the molecular properties of the shell to discover how to improve commercial light diffusers.

Lord, how can I be a super diffuser of the light from Your Word and the light of Your love? My desire is to be effective in letting Your light shine to others.

The Never-Been-Ridden Donkey Colt

When they brought the colt to Jesus and threw their cloaks over it, he sat on it. Mark 11:7, NIV.

Where I grew up in Ethiopia, domesticated donkeys were quite common. I would frequently see a donkey driver with a half-dozen donkeys heavily loaded with firewood or coal clip-clopping to market. Occasionally I would see adults riding donkeys, their feet nearly touching the ground on each side. The friendly little animals stand a little more than three feet at the shoulder. Since their size can vary drastically, however, some donkeys can be almost the size of small horses at four and a half feet. With very large ears, donkeys are good at hearing predators, and the ears presumably help them keep cool in the hot arid climates in which they live. Donkeys must have a tough digestive system, because they can eat almost anything and are very efficient at extracting water and nourishment from it. Thus they require relatively little food and can go long periods without water.

All donkeys have a dark-colored stripe that runs down the middle of their back. Some have a dark stripe across the shoulders, giving them the mark of a cross. They have a light-colored nose, a light ring around the eye, light fur inside their ears, and a light underside.

For a time people considered owning them to be a sign of wealth. However by the time of Christ the animals were the most likely form of transportation for poor people. When pregnant with Jesus, Mary rode to Bethlehem on a donkey. Chances are that Jesus had ridden donkeys often as a youngster, so to ride one during His triumphal entry to Jerusalem was probably not new. His choice of a young donkey suggests that Jesus was coming in peace. Warriors rode horses into battle. Though the Jews were praying for a conquering hero, Jesus was establishing a different kind of kingdom. The symbolism is gentle, common, lowly, and peaceful.

Though donkeys seem oblivious to it, what an honor to their kind to be selected to carry the Creator of our world on not one but two momentous events—first to His impending birth, and then again on His triumphal entry into Jerusalem, shortly before His crucifixion.

Lord, even if ridiculed for being one of Your followers, I choose to carry Your love in my heart and Your Word on my tongue as I live a gentle and peaceful life for You today.

Wawaiah (Pronounced wah-way-yah)

I said, "You are my servant"; I have chosen you and have not rejected you. Isa. 41:9, NIV.

My earliest memories of life include Wawaiah, standing there with a big ear-to-ear grin, anticipating my every need, and quickly acting to help. I was a missionaries' kid growing up in Ethiopia. Wawaiah was our houseboy, a servant in the truest sense of the word. My parents had chosen him to work for them. He must have been a teenager at the time. Uneducated, desperately poor, thin, clothed in rags, but bush-smart and with a huge heart, Wawaiah seemed to know instinctively what it meant to serve. When my missionary family came into his life in Gimbie, life was no longer about him. For him, it was all about the missionary family with the two little boys that he served, and serve he did, with style and panache. He seemed ever-present, ever ready to help. I remember him watching us intently, and listening carefully. Our slightest wish was his command, and he would spring into action. It was obvious that Wawaiah derived great pleasure in serving and serving well. That became his life. And his relationship with us made a huge difference both in his life and in ours.

My family took care of Wawaiah. He no longer had to wonder where his next meal was coming from or where he would sleep. It wasn't long before he was well dressed, healthy, and successful by local standards. As he served generously, my parents responded in kind.

According to Isaiah, God chose me to serve Him. The parallel is powerful. Before God came into my life, I was poor, lost, wretched, spiritually blind, and naked. God chose me to be His servant. I consider that to be a privilege and a profound honor. Suddenly my life is no longer about me, but rather about how I, as His servant, can best serve my Lord and Master. If I have learned anything from Wawaiah, I too should be ever watchful, alert to my Master's beck and call, always on duty. For task instructions, I read His Word and listen carefully to His voice in my heart. Then it is an automatic "Yes, my Lord—anything You wish, my Lord—as You wish, my Lord." Isaiah continues in verse 10: "So do not fear, for I am with you; do not be dismayed, for I am your God. I will strengthen you and help you; I will uphold you with my righteous right hand" (NIV).

My Maker and my King, thank You for choosing me to serve You. Thank You for strengthening, helping, and upholding me in that service.

January 9

Free to Choose

How long will you waver between two opinions? If the Lord is God, follow him; but if Baal is God, follow him. 1 Kings 18:21, NIV. You adulterous people, don't you know that friendship with the world means enmity against God? Therefore, anyone who chooses to be a friend of the world becomes an enemy of God. James 4:4, NIV.

When I stop and ponder deeply how the Creator chooses to interact with you and me, it takes my breath away. The source-of-life Creator is all-powerful, all-knowing, all-loving, and everywhere present. He gave us life, and then chooses to love you and me unconditionally and have a close personal relationship with us, His dearly beloved. But He doesn't force, cajole, or even coerce us to have that relationship with Him, one that He longs for. Rather, He leaves us completely free to choose Him—but only if we want to. Since He is the source of life, becoming His friend leads to even greater life. But refusing a relationship with Him is, in fact, selecting death. Embedded within each one of us is a still small voice (moral compass) to help us choose life rather than death. It gives us reliable directions as long as we regularly download updates through Bible study and prayer. If we choose not to download updates and choose to ignore the directions, the voice tends to go away and not bother us anymore.

Sometimes I wonder why God doesn't simply give us a DVD that shows us how and when He created this world. No doubt He has even better wireless technology than we do, making it easy for Him to give each of us a personal, full-color, 3-D, surround-sound-with-mega-bass movie of what He did at Creation. Oh, I can feel the floor shaking as the thunder crashes on the fifth day. Of course the movie would have full documentation. With that information there would be no question that God is the Creator-God. The entire devil-designed flimflam yarn of naturalistic origins wouldn't stand a chance, and all of us would be convinced of the Creator's authenticity and rally around Him, electing to have that personal relationship.

He gave us life, and then chooses to love you and me unconditionally and have a close personal relationship with us, His dearly beloved.

But then I realize that this kind of proof would take away real choice. I would be forced to decide. But a true lover never forces. The beauty is that God gives me enough evidence to choose Him if I like, but He will not erase all doubt. I get to decide for myself. What a lover!

Lord Jesus, what a freedom is mine when I realize that I am free to choose to believe or not. Just now, for this day, I choose to believe.

January 10

Purr Pleasure

The Lord delights in those who fear him, who put their hope in his unfailing love. Ps. 147:11, NIV.

No doubt you have listened to the contented purring of a house cat and wondered, *How do they do that? Where does that low fluttering noise come from?* Since there are about 70 different breeds of domesticated cats with an estimated world population of more than a half billion domesticated felines, scientific studies of cats should be easy to do. In fact, many of you have no doubt dissected formalin-preserved cats in cat lab during a college anatomy class. So if there were a special purr-generating apparatus we should know about it—right? But what makes the sound of a purring cat and even the reason that it purrs remains shrouded in mystery.

Just put your ear to your purring cat, and you will hear the sound during both breathing in and breathing out—a defining characteristic of purring. Some cats purr so loudly that you can hear them across the room (or across the yard in the case of the cheetah). Not only do we not know for sure how cats produce the rattle-like sounds—we are still not certain which members of the cat family can or cannot purr.

People have hypothesized lots of reasons as to why cats might purr. But since we can't ask them why they do it nor can we get inside their head, all we can do is guess. Could it be a way for kittens and mother cats to communicate, for injured or cornered cats to signal that they are not going to fight anymore? Cat lovers, of course, know that cats purr because they are contented and find great delight in having their ears scratched, their head and back petted, and their belly rubbed gently. For me, the sweet vibrations and sounds of a purring cat snuggled in my lap give me great pleasure.

I sometimes wonder, "*Do I rob God of pleasure by my prideful self-denial, by my tight-lipped piety?*" Malachi 3:7-12 says: "Return to me, and I will return to you . . . Then all the nations will call you blessed, for yours will be a delightful land" (NIV). Clearly the Lord desires my happiness. John 17:13 shows Him as wanting us to have "the full measure of my joy" (NIV). Let us worship the giver of every good gift with our loud and contented purring. With great gratitude, with guilt-free exuberance, revel in the joy of the one who lavishes us with His love and goodness.

Lord, I trust You fully, knowing that You have supplied all my needs and have given me more than I could ask or imagine. Hear the purring of my heart as worship to You.

Marriage as a Model

That is why a man leaves his father and mother and is united to his wife, and they become one flesh. Gen. 2:24, NIV.

The story of the first marriage is an integral part of the Creation story. God had just finished making "every beast of the field" and all the "birds of the air" (Gen. 2:20, NKJV), and He brought them to the newly created Adam to see what he would name them. Whatever Adam decided on, that was its name. During this process, Adam couldn't help noticing that all of the birds and beasts had male and female counterparts. Where was Adam's other half? So the Lord administered the first anesthetic and performed the first organ donor surgery by removing a rib and seamlessly closing the wound. From Adam's rib the Lord God made the first woman and brought her to him.

I try to imagine the tenderness and love between that first couple during the days and weeks of their honeymoon. How carefully did they listen to each other in their animated conversation? Did they share their deepest feelings? Were they closely focused and attentive in meeting each other's needs? Did they get instructions from God Himself? I can almost hear the Lord telling Adam that his job was to love Eve. He lets Adam know that it won't be easy to determine what feels like love to her. However, that will be his happy task. Figure it out and then love her dearly. God must have said, "Do it for Me." And to Eve, God explains that what Adam needed most is respect. Again, that will be Eve's task, to ascertain what respect is to Adam and then give him lots of it. "Do it for Me."

And so marriage becomes a model. The mysterious bond between a loving husband and a respectful wife (Eph. 5:33) is the best illustration that we have of the love bond between Christ and His people. I try to get my mind around what this means. When my wife and I are experiencing and enjoying the closest intimacy possible in a marriage, Christ is there letting me know that this is the kind of relationship that He wants to have with me. "As a bridegroom rejoices over his bride, so will your God rejoice over you" (Isa. 62:5, NIV). Marriage is indeed a precious gift of Creation.

Is it any wonder that God hates divorce? Or that the arch-deceiver is doing his best to wreck every marriage that he can?

Lord of love and marriage, help me to carefully follow Your marriage instructions so that I can have a model marriage to Your honor and glory.

Dust to Dust

By the sweat of your brow you will eat your food until you return to the ground, since from it you were taken; for dust you are and to dust you will return. Gen. 3:19. NIV.

You know, of course, that God formed Adam from dust—the Hebrew word for "dust" also means "dirt." When we die, our body will recycle back to dust again. Everybody knows that. But I learned something recently that I found hard to believe. Estimates vary widely, but it is safe to say that much (possibly 80 percent) of the dust that floats in the sunbeams and settles on the furniture in my house is my skin cells that have flaked off. What this means is that, little by little, every day, I am constantly returning to the dust of the ground. You see, it takes only a few days for the whole outer layer of skin to flake off, producing almost 30 grams of dust per day. Depending on how many people and pets live in the house, house dust can contain lots of dead skin cells.

Now, here is the scary part. Dust mites—tiny critters that you can see only with a microscope—live by eating these flaked-off skin cells. For most people the mites are completely harmless, and it's a good thing for us that they don't carry diseases. Most of the time we don't even know they are around. But when dust mites grow, they shed their skin too, and they are not housebroken, so they defecate all over. Some people are really allergic to the waste products and skin of the tiny critters. For people who are allergic, mites can be a huge problem, and such individuals can easily tell when the creatures are around. Their eyes itch, their noses itch and run, and they might have a hard time breathing. Maybe you have such allergies.

Whether or not you have them, allergies can be really annoying, as can many other challenges and losses in life. Are you finding yourself arguing and fighting? Maybe someone in the family is getting a divorce. Have some of your friends turned against you? Quite often difficulties, problems, and irritations can trip us up and lay us low in the dust (see Ps. 119:25). But the psalmist goes on to say (verses 26-32) that even though my soul is really tired, I can go to God's Word for strength and courage. Best of all, His Word sets my heart free. I hope that sounds as encouraging to you as it does to me.

Jesus, thank You for Your Word, which gives me strength and frees my heart.

Lessons From Leprosy

A man with leprosy came and knelt before him and said, "Lord, if you are willing, you can make me clean." Jesus reached out his hand and touched the man. "I am willing," he said. "Be clean!" Immediately he was cleansed of his leprosy. Matt. 8:2, 3, NIV.

Bible translators apparently didn't know about vitiligo, an autoimmune disease that shows itself as white patches on the skin where pigment cells have quit working. If translators had known about the condition, the "lepers" that Jesus healed, and Miriam, and Naaman, may have had a different biblical (medical) diagnosis. Leprosy, now called Hansen's disease, may lighten the skin slightly but is better known for the awful body deformities it causes. You probably have never seen anybody with Hansen's disease. I have, and it's not pretty. I first saw the man painfully hobbling with a cane that he struggled to hold with his fingerless hands. His face, bubbled with great blisters, seemed frozen in a painful grimace behind sightless eyes. He had missing toes and lips. I felt so sorry for him. Disease had made him an outcast of society.

Hansen's is one of the oldest-known diseases, with some of the first written records about it dating back to 600 years before Christ. Gerhard Henrik Armauer Hansen, a Norwegian physician, first described the bacteria, *Mycobacterium leprae*, that causes the condition. The bacterium is now well known and carefully studied. Its 3,268,203 base pairs of DNA have been sequenced, and we now have good antibiotics that reliably cure the disease. Left untreated, the bacteria cause nerve damage that eventually results in horrible disfigurement.

Meanwhile, the vitiligo that turns patches of skin white in about 2 percent of the population is quite harmless except for the stigma that goes along with it. Remember how ancient society treated lepers in Bible stories? People with patchy skin are stigmatized even today. So what is the lesson? Jesus is willing to cure every disease. He reaches out and touches us with His powerful love that cures the medical problems of our broken-down world, heals the mental anguish of every stigma, and even frees us from the desire to break His laws.

Lord Jesus, are You still willing to touch all the sickness in my life and make me clean? Is Your healing touch still immediate? Lord, I believe! Help my unbelief.

Antidote for Anger

David burned with anger against the man and said to Nathan, "As surely as the Lord lives, the man who did this must die!" 2 Sam. 12:5, NIV.

When was the last time that you got really angry? Did you punch a hole in the wall—or maybe it was somebody's face? Did you, as did King David, want to kill somebody?

I remember getting so angry at my brother that I threw rocks at him. Luckily for him, he was good at dodging. Once I threw a pillow—backhanded— and accidentally smashed my elbow into the edge of an open door. It hit my funny bone (the ulnar nerve) so hard that it is still tender even now years later. Every time I feel that sensitive elbow it reminds me to cool down and take it easy.

What if you had spent a lot of time on an important assignment at school? You did the best job possible. As you proudly laid the masterpiece on the teacher's desk a whole day before the essay was due, you just knew that you had an A. Then a few days later you got your paper back and learned that it had been graded by "a fellow student." A big F decorated your paper. Scrawled across the title page were big, bright-red letters that said, "This is one of the worst essays I ever read." Would you have felt really hurt . . . and angry?

This is exactly what happened to 700 undergraduate students who didn't know that they were subjects of a research study on anger. The researchers told half the students to work out their anger on a punching bag and the other half to distract themselves by reading a story or listening to music. Then the angry students had a chance to talk to the "student" who had supposedly done the grading. Those who had been punching the bag were much more likely to shout and say angry words than the ones who had been quietly reading or listening to music.

Things will happen to you today that will stir up your anger. Life is just not fair. The wisest man who ever lived said that gentle answers turn away wrath, but harsh words stir up anger. The effective antidote for anger is not only biblical, but research shows that it works. So chill out for a while, give a soft answer, and watch the anger melt away.

My gentle Jesus, put soft answers into my mouth today. I can't do it on my own.

January 15

Blackpoll Warblers

Look at the birds of the air; they do not sow or reap or store away in barns, and yet your heavenly Father feeds them. Matt. 6:26, NIV.

The tiny blackpoll warbler landed exhausted on the bare spit of rocky sand after a stormy crossing of Lake Erie. For now it was safe on Point Pelee, the southernmost point of mainland Canada. Thousands of migrating birds funnel through this narrow point, taking advantage of an important resting and refueling stop on their long northward migration to summer nesting grounds. Blackpolls, named for the patch of black feathers on the top of their head, spend the winter in South America but migrate back to the spruce forests of northern Canada where they raise their young.

The crossing of Lake Erie seems to be a problem only when a storm gives the tiny birds a strong headwind. Though it is hard for them, these birds regularly fly across nearly 2,000 miles of the Atlantic Ocean from the northern coast of South America to Florida. We know it is hard because during the journey blackpolls can lose almost half their body weight. So every chance they get they take advantage of prevailing winds to help them on their way.

With one of the highest-pitched songs of any songbird, the blackpoll's quick tsit tsit tsit calls have such a high frequency that some people have a hard time even hearing them. Blackpolls communicate with each other as they feed on insects and spiders.

As you can guess, migrating birds face many hazards. Some predatory birds that catch and eat other birds time the raising of their young to take advantage of the increased food supply as migrants pass through their area. Bright lights, especially during foggy conditions, confuse and mesmerize migrants so that they crash into lighted buildings, towers, or monuments.

The Bible is clear—God cares for even the cheap little throwaway birds. But He cares for us ever so much more.

Getting enough food along the way can be a big problem, but birds do not worry—they simply depend on God to provide for all their needs. The Bible is clear—God cares for even the cheap little throwaway birds. But He cares for us ever so much more. He knows every detail of my life, and He wants only the best for me.

Creator God, have You really counted all the hairs of my head? I am confident then that You know all about me and that I can trust You to care for my needs this day.

January 16

Ultra-high Mileage

It is hidden from the eyes of every living thing, concealed even from the birds in the sky. Job 28:21, NIV.

D o you have any idea how many different kinds of birds exist on our planet? I have no doubt that the answer to that question depends on whom you ask. Ornithologists who study birds carefully have recorded nearly 9,000 different species of birds. About half of those birds migrate each year to spend the winter in milder climates, where food is more available.

The tiny blackpoll warbler is one of the most common birds in northern boreal forests of Canada. In summer it ranges throughout most of Alaska, across the northern tiers of all of Canada's provinces, down east through the Midwestern United States, and all of the eastern United States and Canada. When it starts getting cold, this tiny bird, that weighs less than a half ounce (approximately the weight of two nickels and one dime), fuels up by adding fruit and berries to its normal diet of spiders and insects.

They feed continuously until the winds are just right. Then they launch their long flight across the Atlantic Ocean. Whether guided by stars, magnetic sensors in their brain cells, or perhaps by the angle of ultraviolet light at sunset, the tiny birds somehow navigate nonstop for 80 to 90 hours. During the trip, how do they know when to climb to 20,000 feet while flying over Antigua? Who instructs them to fly at 2,500 feet for both the first and last parts of their journey? Apparently they vary their altitude to catch the best tailwinds and conserve their energy as they wing southward at about 25 miles per hour.

Ornithologists have calculated exercise equivalents for humans. Try running four-minute miles for 80 hours. That is the best metabolic approximation for the blackpolls' trip. Their fuel efficiency, if compared to gasoline consumption, calculates out to 720,000 miles per gallon.

No matter which migrating bird we choose to study, we find ourselves continually amazed at the precision and beauty of each factor in their journey. What determines the crucial itinerary for preparation, fueling, and departure? How do the birds navigate with such accuracy? How do they use energy so efficiently during their long flights? The latter question makes me wonder how I can learn to be more effective in service to God. Where can I get this kind of wisdom? How can I receive this kind of transformation? (See Rom. 12:1, 2.)

Lord, like the birds, I don't have a clue as to how to serve You best. Transform my mind.

The Sun Seeker

So God created the great creatures of the sea and every living thing with which the water teems and moves about in it, according to their kinds, and every winged bird according to its kind. And God saw that it was good. Gen. 1:21, NIV.

The arctic tern is a beautiful bird that spends most of its life flying over the ocean in search of food. As birds go, it is medium sized, mostly white, with light-gray upper parts but with a striking black cap pulled way down below its black eyes. It has a bright-red bill, tiny red legs, and red webbed feet. Since it spends most of its life in the air, you can't miss the fact that it has a forked tail. Should you put an average-sized arctic tern on one side of a balance, you will need about 40 pennies on the other side to make it level out. Hold 40 pennies in your hand. They weigh only 3.5 ounces.

Arctic terns enjoy perpetual summer. When it is summer in the far north, they are there raising their young on a rocky beach of northern Greenland or Iceland. Then, when summer starts to leave, they and their youngsters begin heading toward the Weddell Sea in Antarctica some 12,000 miles to the south. Research data from minuscule data loggers strapped to their legs show that they take big looping S curves across the ocean. By the time they arrive in the far south summer has arrived, so they spend endless daylight hours there flying and eating. Their lifestyle gives the arctic tern the distinction of being the one animal that enjoys the most daylight hours of any creature on earth. Because they have to travel so far, they get a second award: Arctic terns log the most mileage during their annual migrations. Researchers knew that the terns were flying at least 24,000-30,000 miles each year in their pole-to-pole-to-pole round trips. But the data loggers showed that they were covering more like 40,000 to 50,000 miles each year. Since the birds live for about 30 years, they probably fly about 1.5 million miles during their lifetime—an amazing statistic for a bird that weighs in at only 40 pennies. What is more, researchers discovered that, even though terns do not travel together, they all departed their wintering areas, crossed the equator, left ocean feeding and stopover sites, and arrived at their summer sites within days of each other—not in sight of each other but doing things together.

Lord of all, Creator of the arctic tern, how did You program these amazing fliers to be at the right place at the right time? Where do You want me to show up today? Just tell me the time and the place. I too seek the Son and long to bask in the light of His glory.

Roaring Lions

Be alert and of sober mind. Your enemy the devil prowls around like a roaring lion looking for someone to devour. 1 Peter 5:8, NIV.

I well remember lying in bed at night as a young boy, listening to lions roaring outside our home. My parents were missionaries in Ethiopia. Dad started the hospital in Gimbie, deep in the bush where, in the late 1940s, one could occasionally hear lions at night.

The roar would usually start as a deep bellowing grunting sound that would rise in pitch and loudness. Again and again the roar would travel through the still night air, announcing a male lion on the prowl or defending his territory. The roar was loud and could easily carry for three to six miles, depending on the night breezes. Since lions can hear a lot better than we can, the roar is the way that both male and female lions communicate with each other over long distances.

Lions are the second-largest of the big cats, exceeded in size only by tigers. Extremely social animals, they live in groups called a pride. From the safety of a car I remember watching a pride of lions sleeping under the shade of a thorn tree. When we were lucky, we would see them licking each other or rubbing their heads on each other. If you have house cats, no doubt you have had your cat rub its head on you too.

Lions are amazingly skilled hunters. Females get more practice than males because they tend to be the providers for the pride. Though they usually hunt alone, groups of females may go out at night looking for prey. When they locate an antelope or gazelle or zebra, they will split up and set a trap. With cunning, cooperation, and a roar they will drive the startled prey into the jaws of silently waiting members of the pride.

The devil and his gang of fallen angels prowl around like lions, searching for hapless victims to ambush. Though at times we smell the hot breath and see the glistening teeth of the roaring lions with their mouths wide open against us (Ps. 22:13), we need not fear. "The Lord is my strength . . . and he will rescue me from the mouth of the lion . . . for dominion belongs to the Lord" (see verses 19-28, NIV).

Thank You, Lord, for being my strength and safety. I trust in You today.

The Mane Story

Therefore, as God's chosen people, holy and dearly loved, clothe yourselves with compassion, kindness, humility, gentleness and patience. Col. 3:12, NIV.

U nless you know exactly where and what to look for, it is sometimes hard to figure out if a house cat is male or female. Not so with lions. Lions are the only cats that have males that appear distinctly different than females. Can you guess what that characteristic is?

We admire the magnificent mane of golden hair tipped with black and marvel at what a regal look it gives to a male lion. In our mind's eye we see the lion perched on a prominent outcrop of rock surveying the landscape at sunset, its mane blowing in the breeze. No wonder people refer to the lion as the king of beasts.

Scientists look at that mane and wonder why the male has a thick mane of hair on his head and neck. What could its purpose be? It certainly isn't there to keep them warm, because they live in hot climates. A long, dark mane absorbs more heat and is hard on lions during the hottest part of the year. (Lions do grow longer manes when the temperatures are cooler.) Does the lion's mane protect his neck when fighting other males? Scientists conclude probably not, because while all types of cats are armed with lethal teeth and claws, only lions have manes. Nor do researchers find any evidence that lions without manes have more wounds to their head and neck. Thus the mane is probably not for protection in battle either. So what is its purpose?

After many years of careful study, biologists now believe that a lion's mane gives other lions a message. When a lion has a long dark mane, it lets females know that he is strong and healthy. It attracts females, while *How do you signal others to let them know that you are a Christian?* males keep their distance. Males choose not to fight a lion with a long dark mane because it is a clear signal of his victory in battle.

How do you signal others to let them know that you are a Christian? Is it the way you dress or what you eat, or the fact that you carry your Bible? Some might think so. But the clearest signal that you can give is the way you treat others.

King of kings and Lord of lords, may my love, kindness, and compassion for others be as easy to detect as the mane on a lion. Empower me to be a good ambassador for You today.

Nature's Nonstick Surface

Wash away all my iniquity and cleanse me from my sin. Ps. 51:2, NIV.

W hy does it rain just after I wash my car? And why does the rain get my car dirty again so quickly? You know how it goes. You get the car (or windows in your home, or your outdoor furniture, or . . . well you name it) all shiny and clean, and along comes the rain. And just like magic, your stuff gets all rain spattered and spotted, and you have to do it all over again if you want to keep it looking nice.

I guess we all need to take a lesson from the lowly lotus plant (*Nelumbo nucifera*) that lives way down in the mud and the slime of lowland tropical wetlands. Although it rains frequently there, creating plenty of mud and dirt to splatter around, lotus leaves and flowers stay pristine clean and beautiful. So pretty, in fact, that lotus (or sacred lotus, as it is often called) is the national flower of India and Vietnam. So how does the lotus manage to stay clean after a rain when other things, such as cars and windows and furniture seem to get mud-spattered and dirty?

That is a question that scientists have been asking and researching. After it lands on most surfaces, a raindrop flattens, and the surface gets wet. On waxy plant leaves (or a freshly waxed car) the water will bead up, and most of the drop will roll off. But even waxy leaves and cars do get wet, which tends to hold the dust and dirt and leave watermarks behind. The lotus leaf doesn't look or feel waxy, but water beads up on its surface big-time. On a lotus leaf a water drop stands tall almost like a marble and rolls around on the surface like one. It just doesn't flatten out and get the leaf wet. As a result, water drops roll off the leaf, carrying away dust, dirt, or pollen and always leaving the leaf clean and dry. It is known as the lotus effect.

The secret is in the structure of the leaf surface that we can see only with a high-powered electron microscope. The electron microscope shows that the leaf surface is actually rough because of extremely tiny pegs that stick straight up. So the physics of the nanometer-sized pegs makes water drops bead up and roll off, keeping the lotus leaf clean.

Lord, please give me the nonstick "pegs" of humility, earnest prayer, sincerity in seeking Your face, and a resolute turning from my wicked ways. I need Your cleansing.

Cells on the Move

For I myself am a man under authority, with soldiers under me. I tell this one, "Go," and he goes; and that one, "Come," and he comes. I say to my servant, "Do this," and he does it. Matt. 8:9, NIV.

I teach a university course called Tissue Culture. My students and I grow all kinds of cells in specially designed plastic culture flasks that keep the cells happy with perfect growing conditions. The cells are extremely interesting to watch, because they move and respond to the changing conditions that we provide for them.

The beauty and complexity of cellular movement and activity stun those who study it. Many cells are constantly on the move, squirming, ruffling their edges, squeezing into new regions, or chasing down bacteria. That cells move is not news, because even in the 1600s Antonie van Leeuwenhoek wrote in his notebook that he saw "pleasing and nimble" movements after squinting into his homemade microscope. (Google "Cell Movement" and click on "video" to see some exciting action.) Only recently, with several new tools in our labs, are we now beginning to find out how cells move.

Inside a cell we see frantic activity, something like a construction site where a huge building is being put together overnight. Or we could describe it as a humming and highly coordinated beehive. Or it has similarities to a bustling city. It is like all of these. Yet it is also like none of them because it is so incredibly tiny, the activity is unimaginably fast, and the director of all the precisely orchestrated activity are long stringy molecules of DNA. Under the direction of DNA a cell builds and dismantles thousands of proteins and moves them around to accomplish the cell's various functions. And because of the precision and orderliness of such moving proteins in cells we have life and can think about life and worship the Creator of life.

When my life becomes chaotic or appears dead and lifeless, it is usually because I am not listening to or following the instructions of the One who knows the desires of my heart. Jesus was "astonished" by the faith of the centurion, because he understood that orders were to be followed.

Lord, fill my heart with trust as I follow the instructions of Your still small voice and get my life moving in Your direction today.

January 22

Cleaner Wrasse

Each of you should use whatever gift you have received to serve others, as faithful stewards of God's grace in its various forms. 1 Peter 4:10, NIV.

I once had the privilege of snorkeling in the Red Sea and observing the bluestreak cleaner wrasse fish doing their thing. In amazement I watched as a big grouper edged into a cleaning station where several of the brightly colored wrasse waited. The grouper opened its mouth and flared its gills, and the wrasse swam into the monstrous mouth cavity and began cleaning the teeth and picking off dead skin and mucous around the lips, gills, and fins of a fish much larger than they were. The grouper is a slow swimming fish that does not chase its food. Rather, it waits quietly for other fish or crabs or octopi to come near, then it suddenly opens its mouth and with a powerful sucking action it simply vacuums the hapless prey into it. So I stared, fascinated, as the tiny fish swam in and out of the grouper's mouth and gills, providing a service to the larger fish. In return the grouper didn't eat or even snack on them. It seemed to know that the wrasse were helping it to have a healthier life. When two different species aid each other like this, biologists dub the relationship as "mutualism."

In reality we were created to serve others. It is a fact that our greatest joy as humans comes when we help others with no thought of gain for ourselves. We call this kind of unselfish service altruistic behavior. It would be nice to think that the bluestreak cleaner wrasse are giving altruistic service to the grouper and other fish that come to their cleaning station. They aren't, though, because the wrasse actually benefit. Cleaning other fish is the way they survive—by eating parasites, bits of food particles in the teeth of the bigger fish, and dead skin and mucous on those big fish that cruise in for a cleaning.

Martin Luther King, Jr., said, "Everybody can be great . . . because anybody can serve. You don't have to have a college degree to serve. You don't have to make your subject and verb agree to serve. You only need a heart full of grace. A soul generated by love."

Our Father in heaven, bring me an opportunity for altruistic service today. And then help me to recognize that opportunity and to serve joyfully as if I am serving You.

Singing Trees

Let all the trees of the forest sing for joy. Let all creation rejoice before the Lord, for he comes. Ps. 96:12, 13, NIV.

I just can't be down in the dumps after reading Psalm 96. What an inspiring song of wondrous praise to our God and Creator! As a plant biologist I frequently wonder how the trees of the forest can sing for joy (see also 1 Chron. 16:33) or clap their hands (Isa. 55:12). Conventional scientific understanding simply doesn't account for trees having or showing any emotions such as joy or sadness. Trees don't have muscles or hands or a brain to control them, so obviously they can't clap. But wait. Could there be other ways to think about this unusual biblical tree behavior? Certainly poetic license would allow for wind rustling the leaves, clapping branches together, or sighing through the treetops. That could be singing or clapping.

Another perspective is that if living things that don't have thoughts or feelings can indeed praise God, then how much more reason we have for extolling Him, since we are endowed with far greater emotional capabilities than trees.

Yet another way to think about it is this: every entity praises God by fulfilling the purpose for which it was created. In this way animate and inanimate alike honor the Creator. Following this logic, even a water molecule sings for joy and praises God with clapping hands when it does what He intended water molecules to do. He designed trees to make leaves, wood, and fruit, among other things. They purify, humidify, and cool the air and enrich the soil with their fallen leaves. Besides feeding critters of all types, they provide a place for innumerable species to call home. We even use them to make our homes as well as unnumbered other wood, fiber, and chemical products. The list goes on and on. So as trees do what they were created to do, in a way they do sing for joy and clap their hands and praise their Creator.

What were you created to do? If your Creator walked up to you right now and had a heart-to-heart talk with you, what would He ask you to do for Him? I think that in fulfilling His wishes today, your heart, your voice, and your actions would all be giving praise to God.

Lord, please clarify Your purpose for me today. What would You have me do? Whatever You have in mind for me, let me be receptive and open to Your quiet Spirit.

Sharing Gifts

If you come with us, we will share with you whatever good things the Lord gives us. Num. 10:32, NIV.

This morning at our bird feeder I watched a mother downy woodpecker feeding one of her youngsters. Just as some teenage boys, the nestling was clearly bigger than its mother and much less industrious, too. The thin, harried mother bird pecked repeatedly at the large suet chunk, gathering a beak full of the energy-rich beef fat. Then, turning to the plump, squawking youngster at her shoulder, she proceeded to feed it. Back and forth she went, transferring the food the few inches from the suet chunk to the feathery teenager's open mouth. The nestling was either too lazy or too inexperienced to join its mother in a high-quality, sit-down meal together. For a few days this interesting lopsided sharing took place—the younger bird following its mom around begging for the food to be put right into its gaping mouth. After a few days, although it continued to follow her from food source to food source, they now both ate together. Instead of driving it off as she does with most other members of her species, she welcomed it to be by her side and getting its own food.

In our text for today Moses invited his brother-in-law, Hobab, to go with him to Canaan, indicating that, like the mother woodpecker, he would share whatever good things the Lord had presented them. You see, just like the big chunk of suet on the feeder—more than enough for all the downy woodpeckers in the surrounding woods—God was providing all the good things for His traveling-to-Canaan children. Since God supplies in abundance, there are more than enough good things for everyone. I think that I will take a cue from Moses and invite and encourage more of my friends and relatives to go with me to heaven, where there will be boundless good gifts from the Lord. And in the sharing of those gifts there won't be any less joy, because the supply is inexhaustible.

Lord, sharing sometimes seems hard for me until I stop to realize that You are the giver of every good and perfect gift. Open my eyes today so that I can see the needs of others, and then give me a soft heart that loves to share the gifts freely that You have bestowed on me.

The Case of Fake Eggs

Woe to those who call evil good and good evil, who put darkness for light and light for darkness, who put bitter for sweet and sweet for bitter. Isa. 5:20, NIV.

T his story is complex, so you will have to concentrate. About 500 different species of passion vines exist around the world. A few of them grow like herbs, some are shrubby, but most are vines with big beautiful flowers that turn into a fruit from which we can make an amazingly flavorful tropical juice. Passion vine leaves make scores of interesting and complex organic chemicals, such as flavonoids, alkaloids, flavones, and even some poisonous glycosides. The deadly poisons apparently protect leaves of the passion vine from being eaten by most insect herbivores. But some species of longwing butterfly larvae (*Heliconius*) can bypass the plant's defense by neutralizing the poison—or perhaps they can store it for their own protection.

Now the plot thickens. Not only do the longwing larvae avoid poisoning from the toxic leaves, but the adults prefer to lay their eggs (in a stalked egg case) on the leaves of the vines. A curious aside: longwing larvae are cannibalistic in that the first ones to hatch try to eat egg cases not yet hatched.

All I know for sure is that I want my life to be authentic and transparent. I don't want to deceive anybody.

That behavior certainly reduces competition and helps protect some plants. But the passion vine is capable of fighting back on its own. It has the genetic code to make egg case decoys (fake egg cases) on their leaves. Longwing butterflies will pass up a leaf that looks like it has already been populated with egg cases. What's more, the fake egg cases are actually plant glands that make and secrete a chemical that attracts wasps that prey on longwing larvae. So the plant has two lines of defense against what bugs them: recruiting wasps to kill the leaf eaters and faking out the would-be eaters by making them think that the territory is already taken.

Is this complicated or what? Could the great deceiver be involved here somewhere? Perhaps. All I know for sure is that I want my life to be authentic and transparent. I don't want to deceive anybody.

I am earnestly asking for Your help today, Lord, to be true and honest in every aspect of my life. May Your sweetness, Your goodness, and Your light flow through me.

Seventy Sextillion and Still Counting

He determines the number of the stars and calls them each by name. Ps. 147:4, NIV.

W hen I last counted, I found 55 texts in the Bible that mention stars— the kind that twinkle in the sky on a crystal-clear night. Thirteen of them refer to the number of stars in the sky. Most of those numerical references make the kind of comparison we find in Genesis 22:17: "I will surely bless you and make your descendants as numerous as the stars in the sky and as the sand on the seashore" (NIV).

So how many stars are there? And how many sand grains exist on earth? The reality is that nobody has or ever can count them. Somewhere in the process one star or grain of sand is bound to slip by uncounted, or one or two might get counted twice. The point is that we simply can't enumerate all of God's blessings. But making estimates of how many stars in our known universe and the grains of sand on Planet Earth is a mental exercise that many seem to enjoy.

The current estimate of the number of stars in our own Milky Way Galaxy is 200 billion. What if you had a machine that could count one star every second 24/7? How long would it take it to number all the stars in just our galaxy? OK—why don't you do the math? Write down 2 followed by 11 zeros. That is how you write 200 billion. Now divide 200 billion by the number of seconds in a year. Remember that a year is 365.25 days— the reason we have a leap year every four years. If you do the calculations right, you should get 31,557,600 seconds in a year. You will probably need a scientific calculator, because we are working with such big numbers. But when you divide 200 billion by 31,557,600 you should get 6,337.62 years. That is all of recorded history for our machine just to tabulate the stars "closest" to us. We have a very long way to go, because there are stars in billions of other galaxies to count. The current estimate is that the universe has 70 sextillion stars. Write that number with a 7 followed by 22 zeros. Our star-counting machine would have to count for more than a sextillion years. What an amazing God!

My Lord and Savior, You made each star and called it by name? What an amazing God You are. I bow down and worship You because I simply can't comprehend Your greatness, Your creativity, and Your majesty. I exalt You and worship at Your footstool.

An "Empty" Spot in the Night Sky

Lord, our Lord, how majestic is your name in all the earth! You have set your glory in the heavens. Ps. 8:1, NIV.

After more than 15 years of dreaming, designing, and planning, the Hubble Space Telescope was launched into space on April 24, 1990, aboard the space shuttle Discovery. With a relatively small mirror of almost 95 inches (several mountaintop observatories have telescopes with mirrors of 400 or more inches), Hubble's great advantage is in being outside of earth's atmosphere, thus giving the telescope clear and stable picture taking ability. Hubble travels at about five miles per second, which gets it around the earth in just a little more than an hour and a half. During each orbit scientists have about 45 minutes while Hubble is in the shadow of the earth. The dark night sky is the best time for collecting light from the astronomical features that they want to investigate.

After studying many thousands of images of beautiful galaxies and supernovas, some scientists decided to pick a relatively empty part of the sky to look at. They chose a tiny dark spot in the night sky in the constellation Fornax. The tiny spot is so small that it is like looking through an eight foot soda straw. Or another way to imagine it is staring at a dime 75 feet away. Then, during the course of 400 orbits, they programmed the Hubble cameras to collect light coming from the "empty" spot. The camera took 800 shots between September 24, 2003, and January 16, 2004, giving a total exposure time of 11.3 days. What that long time exposure shows takes my breath away. For even with our feeble instrument, that picture reveals nearly 10,000 galaxies that we didn't know existed. Many of the galaxies are interacting with each other. Some of them are distorted from galactic collisions. Others appear normal and unaffected by each other, majestic spirals with hundreds of billions of stars. How little we really know about what is out there!

I can't wait to travel to some of these distant galaxies and visit other worlds where the inhabitants have been living unaffected by the disease, death, dishonesty, and deceitfulness of sin. Won't it be interesting to ask them about their life and interactions with their Creator-God?

Lord Jesus, I long to be able to see with Your eyes. I long to see You as You really are.

Gravity Times 10

We have different gifts, according to the grace given to each of us. Rom. 12:6, NIV.

Chris Clark studies hummingbird flight at the University of California at Berkeley. Using high-speed cameras, bird decoys, and caged birds, he manages to get the male Anna's hummingbird to perform its courtship dive for his movie camera. At 500 frames per second Chris can analyze frame by frame what the aerobatic bird is doing during its spectacular flight.

You probably know that female birds are extremely choosy about which male they will allow to mate with them. Depending on the species, males might have to sing a complicated love song or to have just the right color or pattern of brightly colored feathers or to perform just the right courtship dance or to build a nest to exacting specifications or, in the case of the Anna's hummingbird, to put on an air show to die for in order to get chosen.

Perhaps, like me, you have watched a male hummingbird performing his courtship flight. Usually the female is perched on a branch where she can watch. The male will zoom off high into the sky and dive straight for her before pulling up into a tight J-shaped swoop just missing her and wowing her with sun reflecting off his iridescent throat patch and the sound of the wind whooshing through his wings. With many repetitions he shows her what a good mate he will be.

Chris has learned that the Anna's male dives toward the ground at 90 feet per second, or nearly 400 times their body length per second. Relative to their body size, that is faster than a fighter jet flies with its afterburners on or even the space shuttle during atmospheric reentry. And when the bird pulls out of its dive, it experiences nearly 10 g (10 times the force of gravity). Without a special anti-g suit worn by fighter pilots and astronauts, a human can tolerate only 3 to 5 g if in good physical condition and for only very short periods of time. With modern g suits and specially built airplanes, pilots can now endure 9 g, but only with special anti-blackout training and conditioning. Obviously the male Anna's hummingbird is designed with a special gift that pushes the limits beyond what we thought possible. Chris says that the acceleration forces on this bird are "greater than any organism previously recorded."

Lord, what gifts have You given me that You want me to use for Your honor and glory today? Bring hurting people into my life that I can wow with Your love and compassion.

January 29
Speaker Recognition

God's voice thunders in marvelous ways; he does great things beyond our understanding. Job 37:5, NIV.

The phone rings. I answer it. Instantly I know that it is my grandson calling, or my colleague at work. I have spent time with the person, and the voice is unmistakable. I hear somebody coming down the hall behind me talking. Without turning around I know who is approaching because I have heard that voice before, and it is that of a friend. You know what I am talking about, don't you? And for your very close friends, just seeing their picture or reading an e-mail from them will cause their voice to sound in your head. It is as if you can hear them saying what you are reading in the text message or in their hurriedly scribbled note to you.

Speaker recognition is a rapidly expanding and developing field that combines elements of mathematics, physics, acoustics, and computer science in highly technical ways. It is an elegant and sophisticated form of noninvasive biometric used to positively identify an individual for security purposes or to infer an identity in forensic work. Computers can now quickly analyze voice prints to determine with a high degree of precision whether or not the voice belongs to one person or another. But when you know an individual well, the ear and the brain work together to give amazingly precise identifications.

Abraham and God must have spent considerable time in conversation. The patriarch must have known the Lord's voice well. For when God asked him to take his one and only treasured son—the one he had dreamed of his entire life, the one he had prayed for, the one God had promised—when the Lord instructed him to take Isaac up on the mountain and sacrifice him . . . talk about speaker recognition. I think I might have asked for positive ID. But then, I have not spent enough time with God yet to know Him by His voice. What about a running conversation with God throughout each and every day, something akin to shepherds gently talking to their sheep?

Lord, I want to hear Your voice today. My desire is to know You so well that when Your voice speaks to me I will know it is You and not the deceiver/impostor. I want to hear and respond both to Your still small voice and to Your marvelous and magnificent thunderings. Tune my ear to the inimitable beauty of Your voice.

Light Codes

Beware lest any man spoil you through philosophy and vain deceit. Col. 2:8, KJV.

A re you as enchanted as I am by the mysterious blinking flashes of fireflies on a warm summer evening? As darkness deepens the twinkling lights that hover and move, stroking little J-shaped streaks along the edges of the dark woods, are simply fascinating. And of course my children never could resist catching a few to put in a jar beside their bed before falling asleep at night. After they were sleeping I have often peered into those tiny translucent terminal abdominal segments, wondering how they make that amazing light and why they flash it anyway. We will look at the how in tomorrow's devotional. Now for the why.

Biologists have studied some of the 2,000-plus species of fireflies (not really flies–they are actually beetles) and have noted that, in some of the flying types, it is usually the male that flashes while flying and that he is apparently attempting to communicate with female fireflies of his own species who might be watching from the ground or perched on a twig. If the male's light display meets her exacting specifications, she will flash back in a way that the male recognizes as an invitation to get together for mating. The flash code is very precise and varies from species to species. The male's series of flashes and movements has to be just right in order for the female to respond. And her timing is critical too. If she doesn't get the delay between his flashes and her response just right, he will think that she is not his type and will keep on the move, looking for a female of his species. He has to get it right or he could die.

> *Am I sometimes enchanted and attracted to what I believe to be right—what looks like light and truth, only to find that it is the great deceiver's attempts to get me into his grip of death?*

The danger for him is that there is one genus of predatory fireflies called *Photuris*, in which the females hunt for food by mimicking the flash pattern of females of other species. What the deceiver female does is flash back, pretending that she is his type. When he lands, expecting to mate, she attacks and eats him for dinner. At least 12 species of predatory *Photuris* females have mastered the flash code of from two to eight other species. But one species of *Photuris* has the ability to attract 11 other species of males. That is an amazing repertoire of flash codes.

Am I sometimes enchanted and attracted to what I believe to be right—what looks like light and truth, only to find that it is the great deceiver's attempts to get me into his grip of death?

Lord, it is only through Your wisdom and grace that I can avoid the deceiver's snares or escape his grip of death once lured in. Without You I am dead meat. Help me today.

January 31

Bioluminescence

What is the way to the abode of light? And where does darkness reside? Job 38:19, NIV.

"O uch! That light bulb is still hot!" Lighted bulbs are hot because little of the energy they use actually results in light. Most of it gets wasted as heat that can burn fingers. When living cells make light, however, the process is nearly 100 percent efficient. With no wasted heat, not surprisingly we call it cold light. Fireflies (and many hundreds of other life-forms) make cold light. Heat will destroy living cells, so if they make light, it just has to be of the cold kind. We call the light that living cells produce bioluminescence. So how do fireflies make their light? What is the way to the abode of their light?

Bioluminescence in fireflies requires a chemical reaction in a relatively simple biological pigment called luciferin. Luciferin has two forms, a tensed up energetic form labeled oxyluciferin or a relaxed form, the simple luciferin. The enzyme luciferase uses the cell's chemical energy to cram oxygen into the luciferin, making the energetic oxyluciferin. Then oxyluciferin settles back to its relaxed state, giving up the stored energy as a photon of light. Actually luciferin is the name given to any member of a family of light-producing biological pigments. Different forms of the pigment occur in various light-producing life-forms ranging from bacteria to fish to fungi. Some scientists believe that all cells produce some bioluminescence of one sort or another. Though luciferins have been under intense study for about seven decades, we know very little about how critters make the magical stuff. We still have so much to learn.

But not knowing how organisms produce it has not stopped us from artificially making luciferin and employing it in many creative ways. For example, we can use it to detect the presence of blood at a crime scene, cancer in an organ, or pathogenic bacteria in foods. In each case a positive test glows in the dark.

Come to think of it, shining the light of truth is our job in this dark world. When we let our light shine, it brings glory to God, whose face is the ultimate source of bioluminescence in the universe. My greatest hope is to see the light shining from His face.

Lord, make Your face shine upon me and be gracious to me today. Then shall the righteous shine forth as the sun in the kingdom of their Father.

February 1

Always More to Learn

You asked, "Who is this that obscures my plans without knowledge?" Surely I spoke of things I did not understand, things too wonderful for me to know. Job 42:3, NIV.

With a parabolic microphone, headphones, and audio recording equipment, Christina, one of our graduate students, spent hundreds of hours in the field and in the laboratory recording thousands of chirps from three different species of male crickets. For each series of high pitched chirps of the male's courtship song, she also logged the location, time of day, temperature, humidity, and lots of other environmental data. And in one series of experiments, other scientists teamed up with her to record chirps of the same species of crickets hundreds of miles north and south of her on the same day. So what is Christina discovering? She reports a surprising variability in the cricket's calling song and that the song is affected by the age of the cricket, its behavior, environmental factors, and perhaps even the anatomy of the cricket's song-making equipment.

You may be saying, "Duh! Who cares about variability in a cricket's calling song?" I'll tell you who cares—hundreds of scientists in both the United States and Europe who study the extreme complexity of the nervous system have been working for decades trying to understand how nerve cells communicate with each other. Since human or mouse nervous systems are far too complicated, the scientists have used crickets as their model system. They have based decades of research on how female crickets respond to the male cricket calling song. And somewhere way back at the beginning a scientist or two recorded the male calling song, characterized it, described it in the literature, and that one song has been generated electronically millions of times in dozens of labs all over the world to study how the females' nervous system is wired and how they respond to this so-called ideal calling song. Christina's work shows that we have so much more to learn. We don't really understand the systems well at all.

Like all of God's marvelous creation, life is not as simple as we sometimes see it or try to make it. Surprising variety is a fact of life.

Lord Jesus, what surprises do You have in store for me today? Teach me from Your rich knowledge base. As I learn more about the things You made, I worship and honor You.

February 2

Good Stuff

Keep me as the apple of your eye; hide me in the shadow of your wings. Ps. 17:8, NIV.

For me, it is an unforgettable lecture that happened long ago. Yet in my memory I can still hear George Wald describing what a marvelous coincidence it is that a proton has an equal but opposite charge to that of an electron. Wald had received the Nobel Prize in Physiology or Medicine in 1967 for his work on vitamin A and its function in the physiology of vision. Now, after several decades working as a biologist, I have heard other Nobel laureates give lectures. But none remain in my memory as vividly as hearing Wald speak.

So why was Wald so excited about the charge on a proton and an electron, and why is that such a big deal, anyway? Well, one of the first things any budding scientist learns is that everything consists of very small particles called protons, neutrons, and electrons. Protons carry a positive charge and electrons have a negative charge. As you might guess, neutrons are neutral. In their uncharged conditions atoms have exactly the same number of electrons as they have protons. The charges exactly cancel each other. Yet the proton is almost 2,000 times more massive than the tiny electron. That is something like the difference between a small marble and a large bowling ball. Surprisingly, the charge on the two vastly different-sized particles is equal but opposite. So equal in fact that Wald wrote a number on the chalkboard. The number is the difference between the equal and opposite charges. The number is very tiny. He wrote 0.000,000,000,000,000,000,160,217,648,7 coulombs. That is a pretty accurate measurement, wouldn't you say? Wald let us know that if the charges were not that exactly equal and opposite, basic particles would be charged so that they wouldn't come together. There would be no stuff—solar systems, planets, rocks, dirt, or anything else. And without stuff, there would be no life. Wald marveled at the stunning coincidence. I remember his amazement at this "chance" occurrence. I chose to recognize the fingerprints of my Creator. Aren't you glad that the Creator knows what He is doing and that He can make stuff from scratch? Plants, animals, human beings—we are all made from the same basic components of proton, neutron, and electron.

Thank You, Lord, for making the enormous proton and the minuscule electron to such exacting specifications that they can come together and make the stuff of everything—birds, trees, grass, diamonds, stars, and me. Keep me as the apple of Your eye today.

Life Isn't Fair

"An enemy did this," he replied. Matt. 13:28, NIV.

One day on my morning walk I saw a mother field sparrow being closely followed by a big brown bird two to three times her size. The big bird acted as if it was her baby. When mama would find a morsel of food, the big baby would quiver its wings as baby birds do and beg for food from its tiny "mom." Though the big baby towered over her, she would feed it and then move on to search for more food. It was a case of brood parasitism by the brown-headed cowbird.

Two species of cowbirds parasitize the nests of other smaller birds. Of the two, the brown-headed cowbird is much more common and broadly distributed in North America. Female cowbirds can lay an egg almost every day from late May to early July. In fact, cowbirds can produce more eggs per season than any other wild bird. Cowbirds are lazy parents in that they don't build a nest or take care of their own young. A female cowbird will sit on a high branch where she can observe the shrubby edge of the woods, and with her sharp eyes she will spot other smaller birds such as warblers, vireos, or sparrows in the process of building their own nests. Cowbirds parasitize more than 200 species of songbirds. After locating a nest under construction, she will track the progress of nest building. Then, just after the target bird starts to lay eggs in her new nest, the female cowbird will remove one or more of the eggs from the nest and lay one of her own in its place.

As you might guess, cowbird hatchlings emerge first, getting a head start on feeding. Soon they dwarf their other nestlings and simply outcompete them for food. The foster parent's own babies often don't survive. So the end result is that a cowbird female can produce 30 to 40 young in one season because she has so many foster parents working for her. The reality is that life in our world of sin is just not fair.

I am glad that there is a day of judgment coming when the righteous Judge will level the playing field. Until then, I need to take a lesson from the little mother sparrow and treat all with love and grace as I go about doing good.

Lord, I don't understand why others sometimes take advantage of me. I need Your help to treat them with kindness and grace. It has to be Your love that flows through me.

Superglue

Let us hold unswervingly to the hope we profess, for he who promised is faithful. Heb. 10:23, NIV.

Edward Mote was a young cabinetmaker who later turned to hymn writing. One of his popular hymn texts starts out with the words "My hope is built on nothing less than Jesus' blood and righteousness." Could the center of my hope be stated more simply? Jesus died to pay the penalty for my sins that I might have righteousness. That is the good news. But unless I meditate on that gospel reality, accept it gratefully, and hang on to it tightly, I am sure to lose it. Which is why Paul exhorts us to hold unswervingly to this hope. The King James Version and many others say "Let us hold fast the profession of our faith."

When Kodak laboratories accidentally stumbled onto the quick-bonding, tightly adhering superglue properties of cyanoacrylates in the early 1940s, it didn't take long for a whole new industry to spring up. Many companies came out with their own cyanoacrylate formulations for a variety of special-purpose glues. Their perhaps hundreds of uses now range from gluing skin and other body parts back together again after surgery to model building to cementing fragments of live corals to underwater rocks to get a colony started in a marine aquarium. Have you, like me, accidentally glued your fingers together at times? Mine were stuck so tightly once that I had to carefully cut them apart with a razor blade. It was before I learned that nail polish remover is a good superglue softener. The downside of cyanoacrylate-based glues is that the fumes can irritate the eyes, nose, and throat, and some people can become sensitized to them.

The good news is that when we make the decision to hold tight to our faith, the ultimate superglue of the Father kicks in, and He holds on to us. And He will not let us go.

Scientists are busy studying nature's adhesives, because holding fast or clinging unswervingly is what barnacles and oysters do to rocks and other solid structures in the ocean. Their glue is much stronger than anything we can make. It is nontoxic, cures underwater, and resists terrific storms. If we can figure out the chemistry of their glue, someday we may squeeze a drop of barnacle glue out of a tiny bottle when we need a super-strong, quick-setting adhesive. The good news is that when we make the decision to hold tight to our faith, the ultimate superglue of the Father kicks in, and He holds on to us. And He will not let us go. No power can snatch us out of His loving hand.

Lord, how comforting to know that the superglue of Your love can never fail.

February 5

Blessings of Bats

I will tell of the kindnesses of the Lord, the deeds for which he is to be praised, according to all the Lord has done for us. Isa. 63:7, NIV.

I praise God for bats. Most people consider them ugly and dangerous—something to fear. English translations of the Bible apparently mention bats three times (Lev. 11:19; Deut. 14:18; and Isa. 2:20), but only Isaiah specifically refers to the bat. The earlier two texts use a Hebrew word of uncertain meaning that scholars guessed might refer to a bat. That leaves only one reference in the entire Bible to one of God's really amazing and important creations. Let's take a closer look.

Scientists have named more than 1,100 kinds of bats. They are, of course, the only mammal that can fly for hours at a time with great freedom. Wouldn't it be wonderful to have that ability? Most bats eat night-flying insects, many of which damage crops or are pests, such as the corn earworm and mosquitoes. Bracken Cave in central Texas is home to a large bat population of Mexican free-tail bats that eat an estimated 200 tons of insects each night during the summer. Talk about effective pest control. We enjoy watching several little brown bats that regularly patrol around our Michigan home each summer evening. They can scarf down about 1,000 mosquitoes per hour.

The smallest bat, called the bumblebee bat, weighs less than two grams—less than a penny. It lives in Thailand and Myanmar. In contrast, the largest bat inhabits Philippine rain forests, weighs in at almost three pounds, has a wingspan between five and six feet, and bears the name of the giant golden-crowned flying fox. That's because its face looks very much like a fox. The large fruit-eating bat is endangered because of habitat destruction along the rivers where it feeds. Known as the silent planter, their droppings contain seeds, and they are important contributors to reforestation.

Visit batcon.org, the Web site of Bat Conservation International, to learn much more about bats and why their populations are declining the world over. Every kind of creature that God created serves an important purpose. Even the vampire bat produces a salivary enzyme that is a powerful blood clot dissolver now being studied as a potential treatment for stroke victims.

Lord, the more we learn about Your creation, the more we stand in awe of You. You are kind and greatly to be praised.

The Slippery Slope

But you, man of God, flee from all this, and pursue righteousness, godliness, faith, love, endurance and gentleness. Fight the good fight of the faith. Take hold of the eternal life to which you were called when you made your good confession in the presence of many witnesses. 1 Tim. 6:11, 12, NIV.

Have you ever watched an insect scurrying around on a pitcher plant? Hundreds of species of pitcher plants belong to a half dozen different families all over the world. All of them have some part of the plant formed into a rain catcher to make a pool of water in which they can trap and drown insects for food. The plants attract insects to the water with lures of nectar and bright markings pointing the way. In its explorations for some tasty morsel, the insect encounters stiff hairs that point downward toward the good stuff. The slope gets steeper, so the insect naturally turns around to go up to higher ground to get a better look at the situation, but it's too late. Loose waxy scales that make for a very slippery footing cover the slope. Trying to scramble uphill on the loose scree simply doesn't work. Imagine yourself trying to climb up a very steep slope with nothing solid to stand on. All you have underfoot are loose waxy plates. And thousands of sharp spears all pointed down slope block your way. No wonder the insect suddenly loses its footing and falls into the trap. Before it even stops struggling, other denizens of the dark watery pit start chewing on and burrowing into the insect's body. Plant enzymes begin digesting the plant's victim. Bacteria break down high-energy insect chemicals for use by the plant.

For an insect the only hope is to flee at once. Exploration is certain doom. The trap of the pitcher plant is that good.

What is your slippery slope? Is it the love of money that Timothy speaks about? Or is it the lure of prestige, influence, leisure? Timothy's exhortation is to flee, and pursue righteousness, godliness, faith, love, endurance, and gentleness. Take hold of the eternal life to which God calls you.

Lord, plant my feet on solid ground. Help me stay off the myriad slippery slopes of idolatry that lead to certain destruction. Let me take hold of Your offer of eternal life.

Royal Jelly

For you are a people holy to the Lord your God. The Lord your God has chosen you out of all the peoples on the face of the earth to be his people, his treasured possession. Deut. 7:6, NIV.

One of God's more interesting creations is the honeybee, a fact I learned several years ago when I began caring for and maintaining several hives. These little marvels of God's creation are highly social and live in colonies usually with only one queen, zero to several hundred drones (the males), and many thousands of worker bees. The queen lays all the eggs in a beehive and is carefully tended by some of the worker bees who cluster around her, feed her, clean her, and prepare cells for her eggs. They keep her busy laying eggs (a couple thousand per day during peak egg laying in the spring). Like the queen bee, worker bees are all females too, except that their reproductive organs are not fully developed, so they are sterile. The queen bee is the only female with fully mature ovaries.

When a queen bee starts to get old or if she suddenly dies, the worker bees choose a few larvae of the right age and start feeding them with an especially rich diet of a substance called royal jelly. You see, all larvae get a small quantity of royal jelly, a secretion of the hypopharyngeal gland located in the head of every worker bee. But larvae selected to become queens receive an abundant supply of the royal potion. They end up actually swimming in pools of the clear-yellow secretion during their development. And even though both the worker larvae and the queen larvae all have identical genetic makeup, the large doses of royal jelly in the developing queens apparently blocks a larval enzyme that normally shuts down some genes in worker larvae. With those royal genes active again, the queen larvae develop their full reproductive potential. It is the feeding that makes all the difference.

In biology this is a classic example of how two individuals with identical genetic compositions can have very different outcomes because of the developmental environment.

Come to think of it, if you are reading this as well as your Bible and your habit is to spend time in prayer every day, then you are immersed in a rich culture that can develop you into the royal priesthood, a person who can show forth God's praise.

Guide me, O great Jehovah, I am weak, but You are mighty. Hold me with Your powerful hand. Bread of heaven, feed me till I want no more.

February 8

Solitary Bees

The Lord said to me, "Son of man, look carefully, listen closely and give attention to everything I tell you concerning all the regulations and instructions regarding the temple of the Lord. Give attention to the entrance of the temple and all the exits of the sanctuary." Eze. 44:5, NIV.

We usually think of bees living in big, well-organized colonies, and many of the more commonly known bees do just that. But with nearly 20,000 species of bees inhabiting every continent except Antarctica, you might guess correctly that many bees live solitary lives. In fact, roughly 85 percent of all bee species are solitary ones.

A recent study involving two teams of scientists, one group in Turkey and the other in nearby Iran, discovered and described several nests of a little-known solitary bee called *Osmia avosetta*. What most interested these scientists were the brightly colored nests elaborately constructed from freshly cut flower petals layered with fine clay. The reason that science had not described the nests previously is that they are buried underground with only a tiny hole showing at the top, making them very hard to find.

What they learned from days of careful observation was that the female bee digs a hole in loose gravely soil on a steep north-facing slope. She then trims off a flower petal, rolls it up tightly, and carries it into the hole where she unfurls the petal and positions it with the rounded cut end pointing up. The bee collects many more petals, transports them in the same way, and carefully arranges them like shingles going from the bottom up. Then she wets a fine clay layer with something (water, nectar, salivary secretions—they aren't sure what yet) and uses it to glue another shingled layer of petals inside of the first outer layer. Next she provisions the nest before laying one egg on top of the food. Finally, she closes the nest in three precise steps. First she folds the upper ends of the inner layer of petals in toward the middle, sealing the nest. Packing some fine moist clay on top of the folded petals, she finishes off by folding the outer layer of petals over. So how did mother *Osmia* learn to do all this work so precisely?

Have you noticed how the Creator of this vast universe pays attention to the smallest details? It turns out that temperature and humidity in the *Osmia* petal nest have to be just right for the young to develop. Mother *Osmia's* success depends on precision genetic programming.

Lord, are details like this important to You? Are You interested in the details of my life? Is it important that I live a life of order and organization? Teach me Your ways, O Lord.

Mulberries

I am the vine; you are the branches. If you remain in me and I in you, you will bear much fruit; apart from me you can do nothing. John 15:5, NIV.

In our woods and along our street mulberry season lasts for many weeks in late spring and early summer. Whenever I think of "much fruit," mulberries come to mind. It is easy to see when the mulberries are ripening because their berries fall off easily, making a black mess and dark stains on the sidewalks, cars, and streets. Birds and other animals love to eat the fruit, and their droppings add to the stains. During my morning walks I often pause under a thickly fruited branch to pick a handful of berries because they are so sweet and flavorful. Just one handful of the luscious berries will darken my hands and mouth, too. But because the pigments are water-soluble anthocyanins, the color will wash away quickly.

Though botanical names in the Bible vary, it does mention mulberry trees, and we know that they flourished throughout Palestine then as they still do today. The trees grow rapidly at first, then slow to a crawl, which is why you rarely see a tall mulberry tree. Besides the black ones, there are also red and white varieties of mulberry. The white mulberry was grown as food for silkworm moths, because their leaves are the only food that silkworm larvae will eat.

One time we spread a big plastic sheet under a mulberry tree and shook the branches vigorously. The rain of ripe fruit was impressive. Then, to safely reach and shake even higher branches, I used the hook on my telescoping fiberglass pole tree trimmer/pruner. That tool worked so well that I accidentally pruned one of the high branches, and it fell onto our plastic sheet. After picking the cut branch clean, I tossed it off into the weeds. When I passed by a few days later, I noticed that the leaves on the accidentally severed branch were dry and brown. Immediately I thought of today's text. And I thought how quickly I lose spiritual life when I disconnect myself from the source of life. This passage in John speaks of remaining connected, implying that I am the one with the choice of whether or not it will happen.

Lord, I choose to remain joined to You today so that my spiritual life won't wither and die. I want to be a fruitful branch.

High Fashion

And why do you worry about clothes? See how the flowers of the field grow. They do not labor or spin. Yet I tell you that not even Solomon in all his splendor was dressed like one of these. Matt. 6:28, 29, NIV.

I f you get a chance, look at a flower through a hand lens or use a dissecting microscope to study a tiny flower. I have found that even a very humble-looking tiny flower is stunningly beautiful when seen with good magnification. Even better, we can put a flower into the specimen chamber of a scanning electron microscope and study the intricate beauty and architecture of its many surfaces. (My guess, though, is that you don't have access to that kind of microscope and that you will have to settle for simply appreciating the flowers around you.)

Viewing a flower petal as imaged by an electron microscope will reveal how the jigsaw puzzle pieces of the upper epidermis fit together exquisitely. On the lower surface special guard cells control the passage of carbon dioxide and oxygen into and out

God has all His bases covered. He knows what He is doing and cares for every detail.

of air chambers of the leaf. The anthers produce a bountiful supply of exquisitely sculpted pollen grains that germinate after landing on the stigma. A delicate pollen tube will then grow in search of the egg cell. If you could see the highly choreographed activity of sugar and water transport to the cells in the flower, you would know that God has all His bases covered. He knows what He is doing and cares for every detail.

Though the splendor and high fashion dress seen in lilies of the field is impressive, the lesson that Jesus was teaching in Matthew 6 was one that is hard to learn. The poor see what the rich have and struggle to get rich themselves. The rich have much more than they need and spend time figuring out how to get even more or protect, catalog, and preserve what they have. Jesus is saying here that clothing and food are not worth stressing about. Rather, He said, "Seek first his kingdom and his righteousness, and all these things will be given to you as well" (verse 33, NIV). The strategy that Jesus suggests for ridding me of my self-centered priorities involves my realization that God truly loves me, that He has unlimited resources, and that He cares for me.

Lord, why do I spend so much time worrying about the mundane? Teach me to rest in Your love, knowing for sure that You will care for my needs.

February 11

Food

The land produced vegetation: plants bearing seed according to their kinds and trees bearing fruit with seed in it according to their kinds. And God saw that it was good. Gen. 1:12, NIV.

Have you ever thought of food as the most important of all medicines? When I looked at recent world statistics suggesting that nearly 11 million children die each year and that about half of those deaths are because of poor nutrition, it made the link between food and medicine strong in my mind. But there is more. The diseases that kill most children (diarrhea, malaria, pneumonia, and measles) are much more deadly when young people have too little food or lack the right type. Indeed, food is truly our most important medicine.

I can't look at a blueberry, grape, tomato, banana, potato, or grain of rice or wheat, etc., without shaking my head in wonder and awe. First, just think of the packaging. Many have waxy coatings or special skin or coverings that slow evaporation of moisture. Some of them turn color when they get ripe to let us know that they are ready to eat. Ripe means that the sour acids have been converted to sweet sugars and that the hard fruits have become soft and delicious. Then consider their chemical content. To date, food scientists and chemists have identified more than 900 complex chemicals packed into fruits, vegetables, nuts, and grains. Such plant chemicals (phytochemicals) have lots of complicated names such as beta-carotene, lycopene, and isoflavones. No doubt many others still remain undiscovered.

The more we learn about such substances, the more we realize that they protect us from major diseases such as diabetes, hypertension, high cholesterol, hardening of the arteries, cardiovascular disease, poor eyesight, cancer, and so much more. So now I see each sweet glistening berry, tasty nut, shining apple, or crunchy grain of cereal as a loving health packet from my Creator. He made me and knows what I need to eat to stay healthy.

All that I require for life and health is abundantly available in a simple diet of natural plant-based foods. What is more, He didn't put it in a bitter pill form. The best food for me is attractively packaged, feels good in the mouth, tastes and smells delightful, and best of all, it protects me from many diseases. No wonder God called it "good."

Lord, too often I just say "Thank You for this food" without really thinking about all the attention to detail that You have put into it. Forgive me for being so thoughtless.

Aphids, Part I: Seeking

Those who seek the Lord lack no good thing. Ps. 34:10, NIV.

Though it might be hard to believe, some people actually love aphids. Most, however, think of them as pests that spread plant disease and suck the life out of the plants that they so carefully nurture in their garden. The majority of aphids are tiny soft-bodied insects that just mind their own business—eating and reproducing so rapidly that many aphid babies are born pregnant. But we will save that for another time. Today we want to examine how aphids feed.

Aphids have a microscopic feeding tube called a stylet. The stylet isn't just a simple sharp tube like a hypodermic needle. Rather it has complex tubes within a tube with valves so that it can inject saliva through one tube and take in the plant juices through another. Aphids puncture the tender soft parts of a plant and poke their feeding tube down through many layers of cells, tasting the contents of each cell until they find just what they are looking for. Scientists have discovered that aphids have nearly 100 cells of their own tiny body dedicated to taste-testing plant cell contents. What they are looking for are the sieve cells of the plant's phloem pathways. They are the highly specialized plant cells that carry the sugar-rich fluids under high pressure directly from the plant's photosynthetic cells to the places where it is used or stored. So the aphid seeks to tap into the plant's energy-rich supply lines. The insects spend a great deal of time probing for such cells, since they are not particularly abundant. The phloem supply line sieve cells, however, have built-in protective mechanisms to prevent leakage. When a sieve cell gets punctured or cut, the pressure drop triggers plant molecules that expand, gell, and clog so the good stuff won't leak out.

Aphids have a valve in their feeding stylet that prevents the pressure drop that would trigger clogging. So when they finally locate the special sieve cell and their taste test confirms that their stylet is in the right place, they first inject a few micro-drops of aphid saliva rich in chemicals to prevent clogging. Now they can open the valve and the pressure in the plant cell force-feeds them with life-giving fluids.

Lord, I choose to be as focused and diligent in my search for You and Your life-giving Word as the aphid is for the sweet energy-rich phloem sap.

Aphids, Part II: Abundance

Command them to do good, to be rich in good deeds, and to be generous and willing to share. 1 Tim. 6:18, NIV.

Aphids are champions of reproduction. One aphid can produce about 100 offspring in just a few weeks. If you use a microscope to peer into the semi-transparent body of an adult aphid, you can see miniature aphids developing in preparation for birth. Most insects lay eggs. But aphids bear live young. They can squeeze out about five new babies every day for a month or so. And in about a week those newcomers are having their own babies. They can begin reproducing so quickly because at birth they already have the next generation developing inside of them. It reminds me of a Matryoshka doll. You have probably seen a set of brightly painted carved Russian dolls, each one inside another. Aphids are like that in having at least three generations nested one inside the other, making them prodigious in the reproduction department.

How do they do that? It is technically known as parthenogenesis, reproduction without fertilization. No males are produced this way—only females. And all the females are genetically identical to each other. When you look at a bunch of aphids, however, on the lower side of a leaf you will find lots of small wingless aphids (the cloned females), a few larger ones, and even one or two with wings. Quickly you realize that aphids are not all identical. Aphids use several strategies for reproduction, depending on the weather and plant health. When hot summer weather sets in or when the plants are stressed or getting ready to die, some of the females develop wings and fly to healthier plants. Late in the season when cold weather approaches, some of the females turn into males. When the males mate with females, instead of the females bearing live young, eggs are produced that overwinter in some protected spot. Next spring the eggs will hatch into a new batch of females that begin their Russian doll trick all over again.

Because aphids are such soft defenseless, slow-moving creatures, lots of other insects eat them for lunch. Being incredibly prolific is their key to success as a species. By doing well what they can do—reproducing—aphids are widespread.

Lord, though my nature is stingy, I want to learn the lesson of using the gifts that You have given me in generous, magnanimous, and abundant ways.

February 14

Wood Thrush

My tongue will proclaim your righteousness, your praises all day long. Ps. 35:28, NIV.

It may be February on the calendar, but I like to think of a typical early-summer morning in southwest Michigan. The mature beech/maple woods where we live resist the intrusion of the first gray light of dawn an hour or so before sunrise. The high plaintive whistles of the eastern wood pewee fill the air, but the dominant birdsong that I wake up to every morning is the hauntingly beautiful song of the wood thrush. Though I rarely see the secretive bird, I do enjoy the flute-like yodeling every morning and evening when the woods are dark and mysterious. If you take early-morning or late-afternoon walks in or near deep, dark woods anywhere east of the Mississippi River, you may not see this robin-sized bird, but you will likely hear the loud, clear, fluty notes of its melodic song.

World birdsong expert Don Kroodsma once visited southwest Michigan and gave a couple fascinating lectures. I learned that, like many birds, the wood thrush has two voice boxes. But it took my breath away when he played the familiar song of the wood thrush at a very slow speed without changing the pitch. All of us listening in the auditorium heard the raspy chirrrr at the end of the fluty song converted into a melodic duet. Using both voice boxes simultaneously, the wood thrush modulates the sound coming from each voice box separately. The rising and falling whistles that come from the two voice boxes harmonize into a magical blend that is exquisitely beautiful. Hearing this concert of praise from one of God's little creatures made me want to join in with the Doxology.

We know that birds can see much better than we can. That is, they can detect much finer detail (resolution) than the human eye. Apparently they can hear much better too. Kroodsma showed evidence that birds can sense the intricate aspects of their songs. When he compares the recording of a juvenile bird to the same bird later in the season, its song undergoes dramatic changes. Early recordings are much like baby talk with song elements in the wrong order or poorly rendered. Later recordings of the same bird show that practice has changed the song. It is much closer to that of older, practiced adult birds.

Lord, if birds spend so much time rehearsing their songs, how much better could I represent You if I practiced loving others?

Syrinx (pronounced SERE-inks)

The Sovereign Lord has given me a well-instructed tongue, to know the word that sustains the weary. Isa. 50:4, NIV.

Though I often hear people say LAR-nix and FAR-nix when they are speaking about the human larynx and pharynx, the fact is that both of these frequently mispronounced biological terms rhyme with syrinx, the name given to a bird's voice box. Your pharynx is the back of your throat where your nasal passageway and oral cavity come together. The larynx is that pointy little lump that you can feel on the front of your neck that bounces up and down when you swallow or speak. Otherwise known as the Adam's apple, your larynx is at the very top of the trachea, contains the vocal cords, and is the wonderful structure that gives you a voice.

Birds also have a larynx, but for them it only guards the opening to the trachea. They produce their birdsongs in the syrinx, located at the base of the trachea where it splits into the two bronchi. Both the larynx in mammals and the syrinx in birds are amazingly complicated sound-producing organs. When we speak or sing, we employ only about 2 percent of our air to move the vocal folds and make sound. But when birds sing, they use nearly 100 percent of their air to create their sounds. In terms of sound production, that is extraordinary efficiency, perhaps one of the reasons that I always shake my head in wonder when I hear the huge voice that comes out of such a tiny feathered body.

What about me? What words or songs am I practicing today?

The two sides of the bird's syrinx are controlled independently, which is why some birds such as brown thrashers, ducks, bellbirds, grebes, bitterns, or wood thrushes, to name just a few, can sing two different songs simultaneously. Other birds such as canaries use only their left side to sing all their songs. The complex sounds coming from the brown-headed cowbird are made by switching from one side to another for successive notes. No doubt you have heard the familiar northern cardinal perform its loud repeated whistle that starts low and ends high. Scientists who study cardinal vocalization report that male cardinals use the left side of their syrinx for low sounds and seamlessly switch to the right side as the song goes up. It takes a lot of practice for them to perform their song just right. What about me? What words or songs am I practicing today?

Lord, may Your words of comfort and affirmation flow through me today.

February 16

Frankincense

For we are to God the pleasing aroma of Christ among those who are being saved and those who are perishing. 2 Cor. 2:15, NIV.

I well remember as a youngster visiting Aden, then a dusty Yemeni town on the southern tip of the Arabian Peninsula. Not far south, across the Gulf of Aden, Somalia hugs the coast, coating the horn of Africa in a narrow strip. From Aden, travel north and east along the coast of the Arabian Peninsula to the Dhofar region of Oman. Rain is spotty in the dry desert countries bordering the Gulf of Aden. Plants generally struggle for existence, taking advantage of the brief monsoon season to get out some flowers and grow enough so that they can hang on for another season of hot and dry.

The dry calcareous rocky ravines support few plants. But like a root out of dry ground, a gnarly tree named *Boswellia sacra* ekes out a tortured existence on the blistering hot terrain of these three regions bordering the gulf. The tree has compound leaves and small yellow flowers. Cutting the leaf will release a milky-white latex sap. But cut or scrape off some of the paper-thin bark on the trunk, and a gummy edible resin will ooze out and dry as little beads in the desert heat. Highly aromatic, they are prized as an ingredient in incense or various folk medicines. Sold and treasured worldwide as frankincense, one can burn the resin to kill germs, repel mosquitoes, or create an atmosphere for worship. Chewed like gum or rubbed on as oils, people have used frankincense for thousands of years to heal all sorts of diseases from arthritis to digestive problems.

Magi from the East traveled far to see the Baby Jesus and worship Him, presenting Him with their costly gifts of gold, frankincense, and myrrh. God directed Moses to prepare a recipe of spices, gum resins, onycha, galbanum, and pure frankincense to create a special incense for use in the tabernacle. Frankincense, the precious, special gift of *Boswellia sacra*, made by a scrubby tree living under difficult circumstances, is one of the key ingredients in a sacred incense, made according to a recipe handed down by God Himself, with specific restrictions against using the concoction for personal use.

Lord, sometimes I chafe under difficult and trying circumstances. Is my life to produce a sweet perfume that is holy and special to You? Thank You for the encouragement from Boswellia.

February 17

Hyssop

Cleanse me with hyssop, and I will be clean; wash me, and I will be whiter than snow. Ps. 51:7, NIV.

King Solomon was the wisest man that ever lived. First Kings 4 suggests that he was knowledgeable about natural history and delivered lectures about both plants and animals. One of them was about hyssop. I am quite certain that a full-color, surround-sound, 3-D recording of his lecture is archived in the celestial audiovisual center. I hope one day to listen to Solomon's description of this herbaceous to semi-woody shrub in the mint family.

A genus with about a dozen species native to the area from the Mediterranean to central Asia, *Hyssopus* has been cultivated for thousands of years. Perhaps the most important member of the genus *Hyssopus officinalis* well represents this knee-high herb with lots of bright-green, straight, mostly non branching stems arising from a central point. The smell of the plant is strongly minty. When it flowers, each long straight stem sports clusters of light-blue, sometimes pink, rarely white, most often blue to purple flowers. Beekeepers love to put their bees near fields of hyssop because they make a clear, golden honey with a rich aromatic flavor that is highly valued. Those who grow hyssop usually harvest the stems when in full flower and use the herb fresh in cooking or for extracting the essential oils employed in perfumes, soaps, creams, and other cosmetics. More often the stems are dried and then finely chopped for use in cooking as a condiment, for flavoring, as a minty tea, or as an ingredient in herbal medications.

The Bible makes many references to hyssop, though we don't know which particular hyssop that was. Many plants besides the genus *Hyssopus* bear the common name hyssop. In most instances biblical texts link this plant to cleansing rituals in which one dips the plant into blood for sprinkling or for marking—all symbolic pointers to the cleansing blood of Jesus. And while on the cross, spilling His life-blood for us, someone used a stiff straight stem of hyssop to lift the vinegar-soaked sponge to Jesus' dying lips.

Without question, hyssop has a long and important history. Come to think of it, will the Creator of this marvelous plant one day give a lecture on the natural history of hyssop? I want to be there to hear it from His own lips.

Lord, thank You for creating myriads of useful and interesting plants and animals. May I honor and glorify You by the way I care for them and use them to serve others.

The Hiding Place

Set your minds on things above, not on earthly things. For you died, and your life is now hidden with Christ in God. Col. 3:2, 3, NIV.

T alk about hidden. I will never forget the time I put a full-grown adult male American copperhead snake into a small glass terrarium so that we could safely place him on display in the Biology Department for a few weeks. The small glass enclosure with a tight screen top measured only about a cubic foot and had a thin layer of fallen leaves covering the bottom of the glass to make him feel more at home. About an hour later I checked on the pit viper, but it was nowhere to be found. Fortunately for me, I had locked the terrarium in a glass cabinet. The lock was still shut. The screen was still tight—but no snake! Where could it have gone? Copperheads have a poisonous bite and are aggressive when threatened, so I didn't want it loose to wreak havoc with unsuspecting students or faculty. I had to find him, and from all I could figure out, he had to be inside that tiny glass terrarium. But where?

Inch by square inch I carefully and systematically studied the appearance of each dead leaf on the surface of the enclosure. Everything looked like normal leaves to me. Then, after a minute or two of searching, there he was, watching me searching for him. Most of his thick, foot-long body had wriggled down under the leaves, but his head and neck were still visible, and he was alert for anything that might hurt him.

I am still trying to get my head around the sheer futility of watching your footing when you are out hiking in the woods. This rascal was nearly impossible to see even when I knew where he was. For weeks we all had fun trying to find him when we passed by. Each time, it took a bit of looking. But every time he was there, looking right back at us. Fortunately for hikers, copperheads are shy and will slink out of harm's way when humans approach. It seems that they have as much fear of us as we have of them.

Being hidden in Christ is the safest of all hiding places and puts us completely out of harm's way. The devil—the old serpent, Satan—can have no power over us. No matter how long he looks for us, we are safe, surrounded in God's abiding love.

Lord, thank You for protecting me and surrounding me with Your soothing songs of deliverance. Help me to stay safely hidden in You.

A Tenth of Mint

Woe to you Pharisees, because you give God a tenth of your mint, rue and all other kinds of garden herbs, but you neglect justice and the love of God. You should have practiced the latter without leaving the former undone. Luke 11:42, NIV.

We grow peppermint beside our water garden, where it gets the partial shade, moisture, and cool soil that helps it flourish. In fact, like the weed it is, it spreads and grows prolifically right in the water. Because of its high menthol content, mint is a favorite for flavoring candy, ice cream, and tea. Even medications, toothpaste, chewing gums, and mouthwashes often have mint flavoring. The herb is so popular that people have grown it for centuries and use it in all kinds of ways.

So just where is the mint in peppermint? In our lab we have looked at mint leaves with the electron microscope. What we see on the upper surface of the leaf is a typical leaf surface with some hairs sticking up out of a background of epidermal cells. But dotting the normal leaf surface, however, are numerous round blobs, each one nestled into a small depression of the upper leaf surface. Botanists call these fat round blobs peltate glandular trichomes, meaning "shield-shaped" (peltate) hair (trichome) that secretes (glandular). Careful cross-sectioning of the peltate glandular trichomes reveals a flat disk-shaped cluster of eight secretory cells (the shield) attached at the center to one stalk cell, which is itself connected to one basal cell, an epidermal cell of the leaf. During peak production the eight secretory cells produce the peppermint oil, with each of these cells pumping the oils up under the waxy cuticle covering the eight cells. The cuticle swells with the accumulated oils and grows into a fat droplet of oil contained under the fragile coating of wax. Even a gentle touch will break many of the waxy covers, releasing the oil with its refreshing smell and taste.

Mint plants are prolific, each stem producing a new pair of leaves every two or three days. Can you imagine how such productivity must have delighted the obsessive-compulsive Pharisees? While tithing is important, the lesson of the mint and other garden herbs is that some things have an even higher priority. "He has shown you, O mortal, what is good. And what does the Lord require of you? To act justly and to love mercy and to walk humbly with your God" (Micah 6:8).

Lord, thank You for the clarity of Your Word that lets me know what Your important take-home message is. Help me to stay focused on always treating others justly and mercifully as I walk humbly with You day by day.

The Nest Cam

Wait for the Lord; be strong and take heart and wait for the Lord.
Ps. 27:14, NIV.

As I sit here eating breakfast with my wife in quiet conversation, we are both keeping our eyes on the screen of the laptop computer. Our mealtime habit recently has been to log on to a barn owl nest cam so that we can keep up with developments. Hour after hour Molly or McGee (yes, some barn owl parents have names) patiently sit on the nest. We have watched eggs as they were first pipped, then gradually pushed open from inside, and the tiny bobble-headed nestlings emerged, fed, and grew. As if on a two-day schedule, every other day for a week, another egg hatched, revealing another mouth to feed. The discarded fur of rabbits and field mice filled the nest box. In fact, now as we watch, Molly stands, stretches, and picks up a half-eaten rabbit carcass from the corner of the box. The big-eyed fuzzy babies with grotesquely large beaks come alive and begin sounding off with their hungry cries. Still sitting on her brood, Molly places one heavily taloned foot on the carcass, gets a good tight grip, then takes some time to find a bite just the right size. Finally, with considerable strength, she tears away a piece of meat with a strong upward motion of her head. As her head goes up, little heads pop up just under Molly's beak, making it easy for her to pass the little morsels of food to them before tearing off another piece. I love the technology of the nest cam. I sure could have used it years ago when I spent weeks out in the rain, wind, and sun doing a nesting study the old-fashioned way. What was amazing then and now is the patience, the attention, the 24/7 commitment of parent birds.

Much like the attentive wait-staff in a high-class restaurant who serve their patrons, like a mother bird totally focused on caring for her young, we are told to wait on the Lord, serving Him with gladness.

Other versions and commentaries on Psalm 27:14 are clear in asking us to wait patiently on the Lord. Much like the attentive wait-staff in a high-class restaurant who serve their patrons, like a mother bird totally focused on caring for her young, we are told to wait on the Lord, serving Him with gladness. Come to think of it, what an honor it is to attend the King of kings and Lord of lords, the Creator of all. Let us worship Him by fulfilling His every wish for us today.

Lord, what would You like me to do for You today? How can I best serve You? Teach me to wait patiently, totally focused on the task that You have in mind for me.

Quiet Waters

He leads me beside quiet waters, he refreshes my soul. Ps. 23:2, 3, NIV.

We are blessed to share a property line with Love Creek, a 150-acre park managed by Berrien County, Michigan. Whenever we want we can walk out our back door onto miles of trails that wend their way through mature beech/maple forests, open fields, and marshy bogs, and along a gurgling creek with tranquil pools. From mid-March through June the parade of spring wildflowers are spectacular. The brown forest floor erupts into knee-deep green which, when we pause to study it carefully, resolves into scores of species of spring ephemerals that flower in predictable sequences. After a long snowy winter, getting out on the trails to greet the early-spring bloomers as each makes its appearance has been one of God's special blessings to our family.

A news note just published in Environmental Science and Technology confirms yet another blessing of walking our green woodland trails. It also upholds the inspiration of the psalmist David in the opening lines of the familiar lines above. You see, Jo Barton, senior researcher for the Interdisciplinary Centre for Environment and Society and a lead researcher in the Department of Biological Sciences Green Exercise program at Essex University in the U.K., has shown the health benefits of exercise in nature. Working with many other collaborators during the past decade, she has documented that exercise outdoors is really much better than being on a treadmill or stationary bike inside. She reports that just five minutes of exercise each day out in nature can significantly improve mental health. What was most surprising to me was her finding that all exercise in nature is beneficial, but "green areas with water appeared to have a more positive effect."

Barton's conclusion provides yet more evidence suggesting that we live in an exquisitely complex system designed by a loving and caring God who has given us just what we need to make the best connections to Him.

Lord, I invited You to walk with me today in Your garden. Restore my soul as You lead me to quiet waters for meditation and prayer.

Marvelous Deeds

Declare his glory among the nations, his marvelous deeds among all peoples. Ps. 96:3, NIV.

I f you were asked to identify the most marvelous and wonderfully complex system in the known universe, what would you say? My bias says that it would have to be a biological system, perhaps the human brain. An astronomer might choose a galactic system. A molecular biologist might select an elegant enzyme complex. Perhaps your answer to that question depends on how much you have explored or how much you have thought about it.

With its estimated 100 billion neurons (brain cells) with unnumbered connections to each other and variously controlled circuits, the human brain has often been held up as an example of unimaginable beauty and complexity. It is so intricate that even modern neuroscientists are merely playing with pebbles on the shores of a vast ocean of knowledge. One way to study the staggeringly complex, however, is to learn from simpler analogous systems. When we figure out a simple system, we can begin by imagining comparisons, then asking questions about how it might work, and finally testing our hypotheses. Will it ever be possible to understand the human brain fully? It is fairly safe to say that it won't happen in our lifetime.

The tiny fruit flies with red eyes that hover around our ripe peaches during late summer have about 100,000 neurons—a simple system in comparison to human brains. And now, using the power of a new computer-based technique, neuroscientists are beginning to make a digital map of the minuscule fruit fly brain. The cell-by-cell detail emerging from the painstaking work indicates a brain with unbelievably complex and beautiful patterns. As always, such research reveals surprises. Neurons, which science previously thought to look much alike, are showing up with stunning variation in structural detail in various parts of the brain. Different structure usually means different function. How neurons connect to each other—the circuitry of the brain—shows amazing similarity from brain to brain. We find a plan, a purpose, a wonderful design here. Let us worship and honor the Creator who gives us neurons with its connections and ability to think about Him and about the things that He has made.

Lord, does each brain cell actually have a particular function? Have You really arranged for every detail of my life? In what areas of my life have I let You down and failed to carry out Your plan for me? Teach me how to honor and glorify Your name better in my community.

February 23

Alpha-Amylase

Do not neglect your gift, which was given you. 1 Tim. 4:14, NIV.

I love discovering how things are made. Shiny brass hand bells, rough scratchy steel wool, dishwashers, cuckoo clocks, giant tires—the list seems endless on the Discovery Science Channel's "How It's Made" program. What an awesome showcase of human inventive genius. But what draws my attention, though, is the many specialty machines designed to drill, bend, extrude, mold, cap, package, paint, or polish what is being manufactured. Without those machines, the stuff doesn't get made. And somebody had to think about, design, and make those devices.

In some ways the cell is like a giant factory—except that the cell is incredibly small and the many specialty machines inside it are even smaller and are made of protein instead of steel, rubber, and plastic. Like the factories' big rattling steel machines, the cell's specialty protein machines are also designed to punch holes, bend, cut, polish, or do one of a thousand other specialty tasks in the process of making things or taking things apart for recycling or fabricating parts for something else.

The cell's protein machines are known as enzymes. The Creator designed each enzyme to do one task and to do it well. For example, alpha amylase, one component in saliva, trims, cuts, or snips long insoluble starch molecules (such as the starch in rice, cereals, pasta, or potatoes) into shorter soluble starch molecules. And if you chew your food thoroughly enough you will begin to taste some sweetness. That is because the alpha amylase keeps working until it gets the long chains cut down to maltose—grain sugar, a disaccharide. Another enzyme, maltase, easily converts maltose into the blood sugar glucose. So now you know why your mom tells you to chew your food thoroughly.

In the grand scheme of things, what is your specialty job? What has God designed you to do? Perhaps some of you may still be in college or graduate school. The Master Designer may still be building you, preparing you to do a specialty task for Him. Being prepared, qualified, and skilled to do that responsibility at the right time and in the right place where He needs you should make you feel pretty important. But God is always preparing us for His purposes all throughout life. No doubt about it, you are special and, like Queen Esther, you are being prepared for "such a time as this" (Esther 4:14). So be patient and let the Master Designer have His way with you.

Lord, help me to submit patiently as You prepare me to do Your specialty job.

Aphid Pipes

By this everyone will know that you are my disciples, if you love one another. John 13:35, NIV.

Some aphids have actually teamed up with scientists, helping them to make really important discoveries about plant physiology. So why do people hate aphids?

Biologists have classified more than 4,000 species of them. Only about 250 of them cause trouble and give aphids the bad name of pest because they reproduce so incredibly fast. When they feed in large numbers, they can drain the life out of important food and ornamental plants. They can spread plant disease, too. Many species of aphids feed on only one type of plant. Others, though, like great variety and live on hundreds of plant species. How aphids feed is to poke a microscopic feeding tube or pipe into the tender soft parts of a plant until that pipe enters a single high-pressure sugar-conducting cell of the plant known as a sieve cell. But as we saw in a previous reading, the insects don't have to suck on their tiny straw. The high pressure of the sugary solution in the sieve cell force-feeds the aphid. In fact, the sugar solution quickly bloats their soft body, and, to keep from bursting, they have to let it run right through them. To relieve the pressure, the excess sugary solution drips out of the tiny aphid anus in sweet droplets called honeydew. Some ants eat these sweet droplets. To maintain their food supply, ants actually herd and protect aphids and "milk" them for their honeydew.

Scientists who were trying to determine the exact chemical composition of the plant's sieve cells were having trouble getting accurate samples to test. Every time they poked or cut into a sieve cell, the pressure changes would trigger the plant's leak protection system, and the flow quickly stopped. Leak protection chemicals would also contaminate the sample. But when scientists teamed up with aphids they were successful. The insects not only provided the proper size tube, but they also inserted their feeding tubes into exactly the right cells in a way that avoided the plant's leak-protection response. Once the aphids were connected, the botanists cut the aphid loose and collected the plant juices that oozed out. With this innovative method, plant scientists can now accurately sample sieve cell contents and better understand the composition and flow rates of the photosynthetic products being transported.

Lord, flow Your love through me so that another may sample Your sweet, abundant, life-giving love. Today, with Your help, let me be that pipeline.

Pet Hamster

Stop judging by mere appearances, but instead judge correctly.
John 7:24, NIV.

It was a very sad morning in our home. As I dropped my children off at the local church school I couldn't help reliving its events. First, it was an unusually cold winter morning in southern Tennessee, with the cold snap taking the temperatures below zero. The cold must have been what caused my daughter's pet hamster to die sometime during the night. It was strange for us to have to go out in the gray light of dawn with a shovel, break through the frozen ground, dig a shallow grave, and tearfully bury the cold lifeless body of a family pet before heading off to school. Was it my fault that the hamster had died? I wondered. Lisa was an unusually responsible 9-year-old who normally took very good care of her hamster. But for some reason the level of care had gone down, the level of disagreeable odors had gone up, and the poor hamster had been banished to the garage. I had taken the cage that included hamster, fancy exercise wheel, colored tubes, and reeking cage litter to the garage until Lisa could once again pick up her end of the bargain and clean up the cage. That's how the hamster got caught in the garage on a very cold night and paid the supreme price. How tragic.

About noon that day, while at work, a thought popped into my head. Could the hamster be hibernating? There was only one way to find out. Racing home, I grabbed the shovel, went out to the fresh mound of earth, and dug up the cold limp body. Brushing the dirt off the matted fur, I placed the body in a shoebox and placed it behind our woodstove while I fixed a sandwich. Soon the little body started to twitch and shake, and before long the lucky little guy was sitting there with his usual bright eyes and twitchy nose, exploring every nook and cranny. Needless to say, when the kids came home from school that day, there was great rejoicing. And the cage remained quite clean after that. Though I was a hero to my kids, I knew in my heart that, as a professional biologist, I should have thought "hibernation" and been a bit slower in burying the poor critter in the frozen ground.

> *That's how the hamster got caught in the garage on a very cold night and paid the supreme price.*

Lord, how often I rush to judgment. How often I look the other way as I pass the emotionally injured along life's road. How often I even bury someone who appears dead and useless. Teach me to always treat others with warmth and tender care.

Zombie Ants

You will keep in perfect peace those whose minds are steadfast, because they trust in you. Isa. 26:3, NIV.

When the word was first coined, "zombie" referred to a hypnotized individual whose mind was under the control of another. Now entomologists studying carpenter ants in Brazil have stumbled onto some really bizarre ant behavior that appears to be directed by a fungus. The jungles of Brazil are hot, steamy places, providing ideal conditions for molds, mildews, and other fungi to proliferate. One widely distributed fungus called *Ophiocordyceps unilateralis*, first discovered in 1865, seems to have lots of cousins who specialize in parasitizing various kinds of ants. What is coming to light now is that there may be hundreds of species of cordyceps fungi with highly specialized systems, each designed for a certain species of ant. The best studied and most reported zombie ant story goes like this.

A fungal spore gains access through an ant spiracle or respiratory opening along the side of its body. After germinating, the fungal mycelia (reproductive filaments) progress through less-important ant parts, absorbing ant juices and nutrients. As the fungus spreads, the parasitized ant continues to function normally, though it probably doesn't feel well. At some point the fungus invades the ant's brain and produces psychoactive chemicals that take over the insect's behavior in specific and complex ways. First, the ant does the unthinkable—it leaves the colony. Not long after that the ant locates the underside of a leaf on the north side of a tree about 10 inches above the ground where the humidity is constant at 94 or 95 percent and the temperatures vary only a few degrees. The ant then clamps its strong mandibles onto the main vein of the leaf in a death grip. The leaf doesn't die, mind you, but the ant does, because by this time the fungal mycelia have taken over its entire body and a long fungal fruiting body grows out of the top of the insect's head, making it look like a unicorn. Fungal spores thus drop onto foraging ants, continuing the infection. Whole ant colonies can perish this way.

Lord God, Your protection is my only safety from Satan's countless mind-controlling deceptions. I am thankful that You created human beings free to think and choose for themselves. I now choose to trust in You. Solidify that trust.

February 27

Apomixis

Night and day, whether he sleeps or gets up, the seed sprouts and grows, though he does not know how. Mark 4:27, NIV.

Plants normally produce seed as a result of sexual reproduction—that is, pollen grains deliver sperm cells to the ovule, then following fertilization (the fusion of sperm and egg in the ovule) a seed develops that is genetically unique. The blend of parental traits resulting from sexual reproduction is an important survival strategy in a variable environment. In contrast, apomixis refers to seed production without the benefit of fertilization. Without fertilization, a clone of the mother plant results. It seems that the rules governing reproduction in plants get relaxed so that successful reproduction happens in a huge variety of ways—apomixes being one of those interesting responses to God's reproductive designs.

How does that happen? What kinds of plants reproduce that way?

As you may know, dandelions, blackberries, and some meadow grasses are champions when it comes to seed production, and one of the reasons for their success is that they can reproduce both sexually and asexually. That is, though they can propagate the normal way, they don't require pollination for seed formation. It might help to understand that you and I (and most animals, for that matter) have two sets of genes (diploid) in every one of our cells. One set comes from the mother and the other from the father. And for most animals, having two complete sets—no more and no less—is a strict rule. But plants do well with just one set of genes from one parent (haploid). Or they are fine with two sets from each parent (tetraploid), or two sets from one parent and one set from another (triploid).

In particular, dandelions have responded well to their internal "be fruitful" programming and have literally filled the earth. Those dandelions that scientists have most closely studied have turned up as triploid. Though triploid dandelions do produce pollen, most don't use it for reproduction. Instead, cells in the ovule that would normally develop into an egg take a shortcut to the embryonic stage. They don't wait for sperm to arrive and fertilize. The egg simply begins development as an embryo, and the central cell develops into the nutrition for the embryo. The seed becomes a viable and identical copy of all the other seeds on the seed head—a clone of the mother plant and probably a clone of the other dandelions in the yard. So you see, by doing what God designed them to do, dandelions praise God and give Him glory.

Lord, may my life be as productive of good works for You as the dandelions in the field.

Dandelion

For the earth which drinks in the rain that often comes upon it, and bears herbs useful for those by whom it is cultivated, receives blessing from God. Heb. 6:7, NKJV.

Depending on whom you talk to, dandelions are one of the greatest curses of wannabe master gardeners or another of God's bountiful blessings. I actually have friends who revel in the beauty of those golden orbs surrounded by an emerald-green lawn. Others can be uncharacteristically peevish until they have carefully pulled up every long taproot firmly anchoring the offending rosette of deeply toothed leaves.

The name "dandelion" ignores the beautiful golden blooms and the delightfully ornate seed heads and focuses on the toothed leaves instead, which reminded the French of the size and curvature of a lion's big canine teeth. So it is that the Old French phrase dent-de-lion gets morphed into "dandelion."

Depending on whom you talk to, dandelions are one of the greatest curses of wannabe master gardeners or another of God's bountiful blessings.

Dandelions can be found pretty much worldwide, growing well in disturbed habitats wherever there is plenty of sun. Since the base of the plant does not put up a shoot that can be easily grazed or whacked off by a lawn mower, it survives mowing, foot traffic, and all sorts of assaults that other flowering plants simply wouldn't tolerate.

Though every part of the plant exudes a white, milky latex sap when broken, and some may not like the slightly bitter taste, all parts of the plant are edible and actually highly nutritious. The leaves boast more beta-carotene (vitamin A) than carrots themselves, and the vitamin K in one cup of chopped leaves comes in at 535 percent of your daily needs. Vitamin C, calcium, and iron are high as is magnesium, phosphorus, potassium . . . the list goes on and on. Dandelion greens are good in that they are both filling and nutritious while having a glycemic load of only 2, meaning that you metabolize it slowly so that it doesn't spike your blood sugar. Best of all, dandelions are free, growing in your yard, in parks, and along roadsides. All you need to do is fix them and eat.

What a God to give us such a blessing that propagates easily, grows everywhere, is beautiful to look at, and so good to eat!

Lord, I ask You to help me be a great blessing to others.

March 1

Snowflakes

From whose womb comes the ice? Who gives birth to the frost from the heavens? Job 38:29, NIV.

No doubt everyone has heard the statement that no two snowflakes are exactly alike. Can that be true? We just had a huge snowstorm here in Michigan, so I just spent several hours digging out and have personally moved trillions of snowflakes. Surely somewhere in the universe in all the years that it has been snowing, there must have been two ice crystals that are (or at least were) exactly alike. And besides, who would know? Who is checking every snowflake?

Well, according to California Institute of Technology physicist Kenneth G. Libbrecht, who maintains a wonderfully informative and interesting Web site at SnowCrystals.com, the chances of two snowflakes being completely identical at the atomic level is "indistinguishable from zero." Libbrecht explains why. Briefly, he says that a single small snowflake contains roughly 1,000,000,000,000,000,000 (10^{18}) water molecules. Not all water molecules are exactly alike. True, water molecules consist of two hydrogen atoms bonded to one oxygen atom. But hydrogen and oxygen atoms have different isotopes (weight classes). So considering the known frequencies of the isotopes of hydrogen and oxygen, approximately 10^{15} of the 10^{18} molecules in our one small snowflake have heavy hydrogen and/or oxygen. The placement of isotopic water molecules during crystal formation contribute to structural variations in snowflakes. Add to that the fact that temperature and humidity also affect snowflake formation, and it is easy to see that the number of ways to put a snow crystal together is enormous. We can't even guess what it would be. But a 1 followed by anything from 100 to 300 zeros is a good starting point. That number is actually much larger than the number of atoms in the observable universe, which scientists estimate to be a 1 followed by only 80 zeros.

Certainly one of the treasures of the snow that Job may have been asking about (see Job 38:22, KJV) is the beauty and complexity of snow crystals. Our God continually reveals Himself as a lover of beauty, order, indescribable complexity, and unimaginable variety.

And to think, there are even more ways to make a person.

Lord, You knit me together in my mother's womb. I too must be unique and special to You. How precious to me are Your thoughts, O God! How vast is the sum of them!

March 2

Thinking Dirt

And the Lord God formed man of the dust of the ground, and breathed into his nostrils the breath of life; and man became a living being. Gen. 2:7, NKJV.

I never cease to be astonished at what God can make out of dirt. You know, the stuff that you are constantly digging out from under your fingernails after working in the garden, what you have to wash off your hands or sweep out of your house because it keeps coming in on the kids' shoes, yet dirt is a substance that magically turns into corn, or beans, or radishes, or plums, or apples after you bury the seed in the soil. Then it amazes me how He can then convert all this amazing variety of plant material into cows or horses; monkeys, parrots, sunfish or anglerfish; egrets or peacocks, all depending on what it is that eats the plants. But I like to think that the underlying reason for all this flurry of creation was to make a comfortable place, an infinitely interesting home, for what God really wanted to make—dirt that could think about the Creator, dirt that could imagine the future, and remember the past. That thinking dirt is us—*Homo sapiens* (homo is Latin for humus, dirt, earth, and sapiens is Latin for wise or capable of discerning). To be human is to think about how we got here and where we are going. No other life-form does that.

Come to think of it, thinking dirt behaves in some ways like its Creator. We take the dirt in all its forms and the stuff that grows out of it and create other things. Though we are unable to endow our creations with life, our creations from dirt are the stuff around us such as houses, skyscrapers, roads, cars, boats, airplanes, power plants, bone china, crystal goblets, cell phones, iPods, and computers. Think about how dirt or something from the ground is an important component of everything that we eat or wear. Then we even try to program computers to think. But computers can think only as they are programmed to do so. Lacking the power of choice, they can't meditate about their creator, their past, or their future.

Lord, my thoughts turn to You in gratitude and praise for the gift of life. I worship You as my Creator and my best friend. Forgive me for how I have responded badly to You in the past. My desire is to honor You this day and in all my plans for the future.

The Bill of the Toucan

But God chose the foolish things of the world to shame the wise; God chose the weak things of the world to shame the strong. 1 Cor. 1:27, NIV.

G od must have a delightful sense of humor. Consider the toco toucan, a South American bird that I have often seen in zoos. The first thing I notice about a toco toucan is its monstrous bill. It is in fact the largest of all bird bills relative to body size. Though it looks massively heavy, it weighs only one twentieth of the bird's body weight. Structural engineers say that, considering its lightness, it is remarkably strong. The brightly colored outside covering of the bill consists of overlapping tiles of keratin, like our fingernails. The inside of the bill is a rigid closed-cell foam construction— both features much like new car bumpers and glider wings.

At first glance, it seems that such a huge beak would be a serious design defect. Evolutionary biologists obsessed with finding a reason for every structure have really been scratching their heads over this one. What do toucans use this enormous bill for? Employing just their huge bills, the playful birds seem to enjoy wrestling (sort of like arm wrestling) and berry tossing (playing catch by throwing a berry back and forth). They certainly use it for berry and fruit picking and for peeling fruit. Could it be a weapon for fighting or protecting themselves from predators? It doesn't seem to be employed that way except maybe to scare off critters that think such a big brightly colored weapon would be lethal. Could it serve in courtship? That was Charles Darwin's guess, since the bill is brightly colored and makes a nice billboard (no pun intended). Now scientists have discovered that the big bill helps in heat regulation. Birds can't sweat, and toucans live in hot tropical areas. Adult birds can apparently control blood flow to the bill, thus regulating its temperature and the amount of heat loss through its uninsulated structure. In fact, toucan bills are the most efficient heat exchangers yet discovered in any animal, actually four times more efficient than elephant or rabbit ears, other well-known heat exchangers.

Could some of the "defects" in my physical features or personality or life experiences be an important part of God's design for bringing me or others into His kingdom?

Lord, though I simply don't understand why You gave me this _____, let me use it to honor and glorify You as my Creator. Assure me again that You do not make junk.

March 4

Trypanosoma

Watch out for false prophets. They come to you in sheep's clothing, but inwardly they are ferocious wolves. Matt. 7:15, NIV.

A s a kid growing up in Africa, I remember seeing people with various tropical diseases coming to my dad for help. Many had deep, bloody, fly- and maggot-infested tropical sores that make me hurt even now just thinking about them. Some arrived with injuries, others with skin diseases, tuberculosis, and a variety of parasites. One of those parasites, *Trypanosoma brucei*, causes a particularly insidious disease called African sleeping sickness. I didn't know what that was then. But in my biologist-trained mind's eye, I now see microscopic critters looking somewhat like tiny fish swimming among their victims' red blood cells. The blood parasites are what cause the disease.

Trypanosomes have been under intense study for more than a century. And for decades it has been a mystery how the microscopic parasites can live in the bloodstream and wreak havoc without our immune systems detecting and eliminating them. Years of painstaking research is now uncovering their secret. It now looks as if trypanosomes have more than 800 genes dedicated to deception and trickery. You see, our immune system is constantly checking the surface chemistry of all cells. If one shows up in our body with a surface coat that doesn't belong—a surface coat that isn't "you"—your immune system will recognize the cell as foreign and mount an immune response that involves preparing killer cells programmed to recognize the intruder and then destroy it. The 800-gene deception, however, gives the trypanosome an advantage. It alters its own surface chemistry every few days. Like the robber that changes his jacket after a holdup to avoid detection and arrest, the parasite constantly varies its coat. By the time our immune system has mounted a response to one surface layer, the trypanosome has altered it and thus avoids attack. In this way the parasite continues to live in its human host, causing fever, severe headaches, aching joints, brain inflammation, seizures, extreme tiredness, coma, and eventually death.

Come to think of it, the devil's deceptions are all around us in many different forms. Experience shows that they cause brain damage of the worst kind.

Lord, equip me with Your divine insights so that I can detect deceptions. Clarify my understanding so that I will not be caught sleeping under the influence of sin.

Gibson and Boo Boo

Many, O Lord my God, are Your wonderful works which You have done; and Your thoughts which are toward us cannot be recounted to You in order; if I would declare and speak of them, they are more than can be numbered. Ps. 40:5, NKJV.

G oogle the title of today's reading and you will see pictures and stories of the world's tallest dog, Gibson, meeting the world's smallest dog, Boo Boo (as documented in the Guinness Book of World Records). Gibson, a great Dane, and Boo Boo, a toy Chihuahua, are vastly different in size and appearance. And since they are both dogs, classified by biologists in the same species, *Canis familiaris*, they nicely illustrate variations within the created kind. To see a similar contrast in the human species, google "Wilt Chamberlain" and "Willie Shoemaker." My search took 0.13 seconds and found 1,480 hits. The first several show the famous picture of Wilt "the stilt," a National Basketball Association player, towering above Willy Shoemaker, a well-known horse racing jockey. What is interesting to me is that these four examples illustrate the range of differences within kinds or within biological species.

Far more vital, however, is that I come to know the one true Creator-God and that I become one of His people in deed and in truth.

Estimates of how many species exist on earth vary widely. If you look at just one well-known and intensely studied family of plants—the orchids— experts recognize about 450 genera with anywhere from 10,000 to 20,000 different species, with more being discovered and described as I write. Biologists have described 350,000 species of beetles, though beetle specialists think there are probably a million species total—yet that is only a guess. The experts disagree among themselves. Some estimate that we are likely to find 100 million species of beetles. Of course, within each of those 100 million species we may well find additional variations similar to what we find with dogs and people.

What are we going to name them all? What names does God give them? Surely He must have some, because He named all the stars. More important, He knows every detail of our lives. Far more vital, however, is that I come to know the one true Creator-God and that I become one of His people in deed and in truth.

Lord, it is written that You will give me a heart to know You and that I will return to You with all my heart. Give me that knowing heart today.

Healthy Bones

A cheerful heart is good medicine, but a crushed spirit dries up the bones. Prov. 17:22, NIV.

A recent study reported in the journal Psychological Science claims that the intensity of your smile in your photographs is a reliable predictor of how long you might live. How come I have a sudden urge to start looking through my family albums so I can score how many of my pictures have that huge ear-to-ear grin or happy-go-lucky smile? The research scored the smile intensity in pictures of hundreds of professional baseball players. Since health and longevity records were being compared with smile intensity, the researchers used only players who had begun their major league careers before 1950. The athletes who showed up in pictures with the biggest smiles had only half the risk of dying compared to those with a straight face.

We have long known about the detrimental effects of stress. But what about the positive effects of a light and happy spirit? The health effects of humor first broke into my consciousness when Norman Cousins, a noted author, editor, and speaker, wrote his famous Anatomy of an Illness (first published in 1979). Cousins, who suffered from heart disease and painful joint inflammation, described the healing effects of laughter. Since Cousins brought attention to the issue, the scientific literature on laughter and healing increased exponentially. It appears now that having the biblical "merry heart" increases health; reduces the risk of heart disease; decreases the incidence of heart arrhythmias; speeds healing after heart attacks; elevates growth hormone; decreases cortisol, dopamine, and epinephrine (all stress factors); enhances immunological health by increasing the activity of natural killer cells and immunoglobulins; and increases longevity. In fact, many major hospitals now have a clown care unit or something equivalent in which specially trained clowns assist children undergoing serious testing or treatment. For as Groucho Marx once quipped: "A clown is like an asprin, only he works twice as fast." Proverbs 15:30 suggests that simply putting on a happy face changes how I feel inside and brings health and healing. Oh, the power that is mine when I realize that I can choose to discipline my thoughts, think positively, and put on my happy face every day.

Lord, teach me to trust You totally. I choose to give You my cares. I choose to forgive those who have caused me pain. I choose to put on that happy face that brings joy to the heart and healing to my bones.

The Armor Bearer

Praise the Lord from the earth, you great sea creatures and all ocean depths. Ps. 148:7, NIV.

We all know about Lucifer, the former light bearer cast out of heaven. The literal meaning of the Latin words *lucem ferre* means "light bearer." In the news today I read about a newly discovered kind of *Loricifera*, an armor bearer (from the Latin *lorica ferre*). What these two have in common is that God created both, and they both have (or at least had) the privilege of praising God. Lucifer made the idolatrous choice of worshipping himself rather than God, and he will have his reward in hell. The newly discovered loriciferan now lives in a hellish sulfurous environment but praises God just the same.

After closely studying the many life-forms that share space with us on our planet, biologists were pretty certain that only some species of the single-cell bacteria were able to live without oxygen. Animals occasionally enter anoxic (oxygenless) environments for short periods of time, although multicellular organisms need oxygen at least for some of their life functions. But now, from more than 11,500 feet (3,500 meters) below the surface of the Mediterranean Sea, scientists have found a few new species of loriciferan animals living in the freezing cold, dark, sulfurous, seafloor muck and oozes in a totally anoxic, extreme-pressure environment. If true, it is an astounding discovery, because it means that there are ways to live and process energy that we simply don't know about yet. Biologists have dredged up substantial populations of the tiny creatures in all phases of their life cycle, so it appears as if they live and thrive there. To visualize what these animals look like, imagine a tiny transparent thimble less than a half millimeter long. The crystalline thimble is the tiny body armor from whence the organism gets its name. To complete the picture, imagine several dozen tiny tentacles and protrusions sticking out of the thimble and waving in all directions, feeding, reproducing, thriving, faithfully doing what they were created to do.

Praise the Lord from the earth, you great sea creatures and all you creatures that live in the depths of the ocean. The tiny loriciferans praise their Creator by living and thriving where they were placed. What a concept! In simply doing what He created me to do, I praise and honor my Maker.

Lord, when I'm tempted to complain about my lot in life, remind me to take a deep breath and to praise You with simple acts of kindness and love to those around me.

March 8

Still Clueless

Let them praise the name of the Lord, for He commanded and they were created. Ps. 148:5, NKJV.

One of my former college students had a great interest in studying creatures that live in the sea. For many years she was a scientist at the famous Monterey Bay Aquarium Research Institute (MBARI) in California. One of her tasks was to identify or describe the creatures that drifted through the lights of the remotely operated underwater vehicle (ROV) as it traveled to and from the ocean floor miles below. The ROV, a tethered robot with lights and cameras, sample gathering equipment, and many instruments to measure water qualities, temperature, and light, routinely explores the depths where it is too dangerous for human beings to go. The crushing pressures, the total darkness, and the freezing cold prevent us from visiting there ourselves.

Deep-ocean biologists used to think that the ocean floor was nearly devoid of life. ROVs have now spent enough time taking pictures and bringing back samples to prove otherwise. The ocean floor teems with life. In 2003 scientists had identified roughly 6,000 kinds of marine microbes—bacteria, archaea, single-celled protists, and viruses. Late in 2003 a consortium of more than 2,000 scientists from 80 countries led by marine microbiologists from MBARI decided to mount a major initiative to know and understand single-celled organisms in the ocean. The International Census of Marine Microbes (ICoMM) was born. Educated predictions were that they would find as many as 600,000 kinds of marine microbes.

Seven years later samples have been collected from more than 1,200 sites around the world. The flood of new information has filled data banks, and the analysis of that data goes on day and night. The results are astounding. If they had found twice as many microbes as they expected it would be amazing, and 10 times as many would be breathtaking. But no, researchers have discovered nearly 100 times as many types as they expected. Conservative estimates now place the number at 20 million types of marine microbes. When I read these numbers I shake my head in wonder and think to myself, We simply don't have a clue. God's creative thoughts are unfathomable.

Lord, when I am tempted to think that I have it all figured out, humble me with more discoveries that remind me that You are Creator and I am creature.

Morel Hunting

If you seek him, he will be found by you; but if you forsake him, he will reject you forever. 1 Chron. 28:9. NIV.

I well remember the pleasure of finding my first morel mushroom along the edge of our yard one spring morning. Then I saw another, and another. Quickly I picked a generous double handful of the cream-colored beauties, took them inside, sliced them open, washed and blotted them dry, sautéed them in butter, and enjoyed them for breakfast with French toast and fruit. What delectable eating. If you have ever been out morel hunting—and eating—you know the delights that I am talking about.

Morchella esculenta, the yellow morel, and *Morchella elata*, the black, gray, or smoky morel, make the most delicious mushroom eating that you can imagine. Totally hollow, these mushrooms have a deeply pitted cap. The bottom edge of the cap attaches directly and seamlessly to the hollow stem. Pinecone mushroom or sponge mushroom or even honeycomb mushroom are some common names for morels, and for good reason. The names fit. The appearance is so distinctive that you can't mistake a morel for anything else. If you are not used to hunting and eating wild mushrooms, however, it is best to check very carefully with a reliable source, because false morels can poison the unwary.

Morels usually put in their appearance in early spring when daytime temperatures are between 60 and 70 degrees, nighttime temperatures not lower than 45, soil temperature creeping up above 50, and the soil has moderate moisture. Experienced morel hunters have a feel for when conditions are right. They simply disappear into the woods and spend a great deal of time out of sight. When they emerge they will generally have a big open netting onion bagful of beautiful morels. Could it be that the really successful morel hunters are the ones who just keep at it, won't give up, and are much more determined than the average?

And could it be that our search for God demands an even higher determination and passion? Might it be important that we disappear into our closet for quality time together with our Creator and Savior? "Taste and see that the Lord is good; blessed is the one who takes refuge in him" (Ps. 34:8, NIV).

Lord, give me a powerful hunger for connecting with You. I choose to seek You with all my heart, because You have promised that You will be found. Keep me searching.

Sweeter Than Honey

How sweet are your words to my taste, sweeter than honey to my mouth! Ps. 119:103, NIV.

D o you have a sweet tooth? I know that I do. For as long as I can remember I have always enjoyed eating anything that is sweet. Sometimes a dessert passes by and others at the table describe it as just too rich. But there is no such thing as being too rich for my taste. If you have the so-called sweet tooth, you understand what I am talking about.

For a long time we have known that we detect sweetness when it comes in contact with taste buds on the tip of the tongue. So how does it work? What has to happen for a drop of honey on your tongue to register as sweet pleasure in your brain? It is really quite simple.

First you have to have gene T1R2 and gene T1R3 in your DNA. Most of us have that. Each gene makes its own protein. The two proteins come together to make a special G protein coupled receptor called gustadin, which is your sweet receptor in the cell membrane of sweet-detecting cells of a taste bud. Sugar molecules in the honey have multiple parts that dock in corresponding multiple parts of the receptor. It is sort of like a three-prong plug going into a wall receptacle. Until the three prongs fit into the right holes, the light doesn't come on. When the sugar molecule is connected properly in all its parts—that is, when it fits correctly—the G protein gustadin changes shape. That shape change activates adenylate cyclase, a nearby enzyme. Adenylate cyclase alters ATP to cAMP, and cAMP activates a protein kinase, whose job it is to add phosphate to a potassium channel. That addition snaps the channel closed. With the potassium channel closed, positively charged phosphate ions build up inside the cell. It helps to know that normal cells have a negative charge inside so the buildup of a positive charge is a shift from normal. As soon as a certain charge threshold is reached, voltage-gated calcium ion channels pop open, which floods the cell with even more positive ions. This flood of positive charge generates a signal that ultimately reaches the sweetness pleasure center of your brain.

Even sweeter and more pleasurable, however, are God's words of love, encouragement, and hope for me in this sin-sick world.

Since I seem to have particularly good T1R2 and T1R3 genes, I worship Him who made this amazing system of sweet detection and enjoyment. Even sweeter and more pleasurable, however, are God's words of love, encouragement, and hope for me in this sin-sick world.

Lord, thank You for inviting me to taste and see that You are a good and loving God. I long to sit at Your banquet table and hear the sweetness of Your words with my own ears.

March 11

Umami

Isaac, who had a taste for wild game, loved Esau, but Rebekah loved Jacob. Gen. 25:28, NIV.

I am told that we have about 9,000 taste buds on our tongue that are apparently "tuned" to one of five different flavors. Those flavor groups are salty, sour, sweet, bitter, and umami. Wait you say? U-what? What is umami? It is the savory taste in meats and in aged or fermented products such as cheeses or soy sauce. Mushrooms also have umami. In 2002 science formally added it to the list of what taste experts believed that taste buds detect. I understand that the sweet, salty, and sour tastes have been standard from the beginning. Then thousands of years ago Greek philosophers Leucippus and his student Democritus added the bitter flavor to the tongue's repertoire. So adding umami in 2002 appears to be a significant advance in our understanding of something as basic as taste.

Umami is a Japanese word for "yummy" or "delicious." Other descriptors would be "meaty" or "savory." In 1908 Kikunae Ikeda, a Japanese chemist, identified L-glutamate as the tasty ingredient in dashi, a Japanese soup made from seaweed. The delightful tastes of dashi and seaweed extracts popular in Asian cuisine, however, were similar to some of the world-famous haute cuisine flavors created by Auguste Escoffier, legendary French chef and contemporary of Ikeda. Escoffier was so good at coming up with his tasty creations that the French press called him the "king of chefs and chef of kings." After identifying L-glutamate as the heart and soul of umami, Ikeda went on to create monosodium glutamate (MSG), patented in 1909 by the Japanese company that even today specializes in producing MSG. A report in the American Journal of Clinical Nutrition reports that the 2009 world production of MSG was 2 billion kilograms and rising. That is a lot of interest and effort to enhance flavor and taste.

It seems to me that God created healthful and nutritious foods with the amino acid glutamine and then gave us taste buds on our tongue that give us pleasurable sensations to signal that we are eating what is good. I thank Him for giving you and me this built-in detector of the good and the healthful. I often wonder what God thinks when we sprinkle that signal on highly processed foods. Isn't that a misrepresentation to our brain and a fraud to our body that stands in need of the good stuff? What do you think?

Lord, in our age of over-commercialization and marketing of highly processed foods, help me to make wise and healthy choices. Remind me again that my body is Your temple.

March 12

The Taste of Bitter

Woe to those who call evil good, and good evil; who put darkness for light, and light for darkness; who put bitter for sweet, and sweet for bitter! Isa. 5:20, NKJV.

H ave you ever confused the taste of bitter and sweet? Normally it would never be a problem because a sweet flavor tastes good to most people, and most sweet-tasting chemicals are rich in calories and turn out to be good food sources. Bitter chemicals, on the other hand, we generally judge as quite unpleasant. Many plant alkaloids, amines, and ammonium salts, among others, taste bitter, and most are toxic or poisonous. So the bitter taste is an excellent warning sign boldly proclaiming "Do Not Eat." One interesting similarity shared by the sweet-and-bitter-detecting cells is that both have a very wide variety of chemicals that will cause them to fire off signals to the brain. And though we still have much to learn about exactly how the two contrasting chemical-detecting systems work, both appear to have multiple methods of alerting us to the taste of either the pleasant and sweet or the disagreeable and bitter. Evidence suggests that both systems work when taste molecules "plug" into cell surface receptors and trigger the taste sensation. But other evidence strongly supports the conclusion that, in the multiplicity of taste molecules that produce a response, at least some of them rapidly cross the cell membrane and work on the various parts of the signal transduction pathway inside the cell.

Many people use certain bitter plant alkaloids. One is the highly addictive and poisonous alkaloid called nicotine made by the roots of the tobacco plant. Its leaves store the poison in order to kill insects that eat them. People who smoke receive small enough doses of nicotine that its primary effect is to make them highly dependent on smoking. Coffee beans are another source of numerous alkaloids, including caffeine, various xanthines, theophylline, theobromine, and trigonelline, to name a few. Some of these substances are extremely bitter, but because of masking by other chemicals, many enjoy the coffee flavor. Caffeine is also slightly addictive in that heavy drinkers get headaches and do not function well without the morning fix. I am thankful to the Creator for giving us such reliable taste systems that rarely confuse the good and the bad. The great deceiver, of course, is on a mission to redefine good and evil.

My Creator and my God, I invite You into my life and into my sensory receptors so that I will always know the difference between good and evil. Strengthen my will to do good and to shun evil.

March 13

Breastfeeding

Like newborn babies, crave pure spiritual milk, so that by it you may grow up in your salvation, now that you have tasted that the Lord is good. 1 Peter 2:2, 3, NIV.

T he birth of a baby has to be one of the greatest miracles of life. On average, about four babies enter our world every second. During that same second approximately two people die, so that the world population is increasing at the rate of about two people per second. It is a statistic that I have a hard time with, because I know how much pain and sadness there is in our sin-sick world. My prayer is Lord, take care of all those precious lives. A human life is a unit with the greatest known value.

A human life is a unit with the greatest known value.

As each healthy baby comes into the world kicking and screaming, it is generally hungry and is ready to eat. When mother cradles baby in her arms, the food is right there at the infant's mouth, and baby is programmed to root around and latch on and start sucking, drinking in that life-giving milk—another profound miracle story of production. When you study the system from a designer's perspective, it looks "very good."

So what is in mother's milk? Is it good nutrition for the newborn? Does it meet specifications for growth and development? Much research done during the past two decades clearly shows that it is the perfect baby food. It appears to be designed by a loving Creator who knows what He is doing. Consider these observations.

For the first few days mother's milk (called colostrum) is rich in proteins and low in sugar and fats. A perfect nutritional blend, it boosts the baby's immune system and kick-starts the function of the infant's fairly inactive and inexperienced digestive tract. For the next few days the milk changes to a sweet watery liquid called transitional milk. The baby gets fully hydrated, and the sweetness appeals to the baby's awakening senses. Roughly two weeks into life, mother's milk composition shifts again to the so-called mature milk with watery foremilk and thicker, creamier hindmilk. The fat and sugar content continue to rise, and the immunoglobulin levels fall. After about six months babies begin supplementing their diets with a little solid food as they continue their growth and development. What an analogy. God calls us out of darkness into marvelous light. Born again, we grow unto salvation by feeding on the pure milk of the gospel. It too is just what we need for spiritual development.

Lord, may I hunger and thirst after righteousness. Feed me till I want no more.

On Hunger

Quick, let me have some of that red stew! I'm famished!
Gen. 25:30, NIV.

H ot, sweaty, thirsty, and very hungry from his long hike carrying a full-grown antelope, Esau staggers home, exhausted and irritable. It's no wonder. His blood sugar is at rock bottom. The hunger center in the hypothalamus of his brain is screaming, "Feed me. Let's get some food in here—and quickly."

You know the feeling, don't you? Stomach growling in pain from its contractions, you are weak and grouchy and need to eat. If you are lucky, you sit down to a wonderful meal, taking your time to enjoy the food until you are satisfied. Even after decades of research and thousands of scientific papers we still have so much to learn about the complicated process of hunger and satiety.

What we do know is that the feelings of hunger happen, in part, from an empty and contracting stomach. Blood chemistry will now reveal low levels of important nutrients such as triglycerides, glucose, and amino acids. Lots of physiological and psychological factors play a role here. Smelling the aroma of food gets the salivary juices flowing. Then, as food enters the mouth, certain food molecules plug into receptor sites on the surface of cells in taste buds, letting the brain know that nourishment is coming. Relief is on the way. Simply chewing food sends signals to the brain that start the process of telling it that food is on its way. Significant digestion has to take place before blood chemistry rises to normal, so other factors have to let you know that your needs have been satisfied during the lag time. That's why stretch receptors in the stomach start firing as the stomach gets full. If they are working well enough, they inhibit the feeding center, and before long, the food doesn't look as tempting as it used to. It doesn't smell as attractive. Becoming aware of those important stop signs, you push back from the table and say, "I'm full and couldn't eat another bite."

Eating too fast makes us overshoot the stop signs so that we eat too much, one cause of obesity. Stop signs that don't function well or at all often need both psychological and physiological treatment.

Lord, thank You for the integrated system of chemical sensors, stretch receptors, and control devices that help to keep me nourished. May I use them to honor and glorify You.

Weather Forecasting

When evening comes, you say, "It will be fair weather, for the sky is red." Matt. 16:2, NIV.

What will the weather be like tomorrow? What about three or five days from now? Will we be able to enjoy our garden wedding? What about the camping trip next weekend? Will that be a "sit-in-a-leaky-tent-all-weekend-bonding experience" or will it be a fine weekend of hiking and bird-watching?

Modern weather forecasting relies on a combination of many methods. The type we see in Matthew 16:2 above is the "analog" method. In the past, fair weather usually followed a red evening sky. So using the past as our pattern, we figure that if we see a red evening sky tonight, we will have fair weather tomorrow. People still use the analog method today. But instead of looking at just sky color, for example, we take thousands of other factors into consideration. The method is good but suffers from the fact that no two days are just alike in all the thousands of other factors involved.

Other methods go by such terms as persistence, trends, climatology, and numerical weather prediction (NWP). Briefly, the persistence method states that the weather we are having today will most likely continue tomorrow. And barring strong winds or other changes, that works pretty well. The trends method looks at wind directions and speeds and suggests that what they are experiencing 50 miles west of here will arrive in a couple hours. The climatology method simply averages what has happened at this time and place for the past 100 years or so. The best method is the NWP method. This method utilizes current data from thousands of weather stations all over the world: temperature, humidity, wind, barometric pressure, water temperature, current, cloud cover, and so much more. The data comes from the surface and from many different altitudes and ocean depths. All the numbers go into giant supercomputers that crunch them using mathematical formulas, and out comes the forecasts. But because of missing data and flaws in the mathematical assumptions and understandings, forecasts are still not completely reliable.

In an attempt to elicit more dependence on God in his people, the prophet Samuel prayed for the rain to come during the wheat harvest, a time when rain was unheard of based on the climatology method. That same day rain fell, and all the people stood in awe of the Lord (see 1 Sam. 12:17, 18).

Lord, we acknowledge that You control the weather. It does what You tell it to do. If need be, use it to teach us to depend totally on You. Bid the storm in our heart, "Peace, be still!"

March 16

The Perfect Storm

His thunder announces the coming storm; even the cattle make known its approach. Job 36:33, NIV.

I love a good thunderstorm, especially one that develops on those hot, humid dog days of summer. The air is so humid that nobody feels like moving. While man and beast lethargically move about, the hot, sticky air rises, expands, and cools as it gets higher. Cooling water vapor condenses and forms a cloud. The process of condensation, however, releases heat, which can keep the inside of the cloud warm enough to keep it expanding and rising even higher—miles up. The condensed water drops begin to fall, but strong updrafts hold them aloft, carrying the warm air mass up through miles of troposphere, near its boundary with the stratosphere, which we call the tropopause—the layer in which strong jet streams blow. The jet stream stretches the massive cloud into a typical anvil shape that we recognize as a thunderhead or cumulonimbus. Static charges build up between the rising wet, negatively charged warm air and the sinking positively charged colder, drier air.

When the charge difference is sufficient, great bolts of lightning streak back and forth, helping to equalize the charge. Or the lightning discharge might strike between the negatively charged clouds and the positively charged ground. The heat of lightning causes air to expand at supersonic speeds. Like jets breaking the sound barrier, we hear the sonic booms of mighty thunder that rattles the windows and pounds in your chest. Before the rain hits, you feel the cold downdraft of air from the clouds piled high above, and the trees start to bend back and forth as the wind picks up—then the big drops begin plopping all around, kicking up little clouds of dust. Quickly the rain intensifies into one of God's sweetest gifts to humanity—moisture falling out of the clouds in abundance. Sweet, clean, cold, solar-distilled water pours down in torrents in a complicated process that happens many times every day all over the earth. Recent satellite data shows that on average, about 3 million lightning strikes occur each day. In Psalm 29 David describes the voice of the Lord as powerful, majestic, and striking with flashes of lightning. When I see a good thunderstorm, I hear the voice of the Lord and thank Him for His power and glory and long for the time He will appear accompanied with thunder and lightning. Even so, come, Lord Jesus.

I acknowledge You as King of kings and Lord of lords. How I long to see Your throne high and lifted up, giving off lightning, rumblings, and peals of thunder (Rev. 4:4).

Green Green Grass

He unleashes his lightning beneath the whole heaven and sends it to the ends of the earth. Job 37:3, NIV. He fills his hands with lightning and commands it to strike its mark. Job 36:32, NIV.

Have you noticed how fresh and green the grass is after a thunderstorm crashes through your neighborhood? It seems as if the darker and noisier the storm and the more lightning and thunder that happens during the storm, the more green and beautiful the grass is afterward. Some of this effect obviously results because of the deep watering of a thirsty lawn. And perhaps some of the effect may simply be the contrast between the dark, brooding, stormy sky and the brilliant sunshine highlighting the emerald grass as it peeks out after the storm.

My experience is that few are aware of the bonus gift received from every passing lightning storm. The fact is that your lawn, shrubs, trees, and garden get a dose of nitrogen fertilizer thanks to a wonderful chemical reactions powered by lightning. Here is how it works.

Normal dry air consists of 78.1 percent molecular nitrogen, 20.9 percent molecular oxygen, with the remainder consisting of lots of other gases, such as hydrogen, argon, helium, ozone, and carbon dioxide, all in much, much smaller quantities. Molecular nitrogen is a diatomic molecule designated as N_2. The two atoms of N_2 are connected by a triple covalent bond, a very strong bond indeed, which is why plants can't use atmospheric nitrogen. Commercial fertilizer production starts with hydrogen from methane or coal, nitrogen from the air, high temperatures and high pressures to help break the triple bond, and several catalysts to convert atmospheric nitrogen into ammonia NH_4, which is then oxidized into the nitrates and nitrites that plants use. Making commercial fertilizer is a time- and fossil fuel-consuming process, which explains why the price of fertilizer keeps rising along with energy costs.

I am grateful that God in His wisdom asks lightning to hit its mark, and quicker than you can say "Ka-boom," the great heat and pressure of lightning converts atmospheric nitrogen directly into ammonia, nitrates, and nitrites. In God's reaction chamber these molecules quickly combine with raindrops that fertilize your grass. This bonus gift comes with each lightning storm. Let us worship and praise Him for His wonderful works.

Lord, thank You for the example of King David, who ruled in the fear of God like the light of the morning, like brightness after a rain that brings the grass from the earth.

March 18

Programmed Cell Death

For if you live according to the flesh you will die; but if by the Spirit you put to death the deeds of the body, you will live. Rom. 8:13, NKJV.

A re you aware that, day in and day out, your body may be replacing cells at the rate of about 1 million cells per second? Sometimes cells have to die so that other cells (and the rest of the body) may live—a concept first studied in tadpole tail shortening as early as 1842. But it wasn't until 1990 that science had the tools to explore programmed cell death systems in detail. Some of those studies resulted in Sydney Brenner, Robert Horvitz, and John Sulston receiving a 2002 Nobel Prize in Medicine for what we now call apoptosis or programmed cell death. Ongoing research continues to demonstrate the importance of apoptosis in understanding various types of cancer, autoimmune diseases, and normal growth and development. That apoptosis does not refer to cells that die because of some type of injury I emphasize by the title to this reading. What is going on here is a natural, multiple, sequential step (programmed) process in which a cell kills itself or commits suicide. When embryos develop normally, some early cells have to be removed, akin to taking down the scaffolding and concrete forms after we have completed parts of a building. Normal genes in these cells turn on and start the program that leads to their removal. Some non-developmental cells may be affected by external stimuli that trigger apoptosis that leads to their demise. Examples here would be cells infected by a virus, cells that incur DNA damage, or cells that have turned cancerous. Each of these scenarios would normally start apoptosis in the affected cells, thus removing them from the cell population.

A number of highly complex mechanisms may initiate apoptosis, but once that happens, the sequential steps begin with the cell shrinking, its surface bubbling outward, and its DNA and some cell proteins digested and recycled. The mitochondria within break down and release cytochrome c as the cell collapses into tiny vesicles releasing both ATP and UTP, which signal passing phagocytic cells (cells that consume microorganisms and debris of dead cells) to gather around and eat. The complexity of mechanisms, receptors, and choreography of events for accomplishing apoptosis is stunning and appears to be a carefully designed system to protect cells from disease and enable them to undergo normal growth and development. Once again we see the fingerprints of a loving Creator-God.

Lord, You too died so that I might live. My heart responds in gratitude and praise.

March 19

Splendor of Lilies

And why do you worry about clothes? See how the flowers of the field grow. They do not labor or spin. Yet I tell you that not even Solomon in all his splendor was dressed like one of these. Matt. 6:28, 29, NIV.

I n His sermon on the mount Jesus included a section on worry. None of us want our children to wonder where they will find their next meal or if we are going to provide clothes. So, as parents, we can relate to a loving God who asks us not to fret about such things. In this context Jesus described the lilies of the field as not worrying about what they should wear, yet, thanks to their Creator, they are dressed far better than Solomon when in his finest. That illustration must have meant a lot to His listeners. I can only imagine what Solomon looked like in his royal robes.

Several thousand species of lilies comprise more than 300 genera, 108 of those native in the United States. Needless to say, as a group they would make quite a stunning array. The lily family includes lots of little spring flowers such as the hyacinth, tiger and Easter lilies, onions, garlic, and others all the way up to tree-sized plants such as the Yucca plant.

> **None of us want our children to wonder where they will find their next meal or if we are going to provide clothes.**

I think that one of the most beautiful lily genera is *Calochortus*. With 78 different species and varieties of *Calochortus*, we certainly have lots to choose from. Most of them are the various types of mariposa lilies. Some of them are called star lilies or star tulip. Check them out in garden magazines or in photos on the Internet. Their flowers are elegant and colorful. But of course, beauty is always "in the eye of the beholder."

Wildflower photography is one hobby to which I have devoted considerable time and money. Focusing carefully on the beauty of flowering plants in all types of lighting and stages of life cycle has helped me to see and appreciate much more beauty than I had ever imagined. My lifetime of studying the molecular biology and the ultrastructure of these same plants as evidenced by both transmission and scanning electron microscopy has heightened my awe and wonder even more. No doubt an eternity in heaven will be a place to continue this trend, because "no eye has seen, . . . no ear has heard, . . . no human mind has conceived the things God has prepared for those who love him" (1 Cor. 2:9, NIV). What a "No Worry" God is ours!

Praise the Lord, O my soul. O Lord my God, You are very great—You are clothed with splendor and majesty.

This Is My Father's World

The earth is the Lord's, and everything in it, the world, and all who live in it; for he founded it on the seas and established it on the waters. Ps. 24:1, 2, NIV.

I f you ever visit downtown Baltimore, Maryland, you may enjoy the Brown Memorial Park Avenue Presbyterian Church on the corner of Park and Lafayette avenues. An excellent example of Gothic Revival architecture, the church was dedicated in 1870. Its soaring vaulted arches support a blue ceiling that covers "the most magnificent interior space in Baltimore City," according to one Baltimore news writer. Among its many stained-glass windows are 11 original ones designed by Louis Comfort Tiffany, son of Charles Lewis Tiffany, founder of Tiffany and Company, famous the world over for jewelry and silverware. Son Louis is known best for his artistry and creativity in stained-glass windows.

One of the largest and most beautiful windows that he ever created was installed in the Baltimore church in 1905. Entitled "The Holy City," its 58 panels depict the apostle John in vision on the isle of Patmos as well as imagined scenes from the vision itself. This magnificent glass creation was dedicated to Maltbie Davenport Babcock, talented and beloved minister who for nearly 14 years enthusiastically led his flock of prominent Baltimorians to the Creator but who died prematurely in 1901, little more than a year after moving to the Brick Church of New York City. Though Babcock didn't publish his writings, his wife, Catherine, assembled a collection of his poems and sermons after his death. One of those poems contains the words for the popular hymn "This Is My Father's World." Described as athletic, Babcock enjoyed frequent hikes. After his death, Catherine said that her husband's parting words on leaving for a hike were that he was "going out to see the Father's world."

In the hymn text Babcock properly and eloquently worships and gives credit to the Creator-God. The next 22 readings will expand on individual lines from Babcock's text, because the vignettes from nature "declare their maker's praise." Simply put, idolatry is misplaced worship—i.e., worship of the creature rather than the Creator. Psalm 24:4 states that those who will enjoy heaven will be those who have not misplaced their worship: "He who has clean hands and a pure heart, who has not lifted up his soul to an idol, nor sworn deceitfully" (NKJV) will be the ones who stand in his holy place.

Lord, may I ever know that You are the King of glory.

And to My Listening Ears

How great you are, Sovereign Lord! There is no one like you, and there is no God but you, as we have heard with our own ears. 2 Sam. 7:22, NIV.

Come walk with me early on a spring morning. A cacophony of bird song fills the air. I say "cacophony," because to my untrained ear it somewhat reminds me of an orchestra tuning up—lots of sounds that don't make much sense or have any melody. We notice that as we advance into one bird's territory its oft-repeated song grows louder and louder and then fades away as we move on into another bird's space. Occasionally I have had the privilege of going out with a birder who has an intimate knowledge of bird calls. Without having to see the bird, my friend can identify numerous species, picking the individual bird out of the bewildering array of calls. Much as an experienced conductor knows the sound of every instrument in the orchestra and can hear if they are playing their line correctly, a good birder can pick out a rare bird's call even when it is jumbled in with all the other common morning songs.

One bird I have learned to recognize by sound is the common house wren. I hear its loud, energetic burst of melody long before I can spot its tiny body with quivering throat perched in a garden shrub, singing its heart out. When at last I spot the little brown bird with its relatively long curved bill and perky upturned tail and compare it to the loud song filling the air, I wonder how such a tiny body can pump out so much energetic music. It sits on a branch and chortles its song several times before quickly moving to another spot to repeat the joyful chorus. I find it interesting that the Chippewa Indians named this little bird O-du-na-mis-sug-ud-da-weshi, meaning "A big noise for its size." How appropriate! The male can even sing this song in flight and while landing without missing a syllable. And the repetition is amazing. They often perform the song three or four times a minute—sometimes even more.

I want my life to be equally energetic and exuberant in my praise to my Creator. When the male is bringing a beak full of worms to the nest for the young, he will often sing his song without dropping a morsel. His singing is incessant, energetic, bold, and loud. What a model for my praises to God!

Lord, what can I learn from Your creatures by keeping my ears open and by carefully observing their industrious and exuberant attention to detail? Teach me Your way.

All Nature Sings

It is good to praise the Lord and make music to your name, O Most High. . . . For you make me glad by your deeds, Lord; I sing for joy at what your hands have done. Ps. 92:1-4, NIV.

D o you realize what a privilege it is to praise the Lord? Many don't even know that He exists. Some have never heard of Him while others have but choose not to believe. So if you have heard and have chosen to believe, what a privilege and honor it is to lift one's heart and voice in praise and heartfelt worship to the Creator.

It seems to me that nature is never quiet about praising God. For example, animate and inanimate alike glorify Him by fulfilling the purpose for which He created them. So when the thunder crashes or the ocean roars; when raindrops splat or gentle breezes rustle the leaves; when birds call or chipmunks chip; when frogs croak or seals bark, I like to think of this as praise to God, and my heart wants to join in. For that matter, how often have you ever heard complete silence when you were out in nature? Many times I have been in what I believed was total wilderness and have listened to "all nature" singing. Animate and inanimate alike generate sounds that can be interpreted as praise. Even deep in a cave where you would assume silence would prevail, I have heard water dripping or flowing and the gentle sound of air wafting through the many channels and caverns. Yes, even the inarticulate sound of hands clapping is universally interpreted as praise and honor.

So how much more meaningful and precious to God, then, is the use of His gift of mind and voice and tongue to express our gratitude for life and our heartfelt praise to Him. Just consider, of all creation we are the only species that even has the neural pathways to contemplate and think about our Maker. But more than that, we have the ability to employ meaningful words and thoughtful phrases that express our joyful hearts. Taking our cues and inspiration from David, we can "proclaim your love in the morning and your faithfulness at night" (Ps. 92:2, NIV). We can even use all types of musical instruments to show our praise. "For you make me glad by your deeds, Lord; I sing for joy at what your hands have done. How great are your works, Lord, how profound your thoughts!" (verses 4, 5, NIV). Come to think of it, God uses all the songs of nature to get our attention "so that all the peoples of the earth may know that the Lord is God and that there is no other" (1 Kings 8:60, NIV).

Put Your song in my heart today, Lord, so that I can proclaim Your faithfulness to me.

And Round Me Rings the Music of the Spheres

Where were you when I laid the earth's foundation? Tell me, if you understand. Who marked off its dimensions? Surely you know! Who stretched a measuring line across it? On what were its footings set, or who laid its cornerstone—while the morning stars sang together and all the angels shouted for joy? Job 38:4-7, NIV.

Just a few minutes' drive from the campus of Mountain View Academy sits another beautiful campus with a big sign out front declaring SETI Institute. Founded as a private endeavor in 1984, the passion of SETI has focused on detecting some sign or shred of evidence that would suggest that intelligent life exists beyond the limits of our blue sky. SETI, of course, is an acronym for Search for Extraterrestrial Intelligence. Its activities actually began around 1960 with an initial radio recording from space, a first SETI conference, and then Soviet and American government interests funding various projects. Not long after the inception of SETI, Jerry Ehman worked the Big Ear radio telescope at the Perkins Observatory in Delaware, Ohio. With that radio telescope, on August 15, 1977, he picked up and recorded a radio signal that had all the earmarks of coming from some intelligent life. It may have been some kind of code. But since the signal lasted for only 72 seconds and has never been repeated, we have no way to tell what it actually was. On the automatic data logging sheet, Jerry circled the printout in red and scrawled a big red WOW! It has become famous as "the WOW! signal."

Though it has failed to find the kind of radio signals they hope for, the mission of the SETI Institute continues. As described on their Web site, the SETI Institute seeks "to explore, understand and explain the origin, nature and prevalence of life in the universe." They go on to say that "we believe we are conducting the most profound search in human history—to know our beginnings and our place among the stars."

But is the SETI quest becoming the prime illustration of Einstein's definition of insanity? The best technology available has been tuned to space for more than 50 years. Einstein said it best when he defined insanity as doing the same thing while expecting different results. What "music of the spheres" are you tuned to? Are you searching the Word of God to know your beginnings and to know your place among the stars?

Keep me surrounded, Lord, with the assurance of Your love. Filter out the deceiver's confusing signals. Let me hear the angels shouting for joy.

I Rest Me in the Thought

Then the land had rest from war. Joshua 11:23, NIV.

Frequently when I log in to read science news or check out the latest discoveries, I find myself being asked to adjust my thinking radically yet again
as science revises its current theories. For example, on the origin of human
beings: they are most likely evolved from apes; actually, chimpanzees are our closest
living relatives; correction, apes came from humans; correction again, we evolved
from one of several australopiths (which one we don't know for sure) that lived
in Africa 2-4 million years ago. On the age of the earth: by 1860 there were about
100 different estimates on the age of the earth placing its age anywhere from 5,400
to almost 9,000 years old; correction, Lord Kelvin calculated that it would take
100 million years for a molten earth to cool to the state that it is now (1 degree C
hotter for every 50 feet down) but then, he didn't know anything about radioactive
decay that itself produces additional heat; another correction, a variety of chemical
analyses currently dates rocks approximately 4.5 billion years. On the origin of
our home galaxy, the Milky Way: following the big bang 12 or 13 billion years ago,
primordial gravitational fluctuations began the clumping process. Clumps grew by
gathering intergalactic gas and dust. Then today I read that I should probably alter
my thinking about the origin of the Milky Way because new data shows some large
unrelated chunks of the Milky Way formed at the same time when a big mass of
dust and gas collapsed. Dear me—all the theories wear me out. The big question I
keep asking is: "Are we any closer to truth now than we were 50 or 100 years ago?"

The Bible has a story that gives me comfort. The record shows that the desert
wanderers had endured a long struggle. God asked His people to depend on Him
as they drove idolaters out of the Promised Land, but they failed to follow His
command. When Joshua assumed a leadership position, however, he placed his
dependence on God and defeated the enemy city by city. Read about it in Joshua
11. In short, Joshua cleaned house just as the Lord had directed Moses. When the
job was done, then the "land had rest from war."

Wouldn't you like to have rest from the war of competing theories? With
humility and a realization that we simply can't know all the details, are you willing
to trust God's Word?

*Lord, Your Word says again and again that the just shall live by faith. I am ready
now to rest in the thought that You know what You are doing. I choose to have faith
in You.*

March 25

Of Rocks and Trees

For every house is built by someone, but God is the builder of everything. Heb. 3:4, NIV.

Take a quick look around you. Chances are that you are sitting around your breakfast table or perhaps gathered in your living room right now. No doubt the house that you live in is built primarily, if not entirely, from substances obtained from rocks and trees.

When taken totally apart and sorted into three piles, one labeled "rocks," another "trees," and yet another "neither rocks nor trees," most houses would have very little that would fit into that last "neither" category. In contrast, the rock and the tree piles would be quite sizable. Just think, all of the wood, paper, and fiber products would fall into the tree category—probably the largest of the three piles when you consider all the framing, cabinetry, wallboard, wallpaper, and finish carpentry that goes into a house. The second pile would get all the brick, tile, mortar, ceramics, glass, steel, aluminum, nails, staples, screws, paint, wire, gypsum, and the aggregate in your shingles. Various types of rocks, ores, or sands (crushed rock) are used to make many diverse products. (One house that we built had 25 tons of sandstone as a rock veneer on the outside.) OK, now for the last pile. The "neither" one might have some plastic, perhaps parts of the roofing shingles, and some of the caulking and fiberglass resins. But when you stop and think about it carefully, you should probably put these items on the woodpile, because they are all made from petroleum products that used to be wood long ago. Geologists would argue that the items on the last pile should be added to the rock pile, because it is stuff mined from the ground. Oh well, we won't try to settle that argument.

Every single thing comes from His beneficent hand. God has taken meticulous care in preparing everything down to the atomic level.

The point is that we live in houses built out of products that God made. Every single thing comes from His beneficent hand. God has taken meticulous care in preparing everything down to the atomic level. As our text states, "every house is built by someone, but God is the builder of everything." I do look forward to the time when "no longer will they build houses and others live in them, or plant and others eat. For as the days of a tree, so will be the days of my people; my chosen ones will long enjoy the work of their hands" (Isa. 65:22). So, while we wait, how do we grow fruit of the spirit and build character for the kingdom?

I now see how rocks and trees proclaim Your goodness and Your might in yet another way, O Lord. May the Son shine on my life to grow and build for the kingdom.

Of Skies and Seas

Blessed are those whose help is the God of Jacob, whose hope is in the Lord their God. He is the Maker of heaven and earth, the sea, and everything in them—he remains faithful forever. Ps. 146:5, 6, NIV.

D id asteroids create the oceans? That is a headline question asked by one of my latest news magazines today. The breathless reporter went on to describe surprising recent discoveries on the moon and asteroids that may explain the source of earth's abundant water. You see, ours is the only blue planet in our solar system, bathed in life-giving water of both the liquid (seas) and gaseous (skies) kind. Where did it all come from? We just have to know!

These new discoveries began when several satellites equipped with various types of spectrometers discovered much more frozen water and hydrated rocks on the moon's surface than science had previously believed to exist. Then, more recently, astronomers have used NASA's Infrared Telescope in Hawaii to study the asteroid named 24 Themis, which orbits between Mars and Jupiter. Evidence collected by it suggests that the asteroid has a thin film of ice on its surface along with some of the building block molecules for life. (The results are surprising in view of the fact that the surface temperature of the 125-mile-wide asteroid is too warm to support ice for any length of time.) Some theorize that one or more celestial bodies crashed into the earth, giving it not only the water but some of the organic building blocks for life. But where did that water originate? It had to start somewhere.

The molecular structure of water is simple enough, yet it has special design touches that are the reason for its unique properties among other similar sized and shaped molecules. Water is perfectly suited for living systems. In fact, life requires water. Remove it, and life perishes. The nature and role of water is a powerful testimony of God's love and care for His creation.

The inspired Word is clear. God made the sea, the sky, and all that is in them. He not only created the water, but He has set its boundaries and controls the tempests that may rage over it. Psalm 19 can't be misunderstood: "The heavens declare the glory of God; the skies proclaim the work of his hands. Day after day they pour forth speech; night after night they reveal knowledge" (Ps. 19:1, 2, NIV).

Lord, may my senses be open to Your voice, which clearly speaks through nature. Make me teachable as the seas and skies describe Your character of love.

March 27

His Hand the Wonders Wrought

Your hands made me and formed me; give me understanding to learn your commands. Ps. 119:73, NIV.

D o you enjoy going to craft fairs as much as I do? Every summer nearly every little town and community in this country puts on a craft fair or show to display the creative artistry and ingenuity of local craftspeople. I just checked the Internet, and one Web site alone lists more than 20,000 craft events scheduled for this summer. Michigan, my home state, has 158 craft fairs coming up in just the next two months! Many of them are juried craft shows that offer prize money for the best entries. When you travel, what kinds of memorabilia do you purchase to remember your trip? Probably only rarely is it commercially manufactured products. Usually you stop at roadside stands or little shops in which local artisans have made something with their hands.

Come to think of it, the work of our hands shows who we are. Those of violent people are raised to hurt, maim, and destroy, while physicians, veterinarians, physical therapists, and nurses reach out with gentle hands to heal and bring relief. Musical artists use their supple hands along with their mouths and feet to make music that awes or inspires. Writers employ their flying fingers or cramped hands to translate thoughts and ideas into words and stories on paper. Teachers and conductors wave their hands about as they communicate ideas and keep groups organized. Painters and artists create their visual arts with their paint-stained hands, and gardeners and farmers prepare the ground, plant the seed, and harvest the crops with soil-encrusted ones. The calloused hands of carpenters and woodworkers cut, shape, and smooth the wood into functional or beautiful pieces. Mechanics with their often greasy hands fix or replace broken or worn-out parts, and textile artists and seamstresses use their flying fingers to create clothes, curtains, bedding, and thousands of other items for body and home.

Hands are willing servants of the mind. They bring reality to our thoughts and turn them into amazing creations of all types. Since we are made in the image of God, think of what His hands have done! But the most wondrous thing that His hands have done for me is for Him to lay them, palm up, on the rough cross to demonstrate His unfathomable love for me.

When I consider what Your loving hands have done for me, I stand in awe and humbly worship You as my Lord and Savior. Your name is greatly to be praised and honored.

The Birds Their Carols Raise

. . . when people rise up at the sound of birds, but all their songs grow faint. Eccl. 12:4, NIV.

W hy do birds sing, call, whistle, twitter, cheep, yodel, or otherwise make noise? To locate each other at any given moment? To call each other to lunch? Or do they do it to let us know who they are and where they are? Maybe, as Ecclesiastes 12:4 states, they are God's alarm clock that helps wake us up every morning. Since different birds have many different calls (short cheeps or chirps) or songs (more musical sounds of longer duration), could it be that they produce the various sounds for different reasons—i.e., to warn of predators, to express joy of life, to mark boundaries or territories, to praise God, to attract mates, to instruct the young, etc.?

The Bible has more than 50 references to the word "bird." Depending on the version you use, Scripture mentions more than 30 bird types by name. But interestingly, in the NIV I can find only two references to birdsongs (Ps. 104:12 and Eccl. 12:4). The Synoptic Gospels have five references to the cock crowing on the morning of Peter's test. So the Bible isn't much help in answering the question of why birds sing. They just sing— perhaps that is enough.

Biologists have carefully studied bird songs for decades (males vocalize the most). The songs of young birds, like baby talk, need lots of practice to attain perfection. Female birds judge the quality of a male by his song. She refuses to allow mating until the song meets her specifications. Since our ears can't hear all bird sound frequencies, and we can't resolve the rapid syllables of a call, we need specialized recording equipment and digital sound analyzers to appreciate the complexities that birds hear and respond to. Bird vocalizations have local dialects that vary from region to region. Some birds have individual differences that let neighbor birds keep track of who's who. Since biologists carefully avoid giving animals human motivations (such as excitement, fear, joy, and hope), the scientific literature is totally silent concerning the emotions or feelings that birds might have as they vocalize. And sadly, since many biologists don't accept the reality of God much less His creative power and glory, the literature ignores the Creator except for occasional ridicule or scoffing. Yet in faithfully performing the function that they were created for, I like to think that birds praise their Creator.

Lord, if we keep quiet in our praise, even the stones will shout praise and honor. Surely You have given the birds of the air songs of praise. May my voice join with their songs today.

March 29

The Morning Light

The God of Israel spoke, the Rock of Israel said to me: "When one rules over people in righteousness, when he rules in the fear of God, he is like the light of morning at sunrise on a cloudless morning, like the brightness after rain that brings grass from the earth." 2 Sam. 23:3, 4, NIV.

The darkness of the night broke into barely perceptible shades of gray. I was already up and dressed, packing the last of the gear into my bulky camera bag and strapping the tripod to the outside. A weather front had passed through during the night. It should be a wonderful morning for getting dramatic lighthouse pictures. With a few miles to drive, I knew that I would be racing the morning light. All real photographers have been in that race.

Morning light has something magical about it. It comes on slowly, is constantly changing, and is soft, luminous, and luxuriant. And it adds that special touch to a photograph that makes it a piece of art instead of just another picture. When used by a professional, morning light has that much power.

My guess is that the aging King David, at the end of his reign, didn't know much about aperture, focal length, or F-stops. I doubt he understood color temperature, depth of field, or film speed. After all, he didn't even have a camera. But, at the close of his life, in his last words (recorded in 2 Samuel 23), David did know what was important. He knew God well. The two of them had had a long and close relationship. Even though David had his defects, he knew his Lord and Savior and was certain of his covenant relationship with God. He recognized that God was speaking through him, giving him inspired thoughts. So in one of the most beautiful word pictures possible, King David describes what it is like to be right with God, to rule in the fear of God and in righteousness. David said that it is like the light of morning at sunrise on a cloudless morning, like the brightness after rain that nourishes the grass.

Lord, like King David, I too have failed You. But I do know You and have confessed my sins to You. That is what assures me that I am right with You. In the areas of life that You have asked me to rule, teach me to do as You would, soft and gentle as the morning light, but firm and steady like growing grass after a rain. May my rule today be a word picture to Your honor and glory.

The Lily White

Religion that God our Father accepts as pure and faultless is this: to look after orphans and widows in their distress and to keep oneself from being polluted by the world. James 1:27, NIV.

Most of us pick up a potted Easter lily or two as they appear in markets and flower shops, pay the few dollars they cost, and don't give any thought to the great care and attention to detail that it took to produce the plant. Every characteristic of the plants you bought has been critically analyzed and carefully nurtured and planned for.

Easter lilies normally bloom in late summer, so getting them to bloom during the two-week window when people are buying them for Easter is a real challenge. To further complicate matters, Easter is not a set day on the calendar. Since Easter Sunday is defined as the first Sunday after the first full moon after the vernal equinox, it can happen any time between March 22 and April 25. And since growing Easter lilies is an exacting business in which one has to pay a great deal of attention to details, only specialists can stay in business.

The Easter lilies that you buy are the culmination of three or four years of hard and precise planning and work. First little baby Easter lily bulblets are removed from mother plants and planted in great fields. A year later, yearling plants are replanted in another field, where they get special care for a second year. After the second year the mature plants are dug again. This time baby bulblets are removed for continuing the cycle and the mature bulbs are shipped to growers who pot them and spend many more months growing and conditioning the brown scaly bulbs to grow and flower under very precise conditions of temperature, soil moisture, light quality, and photoperiod so as to be perfect for market during the ever-shifting two-week window.

Pure, faultless, helpful to those in need, unpolluted by the world—topgrade Easter lilies don't happen by chance. With God as our gardener, our help, and our purifying substitution, He can make us like the lilies, which will declare our Maker's praise.

Lord, take all the time You need to get me pure and blameless. I submit my stubborn will to You today.

Declare Their Maker's Praise

Then I heard every creature in heaven and on earth and under the earth and on the sea, and all that is in them, saying: "To him who sits on the throne and to the Lamb be praise and honor and glory and power, for ever and ever!" Rev. 5:13, NIV.

C an this text actually mean what it says? Every creature in heaven? and on earth? and under the earth? and on the sea? and all that is within them? Singing? Once again look at the words that suggest that the earthworms and moles will be singing along with whales and starfish, monkeys and spiders, peacocks and hummingbirds. We will all be singing together. All the people singing with every creature—singing praise, "To him who sits on the throne and to the Lamb be praise and honor and glory and power, for ever and ever!" What an amazing chorus. I do want to be there to join my voice in praise. But what is the setting to this amazing song of all creatures?

We will all be singing together. All the people singing with every creature—singing praise.

On the windswept isle of Patmos, John is in vision. What he sees is the throne room of heaven with One sitting on the throne holding a scroll with seven seals. The call goes out, "Who is worthy to break the seals and open the scroll?" (Rev. 5:2, NIV). Apparently not the One on the throne. John starts weeping because it seems as if no one is worthy. But then one of the 24 elders steps up to comfort John and tells him, "Do not weep! See, the Lion of the tribe of Judah, the Root of David, has triumphed. He is able to open the scroll and its seven seals" (verse 5, NIV). John sees a Lamb step up to the throne and take the scroll at which time the four creatures and 24 elders that are around the throne fall down in worship, then pick up their harps and golden bowls filled with incense, and sing a new song with these words: "You are worthy to take the scroll and to open its seals, because you were slain, and with your blood you purchased for God persons from every tribe and language and people and nation. You have made them to be a kingdom and priests to serve our God, and they will reign on the earth" (verses 9, 10, NIV). Next the innumerable angels circling the throne chime in with "Worthy is the Lamb, who was slain, to receive power and wealth and wisdom and strength and honor and glory and praise!" (verse 12, NIV). Finally—as a climax of praise—all animate creation joins the grand swelling chorus. "To him who sits on the throne and to the Lamb be praise and honor and glory and power, for ever and ever!" (verse 13, NIV). Jesus, the Lamb of God who takes away the sin of the world, is indeed worthy.

Lord, what a celestial celebration. Holy, holy, holy is the Lamb that was slain. Amen.

April 1

He Shines in All That's Fair

How beautiful on the mountains are the feet of those who bring good news, who proclaim peace, who bring good tidings, who proclaim salvation, who say to Zion, "Your God reigns!" Isa. 52:7, NIV.

It can be downright depressing if you stop and think about it or if you peruse the world news. If the early blight doesn't ruin the lovely tomato plants in your garden, then the late blight will. Loved ones and friends die prematurely from cancer—even young children. Fractured oil wells gush great gobs of goo—actually torrents of black crude—and no one seems to know how to stop it. Beautiful roses sport wicked sharp thorns. And as if to add insult to injury, a gigantic earthquake crumbles homes and businesses, killing and maiming. Far away, the tsunami surprises tourists and residents alike, sweeping them all away. Add to this chaotic scenario war, famine, political instability and you have ample reason to be depressed. No doubt about it. The news in our sin-sick world is depressing. It isn't a pretty picture.

Though it does take mental discipline, let's flip the coin and actively look for the good and the beautiful. Even though sin has horribly marred it, our world is still filled with stunning beauty, evidence of God's creative power and majesty. Thus we can still find an island paradise, a towering magnificent waterfall, a quiet beach, a tranquil forest trail, colorful coral reefs, mirror-smooth lakes, desert sunsets, broad ocean expanses, sun-dappled creeks, sweeping mountain vistas, lakeside parks, etc. When looking for "all that's fair," these count. All these beauties, however, pale in comparison to the demonstration of Christ's love on the cross.

Christ's physical suffering on the cross was nothing compared to His pain of separation from His Father. "My God, my God, why have you forsaken me?" (Matt. 27:46, NIV). Without question, in the cross Christ experienced the natural consequence of sin, which is death (Rom 6:23) exposing the lie, "You will not surely die." (Gen 3:4). But the flip side of His death and resurrection transforms it into the most beautiful story ever. "The gift of God is eternal life" (Rom 6:23) The good news is that Christ defeated the evil one and gives me life. My God—my Savior— reigns. Here is the fairest of all the shining fair.

I simply don't understand all the evil that I see in the world, Lord, but I trust that someday the fog will lift, eternal harmony will break out, and all ills will be justified.

In the Rustling Grass

May grain abound throughout the land; on the tops of the hills may it sway. May the crops flourish like Lebanon and thrive like the grass of the field. Ps. 72:16, NIV. He makes grass grow for the cattle, and plants for people to cultivate—bringing forth food from the earth. Ps. 104:14, NIV.

Today I think it is appropriate to thank God for grass. The blessings of grass are truly amazing. Try this: Lie down on a lawn and feel the softness. Roll over on your belly and take a close robin's-eye view of it. Pull up a single grass plant and study it carefully. Doesn't look like much, does it? Just a few blades coming out of an unimpressive stem with some roots hanging out the bottom. Next, take a wider view. A well-kept and manicured lawn is a thing of beauty and great value as it provides framing and contrast to a formal garden or as a setting for a home. Individually unimpressive plants, when viewed collectively, are impressive indeed.

Finally, think of the various uses of grass. Not only does it convert a dirt yard to emerald green, but it feeds the world's billions with rice, wheat, corn, oats, barley, rye, triticum, sugar cane, and sorghum. Besides that, bamboo, the world's fastest-growing and tallest member of the grass family, not only serves as a food as shoots but people use it in myriad ways much like wood. As the world's fastest-growing woody plant, it can stretch a couple feet per day when conditions are right. Bamboo is the main food of giant pandas in China and the red pandas in Nepal, and is a staple for mountain gorillas in Africa. Just consider how many other animals depend on grasses for their main food source. As you are thinking about it, don't forget all the meat eaters and insect eaters. Meat eaters (such as lions and leopards, owls and eagles) as well as insect eaters (such as bats and shrews) depend on grass, because their food is the grass eater. The list of kinds who depend on grass is endless. Grasses do feed the world.

Furthermore, grasses stabilize dunes, marshes, and other ecologically sensitive areas. People use them to make paper, thatch, fuel, insulation, and sports turf of all types. I think you get the picture. Grasses are a special gift of God. The phrase "in the rustling grass, I hear Him pass, He speaks to me everywhere" takes on new meaning and significance when I stop to meditate on the gift of grass. Each blade of grass is to me a love letter from my Creator.

When I pause to think of Your amazing gift of grass to this world, Lord, I am awed by Your kindness and generosity. You care for all of Your creation with careful attention to detail.

April 3

I Hear Him Pass

Do not let the oppressed retreat in disgrace; may the poor and needy praise your name. Ps. 74:21, NIV. The King will reply, "Truly I tell you, whatever you did for one of the least of these brothers and sisters of mine, you did for me." Matt. 25:40, NIV.

First, let's identify the nature of poverty. Is it a poverty of ideas, of spiritual development, of emotional health, or of wealth? We need to realize that we must always evaluate the word "poor" against some standard. In terms of financial wealth, when compared to the earning power of a dishwasher in a fast-food restaurant, I am rich. But contrasted to a Fortune 500 executive, I am poor.

Second, people and families tend to move in and out of poor. Many rich people have gone to the poorhouse, while many poor have worked hard and become rich.

Third, there will always be poor among us (cf. Deut. 15:11 and Matt. 26:11).

Finally, we must not forget that Christ became poor so that we could become rich (2 Cor. 8:9).

Does Christ allow the poor among us so that we will learn critical lessons about how to love our neighbor as ourselves, how not to show favoritism, how to be kind and generous to all (cf. James 2; Prov. 19:7; Deut. 15:7)?

Doesn't Jesus walk in the worn-out shoes of the poor every day? If we are alert, we will hear Jesus pass in the shuffling gait of a homeless bag lady. When we are tuned to helping our neighbor, we will hear Him pass in the clicking wheels of the near empty grocery cart of the single mom. Or if we are listening carefully, we will hear Him in the groans of the Wall Street investor who's lost his fortune. Listen, do you hear Him pass in the sobs of a just-raped teenager or in the involuntary sniffles of an abandoned child? Do you hear Him in the request of a neighbor who needs help drying out their basement after a flood? How about the student who asks for tutoring or the pleas for help in the primary Sabbath school room, the local food bank or soup kitchen? What about the sound of a newly engaged couple requesting marriage mentoring? Is that, too, the sound of Jesus passing?

Open the ears of my heart, dear Lord. Let me hear Your cry in the needs of those passing me today.

He Speaks to Me Everywhere

The heavens declare the glory of God; the skies proclaim the work of his hands. Day after day they pour forth speech; night after night they reveal knowledge. They have no speech, they use no words; no sound is heard from them. Ps. 19:1-3, NIV.

Yes, God does speak to me everywhere. The important questions are: Am I listening? Do I respond quickly?

I remember a road race that I took part in a few years back. The point of the race was to follow instructions precisely. My partner, J.T., was the driver, and I was the navigator. We were to follow a course as revealed to us one set of instructions at a time, making turns, observing speed instructions, obeying clues often obscured in code. The final challenge was a time trial, driving a convoluted course marked out by pairs of cones on a large parking lot. Which team could cover the course in the shortest period of time without touching any cones? It seemed easy enough. Then we learned that the driver would be blindfolded and would have to follow the navigator's instructions. You can only imagine the fun when driver and navigator have different ideas about what it means to go faster, turn left, turn more, back up, turn right. It was hilarious. Needless to say, lots of cones got squashed. The best teams were those in which driver and navigator had complete trust in each other, in which communication flowed both ways rapidly, and in which the participants heeded instructions without question.

Yes, God does speak to me everywhere. The important questions are: Am I listening? Do I respond quickly?

God speaks to me everywhere. If I am not listening, He may as well save His breath. It's as if He isn't speaking at all. But if I am listening but not responding instantly, I will certainly be off course quickly. "This is the way, walk ye in it!" isn't relevant after I have traveled another 50 feet or half mile down the road. On God's tree, fruit of the Spirit ripens only from instant blindfolded responses. Some of the things that I have heard Him say are: "Here is a person in need of help!" "Oh no, go back and apologize!" "Love that teenager with the baggy pants and the spiky hair!" "Tell her that you can see her in your office right now." "You do remember, don't you, that the cat responds better to petting than to kicking—remember?" "Mr. Wilson is in the hospital—why don't you go visit him?" "Smile and ask that homeless man if he is hungry."

Speak, Lord, for I am listening. Hush the noise of the city. Quiet the clamor of business. Tune my ears to hear Your voice. Quicken my heart to instant response.

April 5

O Let Me Ne'er Forget

Then they remembered his words. Luke 24:8, NIV.

M y mother doesn't know who I am anymore. Every time I go into her room, I say 'Hi, Mom.' Sometimes she smiles with recognition. More and more she stares blankly, as if I am a total stranger. I tell her about my family, but it is clear she doesn't know anybody I am talking about. Mother has great difficulty signing her name. There are days when I wonder if she knows who she is."

This heartbreaking description of a person with Alzheimer's disease illustrates what a precious thing we have in the gift of memory. Memory gives us a past and enables us to plan for a future. We enjoy routines in our daily cycle and retrace our steps. Without memory, all we have is the present— nothing more. Everybody is a stranger. Calendars don't make sense. Even mirrors are confusing, because there is somebody else here in the room.

Ecclesiastes 12:1 suggests that we should remember our Creator when we are young, because days of trouble will come. The implication is that we will forget even our God. Declining mental abilities are well-known symptoms of increasing age. In 1906 Dr. Alois Alzheimer, a German physician, did a brain autopsy on one of his elderly patients who had died after years of severe memory problems. He was surprised to find tangled nerve cells and dense deposits around them. But it wasn't until the 1960s that science positively linked them to memory losses. After that it wasn't long until intense research began to uncover some of the environmental and genetic causes of what is now commonly known as Alzheimer's disease. We still don't have the cure, but we do know some risk factors.

Here is how to avoid Alzheimer's disease. 1. Don't get old. Aging is the number one risk factor. OK, none of us have any say about that. 2. Don't have parents or siblings that have the disease. A known gene increases risk but is not a guarantee of getting the disease. We don't have a choice about that issue, either. 3. Avoid serious head injuries. They increase risk, so be careful. 4. Exercise regularly—something that we do have control over. 5. Eat a healthy balanced diet. 6. Avoid tobacco. 7. Stay socially active. 8. Play games and regularly participate in intellectually stimulating activities. All of the last five are lifestyle issues that we can control. Most of all, enjoy every day we have as a special gift from our Creator.

Thank You, Lord, for Your instructions to begin life early. I will rejoice in You today.

That Though the Wrong Seems Oft So Strong

For I do not do the good I want to do, but the evil I do not want to do— this I keep on doing. Rom. 7:19, NIV.

Does the wrong seem oft so strong to you? Do you say "Ditto" to Paul's words in Romans 7:19? Do you really truly want to do good but find yourself repeatedly breaking your own promises, resolutions, and goals? I do too. Discouraging, isn't it? OK, take a deep breath.

The cheetah is an exceptionally skilled predator. In just three strides it can accelerate from 0 to 40 m.p.h. and top out at 70 m.p.h. a few strides later. Built for speed, its heart and circulatory system are super-duty in size and strength. The narrow, sleek body with small head and big prominent eyes gives little wind resistance with maximum vision. The whole musculoskeletal system is adapted for quick, tight turns and exceptionally long strides, up to three of them per second at full speed. And since racers need good traction, the cheetah has semi non-retractable claws that are short and blunt, like cleats on running shoes. The pads on its feet are much harder than those on other cats, giving it much more control. I think you get the idea. The cheetah appears designed for the chase.

The downside is that cheetahs are not aggressive cats. Much smaller than lions and leopards, they defer to other predators. At such fast speeds they tire quickly, so a chase usually lasts only 20 to 40 seconds. If it goes more than a minute, they are winded. Only about half of their pursuits are successful.

At this point I can hear you saying, "Huh? How does cheetah data relate to me not doing what I want to do and doing what I don't want to do?" Like Paul, we have asked God for a new heart, and He has given it to us. The more we allow the Holy Spirit to heal our sin sickness, the more sensitive we are to the selfishness that still lurks in us. Yet the fact that we are struggling means that we have actually been renewed. The unregenerate heart doesn't resist. It just goes along. Like the cheetah, never give up trying. Even though you miss your mark, get up and run again. Keep listening to your conscience and submitting your will to God.

Lord, let me hear You say again, "My grace is sufficient for you, for my power is made perfect in weakness" (2 Cor. 12:9, NIV). Let my life be a demonstration of that reality.

God Is the Ruler Yet

For God is the King of all the earth; sing to him a psalm of praise. God reigns over the nations; God is seated on his holy throne. Ps. 47:7, 8, NIV.

Who or what is in control here, anyway? A terrible auto accident leaves a person bleeding beside the road. Blood loss is significant. The victim's tissues are not getting enough oxygen. In the cells the mitochondria can't produce enough ATP to sustain life. They compensate by switching to anaerobic respiration, which builds up lactic acid, resulting in a drop of blood pH. The low blood oxygen makes cell membranes leaky. Extracellular fluids enter cells. Major neural and chemical regulation centers seek to gain control of the situation. Breathing speeds up to rid the body of carbon dioxide in an attempt to raise blood pH. Pressure sensors in the carotid arteries respond to the low blood pressure, promoting the release of adrenaline and noradrenaline. Adrenaline speeds up the heart rate. Noradrenaline tightens down the blood vessels—measures that usually increase the blood pressure. Antidiuretic hormone levels in the blood get bumped up to enable the kidneys to retain water in the bloodstream and also to divert blood away from noncritical organs to maintain blood flowing to the heart, lungs, and brain. During this critical time, control is all-important. If the ambulance arrives soon enough, the victim may live.

As the victim lies there bleeding, waiting for help, the control mechanisms themselves will soon start to fail for lack of blood in the tissues. Sodium ions leak into cells while potassium ions leak out, just opposite of what they are supposed to do. The blood pH continues to drop, little sphincters at each capillary bed lose their grip so that blood stops moving through them, and fluid and protein start leaking, causing the blood to thicken further and reduce the flow through the capillaries. Because control mechanisms have now failed, the victim is near death. Is anybody or anything in control? What is happening is called hypovolemic shock, or simply shock. There comes a point of no return, when, even if an ambulance arrives, it is too late. Too much damage has already taken place.

Biological systems require delicate control systems. When those fail, death happens. Now, let us imagine the control systems required to keep the universe running smoothly. Fortunately, the Designer and Creator of all the big systems is in control. God is the ruler yet. Recall the disciples' amazement: "Who can this be? For He commands even the winds and water, and they obey Him!" (Luke 8:25, NKJV).

Ruler of this vast domain, take my life and let it be consecrated, Lord, to You.

Why Should My Heart Be Sad?

Why does your face look so sad when you are not ill? This can be nothing but sadness of heart. Neh. 2:2, NIV.

During some winters here in Michigan we can go for weeks without seeing the sun. The lake-effect snow sets in, and day after day it's dark and gloomy. Don't get me wrong. We love the snow. We strap on those skis or snowshoes or hop on our snowmobiles and off we go. It is nice to see the sun once in a while, though. It is the time of the year that some people get SAD—an appropriate acronym for seasonal affective disorder, because the symptoms include feelings of being tired, depressed, sad, and listless. Another name for the condition is seasonal depression. The symptoms set in about the same time every year, usually late fall and winter, though occasionally some get the seasonal blues during spring and early summer.

What causes this seasonal sadness? Some say that the shorter, darker days result in the brain producing lower levels of some important brain hormones. Others suggest that levels of a neurotransmitter called serotonin may be in short supply. A powerful substance, it makes you feel good and has soothing, even calming effects. Yet another theory suggests that our eyes have a third class of light receptors (other than rods or cones) connected to a special region in our brain just above where our optic nerves cross over, aptly called the suprachiasmatic nuclei (SCN). New data suggest that the SCN center of the brain affects our daily rhythms through hormone systems. Whatever the case, SAD is a reality.

Physicians often suggest bright lights for treating SAD. Obviously the best bright light is outdoors in the sunshine at a regular time every day. Since that is in short supply, the next best is bright artificial light, quality sleep, vigorous exercise, and good nutrition, which all help. At times SAD is serious enough to warrant medication and psychiatric intervention. Thankfully, most of the time SAD goes away with the change in season and doesn't pose serious health risks.

What about spiritual sadness? Is there a godly sorrow that actually can be a good thing? In chapter 7 of Paul's second letter to the Corinthians he describes in detail how we grow from pain.

Lord, may I please have a big dose of that godly sorrow that brings repentance, that leads to salvation, and that leaves no regret? That is the kind of spiritual sadness that I crave, because I see now how that pain heightens my sense of justice, passion, and concern for others.

The Lord Is King

Lift up your heads, you gates; be lifted up, you ancient doors, that the King of glory may come in. Who is this King of glory? The Lord strong and mighty, the Lord mighty in battle. Ps. 24:7, 8, NIV.

Climate change has become a political hot potato of late. Some say that the changes we are experiencing result from humans producing excessive amounts of carbon dioxide (CO_2). Numerous laws have been proposed, and many have already been instituted in an attempt to regulate atmospheric CO_2. Truth be told, nature already has marvelous CO_2 regulating systems in place. All living systems produce CO_2 just in the process of being alive. Plants depend on this CO_2 for photosynthesis. When atmospheric CO_2 levels go up, photosynthetic rates rise dramatically and remove it from the air. Another system keeping CO_2 in check is the ocean. It functions as a huge carbon sink, absorbing or releasing CO_2 from and to the atmosphere as needed. The CO_2 cycle is much more complex than any of us know, yet the political debate goes on as if we understand it fully.

Many and varied complex control systems also exist at the ecosystem level. Water evaporates from plants and from water and ground surfaces and goes up into the air. Then it condenses and falls back to the ground again, penetrates into the soil where plants pull it up again. Other minerals such as nitrogen, phosphorus, and sulfur have interesting and varied cycles in which the mineral moves from one reservoir to another in a regular pathway.

Aren't you glad that a Creator-King reigns supreme? That He knows exactly what is going on in all systems and recognizes when things are out of kilter and need tweaking?

Control systems at the population level are a bit simpler, making them easier to study and comprehend. For example, the western spruce budworm *Choristoneura occidentalis* is highly effective in chewing up the spruce needles, and it is found all over the west. Why doesn't it just take over? It runs out of food and has predators, pathogens, and parasites that help keep it in check. They are nature's way of regulating and keeping things in balance.

Individual organisms also have effective control systems that maintain constant body temperature, pH levels, and blood chemistries. Such systems are also well known.

Throughout all these realms, aren't you glad that a Creator-King reigns supreme? That He knows exactly what is going on in all systems and recognizes when things are out of kilter and need tweaking? And that He knows what to tweak? I am.

Almighty King, Creator of all, Lord of my life, teach me trust amid all the apparent chaos.

Let the Heavens Ring!

Sing for joy, you heavens, for the Lord has done this; shout aloud, you earth beneath. Burst into song, you mountains, you forests and all your trees, for the Lord has redeemed Jacob, he displays his glory in Israel. Isa. 44:23, NIV.

During one late spring backpacking trip with students in the Great Smoky Mountains I laid our sleeping bags out on the gentle slope of a bald knob near a slick of blooming rhododendrons and laurel. It was one of those glorious days when a slow-moving high-pressure system provides cloudless skies and cool, dry air. The only civilization in sight or sound was an occasional contrail noiselessly inching across the blue arc above. The weather was so delightful that we didn't pitch tents. As we prepared our evening meal the sun sank low and orange in the west. Then it disappeared behind the hills, and as the shadows pulled across the sky, the stars popped out one by one at first, then by dozens, and finally in a breathtaking display of seeming billions. For one student, it was his first-ever experience under visible stars. He couldn't believe what he saw, and he shrieked with delight as shooting stars streaked across the black canvas of night.

For hours we picked out constellations and identified all those we knew. We found many prominent stars. With our binoculars we searched for and found the faint smudge of the M31 Galaxy and identified the few planets that we found wandering across the backdrop of the Milky Way. Late into the night we watched the heavens slowly spin above us. Sleep didn't come easily. All of us could hear the heavens ringing and singing in majestic splendor. "Shout for joy, you heavens; rejoice, you earth; burst into song, you mountains! For the Lord comforts his people and will have compassion on his afflicted ones" (Isa. 49:13, NIV).

One by one the students drifted off to sleep in their warm sleeping bags. For some time I lay there peering into limitless space, listening to the sounds of silence and rejoicing that my God lives, that He loves me, and that He has compassion on me. My heart was filled with awe as I watched the orderly procession of stars wheeling past my small observation post. As I thought of my guardian angel and how he can flash back and forth from his home base to his assigned post of duty at my side, I wondered what his voice sounded like in the angel choir. How I long to hear that choir breaking out in praise and worship to God. Even so, come, Lord Jesus.

Lord, does Your heart yearn to see me turning to You in love and respect? I long to see You.

April 11

Let the Earth Be Glad

Let the rivers clap their hands, let the mountains sing together for joy. Ps. 98:8, NIV.

"The grasslands of the wilderness overflow; the hills are clothed with gladness. The meadows are covered with flocks and the valleys are mantled with grain; they shout for joy and sing" (Ps. 65:12, 13, NIV). "Let the heavens rejoice, let the earth be glad; let the sea resound, and all that is in it. Let the fields be jubilant, and everything in them; let all the trees of the forest sing for joy" (Ps. 96:11, 12, NIV). "The Lord reigns, let the earth be glad; let the distant shores rejoice" (Ps. 97:1, NIV). "The desert and the parched land will be glad; the wilderness will rejoice and blossom. Like the crocus, it will burst into bloom; it will rejoice greatly and shout for joy. The glory of Lebanon will be given to it, the splendor of Carmel and Sharon; they will see the glory of the Lord, the splendor of our God" (Isa. 35:1, 2, NIV). "You will go out in joy and be led forth in peace; the mountains and hills will burst into song before you, and all the trees of the field will clap their hands" (Isa. 55:12, NIV). "Let the heavens rejoice, let the earth be glad; let them say among the nations, 'The Lord reigns!' Let the sea resound, and all that is in it; let the fields be jubilant, and everything in them! Let the trees of the forest sing, let them sing for joy before the Lord, for he comes to judge the earth" (1 Chron. 16:31-33, NIV). "'Blessed is the king who comes in the name of the Lord.' 'Peace in heaven and glory in the highest!' Some of the Pharisees in the crowd said to Jesus, 'Teacher, rebuke your disciples!' 'I tell you,' he replied, 'if they keep quiet, the stones will cry out'" (Luke 19:38-40, NIV).

Did you have any idea how many biblical passages mention the inanimate creation expressing the emotions of joy, gladness, and jubilation? Above are just a few that popped up in my mind. If these lines are to be believed, the mindless and insensate surely do sense their Creator and respond with gladness. Or am I supposed to write this all off as nothing more than poetry? Is it just pretty-sounding praise words and phrases?

We are the blessed ones who actually do have senses that inform our minds so that we can think about what we see, hear, touch, taste, and smell. Thus we have all the reasons to be glad, to be joyful, even jubilant because our God reigns. If the inanimate and insensate are glad and expressive, how much more should we be praising God and rejoicing because He lives?

Risen Lord, forgive my insensitivity to Your presence. I sing Your praise today.

April 12

Forever

The Lord reigns forever, your God, O Zion, for all generations. Praise the Lord. Ps. 146:10, NIV.

Forever. The concept is foreign to me. Have I been programmed by the deceiver to believe that every forever eventually comes to an end? The royal greeting that I hear again and again throughout the Bible is "O king, live forever." None of them ever did. Museum specimens of shiny bones of the king of dinosaurs, *Tyrannosaurus rex*, are all that remain of the once-terrible, powerful, and wondrous lizard. Even the lofty mountains with their craggy peaks inexorably erode away. It's called weathering. Raindrops, melting snow, and ice seep into microfissures, freeze, and fracture even the strongest rock, leading to exfoliation, cracking, and rockslides. The mountains come down a millimeter at a time. Given long periods of time, the Rocky Mountains, the Alps, and the Himalayas would eventually look like the Appalachians, the Scottish Highlands, or the Russian Urals. Allowed even more time, mountains would flatten out and be replaced by new ones pushed up by mountain building processes such as volcanoes and colliding tectonic plates. So when the psalmist sings, "The Lord reigns forever," I don't really have a clue as to what that means.

After being swallowed by the big fish that the Lord provided, Jonah prayed a rather poetic prayer centered on the "forever" word. No doubt seconds can seem like forever when you are deep in the ocean, trapped in the fetid stomach of a big fish with seaweed wrapped around your head and you don't know where your next breath is coming from. With his life ebbing away, Jonah prayed, and the fish barfed him out on the dry sandy beach. That was a short-lived forever.

The fact is when I read in Hebrews 13:8 that "Jesus Christ is the same yesterday and today and forever" (NIV) or in 1 Timothy 6:15, 16 that "God, the blessed and only Ruler, the King of kings and Lord of lords, who alone is immortal and who lives in unapproachable light, whom no one has seen or can see. To him be honor and might forever. Amen" (NIV), the concept of forever is one that I now have to take by faith. Forever and ever is interesting to think about, but it will certainly take experiencing forever to fully grasp it. Yet it is a concept that I desire to understand.

O King of my life, live forever. When my faith begins to crumble like the mountains, solidify it. To the only wise God be glory forever through Jesus Christ! Amen.

April 13
Own Way Idolatry

They exchanged the truth about God for a lie, and worshiped and served created things rather than the Creator—who is forever praised. Amen. Rom. 1:25, NIV.

House cats just have to be a special creation of God to teach us important lessons of patience and servanthood. My wife and I have not one but two teacher cats. But wait. What am I saying? Let me try that again. A more accurate description is that we are the faithful servants of two cats who have chosen to live in the house that we built for them. The cats let us live here with them as long as we put out food and water for them every day. And as we clean out their litter box and take them to the vet for their medical checkups, they might put up with us. Their most pressing agenda each day? Lazily stand, stretch, and follow the patch of sun that moves across the carpet.

When I think of doing things your own way at your own pace, our cats come to mind. Cats seem totally independent and aloof. They march to the beat of a feline drummer that just doesn't make sense to us human servants. If Boots has been outside for a while, I may open the door for him to come in. He sits there and just looks at me as if to say, "What did you open the door for? I am not ready to come in yet. Give me another 93 seconds and I'll come in—if I want to—when I am good and ready." We have all heard the impossible described as "herding cats." We find no references to house cats in the Bible. They must have been around, but Scripture is totally silent when it comes to them. Could Isaiah have better said it: "We all, like cats, have gone astray, each of us has turned to his own way, and the Lord has laid on him the iniquity of us all" (see Isa. 53:6, NIV)?

When I place any created thing ahead of God, that thing becomes my idol. In the hierarchy of importance, where do my favorite toys come in? Do I spend more time with them than with God? My wife and my family— what priority do I give them? When I put my ideas, choices, or decisions ahead of God's Word, is that not idolatry? And when, like a cat, I do my own thing without regard to God's clear instructions, is that not idolatry? I understand that God is longsuffering and patient. With cats in the house, I sometimes think that I know a little of the frustration that He must feel when I go my own way.

Lord, when the way that seems right isn't, teach me Your way.

April 14

Eye Contact

I will instruct you and teach you in the way you should go; I will counsel you with my loving eye on you. Ps. 32:8, NIV.

I don't know why it is, but we are all extremely eye-conscious. We can tell when someone is looking directly at us. When two people have their gaze locked on each other, we call it eye contact. If, for example, someone diverts their stare to your forehead or your nose, just millimeters off of the locked in position, you wonder if you have a grease mark, an ink stain, or a zit popping out. It takes no special training to know when another has their eyes focused on yours. Perhaps that is why it is so disconcerting to speak with someone who has a "lazy eye"—you know, one of those eyes that won't behave. During a conversation, it is hard to tell which eye to look at. One eye is looking at you, but what is the other one doing?

Lazy eye is a condition that goes by the technical name "amblyopia" and is the most common cause of poor vision in children, affecting about three out of every 100 children. The lazy eye can either turn in or out because of muscle imbalance. Because the muscles in one eye are stronger, the two don't track together. Ignored too long, the condition can lead to permanent vision failure. Treatment is simple and usually corrects the problem.

Observe how someone's eyes track when they are reading. The two eyes move as if they are one. The minute, instantaneous changes in eye position are amazing to watch. No wonder people call the eyes the windows to the soul.

Notice how often we give directions or communicate important messages with our eyes. Someone asks where you left your keys. Without saying a word or even moving our head, we can easily gesture with our eyes, letting them know exactly where the keys are. Should someone make a ridiculous comment or question, we can let them know how stupid it was simply by rolling our eyes. Our eyes inform others whether we are excited about an idea or bored silly. By watching someone's eyes, we can detect if they are telling the truth or lying to us. Some express love while others intimidate with their eyes. In all these cases, however, people have to be close to each other and actually in eye contact with each other for such messages to be successful.

The last half of Psalm 32:8 in the New King James Version and several other translations says that God guides us with His eye. I long to see His beautiful loving eyes face to face.

Lord of my eyes, may I ever be in eye contact with You so that I can see Your guiding gaze.

Memorizing Scripture

I have hidden your word in my heart that I might not sin against you. Ps. 119:11, NIV. Your hands made me and formed me; give me understanding to learn your commands. Ps. 119:73, NIV.

D o you find it hard to memorize Scripture? I do. Even the Bible seems to suggest that the earlier you start memorizing, the easier it is to do. As a child, the boy Jesus placed great importance on learning God's Word. He studied the Scriptures diligently and memorized them carefully. When tempted, "Jesus met Satan with the words of Scripture. 'It is written,' He said. In every temptation the weapon of His warfare was the word of God" (The Desire of Ages, p. 120). Deuteronomy 8:3 emphasizes the importance of learning Scripture in which God Himself said, "Man does not live on bread alone but on every word that comes from the mouth of the Lord" (NIV). Daily feeding on the Word of God and memorizing Scripture is life-changing, because it fundamentally shapes my worldview.

If you are to learn Scripture, you must first place a high value on God's Word. What you value, you will spend time with. It takes both time and focused concentration. So

> **What you value, you will spend time with.**

often we can't memorize because we are simply too busy. We must simplify life, declutter our minds, and focus intently on the joyous task of learning words of life. Once focused, you can employ proven memory strategies. What works for you may not for me, so experiment and use what succeeds for you.

One strategy that I learned from my friend Harold Millikan, a longtime biology professor at La Sierra University, is based on the fact that the mind is not a very good word processor. It is, however, an excellent multisensory processing machine. He taught his students to visualize what they were trying to learn. Picture it in living color. Imagine hearing it in seven-speaker surround sound. Conjure up the smells, the textures, the tastes. Involve the senses to improve learning. Millikan also recommended involving emotions, such as surprise, hate, love, and fear. Exaggerate the size of people, places, and things. Break down what you have to learn into small chunks of information, and then connect everything you memorize to something you already know well. Without mental associations, new memories have no hooks to hang on in our brains. So hang the new on the old. It takes much practice but it can be done and at any age.

Strengthen my desire and quicken my mind to learn and retain Your Word, O Lord. Make Your worldview my own. Let me see You and Your world as it really is.

Christian Environmentalism

The Lord God took the man and put him in the Garden of Eden to work it and take care of it. Gen. 2:15, NIV.

I sometimes hear the argument that Christians are not good stewards of the earth, because they don't plan on inhabiting it for very long. The logic is that Christians know that they are going to heaven soon so they simply don't care about how they treat the earth. To be fair, that may be true of some so-called Christians. But after thinking about it carefully, I reject this notion as uninformed ridicule that certainly does not apply to true Christians.

True followers of Christ actually seek out God's Word, listen to it attentively, and obey it carefully. God placed the first couple in the Garden of Eden to "work it and take care of it" (Gen. 2:15). And like good renters who treat the landlord's property as if it were their own, Christians should bend every effort in caring for God's creation and leaving it better than when we arrived.

Christians also do their best to live lives modeled after their Lord and Savior. Psalm 65 speaks eloquently of a Creator who tenderly cares for His creation, watering it, enriching it abundantly, filling it with grain, blessing its crops, and clothing its hills with gladness. That sounds like good environmental practice. (See also Deut.11:8-21 and 1 Chron. 28:8.)

Finally, Revelation 11:18 ends with judgment, reward, and one important criterion for God's destruction of the wicked. Read this text carefully the next time you think casually about increasing the size of your ecological footprint. It is clearly a statement about end-time events. "The nations were angry; and your wrath has come. The time has come for judging the dead, and for rewarding your servants the prophets and your people who revere your name, both great and small—and for destroying those who destroy the earth" (Rev. 11:18).

So here are three quick reasons that Christians should be the best environmentalists. Caring for the earth is one of our reasons for being here; we follow the model of the Creator in caring for His creation; and in the end God will destroy those who destroy the earth.

Lord of the environment, teach me to want less, share more, and care more for the good land that You have entrusted to my keeping. May I be the best steward possible.

Birth

Jesus replied, "Very truly I tell you, no one can see the kingdom of
God unless they are born again." John 3:3, NIV.

Have you watched a baby being born? Is there anything more incredible? For at least one comparison, I think of the long checklist and thousands of procedures that have to go right in order to get a space shuttle flight launched. If we only knew, my guess is that the birth of a baby has just about as many if not more systems that have to work and be switched on and off in a coordinated fashion to make that happen. Think about it. The baby breathes and gulps placental fluid, is provided all life-support intravenously through the umbilical cord, is constantly held tightly, hears every breath and stomach gurgle from mom, and lives in a dark warm world. Then, in a relatively short period of time, baby's head has to go through six very specific maneuvers as it gets properly positioned in the birth canal. It has to engage, descend and flex, rotate internally, then extend, restore the angle, and rotate externally. During these maneuvers, the cervix has to dilate and efface, and the uterus contracts rhythmically, going top to bottom, as if milking the baby down. Hormone and nerve systems are busy. After some tortuous squeezing, we can have a successful birth. Baby is suddenly out into the blinding lights of the real world—it is much colder, noises are much louder, it has to quickly switch over to its own breathing system, and the nutrition systems are now different. The placenta has to be birthed, mother starts producing milk, and baby learns to feed in a new way. A lot of programmed physiology takes place at every birth. I simply can't imagine the complexity of the checklist it would require. I am not sure even if we know all the steps involved.

The spiritual rebirth is not about physiological switching but rather about a deliberate, well-thought-out decision to turn one's life over to the One who was lifted up on the cross in our behalf. It is about spiritual regeneration. And it is about dying to self, finally realizing that all the good that we have been doing trying to reach heaven doesn't count for anything, that we have to switch over to trusting God fully. Joyfully we have to invite the Holy Spirit to work on our heart. This process too is a mystery. We don't understand it. A total shift from the self-directed life to a God-directed life, it's a birth to spiritual life.

Lord, I choose to die to self so that You can do the switching healing of my mind I require to live in Your kingdom.

Growth and Development

All by itself the soil produces grain—first the stalk, then the head, then the full kernel in the head. Mark 4:28, NIV.

B rooke Greenberg's story breaks my heart. Brooke is a 19-year-old who is old enough to get a driver's license. She should be graduating from high school soon and probably would if she could. But Brooke is a teenage girl trapped in the body of a 1-year-old toddler. Apparently she has a rare disease caused by a mutation in a gene believed to cause aging in the rest of us. That mutation has prevented the normal process of aging to take place in her body so that she has remained a toddler while her younger sister Carly, has grown up normally. Perhaps if Brooke were all toddler it wouldn't be so bad, but she has developed in inconsistent ways. Brooke is only 30 inches tall and weighs 16 pounds. Her bone age is 10. Still with baby teeth, she has not learned to talk yet, because her brain has not developed normally. So it's as if she has lots of disconnected parts. Brooke is becoming the focus of intensive research to see if the mutation in her gene can help us understand more about age-regulating genes. Molecular biologists believe that aging is controlled by a very few genes that have profound effects on many other genes. The hope is that once we understand the process better, we can slow the aging process and improve the quality of life as we get older.

Brooke's story reminds me of Christ's parable of the seed recorded in Mark 4:26-29. It is a very short story that He told the twelve. You plant seed, and its sprouting does not depend on your subsequent actions. It grows into a stalk, then a head of grain, then full kernels of grain. The normal developmental process that happens in grain also takes place in the individual Christian experience. But the parable also applies to the kingdom of God—the world church—as well. Development, whether individual or corporate, is not a process that can or should be rushed. Once the seed is planted, one stage follows another in an orderly succession. You shouldn't look for or expect the mature kernels before the ear has had a chance to form. At maturity there will be fruit: faith, repentance, and obedience. As in Brooke's story, failure to develop will cripple. It is a tragedy. What can I do to make sure that my personal relationship to Christ progresses normally and that the corporate body continues to mature in Christ also?

Lord of the harvest, do You see faith, repentance, and obedience in my life yet? If not, teach me the lessons that I need to learn to continue normal Christian development.

Hands

Sovereign Lord, you have begun to show to your servant your greatness and your strong hand. For what god is there in heaven or on earth who can do the deeds and mighty works you do? Deut. 3:24, NIV.

Having just spent a couple hours studying diagrams of the two dozen bones of the hand along with the muscles that move them (some of them located on the forearm), I do believe that the human hand is one of the most wonderful mechanical creations ever. I have admired the tendons and ligaments that stabilize, hold, and connect; the blood vessels that nourish and cleanse; the nerves that activate and give such fine sensory definition; and the other tissue that makes up the hand. Myriad individual parts are precisely packed into the relatively small space of a supple glove of skin so efficiently that the hand has great flexibility and strength while being highly sensitive to touch. It is a fine tool on the end of a forearm that allows us to move it in a great number of positions around the body. We use this dexterous tool to feed and cloth ourselves, to wash and groom ourselves, to rub where it hurts, to scratch where it itches, to slap what bugs us, and to pet or caress what loves us.

The hand enables us to interact with others. It can bring healing and relief or the fist can instantly clench into a powerful weapon that can do great harm. We use our hands to express love, to manifest self through creations of great music, art, dance, or literature; to do acts of kindness, or to create

We complain and whine that we don't have what others have. But the flip side is that we have what others don't have.

instruments that greatly extend its normal capabilities. No doubt the most important task that our hands can do is to fold them together in prayers of gratitude, prayers of intercession, and prayers of supplication, or to manifest praise to the Creator who gave them to us.

What is in your hand? Use it now to serve God. Too often we complain and whine that we don't have what others have. But the flip side is that we have what others don't have. We each have individual gifts. Use the ones that God has given you to humbly serve Him by helping others. Stop complaining and start serving. God can take those small acts of service and magnify them in ways that you can't imagine.

Lord, thank You for using Your hands to lovingly shape and sculpt me. Thank You for the amazing tools You have given me. May I use my talents now in service to others. Forgive me for my complaining spirit. I pray for a grateful heart and helping hands.

April 20

Seed Germination

Very truly I tell you, unless a kernel of wheat falls to the ground and dies, it remains only a single seed. But if it dies, it produces many seeds. John 12:24, NIV.

We have just been out planting seeds in our garden—big ones such as peas, beans, and squash, and little ones such as lettuce, basil, and radish. After preparing the soil, we made the thin little trenches and dropped the seeds in. The big ones remain visible till we cover them up. The little ones vanish the moment they leave our dirty fingers. Invisible. Dead and gone even before we pull a little fine soil over the trench. As 1 Corinthians 3:6, 7 tells it, the planting and watering are no big deal really. It is God who makes it grow.

Inside every viable seed, no matter how small, is a tiny dormant embryo, living but at a very slow pace, nestled snugly in among the starchy endosperm, its food source until the embryo can raise its head out of the ground. The embryo looks like a miniature plant with a root end and a shoot end. If you open a dried peanut carefully you can see the tiny embryo with its leaves all formed ready to go—except in dry, roasted, or salted peanuts the embryo is dead. OK, then, how does the seed germinate?

Seeds soak up water first. Since seeds are stored quite dry, they can absorb several times their weight in water and will swell to at least double their size when dry. Once they have enough moisture, the embryo's metabolism kicks into high gear, and they need to get nutrients and start growing. The starchy endosperm all around them is in a good energy storage form but not much use for providing energy to the embryo. So the embryo sends out a chemical signal (at least this is what happens in cereal seeds) that triggers the production and release of a starch-digesting enzyme from the aleurone—a layer just under the seed coat. The enzyme goes to work on the starch, breaking it down into sugars that the embryo can use. Though the growth of an embryo does involve cell division, most of the increase in size comes from cell expansion resulting from water uptake. What a marvelous system God has created to provide food for the embryo just when it needs it.

In the text above, the dying of the grain kernel represents the death of Christ. By going into the ground it can grow and produce lots of seeds, Christ's sacrifice made the gift of life possible for many. And in that sacrifice, we receive life.

Hope of glory, does Your life live in me? May I be totally focused on serving You.

April 21

Flight Training

But ask . . . the birds in the sky, and they will tell you. Job 12:7, NIV.

J ust watching birds effortlessly flitting through the air makes me want to mount up on wings as the eagle (Isa. 40:31). Apparently I am not the only one, nor the first with the desire. The first successful manned flights were in hot air balloons (1783). But the monstrous lighter-than-air machines certainly didn't flit. A dozen or so years later Sir George Cayley studied the birds carefully and discovered four important aerodynamic forces of flight: weight, lift, thrust, and drag. He correctly determined that birds got both lift and thrust from their wings to carry their weight and overcome drag. From well before Cayley's day until even now, inventors have been designing and testing a type of flapping wing contraption called an "ornithopter," trying for human-powered flight that would mimic the action of birds. The reason we don't see any ornithopters in common use is that we humans have too much weight and not enough power to develop the lift and thrust that birds do with their favorable power to weight ratios.

Otto Lilienthal is called the first true aviator because he actually launched himself into the air, "flew," and landed safely enough to tell about it—many times. His was a lifetime committed to carefully studying bird flight to figure out what their design secrets were. After crashing three ornithopers, he turned to building gliders. Beginning in the early 1890s Lilienthal built 18 gliders (much like today's hang gliders) and many monoplanes and biplanes. It was in one of these early gliders that he had his first successful flight. Then on August 9, 1896, his glider lost lift and crashed from a height of more than 50 feet. He died the following day.

The Wright brothers, who credited Lilienthal with the inspiration to figure out how to fly, continued their study of bird flight, made glider experiments, conducted wind tunnel tests, and employed their knowledge of engineering to build the first successful flying machine. On December 17, 1903, theirs were the first manned powered flights—four of them, each under 60 seconds. Lessons from the birds were critical in reaching this important starting point. When we take the time to study and listen, birds not only teach us how to fly but let us know the genius of their Designer.

Lord of the skies, Lord of intergalactic space, what other lessons would You like to teach us? Are there lessons that we need to learn first to be safe to travel from one galaxy to another?

Bullhorn (Bull's Horn, or Bullthorn) Protection

If the Lord does not help you, where can I get help for you? 2 Kings 6:27, NIV.

This morning I had to clear fast-growing weeds and young trees that were overwhelming a small dogwood tree that I had planted a few years back. Whether a natural or artificial clearing, the sunshine coming in through the freshly opened sky hole stimulates prolific growth. Cultivated dogwood trees are simply not up to the competition. Their situation reminds me of bullhorn acacia trees.

Most acacia trees grow in arid tropical regions where forage is scarce. As a defense against being eaten, most acacia trees have sharp thorns and produce bitter tasting alkaloids to prevent grazing. Bullhorn acacias (*Acacia cornigera*), native trees of Mexico and Central America, lack the chemical protection but benefit from an army of ant protectors. One species of ants called *Pseudomyrmex ferruginea* live in the hollow swollen thorns that are abundant on the succulent acacia tree. Not only does the tree provide housing for the ants through its thorns but it also provides a nutritious nectar from glands on the stalk of its feathery leaves, and as a bonus, the tips of the leaflets each produce a yellowish protein-lipid nodule called beltian bodies. There is no known function for these leaf tip delights except feeding the ants. So what do the ants do to earn the right to live symbiotically with the tree?

Once they reach the appropriate colony size, squads of *Pseudomyrmex* ants regularly patrol every inch of their tree including the space underneath and overhead. Anything too close to their tree is snipped off, pruned, or pulled up. If the branch of another tree so much as comes near their acacia tree, the ants will prune it away. Should another insect step foot on their tree or an herbivore nose in for a bite, the ants furiously attack. The ants quickly recruit more help by secreting a pheromone that rallies all the troops instantly. Some biologists report that grazing animals can smell the pheromone and save themselves grief by keeping their distance.

Who is your protector in the struggle between good and evil? Is your protector well equipped? Do you stay close to your protector?

The many ways You protect me, Lord, from being overwhelmed by the cares of this life fills my heart with gratitude. May I use the resulting freedom to grow for You and to serve You and Your people with joy and gladness.

Elephants and Acacias

Awake, and rise to my defense! Contend for me, my God and Lord. Ps. 35:23, NIV.

A closely related cousin to the bullhorn acacia (see yesterday's reading) is the whistling-thorn acacia growing on African grasslands. Jacob Goheen of the University of British Columbia in Canada and Todd Palmer of the University of Florida in Gainesville were studying satellite images of the Lewa Wildlife Conservancy in north central Kenya when they noticed something odd about the acacia trees. The ever-present thorny trees were noticeably thinning in the northern part of the 62,000-acre property but not in the southern sections. That was odd, because, with ongoing conservation, elephant populations had soared to three times their normal numbers throughout the region. What was making the big difference?

A trip to the park revealed that the most obvious difference between the northern and southern acacias was the presence of ants living in the hollowed-out thorns of trees in the south. Surely ants couldn't prevent elephant browsing, could they? The ants were known to discourage foraging of smaller animals but it was assumed that acacias protected themselves from the big animals with their thorns. After all, ants are a tiny fraction of the size of an elephant, the largest land animal and one that has no natural predators. And elephants have such thick skin. The elephant's nickname of pachyderm means "thick skin." How would an elephant even know that ants were on its skin? How would an ant bite through such thick skin? For scientists, this was a time to do some experiments. In the controlled environment of an elephant orphanage, Goheen and Palmer tested various trees with and without ants. Sure enough, ants on the foliage discouraged browsing. Then out to the field for further tests. When some southern trees had their ant populations removed, the elephants moved in and browsed their foliage. Their surprising conclusion: *Crematogaster* ants, known to be guardians of the acacias from giraffes and other grazers, also protected the acacias from even the largest plant eaters on our planet. There is power in numbers. Apparently elephants do not like having a trunk full of stinging ants.

Since both the bullhorn and whistling-thorn acacias lack the chemical defenses of their other acacia cousins, they are fortunate to have the ant colonies to defend them from herbivores. Did you know that you have 10,000 guardians in Christ (1 Cor. 4:15)?

My Defender, Guardian, and Guide, teach me Your ways and protect me from all evil.

April 24

Acacia

Bezalel made the ark of acacia wood—two and a half cubits long, a cubit and a half wide, and a cubit and a half high. Ex. 37:1, NIV.

Acacia wood gets significant mention in the Bible, particularly in Exodus. When God asked Moses for a sanctuary so that He could be close to the people He loved, He specified acacia wood for most of the gold-covered wooden items in that beautifully appointed God-ordained place. Acacia wood was what was available in that arid region, and it is a beautiful hard grained wood, rot and insect resistant.

Until the Seventeenth International Botanical Congress convened in Vienna, Austria, in 2005, Acacia was a single genus of plants with about 1,300 species, nearly 1,000 of them native to Australia. After much debate and strong opposition, the session split the acacia genus into five genera with Australia getting to keep the acacia genus. Acacias in Africa, tropical America, and tropical Asia now comprise four new genera. Such changes make it incredibly hard to keep up with the nuances of scientific names. Don't you find the concept of the created "kind" much easier to deal with?

In my recent study of trees I have learned what a gift from God the acacia kind really is. Acacias are members of the bean family and the mimosa subfamily. They have a strong reproductive potential, and are armed with thorns, and many are loaded with poisonous chemicals. Some, as we saw previously, even have armies of ants to protect them from hungry grazers. Where I grew up, acacia was a common tree but one that didn't get climbed because of its wicked thorns.

Those types that are not poisonous serve as foods in many cultures. In southwest Asia, for example, people put the feathery leaves in stir-fries, soups, and curries. The green seed pods and seeds are a favorite in Mexico as they are used in guacamole, sauces, or eaten as snacks. Gum arabic is a complex mixture of glycoproteins and polysaccharides found in hardened sap taken from two species of Acacia. We put these complex sugars and proteins in food as stabilizers and in printing inks, glues, cosmetics, and paints. Acacia honey is prized for its clarity, delicate taste, and the fact that it is the only honey that does not crystallize.

Pharmaceuticals, lumber, land reclamation, incense, tannins—the uses and wonders of acacia go on and on. Let's worship Him who made the gift of acacia.

Lord, thank You for the acacia. May I be as beneficial to those around me.

Arbre du Ténéré

It was majestic in beauty, with its spreading boughs, for its roots went down to abundant waters. Eze. 31:7, NIV.

I t was a single tree, growing all by itself in an immense wide-open space. Then along came a drunk driver and knocked it down. Apparently that 1973 accident was the sad end of the Arbre du Ténéré ("tree of Ténéré") Let's go back and start at the beginning.

Long before recorded history, North Africa was apparently a lush tropical forest. Then the climate changed. For some reason the rains ceased, and it got drier and drier. Great lakes shrank and eventually dried up. Vegetation that could live with less water replaced the forest. The change continued for hundreds of years until just scattered acacia trees and scrubby shrubs remained on the dry dusty soils of the long-ago lakebed. In time even those trees disappeared until only one survived. It stood alone when 1899 turned into 1900. The old lakebed was then just dry blowing sands that the wind sculpted into beautiful dunes. Desert nomads used the tree as an important landmark on their trade route across the great desert now known as the Sahara.

In the early 1930s the solitary tree was "discovered" and written about. A few years later someone dug a well near the tree. They had to go down about 130 feet to find the water. But it was there, and the tree had its roots in it. A single acacia tree spread its green leaves above the dry searing sand

A single acacia tree spread its green leaves above the dry searing sand dunes of the desert because it had sent its roots deep.

dunes of the desert because it had sent its roots deep. It served as a crucial landmark year after year, guiding the camel trains to water. To show what a tenacious survivor this tree was, its nearest neighbor tree was 120 miles away. This acacia had the distinction of being the loneliest tree on the planet.

So after years of hanging on and surviving against all odds, a drunk driver came along and took it out. Those who had been saved by this tree and those who had sat under its shade put the dry remains in a museum and replaced it with a scrap metal sculpture. It was so famous that even to this day, almost 40 years after its demise, both Google Earth and Google Maps mark the spot where it once flourished. Check it out.

Lord, am I the only one left who wants to know You? Are there others who still seek Your glory? Lord, help me hang on and survive this drought of spirituality. May I keep my roots deep in the soil of Your love. May I mark the way for others so they can find Your living water.

Hypochondria

Do not be anxious about anything, but in every situation, by prayer and petition, with thanksgiving, present your requests to God. Phil. 4:6, NIV.

Have you ever had a close friend or two who suffered from hypochondria? If so, then you know that nothing at all is nearly killing them. A pathological fear has them in a tight grip. They worry that they might have a fatal disease because of some body twinges or tingling sensations. For them, a momentary pain that most of us would brush off as a minor irritant, might rise to the level of a serious cancer scare. An intermittent tick in some hand muscles they will suspect as Parkinson's disease or multiple sclerosis. A little coughing? Oh, that is most likely lung cancer, or some other fatal lung disease. As a result, they spend endless hours researching symptoms on the Internet, checking and rechecking to find out what it is that they are about to die from.

Hypochondriacs will often go from doctor to doctor, looking for one that will tell them something other than "There is nothing wrong with you." When a health professional does recommend that they seek help from a mental health provider, they will likely switch doctors and continue to run up medical bills. Don't laugh—it isn't funny. The whole family suffers. And if their doctor does give them some medications to reduce their anxiety and depression, they are sure that side effects of the drugs are evidence of yet another life-threatening disease.

As an outsider it is easy to point to a text such as Philippians 4:6 above and say, "Don't worry! Be happy!" Such statements as that probably won't help your worried friend. What about this, though? Think about asking your friend to join you in a significant service project, such as serving at a local food kitchen or tutoring at an inner city school. Research data proves that the happiest people are those who choose to help others. Focusing a life outward in service to others brings great rewards. Though I don't find it in the research literature, it seems to me that hypochondria is a disease with an obsessive inward focus. The contrast couldn't be greater. Changing that focus to an outward life of service works every time it is tried, because, in fact, God created us to do good works for others, (Ephesians 2:10). Paul exhorts Timothy to "command them to do good, to be rich in good deeds, and to be generous and willing to share" (1 Tim. 6:18, NIV).

Your life here on earth, Lord, modeled generous service to others. Today, lead me to one in need of Your healing touch. In helping the broken, may I be made whole.

April 27

A Mother's Care

As one whom his mother comforts, so I will comfort you. Isa. 66:13, NKJV.

The way that animal parents care for their offspring varies widely depending on the creature in question. For example, pregnant leatherback turtles crawl up on the beach at high tide, scoop out a hole, lay eggs, and trundle back into the ocean without even a backward glance. Their young hatch, never seeing their parents, and have to fend for themselves from day one. As you might guess, many get gobbled down by hungry predators before reaching the water. Crocodiles at least tend their nest and then watch over their young that hatch by protecting them in their mouth, a place of safety for the young, exceedingly dangerous for any other being. Warm-blooded mammals and birds as a group generally give much more care and attention to their brood. In fact, the word "mammals" derives from the milk-producing mammary glands that mothers have for feeding the little ones the perfect infant formula.

Some recent studies of rat mothers show that pups who received the greatest attention (licking and grooming) had the greatest brain development in terms of new synapses made in the hippocampus, the area of the brain responsible for spatial learning and memory—an effect detected as early as the first week after birth. The benefit, of course, was that the pups were better at spatial learning and memory. The effect appeared to be because of more synapses per brain cell and greater brain cell longevity. The researchers ruled out enhanced brain cell proliferation as the reason for the spatial and learning improvements. In contrast, pups who had little maternal interaction actually had lower levels of the types of chemicals that promote brain development and experienced significant loss of brain cells in the hippocampus through programmed cell death, probably because they had lower levels of the types of chemicals that spur brain cell proliferation. It seems every mother/offspring study shows the benefits of maternal care.

The Desire of Ages describes how Mary worked with the child Jesus. "With deep earnestness the mother of Jesus watched the unfolding of His powers, and beheld the impress of perfection upon His character. With delight she sought to encourage that bright, receptive mind. Through the Holy Spirit she received wisdom to cooperate with the heavenly agencies in the development of this child, who could claim only God as His Father" (p. 69).

Lord, fill me with Your Spirit, too, so that I can have wisdom in raising my children.

April 28

Obedience

Even the stork in the sky knows her appointed seasons, and the dove, the swift and the thrush observe the time of their migration. But my people do not know the requirements of the Lord. Jer. 8:7, NIV.

It is nearing the end of April, and today I had an FOY experience. That's extreme birder's coded lingo for "first of the year" sighting or identification of a bird. That is, for the first time this year, I heard the distinctive flutelike call of the wood thrush, *Hylocichla mustelina*, singing in the woods near our home. The call lets me know that at least one of "our" birds has returned safely from its "winter vacation" in Central America or southern Mexico.

Advances in our knowledge of bird migration made a big jump in the past few years with the development of miniaturized recording devices that we can attach to leg bands of large birds or that can be strapped on the backs of smaller songbirds. Depending on the model, such recorders (called geolocators) weigh only a gram or two and record time, temperature, wet/dry conditions, and sunrise and sunset times. The smallest models register only sunrise and sunset times, but with that data it is possible to calculate position within 100 miles.

Canadian ecologist Bridget Stutchbury strapped the tiny data loggers onto 20 purple martins and 14 wood thrushes in northern Pennsylvania during the summer of 2007. The next summer the tiny geolocators were retrieved from five wood thrushes and two purple martins. When the data was downloaded and analyzed, Stutchbury and her associates were astonished to learn that the purple martins reached the Yucatán Peninsula in just five days, a 1,500-mile trip. After a three- or four-week stopover, they continued on to Central and South America. The wood thrushes took their time going south, spending one or two weeks in the southeastern United States before crossing the Gulf of Mexico, and a couple paused for a few weeks on the Yucatan also before going on to their wintering grounds in Honduras and Nicaragua. But the return trips in the spring were two to six times more rapid. One purple martin female flew nearly 5,000 miles from the Amazon basin to northern Pennsylvania in 13 days with four of them being stopover days. Wood thrush data showed a similar hustle on the spring return, with all but one of the thrushes going the short way across the Gulf.

The context of Jeremiah shows him decrying the fact that God's people have His instructions but they are not paying attention. This makes the birds look far wiser because they at least follow directions.

Lord, tune my ear to Your Word. Help me to listen and obey.

April 29

Memory

Remember your Creator in the days of your youth, before the days of trouble come and the years approach when you will say, "I find no pleasure in them."
Eccl. 12:1, NIV.

Memory is at times capricious. Ever been introduced to an important person and two minutes later you have to ask how they spell their name? Yet I clearly remember the details of an illustration in a sermon some 40 years ago. The preacher was Smuts van Rooyen. To portray God's interest and involvement in the little details of our lives, with his thumb and index finger he held up a thin strip of paper by one end. The long end of the strip pointed up or at least was aimed that way. The thin strip of paper couldn't support its weight and arched down past his hand. In his South African accent, he said that the paper strip illustrated a blade of "grahhs"—you know, that green stuff that you have to mow during the summer. I remember him describing how the world would be a pretty ugly place if all the "grahhs" just lay on the ground like his paper model. The Creator/Designer wanted "grahhs" to stand up out of the mud and dirt, where it could collect light and look pretty. So the Creator put a simple fold in it. At this point Smuts creased the flat droopy piece of paper lengthwise. As he did so, the paper now stood upright. You could even blow on it, and it wouldn't give. He explained how this one little design innovation gave "grahhs" the backbone to stand so it could do its job. Just a little detail, but an important detail. If He takes care of each blade of "grahhs," certainly He takes care of us. I remember the illustration vividly.

So how does our memory work? We know how data is encoded in computer memory, in magnetic strips, or in your digital camera or iPhone. But we still don't have a clue about how data gets stored in the neurons of the brain. We do know that making memories involves producing more cell-to-cell connections in the brain, and that DNA is activated and new mRNA and new proteins formed. Various areas of the brain apparently store different types of memories. But we don't know the details of what a memory looks like in the brain. Yet the Bible repeatedly asks us to remember. That is important. Remember the Sabbath. Remember your Creator . . . Remember.

Lord God, Creator of my mind and my memories, my desire is to hide Your Word in my heart so that I might not sin against You.

Magnetic Attraction

No one can come to me unless the Father who sent me draws them, and I will raise them up at the last day. John 6:44, NIV.

Remember those little magnetic Scottish terriers popular years ago? I had a set of them more than 50 years ago as a child in Ethiopia. Less than an inch long, they were black and white plastic dogs, each standing on a small bar magnet. I see that for just a couple bucks they are still available in stores and on the Internet.

Because of the invisible forces between them, magnets have always had a power to fascinate. Perhaps that is why so many different types of magnetic toys are available—toys that appeal to adults as well as children. In fact, some magnetic toys have such powerful magnets that they are not recommended for small children.

Discussions of magnetism go back to the earliest Greek philosophers. We can guess that when ancient peoples found minerals with natural magnetic fields they started playing with them. Pieces of magnetite or loadstone could be suspended in ways that they were used as magnetic compasses. Since that humble but useful beginning, magnetic components are now integral parts of everything from electric motors to audio and video tape players, speakers, microphones, computer data storage disks, and the credit card magnetic strip that records your personal data.

The most powerful attraction in the universe is the drawing power of the Father's relentless and unconditional love.

I am told that magnetism originates with the spin of electrons. In most materials, the spin of electrons is random so that it cancels itself out. But when the spin of electrons is oriented and organized, then the material will have magnetic effects. That is why we can make magnets out of cobalt, nickel, certain rare earth minerals, and a variety of other elements. Just get the spins organized and the attraction happens.

The most powerful attraction in the universe is the drawing power of the Father's relentless and unconditional love.

That God does not force Himself on me or demand my attention is harder for me to understand than trying to grasp the basis for the magnetic power inherent in the spin of elementary particles. The reality is that God draws me to Himself with a power that cannot be broken except through my own choice.

Help me, Lord, to orient and organize my thoughts to think about You and Your love that will not let me go. I choose to be drawn to Your lovingkindness.

Talking to an Idiot

You asked, "Who is this who hides counsel without knowledge?"
Therefore I have uttered what I did not understand, things too
wonderful for me, which I did not know. Job 42:3, NKJV.

Writing devotional thoughts focused on the creatures, systems, and processes that God has made is a daunting and scary task. Because God's creations have endless variety, there is just so much to learn. The wealth and beauty of creative genius and the seemingly unfathomable complexity attracts, fascinates, awes, and teaches us much about the Creator. But even though we may know or think we know much about a topic, compared to what there is to know our knowledge is extremely limited. Late in life the renowned philosopher, astronomer, mathematician, and physicist Sir Isaac Newton put it this way: "I do not know what I may appear to the world, but to myself I seem to have been only like a boy playing on the seashore, and diverting myself in now and then finding a smoother pebble or a prettier shell than ordinary, whilst the great ocean of truth lay all undiscovered before me."

One of the things I tell my classes at the beginning of every semester is that biology is a difficult and constantly changing discipline. Biologists are doing their best to understand life—that most amazing and complex organization of stuff known to humanity. I explain to them that half of the concepts that we will study and learn during the semester will be fairly accurate and correct understandings, and half will be erroneous misconceptions. The only problem is that I simply don't know which is which.

That reality shouldn't keep me from learning all I can about everything that I can. However, I must hold my understandings gently and constantly maintain a teachable spirit. I find that, as I visit with my friends, the more they actually know, the more humility they exhibit. A preacher humorously emphasized this concept as he declared, "When I tell myself that I understand what is going on, I need to remember to follow with, 'Self, you are talking to an idiot!'" Such reality-based humility is too often in short supply. One of the most influential early Christians, Augustine, bishop of Hippo Regius, said it this way: "Do you wish to rise? Begin by descending. You plan a tower that will pierce the clouds? Lay first the foundation of humility."

Lord of the wise and the foolish, there are many things too amazing for me to understand. May it keep me humble and point me to You.

Right Hand

Your right hand, O Lord, has become glorious in power; your right hand, O Lord, has dashed the enemy in pieces. Ex. 15:6, NKJV.

H as anybody ever described you as dexterous, adroit, or skilled with your hands? I watch and listen in utter amazement as the flying fingers of a really skilled concert pianist blur while producing the wonderful music of Rachmaninoff 's third piano concerto or one of the Trancendental Études by Liszt. Or what about the dexterity of a gifted neurosurgeon? Their skillful finger work isn't generally on public display, but what they can do with their gifted hands is pretty amazing. My personal favorite is watching a really skillful artist sketch a quick portrait or a detailed picture of a 3-D object on a 2-D piece of paper. Though the word "dexterous" is defined as "skilled" or "adroit," the root word *dexter* is the Latin word for "right" (in contrast to left). Why is my right hand more dexterous than my left hand, a trait that I share with nine out of 10 people in any given population? Why are only 3 percent of the population ambidextrous, meaning that they can write or throw easily and well with both hands? They have more symmetry to their body in terms of hand skills. So 97 percent of the population shows marked asymmetry in hand skills.

Scientific studies show that keyboard artists who start practicing young have less asymmetry in their hand skill because their left hand received more training while they were young. In general, they still have a more skillful right hand than their left hand. In one grip test study 90 percent of right-handed people had a stronger right hand, while only 10 percent had a stronger left hand. In contrast, 33 percent of left-handed people had a stronger right hand. What about lefties or southpaws? Some studies show that a greater proportion of them are high achievers. Four of the past seven United States presidents have been left handed.

I find it interesting that Bible writers focus on the right hand when they are giving assurance of strength or safety or a more important position. Sitting on the right hand of God often appears in such statements as "In your majesty ride forth victoriously in the cause of truth, humility and justice; let your right hand achieve awesome deeds" (Ps. 45:4, NIV). Right hand or left hand, it doesn't really matter as long as we are in God's hands, for "My Father, who has given them to me, is greater than all; no one can snatch them out of my Father's hand" (John 10:29, NIV).

Dexterous Lord, hold me in Your strong right hand. Never let me go.

One Way

Jesus said to him, "I am the way, the truth, and the life. No one comes to the Father except through Me." John 14:6, NKJV.

"Oh, there it is! Come, stand close, and look carefully. What do you see inside the pouch of this strange little yellow flower? See that tiny bright-metallic green bee struggling for life? Apparently it's drowning. For sure, its life is over—unless."

During graduate school I had the opportunity of spending several weeks studying in the cloud forests of southern Mexico. Plants grow on top of and all over other plants in those hot, humid plant-growing environments. One fascinating plant that grows there is the tiny Bucket orchid named for a big pouch that it fills with a fluid of its own making. Most of the bucket has downward-pointing hairs and a very slick surface. But in one area of the bucket are little pegs or stepping-stones that serve an important function.

You see, Bucket orchids attract some miniature bees—but only the male bees, because they actively gather a scented wax produced by the flower. Male bees gather this wax with their front legs and pack it into a special pocket on their hind leg where they store it for an important future use. That wax is a love potion that the tiny males use to attract females.

Bucket orchid wax is secreted in small quantities on a slender little vertical column centered over the fluid-filled bucket. The column is very slippery. You guessed it. Male bees hover around the flower, trying to figure out how to get the wax. Some of them fall in and get trapped in the fluid. They struggle mightily to escape. But the death trap has only one way to get out. When their flailing feet find the little pegs, they follow that solid footing up into a little chamber, high and dry in the flower, where the plant has hidden a couple pollen sacs. As bees reach the chamber they see the way out—a door or passageway. But the passage is extremely tight, and as he squeezes through, the little pollen sacs stick to his back. The bee works and works at getting out, sometimes requiring 30 minutes to an hour of hard work. During that time the glue that attaches the pollen sac to his back has become dry enough to hold it there. Finally he is released to try his luck with another flower, which gets pollinated in a reenactment.

My Jesus, I am drowning in this world of sin. I've tried all kinds of ways to climb out on my own. I am here now. Take me to the Father.

May 4

Transplanting Trees

It is more blessed to give than to receive. Acts 20:35, NKJV.

That spring it seemed as if the rain would never stop. Creeks and rivers had overflowed their banks. The floodplains were doing what they are supposed to do during high water—holding the excess water till the flooding ceased. Finally the rain stopped and river levels returned to normal. A few weeks later my son and I were exploring along the river and discovered thick plantings of six-inch sugar maple seedlings that had sprouted and were growing on exposed sandbars Apparently the floodwaters had transported millions of maple seeds, sorted them, and then planted them on the sandbars. Since we needed some shade trees for our nearly treeless yard, we decided to take what nature was offering. We were not in a hurry.

In one corner of our garden we planted five or six dozen seedlings about a foot apart, thinking that this would make a good tree nursery. A few years later some of the trees had failed to thrive. Some were contorted and not fit to transplant. But a dozen or so trees were straight and tall. Late one fall we transplanted those select trees to various locations in the yard where they had ample room to continue developing into stately sugar maples. Those left on the sandbar probably didn't survive the next flood. Had we not transplanted a second time, we would have had a crowded stand of weak and spindly trees. As I write it is 22 years later, and the maples have transformed the formerly treeless yard into a beautiful garden.

How about you? Are you contributing in self-sacrificing ways to the church community where you are planted? Or are you losing out in your spiritual life, failing to thrive because of being too crowded? Are there too many Christians doing little more than warming the pews once a week? Are you spindly, dwarfed, not functioning up to the potential that God has in mind for you?

What is your mission in life? Where should you be spreading your branches for Christ?

Think of how you might benefit by being transplanted to a place of service where you will be challenged to grow in ways that you never imagined possible. What is your mission in life? Where should you be spreading your branches for Christ?

Lord, is there somewhere that You would like to transplant me to? You know that I want to serve You by helping others. I realize that when I unselfishly serve others, I am the biggest beneficiary.

Threatened and Endangered Species

Every good gift and every perfect gift is from above, and comes down from the Father of lights, with whom there is no variation or shadow of turning. James 1:17, NKJV.

The United States Fish and Wildlife Service is charged with watching out for threatened and endangered species. Scientists consider a plant or animal type as threatened when it is likely to become endangered in the near future, and it is then listed as endangered if facing extinction throughout all or a significant portion of its range. As of this writing, the constantly changing list of threatened and endangered species in the United States includes 1,374 plants and animals. From time to time the agency will add plants and animals to the list if they meet the strict legal requirements. They are occasionally removed from the list if: (1) they were erroneously placed on the list for one reason or another; (2) they have now gone extinct so that they no longer exist; or (3) their populations have recovered.

As you can imagine, each and every species that is listed and then delisted has an interesting story. For example, the cactus ferruginous pygmy owl joined the list because biologists found very few of them in their range of southern Arizona, Texas, and northern Mexico. But then because of litigation, the owl was delisted. The debate rages on about whether or not they should be listed. The American alligator, on the other hand, was put on the list when its numbers plummeted because of hunting for its valuable hide. But now the numbers have recovered; they are again becoming a pest and have been removed from the list. The most recent delisting because of extinction was the dusky seaside sparrow, a non migratory songbird that used to live and nest in the marshes of Merritt Island and along the St. Johns River in south Florida. First their habitat was flooded to control mosquitoes, then drained to help with highway building. After that one-two punch that nearly took the sparrows out, pesticides and continued habitat destruction from development led to their complete extinction, the last one dying on June 17, 1987.

Habitat destruction, hunting, and collecting are the most common perils to plants and animals that end up on the threatened and endangered species list. To be good stewards of God's creation, we would do well to learn about the plants and animals that He has placed here for our pleasure and care for them to the best of our ability.

Lord, forgive me for my careless indifference. Teach me Your ways.

Invisible Life

For by Him all things were created that are in heaven and that are on earth, visible and invisible, whether thrones or dominions or principalities or powers. All things were created through Him and for Him. Col. 1:16, NKJV.

Have you heard about the oceangoing research vessels on the high seas gulping in huge quantities of seawater to learn what DNA it contains? Did you know that many scientists are processing tons of mud and dirt to discover new species of bacteria that live in soil? It used to be that microbiologists had to grow bacteria in the lab before they could isolate the various types for study. Since many bacteria won't thrive unless you give them the right food and conditions, it was a difficult and tedious process to discover a new type of microorganism. Not anymore.

With the advanced state of today's DNA technology, researchers are mining vast quantities of seawater, mud, sludge, and dirt to isolate and purify the DNA that they contain. You see, DNA is not only unique to life; it is the highly specialized type of chemical that encodes instructions to form the vast collection of molecules that make up life. Each species of life from bacteria to human beings has its own unique sequences of DNA. So analysis of the DNA can lead to a determination of what species the DNA came from.

To do the study, the researchers chop up the DNA into manageable size pieces and sequence them. The sequence of the bases in DNA will let molecular biologists know what molecules the DNA is coding for. What is astounding is that so much of what is being discovered is new to science. Millions of new and unique sequences of DNA mean new and unique forms of life not previously discovered. Most of the sequences currently found come from critters that we have never known about before. New and unique sequences of DNA also represent new and unique proteins that could have useful functions that we have not even imagined yet.

But our Creator-God not only imagined each and every life-form, He made them, blessed them, and commanded them to multiply and fill the earth. As a bonus, He created all life-forms with the ability to adapt to changing conditions, the norm on our planet.

Lord of all life, what protein gifts have You given that we have yet to unwrap? What amazing life-forms are yet to be discovered? We stand in awe of Your creative genius and humbly worship You as the giver of all good gifts.

Quick Trip

Your path led through the sea, your way through the mighty waters, though your footprints were not seen. Ps. 77:19, NIV.

L et's explore a different path together. Because of where we are going we will need to be very small, so in your mind's eye, let's shrink down to the size of a water molecule. Ready? Wait, how big is a water molecule, anyway? It must be very tiny. We are getting smaller and smaller—much, much smaller. Slightly more than 1.5 sextillion water molecules fit into one small drop of water. That's a 1 with 21 zeros after it. Think of it this way. From all the molecules in a single drop of water we could give every person on earth (that's nearly 7 billion people) 240 billion molecules of water each. If you put that much water on your tongue, you wouldn't even know it's there, because it would be only a tiny drop, so to speak, in the ocean of water already on the tongue. Obviously a water molecule is unbelievably tiny.

Now that we have shrunk down small enough, let's travel. Starting out with a bunch of water molecules being pulled up from the ground into the stem of a rose, we find ourselves traveling very fast inside an enormous system of pipes. The walls of the pipes are just a blur because of our speed. WOW, what a ride! We pass thousands of valves, and we keep transferring from one pipe to another in a zigzag pathway. Each transfer to another pipe takes us through another open valve. This is amazing. Notice how with each transfer to another pipe we pass into smaller and smaller ones? Hey, we are going a lot slower now. All of a sudden we pop out of the pipe into a brightly lit cavernous space. Huge crystal-clear columns filled with liquid soar up and connect with a very high ceiling. Inside the columns big green shiny blobs float around. They turn the light coming into the cavern emerald green. The columns are all dripping and wet, and we can feel the humid air rushing past. Where is it going? Everything is moving. Oops, we just got caught up in a jet stream. Before we hit the wall, we can see thousands of tiny openings to the outside. Oh boy, here we go. We just got blown through a little opening in the leaf, and now we are outside again. Time to return to reality.

On earth such magical trips have to be totally imaginary. What will be our travel limitations in heaven and the new earth? I do hope we can explore both the small and the big. Don't you?

Lord, I long to enjoy the guided tour of Your creation from the very small to the very big.

Nanomachines

By faith we understand that the universe was formed at God's command, so that what is seen was not made out of what was visible. Heb. 11:3, NIV.

The word "nanomachine" simply means a tiny machine. How tiny? Nano, as in nanometer, means 10^{-9} meters, or a billionth of a meter. To understand just how small that is, let's start with a meter, roughly the distance from the tip of your outstretched arm to your nose. Cut that distance into 1,000 slices, and you have a millimeter, or 10^{-3} meters. That's roughly the thickness of the period at the end of this sentence. Cut the period up into 1,000 slices, and each of those slices is a micrometer thick, or 10^{-6} meters. Some of the smallest living cells measure one micrometer across. Now slice that one-micrometer cell into 1,000 pieces. One of those slices is a nanometer, or 10^{-9} meters, thick. This is the size of some of the largest molecules. For example, the threadlike DNA is a very long double-stranded molecule two nanometers thick. So the word "nanomachine" refers to molecular-sized machines rather than cell-sized devices.

A good example of a nanomachine is an enzyme that performs a single function such as the enzyme maltase. Maltase is a large protein several nanometers in diameter with a single job of hydrolyzing maltose, a disaccharide found in grains. Think of cutting by adding water—that's what hydrolyzing means. Cutting maltose produces molecules of glucose. Maltase is a membrane-bound enzyme found in the tips of the villi of the small intestines. One molecule of maltase can perform thousands of operations per second. Do you see why we call it a nanomachine? It snips much faster than we can with scissors.

Every cell requires literally thousands of nanomachines to perform its daily functions. Each of the tiny machines do very specific jobs. The job of maltase is cutting. Some of the machines put things together or move things from one place to another. One recent scientific paper I read claimed that there are more than 100 machines whose only job is to do cell division. There is no question in my mind that they are the handiwork of a very smart Inventor. We need make no apology whatsoever for believing in a Creator. After all, He said that He made everything. Makes sense to me.

Lord of my life, thank You for every second of life that You have given me. I dedicate every moment of my life to Your honor and glory.

The Tale of Three Phosphates

For in him we live and move and have our being. Acts 17:28, NIV.

Adenosine triphosphate (ATP) consists of—you guessed it—a molecule of adenosine (A) connected to a tail of three inorganic phosphates (P). We can picture it like this (A)-(P)-(P)-(P). ATP provides energy for nearly every function of the cell. In delivering that energy, the end phosphate of ATP gets snapped off, resulting in adenosine diphosphate (A)-(P)-(P) plus the lone inorganic phosphate (P) plus the energy available for use by the cell. To do what it does, each living cell obtains energy from hundreds of millions of ATP molecules per second. In just sitting and reading this page, your body uses a gram or two of ATP every 10 to 20 seconds, or roughly your body weight in pure ATP every day. Your entire stock of ATP gets recycled three or four times per minute. Which means that if your body stops making ATP now, chances are you wouldn't live long enough to read to the end of this paragraph. When you understand this concept, it gives new meaning to the phrase "Savor every moment of life."

So how is ATP recycled? How does ADP reconnect to the inorganic phosphate (P)? Every living cell makes its own ATP, using thousands of mitochondrial enzymes aptly named ATP synthase. The job of these protein machines is relatively simple. They use the energy from the food we eat to reconnect ADP and (P). Consisting of nearly 40,000 atoms, each ATP synthase is a big protein. Each ATP synthase makes about 100 ATP per second and operates at nearly 100 percent efficiency, an unbelievable level when compared to manmade machines. A well-tuned automotive engine does good to get about 30 percent efficiency. Data in just the last few years from hundreds of research projects show what an amazing protein machine ATP synthase really is. The protein has a stationary component locked in the inner mitochondrial membrane and a rotating part that spins inside the stationary one. Energy to drive the rotating inner core comes from a proton gradient generated by cellular respiration. To see animated models of ATP synthase with the inner core spinning, causing conformational changes in the stationary parts which cram the ADP and (P) back together again, is a thing of beauty. That it does work faithfully and efficiently every second of our lives is truly a blessing. To me, it is God's signature card gracefully tied to His gift of life.

Lord, to see Your nanomachines in action gives me a small glimpse of Your creative genius. To understand how crucial they are to every second of life lets me know how much You love me.

Heart Transplant

I will remove from them their heart of stone and give them a heart of flesh. Eze. 11:19, NIV.

A re you a candidate for heart transplant surgery? According to the American Heart Association, a heart transplant may be indicated for a person who has a damaged heart and is at risk of dying. Isn't that every one of us? The latest data shows that in the United States more than 2,000 people get a heart transplant every year (3,500 worldwide), and long-term survival rates are now about 70 percent.

I well remember the first-ever heart transplant surgery. The world held its breath, and all eyes were on Cape Town, South Africa, on December 3, 1967, as Christiaan Barnard and a team of 30 removed a heart from Denise Darvall, who had been killed the day before while crossing the street. Her heart was connected to the major arteries and veins in the chest of Louis Washkansky, a 55-year-old grocer with incurable heart disease. He lived for 18 days before he died of pneumonia caused by immunosuppressive drugs. Many immediately said, "See there. It can't be done. The heart is a sacred thing." A little more than a year later Philip Blaiberg got a new heart and survived 19 months. The next year Dorothy Fisher received a new heart and lived for 12.5 years. Then two years later Dirk van Zyl had a heart transplant that gave him 23 years of life. Today heart transplants are quite common and are done in many cardiac centers the world over. Thanks to new immunosuppressive drugs and new techniques, the survival rate has steadily increased.

The reality is that all of us have damaged hearts, and we are all at risk of dying.

Normally, a heart has to be stopped in order to work on it. Surgeons have to have steady and skilled hands to do the incredibly precise work required. But just last week I saw reports of computer-controlled robots guided by 3-D imaging that are able to do external heart repair on beating hearts. Cameras detect heart movements. Robots instantaneously follow that movement and are able to perform delicate microvascular surgery on the fly.

The reality is that all of us have damaged hearts, and we are all at risk of dying (Jer. 17:9, 10; Ps. 51:10). The good news is that our heart surgeon has a donor heart ready for us, and His long-term survival rate is 100 percent. Why not give Him your old heart right now.

Lord, though I am simply unable to comprehend Your love that would cause You to transplant Your own heart of love into my feeble body, I thank You and honor You as my heart transplant surgeon and life-giver. May I love others today with the new heart of flesh that you have given me.

May 11

Cyclosporine

For the Lord will not reject his people; he will never forsake his inheritance. Ps. 94:14, NIV.

Have you signed your organ donor card? My good friend Dave is alive today because an Olympic wrestler signed his card. After his accidental death, the wrestler's healthy kidney was transplanted into Dave's body, and it has given my friend a new quality of life and greatly enriched his ministry to young people here on our campus. From about 6,000 organ recipients in 1988 to almost 15,000 recipients in 2009, it is clear that organ donation in the United States is becoming more and more common. Demand for organs far outstrips availability, as evidenced by the almost 108,000 candidates waiting for organs this year. National databases help to connect the appropriate organs and tissues to the best recipients. And with better cross matching, understanding of immunosuppressive drugs, more accurate monitoring, etc., organ recipients are now able to carry on with a fairly normal life.

Under normal circumstances our body's immune system carefully searches out foreign (not self) cells or tissues such as bacteria and viruses and attacks and gets rid of them. Our T-lymphocytes are always on patrol, looking for such invaders. Once they locate them, the T-lymphocytes turn into killer T-lymphocytes. This normally good process can quickly cause havoc, however, for an organ recipient who has just received a new heart, kidney, liver, etc. When the immune system recognizes the new organ as not belonging to self, it will mount the attack using its killer T-lymphocytes, a process called rejection.

Rates of organ rejection dropped dramatically in 1983 with the discovery and approval of cyclosporine, a molecule synthesized by a soil fungus first found in Norway. Before cyclosporine, about the only drug available to suppress the immune system and to prevent rejection were steroid hormones such as corticosteroids. The many side effects of the steroids were, in many cases, worse than the problem, so physicians hailed cyclosporine as a miracle drug. Cyclosporine works by inhibiting calcineurin, an important cell signal that activates T-lymphocytes. Suppress the calcineurin, though, and it effectively handcuffs the T-lymphocytes. I wonder, is there a way to keep friends and family from rejecting me?

Lord, how many times have friends and even my own family members rejected me? The assurance that You will never leave me or forsake me gives me hope. With that security and hope, may I always reach out to others with Your love and acceptance.

May 12

Decorah Eagles

As an eagle stirs up its nest, hovers over its young, spreading out its wings, taking them up, carrying them on its wings. Deut. 32:11, NKJV.

Established as a nonprofit organization based in Decorah, Iowa, in 1988, the Raptor Resource Project (RRP) states that its mission is "the preservation of falcons, eagles, ospreys, hawks, and owls." For convenience, ornithologists lump all of these large birds of prey into one group called raptors. To accomplish their mission, RRP creates, improves, and maintains nest sites and works to "deepen the connection between people and the natural world." One way of doing that is by maintaining cameras at nest sites with 24/7 online streaming so that the world can watch.

For several years thousands of online viewers have observed a famous pair of eagles called the "Decorah Eagles." The pair have maintained a half-ton nest high in a cottonwood tree since 2007. From there they have raised several broods of young eagles, including a brood of two in 2008, and a brood of three each year from 2009 to the present. The three young eaglets today are fully feathered but have not fledged yet. I have been checking in on them periodically from the days that the eggs were laid in late February and early March. As I review some of the numerous video clips about this pair of eagles posted on YouTube, I am impressed again by the parents' commitment and dedication to raising their young. Hour after hour, day after day, 24/7 they are on duty—patiently protecting, feeding, cleaning, and brooding their young. One particularly poignant clip filmed on April 3, 2011, shows one of the young bobble-headed chicks that had somehow slipped out of the nest bowl and was alone on a lower level of the monster nesting platform. The struggling, chirping chick tried again and again to return to the nest, but the upslope was too steep and the chick too small and too weak. The tension builds. Then mother eagle simply stretched out her neck, put her massive hooked bill behind the chick, and gently drew it back under her wing and into the protection of the nest bowl.

Mothers of so many species demonstrate commitment and care that is powerful and touching. Most are hardwired for such behavior—it is something that they do without any instruction or training. For all we know, animals are incapable of loving. Come to think of it, without the fruit of the Spirit, we also are incapable of loving as God does.

Lord, fill me with Your Spirit so that I can love and care for others as You have in mind for me.

May 13

Ungulates and Water

As the deer pants for streams of water, so my soul pants for you, my God. My soul thirsts for God, for the living God. When can I go and meet with God? Ps. 42:1, 2, NIV.

Hoofed mammals such as horses, cows, llamas, deer, sheep, moose, giraffe, elephants, and camels comprise ungulates, an artificial assemblage of about six orders of mammals that commonly walk on hoofed toes and have reduced canine teeth. Most of the animals that one sees in the big African game parks fall into this category.

Of all the ungulates, camels and Bedouin goats take the award for being able to lose the most water (30-40 percent of their body mass) and still survive. These phenomenal numbers are because of special physiological adaptations. They can go several days without drinking. Most ungulates, however, die once they lose about 15 percent of their body mass. Many arid-adapted ungulates can go two or three days between water holes. Domesticated ungulates such as farm animals and deer typically need to drink several liters of water every day. In comparison, when we lose water equivalent to 10-15 percent of our body mass, death is likely. For example, people trapped in collapsed buildings usually die from dehydration after just a few days. If they have water, it takes weeks to die from starvation. Water is far more critical.

The mechanisms that determine how long ungulates can go without water include several physiological factors such as how much fluid they lose in their feces and urine, the water content of their forage, their metabolic rate, and how much water they can store in their rumen. Several morphological and behavioral factors also play important roles, such as body size and shape, fur thickness, fat deposition, body orientation, and timing of reproduction.

All ungulates need water sooner or later. Camels and goats, noted for being able to go many days without water, have the ability to drink much more water when they finally get it. I find it interesting that the psalmist David singled out the deer as panting for water. Did he know that deer need water every day, that they have low drought tolerance? And did he recognize his own low tolerance for going without God's living water? David said, "O God, you are my God; early will I seek You; my soul thirsts for you; my flesh longs for You in a dry and thirsty land where there is no water" (Ps. 63:1, NKJV). Do you thirst for the living water?

Lord, my soul thirsts for that close intimate relationship with You. It's no wonder, often going days without the water of life, that my service to others is parched, my song dusty and dry.

The Fullness of God

And I pray that you, being rooted and established in love, may have power, together with all the Lord's holy people, to grasp how wide and long and high and deep is the love of Christ, and to know this love that surpasses knowledge—that you may be filled to the measure of all the fullness of God. Eph. 3:17-19, NIV.

For decades my brother Philip and his family have depended on a spring for all of their household water needs. It is decidedly low-tech, but it works like a charm—most of the time. They live way up in the mountains of western North Carolina, far from city water but where lots of springs bubble cold pure water out from under rocks or well up in low spots in mountain meadows. I have been to his place many times and have inspected the system he uses. Philip searches for good springs with the following criteria. It has to be a suitable distance up the mountain from the house so that gravity will bring the water home, must produce an ample flow even during long dry spells, and needs to come from a single consolidated source, not lots of little seepages flowing together.

When he locates a good spring, Philip digs deep into the mountain toward the source. When he is satisfied that he has isolated the strongest flow, he builds a little collection area with a strong roof and connects a sturdy pipe to the basin. Then he buries the collection area and its pipe connection to keep all the varmints out. Next he positions a big plastic tank just downhill from the spring and runs the pipe from the basin into the reservoir that is aboveground where he can inspect it regularly. The last connection involves nothing more than running a pipe from the bottom of the reservoir to the house. Water pressure depends on the elevation of the reservoir above the house.

The big plastic reservoir quickly fills, and an overflow directs the excess water back into the spring-fed creek bed. Philip just takes a little for his home use while restricting access to critters who would root around at the source.

One long dry summer, however, the unthinkable happened. The spring dried up. Philip brought in his heavy equipment and dug the hole deeper into the mountain toward the source, but to no avail. Being a man of God, Philip spent much time on his knees at the spring, asking the Lord to restore the water. Fasting and much soul-searching accompanied his request. God honored the prayers. The water started flowing again with more abundance and purity than ever.

Blessed be the name of the Lord, whose love is high, deep, and wide.

May 15

How Sweet Is God's Word

They are more precious than gold, than much pure gold; they are sweeter than honey, than honey from the honeycomb. Ps. 19:10, NIV.

For some years I kept bees. Periodically during the summer I would visit my hives, dressed in my beekeeper's veil, gloves, all the while keeping the smoker puffing. Removing the telescoping cover and the inner cover, I would inspect the frames to see how the bees were doing. I would search for the queen on the brood combs and check to see if she was on duty laying eggs, surrounded by her retinue of workers who fed and cared for her. With fascination I watched as bees returning from the field would perform their round dance to communicate both the distance and direction of good nectar sources to other workers gathered around them. The bees' constant activity and attention to their task of collecting and processing the nectar always intrigued me.

From the research I had read, I figured that my field worker bees were foraging for nectar within a few miles of my house, obtaining it from neighbors' gardens and from flowering trees and nearby wildflowers. The nectar that they were gathering would typically have a fairly low sugar concentration, tasting just slightly sweet with only a fraction of a drop per flower.

The bees' constant activity and attention to their task of collecting and processing the nectar always intrigued me.

Thus the bees out foraging would visit many hundreds of flowers to get a load of nectar in their special honey stomach. When low on energy, she might open a little valve between stomachs and let a little of the nectar into her own stomach to fuel the trip home. Then, with a load nearly equal to her own weight, the field worker struggles home, to be quickly met by hive workers. A quick mouth-to-mouth transfer moves her load to the honey stomachs of several sisters who add enzymes to the nectar and work it in their jaws before depositing it in small drops along the top edge of open honey cells. Other workers force large volumes of air through the hive and maintain hive temperatures at a constant 95°F, which evaporates most of the water from the small drops of bee spit. Evaporation reduces the original nectar from 80 percent moisture down to 17.5 percent moisture. Complex sugars convert to simple sugars. In this way, flower nectar becomes honey that is viscous, has a long shelf life, and tastes very sweet. I prefer honey directly from the comb. Too much of it, though, can turn off my desire.

The extraordinary effort and care expended in providing God's Word for me in readily available formats reminds me of the work of bees to make a drop of honey.

Lord, Your Word is so sweet. Can I ever get too much? Help me to receive it by faith.

Casual Sex

Flee from sexual immorality. All other sins a person commits are outside the body, but whoever sins sexually, sins against their own body. 1 Cor. 6:18, NIV.

C asual sex? Really? Could casual sex be something like a casual house fire or a casual head-on collision! I don't want to get overly dramatic, but let's just look at the evidence and then you decide. You conclude if there is anything casual about sex—in or out of marriage.

God created the magnificent gift of sex. When regularly unwrapped and savored within the sacred circle of a committed marriage, sex is good—even very good. Carefully read the Song of Solomon, and you get a lucid picture of the joy that God intends it to be. There can be no misunderstanding, because God's Word is clear and unambiguous—sex outside of marriage is sin and has heart-wrenching consequences. Since God gave us both the positives (in marriage) and the negatives (outside of marriage) the divine instructions present a clear, sharp line.

What makes the line even sharper is that He uses the metaphor of a committed marriage as a model of the wonderful and mysterious loving relationship that He wants to have with us, His church (Isa. 62:5). Using this same metaphor, Ezekiel 16 tells the heartbreaking story of an unfaithful bride. It is imagery that appears repeatedly in the Bible.

God designed sex—the joining of two bodies—to be a very big thing, much more than just physical union. Scientific experiments now show that during sex, powerful neurotransmitters such as serotonin and dopamine and hormones such as oxytocin and vasopressin flood the brains of the connected couple. The neurotransmitters create magnificent feelings of excitement and euphoria much stronger than any other experience. Add to that the hormones busily cementing powerful emotional attachments and lifelong bonds, and it's no wonder the Bible says, "What God has joined together, let no one separate" (Matt. 19:6, NIV). God's mental superglue is powerful. So you think you can casually connect to another just for fun?

Sex outside of marriage has additional factors that make it a huge negative deal. Guilt, grieving the loss of "the gift as God created it to be," risk of pregnancy, the threat of terrible sexually transmitted diseases, damaged relationships both human and divine/human, polluting the body temple, etc. What do you think? Is there such a thing as casual sex?

Lord, what an amazing gift You have given to me and _____ for "becoming one." Help me to hold it as sacred. I choose to honor You.

Flax

She seeks wool and flax, and willingly works with her hands. Prov. 31:13, NKJV.

Today let us worship Him who made flax. Where I grew up in Ethiopia, growing flax (also known as linseed) was (and continues to be) a major cash crop. Seeds for the tall slender annual plant with the beautiful blue flowers are planted in rich loamy soil. Slightly more than three months later the plants are harvested either by cutting close to the ground or by pulling them up by the roots. And what a rich harvest it is. God has provided amazing gifts with flax.

The seeds contain a rich oil that painters employ for thinning oil-based paints and furniture makers use for varnishes. It is one of the earliest produced commercial oils. We add a small amount of freshly ground flaxseed to our breakfast every morning, because it is rich in omega-3 fatty acids that lower blood cholesterol, fight breast and prostate cancers, and are a good source of fiber.

The stem of flax plants have long supple fibers used to make linen. The name "linen" comes from the scientific name of flax (*Linum usitatissimum*). Linen cloth and fibers date to earliest human history. Because linen is cool to the touch and makes an elegant fabric, ancient Egyptian texts described royalty as wearing the finest linens. During the hot summer months we enjoy slipping into bed between cool linen sheets. The woman in Proverbs 31 also "makes coverings for her bed; she is clothed in fine linen and purple" (verse 22, NIV). "She makes linen garments and sells them, and supplies the merchants with sashes" (verse 24, NIV). Doubtless she must have known about harvesting and retting the flax stalks, extracting the fibers, and spinning them into thread, because verse 19 says that "in her hand she holds the distaff and grasps the spindle with her fingers." The distaff is the part of the spindle that holds the unspun flax during the process of spinning it into thread. Even today some of the finest materials for clothing come from linen.

Besides excellent cloth, *Linum* fibers make some of the longest-lasting paper products. Money is printed on paper containing 25 percent linen and 75 percent cotton. The preferred canvasses for oil paintings consist of linen stretched on wooden frames.

Creator of Linum usitatissimum, thank You for making such a useful plant.

Silk

Your clothing was of fine linen, silk, and embroidered cloth. Eze. 16:13, NKJV.

D on't you just love the look and feel of silk? It feels so soft. The flat sides of the triangular silk fibers create its iridescent shine. Many species of insects and spiders make silk, most spinning it from complicated glands that produce a mixture of protein polymers, sticky components, and hardeners. Some of the best known are the silks of spiders that spin webs from two to four pairs of glands at the tip of their abdomen, and the fibers made by the silkworm moth larvae that spins a cocoon from two glands in its head. To make the luxuriant silk fabrics, cocoons of the silkworm moth larvae are boiled to dissolve the glue that cements the windings of the single mile-long silk fiber of one cocoon so it can be unwound and combined with fibers from other cocoons to make a strand big enough to be a thread. Other critters that make silk include various leaf rollers, web spinners, and the like in the ants/bees/wasps order of insects.

Materials scientists are particularly interested in how to make strong fibers in more environmentally sensitive ways. Making artificial fibers requires strong chemicals and great energy, both of which cause pollution. Spiders and moth larvae do their silk production at environmental temperatures in watery solutions. Scientists now study the complicated products of the silk glands to determine molecular structure and to learn how the fibers form.

One recent research study focused on silk made by the common Australian green lacewing. When a female lacewing gets ready to lay an egg, she first secretes a pool of liquid silk from a gland. Then she pulls the liquid silk up into a very thin stalk that hardens in seconds before laying a single egg on the top of the stalk to keep it out of the way of predators. Lacewing silk happens to be much stronger and thicker than other kinds of silk and has more elasticity and lateral stiffness. Since lacewing silk starts out as a liquid it may very well turn out to be easier to produce than the complicated multistep processes of spiders and silkworms. We would like to know what that simpler process might involve. So far the researchers have identified and sequenced the genes that make the liquid and now know that the proteins in the silk are fibrous proteins that fold much like a set of folding doors. So the search goes on.

"O Lord, how manifold are thy works! in wisdom hast thou made them all: the earth is full of thy riches" (Ps. 104:24, KJV).

Sabbath

Six days shall work be done, but the seventh day is a Sabbath of solemn rest, a holy convocation. You shall do no work on it; it is the Sabbath of the Lord in all your dwellings. Lev. 23:3, NKJV.

S eems as if everyone I talk to knows Billy and has been a beneficiary of his kindness, grace, and magnanimous enthusiasm. I am certainly privileged to count him as one of my best friends. After all, we work closely together nearly every day. So when Billy casually mentions in passing that he is having trouble with a faulty light switch at home or is struggling to format a document on his computer at work, my practice is to stop by his home and take a look, or visit his office to help. It is what friends do. Friends care about friends.

Not too long ago I received an e-mail from the president of Andrews University asking me to come by his office to chat about a matter that we were working on. I quickly responded by making sure that appointment time was clear on my calendar. I arrived on time, prepared to work on resolving the issue. When an individual with authority makes a request, we listen.

Though it hasn't happened yet, should the governor of the state of Michigan ask me to show up at a specific time or place, I would certainly make sure no other appointment conflicted with the requests of such a higher authority.

So when my dear friend and wise counselor, Jesus, makes a request, I pay close attention. When the King of kings and Lord of lords, Creator of everything there is, issues a crystal-clear command to show up for an appointment, you can bet that I am going to clear my calendar and be there. He is not only a friend with a request— He is the highest authority with a command. That trumps all other requests.

His request/command to me is clear and unambiguous: "Work shall be done for six days, but the seventh is the Sabbath of rest, holy to the Lord" (Ex. 31:15, NKJV). Week after week, as I meet this appointment, I discover the great blessings of the Sabbath rest and become convinced of the reality that "the Sabbath was made for man, and not man for the Sabbath" (Mark 2:27, NKJV).

Lord of the Sabbath, do You still have more to show me about the rich blessings of the Sabbath? Would You like me to do more good to others on Your holy day? Teach me Your will.

Saying Grace

When you have eaten and are full, then you shall bless the Lord your God for the good land which He has given you. Deut. 8:10, NKJV.

When I sit down hungry in front of a beautifully prepared meal, I don't ever think of it as possibly the last meal that I will ever eat, much less that a contaminant in the food in front of me will cause violent illness or even death. That just never crosses my mind. News stories abound, however, about food-borne illness and death even in this modern age. I can understand how people were sickened and died because of their food long ago, before the discovery of bacteria and other harmful microorganisms, before refrigeration, and before microwaves. But today we know better. Not only do we know that bacteria and fungi exist, but we can identify them by species and even by multiple strains. Furthermore, we know how to kill them and control them so as to make food safe for human consumption. So why are people still getting ill and even dying from eating contaminated food?

Bad food choices, misplaced trust, ever-evolving bacteria—there are no doubt many reasons for ongoing health concerns in our modern age.

Bad food choices, misplaced trust, ever-evolving bacteria—there are no doubt many reasons for ongoing health concerns in our modern age. When we choose to eat high-risk foods such as raw milk, meats, poultry, and cheeses, really bad bacteria may be in the mix. And when we give others the responsibility for our food safety, we are placing great trust in them. Because food processors sometimes cut corners, because of food sabotage, because of poor personal hygiene by food handlers, because of equipment failure, that trust might be misplaced at times. Think about some of this the next time you eat out. Bacteria seem to have great flexibility in the way they pick up environmental DNA and swap it around the bacterial community. As a result, new and toxic strains of bacteria do show up occasionally. Some of them are deadly killers.

How often my prayer before a meal is quick and perfunctory. Shouldn't I seriously think about where I am placing my food safety trust? Would it be a good idea to tell my Food Supplier that I confidently place my trust in Him? Does He know when the food I am about to eat is tainted? Has He promised to protect me from all harm? Should I thank Him for that?

Thank You for this food, Lord. You made it and packed it with just the right blend of important vitamins, minerals, healing phytochemicals, and antioxidants. You also made it delightful to my senses. May this food be safe for me to eat, and may I use the energy in it to honor and glorify Your holy name.

Violets

The grass withers, the flower fades, but the word of our God stands forever. Isa. 40:8, NKJV.

Just off of our back steps we have a lovely violet blooming this time of year. Its foliage is characteristic of the common blue violet, but its five soft white petals are equally speckled and streaked front and back with fine stippled blue to violet dots and thin lines radiating out from the center. It looks as if a small vial of paint might have exploded deep inside the corolla tube, leaving the fine misty splatter on the petals. It is the thin splatter lines that help to guide insects in to where a nectar award waits for them at the back of the lower petal. Apparently the lines are much more prominent when seen by insect eyes that work best in the ultraviolet range.

Duane Ford, greatly beloved but now retired chemistry professor who still lives in our community, gave me a couple pots of the plant about a decade ago. I remember Duane dubbing it the Battle Creek violet, and, from what he told me, I understood that Ellen White grew the variety in her yard. That may have been. Violets have been exceedingly popular for centuries, having grown in the yard of nearly every resident of ancient Athens. Though I wonder about their accuracy, stories of ancient Greeks and Romans wearing wreaths of violets to cure hangovers after their banquets have filtered down to us. Could that be the "crown of pride" referenced in Isaiah 28:1? According to mythology, violets poured out of the lyre of Orpheus, the sixth-century father of songs. And Napoleon Bonaparte appeared to have a very public love affair with both violets and Josephine, his empress for a time. According to tradition, Josephine always had a violet pinned to her dress and had them embroidered on her wedding dress. French gardeners did much to popularize and hybridize violets.

The Mediterranean region reportedly has 400 or so species of violets. North America has at least 75 native species that have apparently produced more than 300 varieties just in the United States and Canada and hundreds more south of the Rio Grande. The ease with which they interbreed makes a horribly confusing mess for professional botanists, who like to keep things nice and tidy. However, violets just stay on task producing their sweet-smelling blooms that actually make a colorful and tasty garnish in salads. Some varieties have a high sugar content and can be used crystallized in candy, cake decorations, and other confections.

Lord, flowers are so ornate and beautiful, yet so transient. How much more You must care for Your Word, which never changes.

Sleep

There I was! In the day the drought consumed me, and the frost by night, and my sleep departed from my eyes. Gen. 31:40, NKJV.

So . . . what's keeping you from getting a good night's sleep? Is it exhausting work, such as Jacob complained to his uncle Laban about? Is it too much food late at night? Perhaps it is family stress, or grief, or . . . you name it. If you're an adult, you know that you need seven to eight hours of sleep each night, plus an additional two for teenagers. At least that's what the research seems to indicate. Furthermore, it reveals that a major portion of that sleep should be well before midnight. We also know that not getting enough sleep can be fatal in many different ways. Sleep-deprived lab animals will simply die. People that don't get enough sleep often fall asleep at the wheel and kill themselves and others in horrific vehicle crashes, or they doze off at the controls and cause major industrial accidents. Sleep deprivation was a major factor in the loss of the space shuttle Challenger, the grounding of the Exxon Valdez, and the first Staten Island Ferry crash, to name a few. Other documented effects of sleep deprivation are forgetfulness, emotional problems, lower stress tolerance, lower resistance to infections such as colds and flu, mood swings, increased risk of obesity, diabetes, heart disease, and faster aging. We all know these facts. But there is a lot we don't know yet.

What does the body do during sleep? I mean, our heart keeps beating, we keep breathing (respiration and heart rate actually speed up during rapid eye movement [REM] sleep, as does brain activity), we keep making urine, and while cellular metabolism slows, it is not that much. So where does the rest part of sleep come in? Oh yes, our muscles get paralyzed during REM except for those sudden annoying jerks!

What really happens during sleep? When you read the scientific literature, you learn about the body getting rest, the bones and muscles being rebuilt, tissue being regenerated, the immune system being strengthened, the memory being reconsolidated, and energy levels being restored. But what does that all mean? Most of that happens when we are awake, too. Science has found different levels of sleep and what the brain waves are doing, but we don't know what is actually going on in the body that accompanies those waves. We have so much to learn about why sleep is so sweet.

Lord of sweet sleep, You put us to bed each night, and something happens. Then You wake us rested and refreshed in the morning. Thank You. We praise and honor You.

May 23

Unity in Community

Locusts have no king, yet they advance together in ranks. Prov. 30:27, NIV.

I will never forget the horror of flying through a swarm of locust and watching utter devastation as the hungry eaters crept along at ground level. The first image formed when, as a child, I was in the cockpit of an old DC-3 flying over Ethiopia. Ahead in the distance we could see a huge brown cloud looming before us as an ever-changing amorphous mass. The pilot steered well off course to avoid the cloud, but we still took enough loud hits on the airplane for it to be frightening and enough splatters on the windshield to make it difficult to see out. It sounded like a very hard hailstorm. The second image I have is of a brown cloud of locusts touching down and morphing into an ever-moving carpet of insects inexorably advancing across the ground and devouring everything green. They covered every tree, every bush, and every little green plant. I remember the local farmers out with burlap bags and sticks, flailing the air and beating the ground to kill as many as they could. Locust droppings fell like rain. Fighting this army was futile.

In the text above, Solomon described four things that are small but wise. One are locusts who have no king but work together as if they had a plan. Because they are so devastating, many scientists have worked hard on understanding locusts in an attempt to control them better. Originally thought to be a different species, locusts are actually short-horned grasshoppers that have gotten too crowded and go into reproductive overdrive. When conditions are right, they reproduce explosively and travel great distances, consuming the vegetation as they go. Scientists have learned much about their olfactory, visual, and locomotor neurophysiology. No doubt the insects have much more to teach us.

I have learned two important lessons from locusts. First, it is truly amazing how much a group can accomplish when it works cooperatively together on a task. The locusts are small, but they get a lot done. Second, God is unbelievably gracious and forgiving. When we really blow it, we can equate the consequences to the devastation of locusts moving through. What has overwhelmed and devastated you? What sickens your heart?

What an amazing promise to me, Lord, that You will restore or repay the years that the locust has eaten (Joel 2:25). Help me to believe this promise. I have wasted so much of the time that You have given me. Lord, I rededicate my heart to You and Your mission for Your church.

The Summer Rain

Give ear, O heavens, and I will speak; and hear, O earth, the words of my mouth. Let my teaching drop as the rain, my speech distill as the dew, as raindrops on the tender herb, and as showers on the grass. Deut. 32:1, 2, NKJV.

For weeks the rain clouds have been elsewhere. The ground is parched and dusty. Lawns are stressed. Leaves on trees hang limp and partially wilted. The vegetable garden and flower gardens are not thriving. You end up dragging hoses from place to place every day, just trying to keep plants in the driest areas from dying. All your sprinkling and irrigation seems too little. When will we get some rain? Then off in the distant west you hear the quietest murmurings of what sounds like high cloud-to-cloud thunder. During the next half hour the clouds thicken, the thunder intensifies, and light goes into hiding. Then splat. Another splat. A few giant raindrops fall, puffing up little clouds of dust. The gentle sound is music to the ears. The smell of fresh rain on dry soil and baked grass is sweet to the senses. But it isn't enough. Don't stop now! The ground isn't even wet yet. And the rain spattered dusty lawn furniture needs a good washing.

O wonder of wonders, the sky suddenly opens up, and every square inch of grass, garden, and soil has lightly dancing raindrops. The rain falls straight down in abundance for five minutes, 10 minutes, 30 minutes. The thirsty soil drinks it in. Leaves start to tighten up in minutes. All nature is sighing ahhhhh. Watering all day wouldn't provide the refreshing blessing that has come in the past 30 minutes. The intensity of the rain slows as it grows even darker. Something more is about to happen. Then lightning crashes again, and water begins to pour down in torrents. Strong winds drive sheets of water ahead of them. Even large trees sway back and forth, their leaves hanging on for dear life. For another 30 minutes God's abundance is beautifully demonstrated. What a gift!

God's Word—His instructions given through Moses—were clear, understandable, abundant. Like the rain they brought great blessings, but the words also warned of danger through disobedience. After the recitation of this beautiful song of love and devotion to His people, Moses hiked up the mountain for the last time, and angels buried him there.

"For I proclaim the name of the Lord: ascribe greatness to our God. He is the Rock, His work is perfect; for all His ways are justice, a God of truth and without injustice; righteous and upright is He" (Deut. 32:3, 4, NKJV).

Semamith

A lizard can be caught with the hand, yet it is found in kings' palaces. Prov. 30:28, NIV.

T his text in Proverbs is curious, to say the least. The literal translation of the six Hebrew words of it are: | the lizard | the hands | may grasp | he | palaces | kings' |. The New King James Version and Strong's Concordance translate the first word, semamith, as "spider." Biologists don't ever confuse a lizard with a spider, which tells me that we really don't know the meaning of semamith for sure. I'll go with spider, because of all the critters that I have studied in the scanning electron microscope, spiders get more time from me than any other. I find them more than fascinating.

More than 40,000 species of spiders share our world with us. And no matter how you may hate them and try to keep your home and garden free of them, spiders are there, all around you, in abundance, relentlessly spinning their webs in great variety, ever showing what a poor housekeeper you really are. But don't feel too bad. They inhabit even the palaces of kings.

They know how to get around. Even though they don't have wings, just-out-of-the-cocoon baby spiders will spin a length of web that the wind picks up and away they go. Sometimes the breeze drops them a few yards from the nest. But at times they have been found thousands of feet up traveling the jet streams, or far out to sea wafted along on the breezes.

I hope to spend 1,000 years of eternity just studying spiders because of their beautifully complex and exquisite sensory systems.

The images of spiders that I get with the electron microscope show extremely hairy bodies and eight hairy legs. And if I look carefully, I can usually find all eight eyes. As you can imagine, with eight eyes some spiders have excellent vision and excellent hearing, too, even though they don't have ears. Spider hearing comes though extremely sensitive pressure sensors in some of the many and varied types of hairs that I find on them. The hairs pick up not only sound but also wind speed and direction, and detect chemicals (giving them acute taste and smell). Some hairs are good for defense. For example, tarantula spiders have tiny, sharp, barbed hairs like harpoons on their abdomen that easily stick into your skin and then break off. They cause itching—but that's all.

I hope to spend 1,000 years of eternity just studying spiders because of their beautifully complex and exquisite sensory systems. Spinning webs and catching an occasional insect, they seem common and unimpressive, yet they get to live in kings' palaces. When have I ever had that honor?

I needed this lesson on humility, Lord. Thank You for Your minuscule semamith teachers.

The Spider's Web

I drew them with gentle cords, with bands of love, and I was to them as those who take the yoke from their neck. I stooped and fed them. Hosea 11:4, NKJV.

No doubt you have observed a spider pulling silk out of its abdomen with its hind legs as it constructs its web. If you haven't watched lately, try to spend a few minutes in quiet contemplation to see the fascinating process for yourself. Of the thousands of kinds of spiders, most of them build webs. Scientists have classified the webs into about six different types, depending on who is deciding. Web-building spiders have pairs of swollen nozzles or spinnerets at the tip of their abdomen, each spinneret serving as the external part of a gland or glands. Most spiders that make silk have three pairs of these spinnerets, though some have four or perhaps only one pair depending on how many types of silk they make.

As one of my students found out when he collected strands of spider web for examination with the scanning electron microscope, spiders spin five types of silk. Depending on what kind of silk they need at the moment, spiders can produce silk with varying degrees of toughness, stickiness, and stretchiness. For example, dragline silk is tough. Capture silk is not only tough, it's sticky, and stretchable, too. Egg sack silk is the most stretchable. And silk used to wrap up captured insects is several times stronger than even dragline silk.

So what is the silk made out of? How strong is it? The answers depend on which of the 40,000 species of spider we are talking about. The chemical makeup of silk is extremely complex. In general, it is a protein with repeating similar segments of crystalline structure interspersed with segments of little to no structure. The way the two segments interact is what gives spider silk its great strength. By all accounts, it is much stronger than high-grade steel of the same thread size and about as strong as Kevlar, though of lighter weight. And it can stretch up to 140 percent of its length without breaking. As you can imagine, the process of spinning this magic filament is utterly amazing. The many glands working together produce a gel in the spider's body that turns into a strong, solid fiber as it is pulled out into the air. Engineers study spider silk to learn how to make artificial fibers in a non-polluting, low-energy way. We are just babes in our understanding here.

You have bound me to You, Lord, with cords of love that will not let me go. Since You designed spider silk so well, I trust that You use even better technology for making my love knots.

Older and Wiser

I said, "Age should speak; and multitude of years should teach wisdom." Job 32:7, NKJV.

I s it really true that old people are wiser? I didn't used to think so. But now that I have three teenagers calling me Grandpa, I've changed my mind. It must be true. When you read young Elihu's argument to Job (Job 32:6-10), he reasons that older people should be wiser—but that isn't a guarantee. It is God's Spirit that imparts wisdom. So, Elihu concludes, though he is young, he is going to share a piece of his mind. So who is wisest?

I suppose that depends on how you define wisdom. If you regard it as knowing how to send text messages, how to program the TV remote, how to find information on the Internet, or how to send attachments in your e-mail messages, then youth definitely have the edge. OK, not just the edge. The race is over before the echoes of the starting gun have died.

A research group at the University of Michigan attempted to determine who had the advantage on wisdom. Was it the young or the old? Their definition of wisdom centered less on the use of technology and more on understanding and managing human relationships. Wiser people, they reasoned, were the ones who could best cope with change and uncertainty in life—those who could best manage life's conflicts, disagreements, surprises, and shattered dreams. Data that they collected across different socioeconomic groups, a wide range of ethnic groups, and a broad spread of education and IQ levels shows that age trumps all these factors and does indeed give a significant edge to those who are older. From the outset of the multi-year study, the team of researchers thought that they would find an age advantage. But as often happens in research, they were surprised by how strong it actually was.

What the study suggests is that while we can all learn from each other, we need to pay particular attention to the advice of our elders, especially when it involves relationships and things of the heart. When grandma suggests that it isn't a good idea for a young person to give her heart and body to her pimply faced boyfriend, she may be right. When grandpa observes that perhaps it wasn't so tragic to lose that dream job, because it makes you free to get an even better one, he may be right. Young people would do well to listen carefully to what their elders say. Scientific research and the Bible are in agreement.

So often, Lord, I am sure that the advice others are giving me is wrong. Help me, Father, to hear Your voice in that of experienced godly people.

Gashing Figs

Amos answered Amaziah, "I was neither a prophet nor the son of a prophet, but I was a shepherd, and I also took care of sycamore-fig trees." Amos 7:14, NIV.

Ethylene is such a tiny molecule. But what a long and notable history it has had with people's lives and fortunes. 1. In early Egypt fig growers would cut a small hole in their figs with a special knife. They didn't know why, but by gashing a hole in their figs a certain way, figs would ripen in four days. Figs that were not cut took too long to ripen and would get invaded and spoiled by insects. Amos may have used this technique. 2. The Chinese didn't know why their pears ripened rapidly when placed in a room with smoking incense, but they stumbled on to this trick and regularly used it to make pears ripen on command. 3. People didn't know why, but trees near leaking gas lights in the late 1800s would lose their leaves, get gnarly, and develop swellings on their upper branches. 4. When it first happened in the 1960s, they didn't know why, but carnation growers near San Francisco lost millions of dollars' worth of flowers because of nearby polyethylene production plants. Later they learned that a little ethylene gas leaked from the factories. Tiny ethylene molecules have powerful effects on plants. The history of understanding ethylene and its many uses goes back many decades.

Research by a Russian chemist in the early 1900s identified ethylene as the active ingredient in illuminating gas that was causing tree damage. A few years later scientists isolated ethylene as the component that makes leaves drop off of other plants. Then around the time of World War I researchers recognized it as a plant hormone (produced by the plant) that causes fruit ripening. We now know that ethylene causes at least a couple dozen effects on plants. At various stages in their life, a plant part may produce ethylene to help regulate important growth and development factors.

Nowadays commercial fruit growers regularly ripen their crops with ethylene to prepare them for market at predictable times. You can do it too. Place a ripe apple slice in a plastic bag of green bananas, and it will speed their ripening significantly. Use that trick, and you have a link to Amos, who gashed figs to make them produce ethylene to promote ripening.

Breathe on me, breath of God; mature my relationship with You so that my fruit of the Spirit will ripen into good works for You.

Docosahexaenoic Acid (pronounced doe-coe-sah-hexah-nowick acid)

Who has put wisdom in the mind? Or who has given understanding to the heart? Job 38:36, NKJV.

A slightly-difficult-to-pronounce word has been cropping up in popular print more and more frequently these days. In May 2010 a two-day scientific conference at the Royal Society of Medicine in London totally devoted itself to it. The word is docosahexaenoic acid, also known by the acronym DHA, but more popularly called omega-3 fatty acid, the name for a family of unsaturated fatty acids found in fish oils and in freshly ground flaxseed. Our bodies can make some DHA, but we do need to get some in our diet, too. The concern is that some populations receive too little DHA. The good omega-3 has been replaced by the not-so-good-but-easier-to-get omega-6 fatty acids in popular cooking oils. Most DHA occurs in the eyes (60 percent) and in the brain (40 percent), particularly at the synapses.

Presentations at the London conference reported on the research of prominent neuroscientists working to understand DHA. Their findings were mostly in their early stages, and many involved correlative studies between fish consumption and incidence of various disease conditions. For example, groups that eat less fish suffer more from severe depression, cognitive decline, Alzheimer's disease (AD), violent behavior, memory loss, schizophrenia, and attention-deficit disorder. Tragically, babies unable to get or make enough DHA have lower IQs.

Some studies presented at the conference looked at nutrients that the brain especially needs to develop properly: iodine (which is in iodized salt), iron, and DHA. All three are more abundant in seafoods. Roughly 1 billion people in the world are deficient in both iodine and iron and as a result suffer from poor brain development. DHA slows the age-related loss of brain cells and prevents the AD brain cell tangles and plaques. People with AD have less than half the normal level of DHA in their brains.

The concern I have is that the mind is the pathway that God uses to communicate with us. Any loss of synaptic function or decline in cognitive function or decrease in IQ is going to solidify the great deceiver's grip on God's greatest love, His people. How important it is then for us to get good nutrition and carefully steward the body and mind that God gave us.

Lord, I dedicate my mind to You. Help me to care for it to Your glory.

Death

O Death, where is your sting? 1 Cor. 15:55, NKJV.

The sting? Where is the sting you ask? All who knew and loved Genevieve Starkey felt the sting, and it didn't feel good. After 94 years of a life filled with generous service in the community, Gen was at rest. She was at peace. But Tom Starkey, her faithful husband for 74 of those years, felt the sting, and it didn't feel good to Tom, either. Until death closed the door between them, Gen always kept her promise to love Tom for better or worse, in sickness and in health. And they certainly had more than their share of "worse" and "sickness." Tom kept his promise too. A promise kept, no matter what, is a beautiful thing. Genevieve's family gathered with friends to celebrate a well-lived life. All who knew Gen loved her, because of her kind and giving spirit. She unselfishly and generously served the community all of her life. Her volunteerism was legendary. Though Gen is not now feeling the sting, her family and friends who live on know the sting of emptiness and loss as they grieve. The sting is acute for those who live.

> *Though Gen is not now feeling the sting, her family and friends who live on know the sting of emptiness and loss as they grieve. The sting is acute for those who live.*

For all practical purposes, the living and the dead have the same chemical composition and appearance. But there are profound differences. The dead no longer have to breathe every few seconds, or pump blood incessantly, or eat occasionally, or keep their body warm. Their systems have come to a full and complete stop. Jesus used the word "sleeping" for this full-stop rest. To borrow an analogy from our computer age, we would describe their systems as "shut down" rather than "hibernating" or "sleeping." Because none of us still living have been there, we don't fully understand the realm of the dead. But Jesus has been there, and He knows. He calls it a sleep.

Jesus is the only one who has power to move Himself or others across that fine sharp line between the living and the dead. He said, "Therefore My Father loves Me, because I lay down My life that I may take it again. No one takes it from Me, but I lay it down of Myself. I have power to lay it down, and I have power to take it again. This command I have received from My Father" (John 10:17, 18, NKJV).

Gen Starkey knew Jesus, believed Jesus, and took Him at His word. The next thing she will hear is that shout of the Lord Himself and the loud trumpet call. The reunions with family and friends will certainly follow, and that is why the sting ultimately is just a minor one.

Lord, always with You, by Your side, is the place I long to be.

Blame Game

In all this Job did not sin nor charge God with wrong. Job 1:22, NKJV.

O n April 20, 2010, the Deepwater Horizon oil rig caught fire during a drilling operation. Before the terrible accident, Deepwater Horizon had drilled many successful wells. One of those wells in the Tiber oilfield reached a depth of 35,055 feet, 4,132 feet of that through water. Chevron Canada is working on a well now at Orphan Basin that begins 1.5 miles below sea level. Just how far down that well will go remains to be seen. Temperatures at such extreme depths are about 250°F, and rocks are under extreme pressure, which is what caused the blowout at the Macondo Prospect, where Deepwater Horizon was drilling the exploratory well before the accident.

Despite many attempts at plugging the leak or diverting the oil, the broken pipe continued to spew oil with great pressure. Black tar balls began showing up on the beaches hundreds of miles away, and the toxic brew killed much marine life. The disaster was huge. Who was to blame?

The giant oil company British Petroleum has been blamed, as has Transocean, the drilling company, and Halliburton, the company cementing the wellhead in place. Others accused the United States Coast Guard. Still others have blamed various United States government entities, including the president himself. I have even been declared responsible. Some talking head on television said that because I use petroleum products, I bear the blame for the blowout under Deepwater Horizon.

It is so easy to blame, isn't it? It isn't my fault. He did it. Or, she made me do it. In this litigious society someone must be responsible for everything that happens, and that someone must be identified and held accountable. There can be no accidents. And if we can't determine somebody or some company to blame, then we call it an "act of God," and He gets the blame. Which makes me wonder: Who has been pointing fingers and blaming God from the get-go?

Have you ever blamed God for something you think He did or perhaps didn't do but should have? Without all the facts, can we ever properly place the blame for anything? Do we ever have all the facts? Do you think the great deceiver ever destroys or taints the evidence?

Lord, at times I have blamed You. I put my hand over my mouth. You know all the facts, and You alone are good. From now on, may I, like Job, never sin by ever blaming You again.

June 1

Goose Bumps

A spirit glided past my face, and the hair on my body stood on end. Job 4:15, NIV.

We live in the deep dark woods where the trees are really tall. Recently we have read in the local papers about cougar sightings near our home. If I don't think of it till near bedtime, I sometimes have to walk the trash out to the road about 300 feet away on dark moonless nights. My mind wanders to cougar, and there goes the hair thing. The chill down the spine. The hair on the back of the neck and the scalp snaps to attention. You know the feeling. Admit it.

Centuries after Eliphas described it, William Shakespeare included these lines in Hamlet: "I could a tale unfold whose lightest word would harrow up thy soul, freeze thy young blood, make thy two eyes, like stars, start from their spheres, thy knotted and combined locks to part and each particular hair to stand an end like quills upon the fretful porpentine." So why do we get the "fretful porcupine" sensation? Why does our hair literally stand on end sometimes when we are scared spitless or horrified? But wait, the very word "horror" comes from the Latin word *horrere*, meaning "to bristle." You guessed it—hair standing on end, or in the case of the porcupine, its quills all aquiver and raised.

No doubt you have watched birds preening and caring for their feathers. Perhaps you may have seen them fluff all of them. The bird looks as if it is swelling up because the feathers are standing more erect, then they lay them all down smooth again. What they did was just comb their hair, so to speak. All the feathers are now arranged as they should be once again.

Goose bumps happen because of a little muscle at the base of every hair. But we don't have conscious control of them. They contract automatically when the sympathetic side of the autonomic nervous system is especially active. That happens when we are cold or scared or when the emotions are running high, as in anger or great joy. You observe it in scared cats and fighting dogs. Even the hair of a sea otter stands on end when confronting a predator. But why does it happen to us? Lots of theories have attempted to explain it, but none are convincing. I keep reminding myself that I have a lot to learn and that one of the joys of heaven will be ongoing research and exploration.

Lord of my arrectores pilorum muscles, teach me to trust in You when scared or driven by emotion. Those little muscles send me clear signals from You, Lord, giving me messages of love, care, and chastening.

Stinkpots

He performs wonders that cannot be fathomed, miracles that cannot be counted. Job 5:9, NIV.

Perhaps you have seen or at least heard about the common musk turtle. It is, after all, quite common and lives in slow-moving streams or ponds from south Florida through to central Texas, up to central Wisconsin, and all the way to the east coast and up into southern Ontario and Quebec in Canada. Common musk turtles are usually less than four inches long. They acquired the "musk" part of their name because they can put out a powerful stink from glands just under their shell back by their tail when they feel threatened. Some people call them stinkpot turtles.

Now, the really curious part about them is that they can stay underwater indefinitely. Whereas most turtles have to come to the surface to breathe every now and again, stinkpots can remain underwater for months at a time. A few other turtles that live underwater for long periods at least have thin vascular skin or some sacs at their rear ends called cloacal bursae that act sort of like gills. But not the stinkpots. They have thick skin and no bursae. So for the longest time, stinkpot respiration was a profound mystery. How do they survive?

The answer to that question came quite by accident. Graduate student Egon Heiss was studying the feeding habits of stinkpots using high-speed photography. It helped that young turtles sometimes climb out on land to feed. But clumsy at feeding, they always had to drag their food back into the water before they could get it down. Egon and his research colleagues noticed that the turtle tongues were different and not very helpful for eating, so they studied them with high powered microscopy. They found highly vascular microscopic little buds that looked as if they were designed just for breathing. Furthermore, the little buds were not only on the tongue but down the pharynx, too. Mystery solved—we think. God designed these little stinkpots to be able to stay down in their calm lakes and streams—feeding on worms, crayfish, crustaceans, and anything else that moves slowly—without having to keep bobbing to the surface to breathe. The more we learn about God's creation, the more we realize how much we don't know. Fortunately, we will have an eternity to study and learn. There certainly won't be any boring times.

Lord of the stinkpot turtles, is there even more to this mystery that we have not discovered yet?

June 3
Raining Bacteria

Have you entered the treasury of snow? Job 38:22, NKJV.

One spring I backpacked with a group of students in the Cherokee National Forest up above the Ocoee River in eastern Tennessee. We were a good day and a half into a delightful trip when the temperature plummeted and a freak spring snowstorm dropped more than a foot of snow on us. Since that part of Tennessee just doesn't get very much snow, we were at first awed by the beauty of the freshly fallen snow. The beauty wore off quickly, however, when we realized that most of the students were simply not prepared for cold weather snow hiking, much less snow camping. We decided to cut our itinerary short and take the shortest route to shelter and safety. It wasn't easy, but all did survive. But what made the freak snow in spring?

Meteorologists know that in order for rain or snow to fall, the air needs to be saturated with water vapor (i.e., 100 percent relative humidity), be cold, and have microscopic material for the moisture to condense on. Dust motes, smoke, and tiny particles of soot in the air work well, as do tiny ice crystals. Apparently such nucleation sites help orient water molecules so that they can easily form ice crystals. Scientists refer to the transformation from a supersaturated cold gas to ice crystals as a phase change. Once it has occurred, then the ice crystal can easily grow and start falling. As ice falls it may warm up and become a drop of rain. For years people have attempted to seed clouds with various types of nucleation material with varying degrees of success.

David Sands at Montana State University, Bozeman, Montana, has been working with *Pseudomonas syringae*, a type of bacterium commonly found almost everywhere on outdoor surfaces—especially plants. The bacterium makes a protein in its cell wall that provides thousands of nucleation sites. They orient water molecules effectively, causing freezing even when the temperature is well above normal freezing temperatures. Such bacteria-induced frost on plants causes extensive damage. The bacteria must get swept up into the air, because in 70 percent of snowflakes recently studied the microscopic bacterium and its magic protein turned out to be the nucleation site. This phenomenon, called bioprecipitation, is believed to be widespread, because everywhere Sands has looked, he has found the bacteria at the center of ice crystals. Could this magic icemaker bacteria be one of the treasuries of the snow that God was asking Job about?

Lord of the rain, snow, sleet, and hail, the science behind precipitation is so very complicated, yet You do it with apparent ease. We worship You as the giver of every good gift.

June 4

Yoke

I desire to do your will, my God; your law is within my heart. Ps. 40:8, NIV.

T he mature ox stood patiently while the youngster yoked to him misbehaved badly. Twisting and turning, sitting down in the furrow, head tossing and wild-eyed, the greenhorn must have been experiencing the yoke for the first time. I was a youngster at the time, too, looking on with fascination and learning by careful observation. What I was watching was a teamster out in the field training a young inexperienced ox restrained by a solid yoke to a mature and well-trained steer. When the little guy had worn himself out, the teamster got him turned in the right direction and gave the command to get up. The experienced steer dutifully obeyed and started moving. That set the little guy off again with another tantrum. "Whoa." The big guy stopped, waiting for the unruly one to straighten out again. After a few more fitful starts the "get up" command resulted in the two moving together and plowing a fairly decent furrow. The teamster kept one hand on the plow and held the whip in the other, gently touching the rump of one or the other to keep the plow going straight.

When well trained, a nicely matched team of oxen is a joy to work with, because they are responsive, very strong, and incredibly effective in hauling a load or pulling the plow. It takes much consistent work, great patience, knowledge gained by long experience, and regular practice sessions to train a team. But cattle are highly intelligent and willing to serve when they know who is boss and what is expected of them.

It takes much consistent work, great patience, knowledge gained by long experience, and regular practice sessions to train a team.

Just after Jesus described how well He knows the Father and the Father knows Him (how they work together as a team), Jesus offered "rest for the weary," using the analogy of being yoked together with Him in service for "my yoke is easy and my burden is light" (Matt. 11:30, NIV). Those listening to Him may have been watching someone plowing with oxen in a field nearby. The people understood that kind of teamwork. Can you imagine what joy it must be for the green steer (that's me) once it figures out what the task is and how to accomplish it while being yoked with a "gentle and humble in heart" strong and experienced oxen teammate? No wonder the yoke is easy. Look who's pulling with me.

Lord, what did I do to deserve being yoked with You? The way You pull this load makes it so easy for me. The rest for my soul is pleasant and good. Thank You, Lord.

June 5

The Nuclear Pore

Oh, the depth of the riches of the wisdom and knowledge of God! How unsearchable his judgments, and his paths beyond tracing out! Rom. 11:33, NIV.

W hen I first learned about the biological structure decades ago, science regarded it as a simple hole in the nuclear membrane. But then, in time, the nuclear membrane became a nuclear envelope, because it was more complicated and highly structured than a simple membrane. With the first fuzzy pictures from freeze-fractured cells, the hole in the nuclear envelope was no longer just a hole, but a pore with eight indistinct regulating structures of some sort. As the years went by, study tools improved, producing more data to give us a better understanding of the structure and function of the myriad tiny openings in the nuclear envelope that communicated with the cell's cytoplasm. Because of the many proteins working together to transport material through the pore, biologists now call it a nuclear pore complex (NPC). Its job is to transport water-soluble molecules from the nucleus to the cytoplasm or vice versa. They include ribosomes, RNA, proteins, carbohydrates, lipids, and signal molecules. Each NPC accomplishes about 1,000 transports through the pore each second. We still have much more to learn about how this crucial channel of cellular communication works, but let's take a look at what we know now.

Every eukaryotic cell nucleus has from one to a few thousand NPCs, each of which measures about 120 nanometers in diameter and about 200 nanometers from the nuclear side to the cytoplasmic side. The opening in the NPC is highly variable but can change from 9 to 26 nanometers depending on what needs to travel through it. Approximately 30 different proteins (called nucleoporins) in multiple copies (456 in total) form the working structure of the pore complex. Some entirely structural nucleoporins bear the name of inner or outer ring, spoke, basket, or filament. Other nucleoporins function more like doormen or bouncers checking badges or like escorts who take a person from one place to another. Any large molecule that carries what biologists term a nuclear localization signal will get rapidly taken through the complex. Without the special calling card, the large molecule won't get through. The NPC is another example of a nanomolecular machine that unceasingly functions to make life possible.

Designer, Architect, and Builder of the nuclear pore complex, how great and marvelous are Your works. From the gigantic galactic systems to the tiniest nuclear pore, Your unsearchable ways inspire worship, praise, and honor.

Eating With Enemies

You prepare a table before me in the presence of my enemies.
Ps. 23:5, NIV.

Hyenas and lions are deadly enemies. Watching them interact is a fascinating study in animal behavior, but it isn't for the faint of heart. They play for keeps.

In general, when all is going well, a pride of lions can hold their own against a pack of hyenas living in their home range. After making a kill, lions will then sit down for a leisurely meal together. Among lions some squabbling for position is common. Dominant males with their long dark manes always take precedence. The males will allow cubs to eat with them unchallenged, but females often have to wait till the "king of beasts" has dined. That's just the way it is with lions. Hyenas are scavengers, though they are known to bring down their own kills too. Especially when large numbers of them work together, they can defeat large game. When the entire pride of lions has had enough, the hyenas routinely move in to clean up. Often, though, since the lions are still close and may still be possessive of the kill, they will attack the hyenas and won't let them eat in peace. When eating in the presence of their enemies, the two species are always on the alert and extraordinarily wary of each other.

I have never had to eat in the presence of my enemy, but I trained to do just that. After getting drafted into the United States Army in 1969, I had several field training experiences in which we were issued MCIs (meal, combat, individual). As I remember, we called them C-rations, because that's what they looked and tasted like. The armed forces now get MREs (meals ready to eat). A great deal of research now makes such MREs more nutritious and tastier, and they can even be heated with a flameless heater. But I digress. Meals prepared for warriors in the field are meant for eating on the run. As time permits and as hunger dictates, the soldier may hunker down in a foxhole or under some cover of rocks or vegetation and consume them quickly, then get back to what they were trained to do. So sitting down at a table to eat in the presence of your enemies just doesn't make sense in human terms. Could it be that the warrior David was describing the extravagant love and care of a God that could allow for even that strange possibility?

Your love, Lord, is more than I can comprehend. Not only do I get to eat, but You pull out the chair and invite me to sit leisurely while You hold my enemies at bay. How do I respond to a love like that except, as did David, with great gratitude and praise?

Abundance

My cup overflows. Ps. 23:5, NIV.

W hile out on a walk with my wife a few days ago, I asked her if she noticed how plants in our tiny corner of the world seem to fill in every nook and available cranny during our short growing season. If I scratch down to bare soil with bulldozer or shovel, plants of all types will rapidly move in. Given enough undisturbed time, layer after layer of plants and then trees will take over, until it creates a carpet of green nearly 100 feet thick. In the tropics that life force of plants seems to be even stronger.

It seems as if wherever there are appropriate temperatures and watering conditions on our blue planet, plants will grow in abundance. Ecologists attempt to determine the rate of production in an ecosystem (a community of organisms adapted to a particular environment, as in a desert or jungle). One generally accepted way to do that is to measure the amount of new stuff (biomass) or the amount of new energy (kilocalories) added to the ecosystem per unit time. Recording how much carbon dioxide plants take out of the air and convert to leaf tissue gives us a pretty good indicator of how much organic carbon (formed and stored in the plant tissues) is being produced, a measurement called gross primary productivity (GPP). But plants themselves siphon off some of the stuff (or some of the energy) for their own life processes. Subtracting what plants use to maintain themselves from the GPP gives a good value for net primary productivity (NPP). NPP is the amount of stuff or energy that remains to feed all the people and all the animals in the world.

So how much stuff gets made per unit time? From the best calculations that ecologists can figure, annual NPP in the most productive areas of both terrestrial and aquatic systems is approximately equal at 1.8 to 2.8 pounds of carbon per square yard (1 to 1.5 kilograms per square meter) per year. With that type of productivity, a plot the size of a football field would produce roughly 8-13 tons (7,000-12,000 kilograms) of carbon per year. Other places such as deserts or the middle of the ocean form little by comparison. Drastic latitudinal and seasonal differences also exist. But when we put the whole picture as best it can be figured, the biosphere (the living things) of earth produces a staggering 116 billion tons (104.9 petagrams) of carbon per year.

Lord, in every area of life You give abundantly. There is no stinginess or lack of resources. Sometimes when we think we may be running out, there You go again, giving a good measure, pressed down and running over. Thank You.

June 8

Wheat Bread

So Abraham hurried into the tent to Sarah. "Quick," he said, "get three seahs of the finest flour and knead it and bake some bread." Gen. 18:6, NIV.

Today, let us worship Him who makes bread possible. And what a gift it is. It is an important staple food. No doubt you love the aroma and taste of freshly baked homemade bread. Is your mouth watering yet? To understand just how bread comes to be, you have to start by carefully studying a single grain of wheat. Cut a kernel in two lengthwise. Around the outside edge it is easy to see the thin line of the hull. Filling most of the pointy end of the kernel (or berry as some call it) is where the embryo lives. The embryo is in fact a minuscule wheat plant, the next generation. If you were to soak the seed so that it could germinate, the root end of the embryo would grow first and get established. Then the shoot end would push up into the sunshine. To feed this embryo (and us), most of the grain of wheat is filled with endosperm, a tissue consisting of lots of starch granules along with gluten, a protein. The word "gluten" happens to be Latin for "glue." Those Romans couldn't have named it better, because gluten forms when two other proteins, gliadin and glutenin, link together tightly.

So why did Sarah have to knead the bread? Well, if you have made bread, you know that all it takes is the flour, water, and salt (plus a little yeast if you are making a leavened bread). Mixing the flour with a little salt and water makes a stiff gooey mixture. Kneading or mixing the stiff mass causes molecules of glutenin to collide with molecules of gliadin and with each other. Collisions of sulfhydryl groups in these proteins will result in disulfide bond cross bridges linking the protein strands together and thus making gluten. When cross-linked well enough, the gluten is said to be "developed" to a point at which it traps the tiny bubbles of carbon dioxide made by the living yeast, giving the bread lightness and exceptional flavor. Incidentally, letting a lump of dough just sit allows time for collisions and gluten development, as do additions of some other ingredients. One can make bread lots of different ways. But the process takes time—time to gather, measure, and mix ingredients, time to let the yeast reproduce and ferment, time to knead and feel the gluten develop, time to let the dough rest and the gluten relax, time to bake, and time to cool.

Creator of starch granules, gluten, yeast, salt, sugar, and water, thank You for the gift of all the ingredients. Thank You also for the chemical reactions that convert them into bread.

165

The Bread of Life

And he took bread, gave thanks and broke it, and gave it to them, saying, "This is my body given for you; do this in remembrance of me." Luke 22:19, NIV.

They say that food is the fuel for life's engine. Life's motor simply won't run if you don't eat. Like most analogies, the "engine as life" analogy has a point at which it breaks down. For instance, I can park my car and turn the motor off for an extended period of time. I don't need to refuel it constantly. Much later I can restart the engine, and we are off and running again. You just can't park life. Well, that's not quite true. In the laboratory we can freeze specially treated cells at –196°C (–321°F) in liquid nitrogen and keep them indefinitely without having to feed them. Much later we can thaw the cells, and the life processes resume as if nothing had happened. But under normal conditions, every life-form has to eat to live.

In the Bible bread represents food, the energy for fueling life. The Hebrew word pronounced lekh'-em means "bread" or "food" interchangeably. Our bodies digest and process the food we eat, turning it into the blood sugar glucose and amino acids and fatty acids that cells recognize as their food. And at the cellular level, the products of food digestion need to be constantly coming in at precisely regulated levels. An individual can go several hours to several days without food, but your cells can't. They must have a second-by-second supply if they are to live. Cut off their food supply, and cells will die within seconds or minutes.

In the wilderness God sent manna to teach the importance of daily dependence.

The analogy of Jesus as the bread of life to maintain the spiritual life is incredibly significant. Just as I must sustain my physical life by eating or internalizing bread, so I preserve my spiritual life by partaking of or internalizing God, Jesus, and the Holy Spirit through daily prayer, by spending time deeply studying God's Word, and by being filled with the Holy Spirit. Without that moment-by-moment spiritual energy stream, we die spiritually.

In the wilderness God sent manna to teach the importance of daily dependence. It tasted sweet and obviously had excellent nutrition, because His people lived on it for 40 years. Every day it was there, but they had to collect it. How will you gather your manna for this day?

Lord, thank You for the miracle of the grain that feeds my body through the daily bread from Your hand. Feed my soul with a fresh infilling of Your Holy Spirit. May I live, body and soul, for You today.

June 10

Stale Bread

This bread of ours was warm when we packed it at home on the day we left to come to you. But now see how dry and moldy it is. Joshua 9:12, NIV.

D on't you just love the taste, smell, and feel of warm, fresh-out-of-the-oven bread? It is so incredibly good. The temptation is to savor it as soon as it is cool enough to touch. But wait! Most breadmaking instructions suggest a 30-minute cooldown time to let the proteins and starches set up so they are firm enough to hold their shape. Too-warm bread squashes into dough balls. So there is an optimum time when bread is the definition of perfection. Typically bread bakeries begin work very early in the morning to have the bread ready for early shoppers and for eating that day.

By the next day the bread is on the day-old bread shelf and sells for a fraction of the price it did before. Why? Simple. It has lost its freshness. The bread is now stale. So what has happened? Though I have not found anybody who is certain about the details of the process of staling, we can all tell that it has happened. While the bread is still nutritious and will still drive away hunger, it just isn't what it used to be.

Surprisingly, breads lose freshness faster in a refrigerator than at room temperature. What we do know is that getting stale involves continuing changes in starch chemistry. In fresh bread, starch is hydrated, bound to water in some special way, making the texture just right. Some say that this "just right" condition vanishes as water leaves the starch granules and moves into the open spaces of the bread. Mind you, this is different than bread drying out—it is bread getting stale. With water in the wrong place, the texture changes to chewier and tougher.

Stale bread was an important player in the successful ruse that the gang from Gibeon foisted on Joshua. What they gained by deception backfired, and the Gibeonites were relegated to woodcutters and water carriers. Stale bread also reminds us to share God's fresh bountiful blessings every day while they are still new. Storing, hoarding, selfishly saving, only to become stale, is antithetical to Christian living.

Bread of life, I prize the aroma, the taste, and the texture of Your living Word as it reads fresh in my mind every morning. Lead me to someone today who not only hungers for the fresh bread of life but also longs for the freshness of Your good news.

Counterfeit

For we do not wrestle against flesh and blood, but against principalities, against powers, against the rulers of the darkness of this
age, against spiritual hosts of wickedness in the heavenly places.
Eph. 6:12, NKJV.

Have you checked to see if the money in your wallet is genuine? Have you learned the look and feel of genuine currency so that you can spot a counterfeit? Those in the know estimate that, of the 1.1 trillion United States dollars in circulation, less than 1 percent is fake, but that still amounts to $250 million of funny money that isn't worth anything. It used to be that small-time counterfeiters created most counterfeit currency. Now rogue governments intent on creating chaos produce most counterfeit money. How is one to know the difference?

Genuine currency is printed on a proprietary blend of cotton and linen, and the thousands of pounds of pressure used to print each bill makes the thin paper even thinner. The special paper has tiny red and blue threads embedded in it. If you handle a lot of money, your fingers will instantly tell you when you have a fake bill. Besides the paper, genuine currency has several additional security features: a special watermark, a vertical plastic security strip embedded in the paper, micro-printing, light backgrounds with very tiny patterns, exquisitely detailed etchings, various color inks, and color shifting inks that change from metallic copper to metallic green under bright light. Ongoing research seeking ways to make counterfeiting difficult for the bad guys continues. But they continue to study very carefully how to get something for nothing.

The archenemy of God is the ultimate bad guy, and he has introduced numerous counterfeits for good and decent things that God has done for us. Without a thorough knowledge of the genuine article, the forgery looks and feels convincing, good enough to deceive, if possible, the very elect (Mark 13:22). Satan fakes signs and wonders, substitutes Sunday for Sabbath, replaces creation with evolution, originates numerous counterfeit religions that pretend to love and obey God or claim that Jesus was a good man but certainly not God. He teaches moral relativism instead of absolute truth. The question I keep asking myself: Am I deeply studying God's Word, becoming thoroughly familiar with the look and feel of the genuine article?

Creator of all that is genuine, teach me to spot the phony and to accept only Your death on the cross as the payment for my ransom.

Hugs

A time to embrace. Eccl. 3:5, NKJV.

Here at Andrews University my freshman biology course called Foundations of Biology has the reputation of being fairly challenging. Wait. Do I hear laughter? OK, students refer to it as a killer course. Well, why not? Modern biology expands exponentially, and it is tough for even professionals to keep up with new knowledge much less carefree students just out of high school. We have unit tests every two weeks that turn out to be rather stressful events. It isn't unusual for students to call home after a test to get some reassurance and love.

We have long known that blood cortisol levels spike during stressful events. It is, of course, one of the "fight or flight" hormones supposed to help get us out of dangerous situations. For some students it probably does help. Another hormone with a known track record is oxytocin. Some call it the "love hormone" or "cuddle hormone," because its levels rise when people hug and touch. Oxytocin forges powerful emotional bonds.

Researchers from the University of Wisconsin, Madison, stressed 7 to 12 year-old girls by asking them to make an impromptu speech or take a math test in front of strangers. Not surprisingly, their cortisol levels rose significantly. After the stressful situation, a third of the girls got hugs and reassurance from their mothers. Their cortisol levels returned to normal quickly, and their oxytocin levels jumped as a result of the touching and talking. A second third of the girls watched a video for more than an hour. Their cortisol levels took much longer to return to normal, and they showed no oxytocin response. The last third of the girls talked with their moms on the phone. Surprisingly, their cortisol/oxytocin changes were not significantly different than the first third, who got the personal touch from their mothers.

Since previous oxytocin studies seemed to point to personal touch as the critical factor, these unexpected results left the scientists wondering. What is it about a phone call that elicits the same hormonal response as the personal touch? Maybe helicopter parenting does play a role after all, since it can both lower the stress levels and enhance bonding. These results get me to wondering if thoughtful reading of God's Word, meditation on His love and compassion for me, and quiet times alone with God will also affect cortisol and oxytocin levels.

Lord, how I enjoy being held in Your arms and hearing You sing to me (Zeph. 3:17). I am ready to listen.

Meditation

I remember the days of old; I meditate on all Your works; I muse on the work of Your hands. Ps. 143:5, NKJV.

D o you select a Bible text and read it carefully, thoughtfully, praying for God's Spirit to impress you with what the text is saying to you? Do you sometimes rewrite the text in your own words? Do you journal about how God's Holy Word relates to the realities of your daily life with all of its challenges? Do you quietly spend time in prayers of thanksgiving to God for His amazing grace? Do you sometimes get exuberant and dance before the Lord because of His great mercy and goodness? Are there somber times when your sins rise up before you like a dark pall, separating you from Christ's love? Do you spend time grieving losses and begging God for answers? Indeed, biblical meditation takes many forms and has many moods.

One of my favorite passages is Psalm 103. As I go through this beautifully written chapter, my heart resonates and responds to each concept. My mind picks up the ideas, turns them over and around, savoring the thoughts like a starving person tasting food again.

"Bless the Lord, O my soul, and forget not all His benefits" (verse 2, NKJV). I can't begin to recount all the benefits of life in the Spirit. I try to imagine how a truly compassionate father treats his children. That is how God deals with me when I respond to Him in love. Oh, He knows my weaknesses. Having made me, He understands that I am dust. "But the mercy of the Lord is from everlasting to everlasting on those who fear Him, and His righteousness to children's children, to such as keep His covenant, and to those who remember His commandments to do them" (verses 17, 18, NKJV).

I am quite familiar with several of popular culture's models of meditation and mind awareness—i.e., meditation is thinking about not thinking. Empty your mind of thought and stress. Intone a mantra to clear your thoughts. But I choose rather to fill my mind with the profound thoughts of what God has written to me and the things that He has made around me. That brings peace, harmony, and contentment. Seeking a clearer understanding of God's goodness, mercy, and love works for me.

O Lord, my God, You inspired the psalmist to write, "My mouth shall speak wisdom, and the meditation of my heart shall give understanding" (Ps. 49:3, NKJV). Fill my head with Your presence, Lord, for I long to see Your glory and know You as You really are.

Benefits of Meditation

This Book of the Law shall not depart from your mouth, but you shall meditate in it day and night, that you may observe to do according to all that is written in it. For then you will make your way prosperous, and then you will have good success. Joshua 1:8, NKJV.

The June 2010 issue of Mind, Mood and Memory, a newsletter published by Massachusetts General Hospital, carries a lead article entitled "The Neuroscience of Meditation." Here the author reviews findings from several studies that appear to agree that meditation, no matter the type, has huge health benefits. Some of the most notable are (1) protecting working memory from the negative effects of stress, (2) lowering the levels of the stress hormone cortisol and reducing tension, (3) reversing memory loss, (4) increasing tolerance to pain, (5) increasing ability to pay attention and ignore distractions, (6) decreasing the density of gray matter in the amygdala (a brain parameter associated with reduced stress), (7) and thickening of the prefrontal cortex and right anterior insula (regions that normally thin with age and that are known to be involved with processing sensory input as well as memories, thus helping us focus attention and make decisions).

Hundreds of studies have sought scientifically to determine the benefits of meditation. But vigorous debate surrounds their validity. Though many of the studies are peer reviewed (meaning that others in the field have checked to see that they are done right), a strong vein of skepticism persists in scientific circles. How do we know that the meditation training is any better or any different from any other kind of training, such as learning how to control your heart rate and blood pressure?

The best test is obviously to see what works for you. God asks us to prove Him. In this highly stressed modern age, where can we turn for peace? Where do we go to find meaning in life? Where did I come from? Where am I going?

In this highly stressed modern age, where can we turn for peace?

God's Word is true and honest. It declares, "Great peace have those who love your law, and nothing can make them stumble" (Ps. 119:165, NIV). When you put this together with the text above, it is clear that biblical meditation should be carefully and honestly tried. I recommend it to you as one that will produce positive results.

Lord, You made me, so You know what works. Give me the courage to put You to the test.

Stress

I will be glad in the Lord. Ps. 104:34, NKJV.

It was one of those days. The schedule didn't have any empty lines remaining: important presentation for the early morning committee meeting; student appointments; tough budget meeting with the dean; mistakenly double booked on one appointment that I have to change; two lectures, one still in need of refreshing with new material; must do a demo for the evening lab; won't get home till 10:30 at the earliest. This pace is insane.

We all know the feeling. All of us have days like that in which too many tasks and responsibilities conspire together to raise the stress level. But when jam-packed days become the norm month after month, the pressures and demands begin to take their toll.

Our bodies are finely tuned machines. When a pressure situation comes along (say you have to give an important speech or suddenly swerve to avoid hitting a deer), your autonomic nervous system dumps a couple hormones (adrenaline and cortisol) into the bloodstream that immediately ups your heart and breathing rates, blood pressure, and metabolism. Your body is responding perfectly, just as designed—on full emergency alert. Blood vessels to your big muscles open up, as do the pupils of your eyes. Digestion slows. The liver releases stored energy into your bloodstream, and you break out in a sweat even though you aren't doing any heavy physical activity. It is called the fight-or-flight response. Usually the crisis passes quickly, things return to normal, and all is well.

The pressures of life involving money, relationships, job performance, schedules, etc., all may place extraordinary demands on us, making existence feel like one grand emergency. The fight-or-flight hormones don't get a rest. Neither do the bodily systems programmed to respond. They wear down, leading to a weakened immune system, moodiness and irritability, decreased work productivity or failing grades, overeating, insomnia, headaches, stomachaches, anxiety, and depression. If the stress continues, panic attacks or chest pains are not uncommon. High blood pressure followed by heart disease and diabetes are usually not far behind.

Reducing stress and the damaging stress hormones that result is vital for a healthy lifestyle. Get daily vigorous exercise and develop a healthy devotional life. Take two five-minute vacations throughout the day in which you breathe deeply, smile broadly, and picture yourself as relaxed while you think about and count your specific blessings.

Lord, I place my trust and confidence in You. Teach me Your way.

Sigh

He looked up to heaven and with a deep sigh said to him, "Ephphatha!" (which means, "Be opened!"). Mark 7:34, NIV.

Every time I read the story of Hannah, wife of Elkanah, mother of Samuel the prophet, my heart goes out to the godly woman. Her husband had another wife. Stop the story right here! Can you imagine the emotional stress of this picture? And if that weren't enough, in a time when bearing children was perhaps the reason for living, her rival wife was doing it and she wasn't. Oh, she was trying, all right—she wanted nothing more than to have a child. But "the Lord had closed her womb" (1 Sam. 1:6, NIV). After endless taunting by her rival that seemed to peak during the annual religious celebrations, she cried bitterly and wouldn't eat. Her husband, Elkanah, added insult to injury. Dismissing her feelings, he asked if he wasn't better than 10 sons! Oh, no! This guy needed some sensitivity training. But wait. There was more. When Hannah was at the tabernacle pouring her heart out to God in prayer, pleading for a son, old priest Eli, sitting on a stool nearby, woke up from his drooling daydream and, falsely accusing her of being drunk, admonished her to lay off the wine. Poor Hannah.

Though the Bible doesn't say so, I am sure that she had plenty of reasons between cries to sigh—and sigh deeply. Following the sobbing and emotional distress, she needed the benefits of a good sigh. Physiologists tell us that breathing is at best chaotic, especially during times of extreme grief or emotional stress. The body gets oxygen when it can. But now, from the University of Leuven in Belgium, comes a study claiming that a spontaneous sigh does wonders for the body by resetting the depth and rhythm of breathing. Researchers fitted both men and women with high-tech shirts that continuously monitored their heart rate, carbon dioxide level in their blood, and most important, their breathing. The data the magic shirts collected led the scientists to conclude that sighing plays an important role in resetting the respiratory system.

What astonishes me about Hanna's story is her faith. When Eli told her that her wish was to be granted, she washed her face and ate, and for her it was done as her song (1 Sam. 2) confirms. She sang, "My heart rejoices in the Lord . . . for I delight in your deliverance" (verse 1, NIV).

My Lord and Savior, You too felt the depths of human emotions and suffered unjustly. May I, like Hannah, rejoice after my difficult trials. Hold me close.

Power of Positive Thinking or Positive Self-talk

Dear friends, this is now my second letter to you. I have written both of them as reminders to stimulate you to wholesome thinking. 2 Peter 3:1, NIV. Even at night their minds do not rest. Eccl. 2:23, NIV.

The human brain consists of about three pounds of extremely soft tissue encased in a protective bony skull. Its estimated 100 billion neurons along with another 300 to 400 billion support cells are constantly active day and night, processing sensory input, making calculations, and generating corrective output. From sensors all over the body and without you having to think about it, the brain checks your blood pressure, blood chemistry, temperature, body positions, and thousands of other things to keep you upright and healthy. This data comes only to the conscious level when you need to do some important corrective action, such as getting the rock out of your shoe or turning the heat up. Otherwise, the autopilot portions of your brain leave you free to think about other things.

We are constantly talking to ourselves, sometimes verbalizing our thoughts even when nobody else is around. But most of the time, the self talk just goes on in the mind—no one else hears the monologue. Perhaps we might plan what we are going to say to someone, rehearsing various lines of conversation to see which one goes best. Or we might mentally practice the piano or compliment ourselves on how we rocked the interview or how slim we look because our self-discipline is working. Sometimes we complain to ourselves about the weather, criticize ourselves for the blunder at the office, or fuss about the way we look. Both positive and negative self-talk is normal. Positive is good. Negative is not. But both too much positive or negative makes us unrealistic thinkers. Psychologists tell us that the mental illness of grandiosity or narcissism sets in when more than 69 percent of the monologue is positive. In contrast, the pathologies of anxiety, depression, and panic become evident when less than 31 percent of the self-talk is positive.

God asks us to discipline our mind. Given total freedom, the mind usually spirals into negative thinking far too easily. "Fix these words of mine in your hearts and minds" (Deut. 11:18, NIV) is a call for mental discipline. The promise of Isaiah 26:3 is sure: "You will keep in perfect peace those whose minds are steadfast, because they trust in you" (NIV). A steadfast mind is a healthy mind.

Lord, thank You for my mind. May I ever use it to honor and glorify Your holy name. Teach me the habit of mental discipline through trust in You.

The Food Label

Take firm hold of instruction, do not let go; keep her, for she is your life. Prov. 4:13, NKJV.

I n 2000 every single state in the United States reported obesity levels under 25 percent, most less than 15 percent. By 2009, 33 of them reported more than 25 percent of their population were obese. Why are we killing ourselves with too much food? It isn't for lack of knowledge, because all packaged foods bear the nutrition facts label mandated by the U.S. Food and Drug Administration. How did that label get started, anyway?

Food shortages and rationing during World War II brought about a strong interest in knowing just what nutrition a person needed to live. An English chemist named Elsie Widdowson who had determined the sugar content of apples for her Ph.D. thesis was then working with Robert McCance, professor of experimental medicine at Cambridge University and who had previously determined how cooking affects the chemistry of various meats. Together, in 1940, they published a reference book called The Chemical Composition of Foods, which guided the thinking of nutritional scientists in the Western world for many decades. Also in 1940 the United States National Academy of Sciences set up the Food and Nutrition Board to determine the recommended dietary allowance (RDA) for various nutrients. Those RDAs have been revised regularly through the years to account for new findings in nutritional science. Nutritionists now use RDAs and DRIs (dietary reference intake) to calculate the numbers that appear on the nutrition facts label required on all processed foods.

So you see, decades of hard work and study have gone into providing the needed information. Obviously many ignore such labels and continue to consume far too many calories and get too little exercise each day. The reality is that our best guide to healthful eating is simply to eat in moderation from a wide range of colorful plant-based foods that do not have a nutrition facts label. The presence of such a label suggests that much of the nutrition has vanished during the processing.

What about the health of our spiritual life? Is our nation's failing spiritual health the result of a lack of information? No. The Bible, containing all the information that we need for a robust spiritual life, is readily available. But like the nutrition label, the information in it gets ignored.

Lord, thank You for the abundance of information that You have provided for our physical and spiritual health. May we learn to take hold of its instruction before it is too late.

June 19

Gilding

Also he overlaid the cherubim with gold. 1 Kings 6:28, NKJV.

T ry as I might, I just can't imagine the beauty and splendor of Solomon's Temple. The master craftsman that Hiram, king of Tyre, sent to help Solomon with the construction was named Huram. According to 2 Chronicles 2:13 he was "a skillful man, endowed with understanding, Huram my master craftsman (the son of a woman of the daughters of Dan, and his father was a man of Tyre), skilled to work in gold and silver, bronze and iron, stone and wood, purple and blue, fine linen and crimson, and to make any engraving and to accomplish any plan which may be given to him, with your skillful men and with the skillful men of my lord David your father" (NKJV). So not only was Huram proficient in many crafts, he must also have been good in managing people. Solomon had thousands of laborers working on the Temple. Someday, I would like to meet Huram and learn from him.

You see, I have tried my hand at many crafts. I do wood joinery and carving and have enjoyed gilding or overlaying the carved wood with gold, which adds to the brilliance and beauty of the piece. I have learned that when I gold leaf a flat panel, its brilliance shows from only a single vantage point. With the light coming from exactly the right angle, a flat surface will shine. But when I carve the panel and apply gold leaf, the whole panel shines no matter what the angle of view. The panel glows even in a dimly lit room. So I find it highly significant that 1 Kings 6:29, 30 describes what Huram did: "Then he carved all the walls of the temple all around, both the inner and outer sanctuaries, with carved figures of cherubim, palm trees, and open flowers. And the floor of the temple he overlaid with gold, both the inner and outer sanctuaries" (NKJV). I try to imagine the warm glow, the luster, and the beauty of all those carved panels coated with pure gold. It must have been magnificent.

When I do gold leaf, I simply coat the piece with a special oil called sizing. After a few hours it gets tacky to the touch and is ready for the gold leaf. The gold leaf I use has been pressed between steel rollers until it is only a few millionths of an inch thick. It would take about 300,000 sheets to make a stack one inch thick. I lay a sheet onto the tacky surface and smooth it down with a soft camel-hair brush. Huram may have pounded thin sheets of gold onto a carved wood surface with a layer of bitumen (tar) in between. In any case, the effect was beautiful, designed to honor and glorify the Creator of all that is beautiful.

Lord, I am asking You to be the builder of this house, my body temple for You. I don't want to labor in vain. May I use only the best materials and keep it holy to the Lord.

Headaches

So the child grew. Now it happened one day that he went out to his father, to the reapers. And he said to his father, "My head, my head!" So he said to a servant, "Carry him to his mother." 2 Kings 4:18, 19, NKJV.

I have often wondered why we get headaches. After all, the brain is not a sensory organ. When people have brain surgery performed on them, they get nothing more than a local anesthetic to dull the pain of cutting and peeling the scalp back and sawing through the skull to remove a portion of the protective bony skull. But when neurosurgeons actually cut into the brain itself or poke electrodes into it, they want their patient to be fully conscious. Though I find it hard to believe, working on the brain itself is actually painless. So why do some people get splitting headaches and everyone experiences at least some headaches?

Since the brain isn't wired with sensory neurons, headaches result from pain elsewhere. Pain from muscle tension in the neck or from the protective tissues covering the *I have often wondered why we get headaches.* brain feels like a headache. Changes in blood chemistry or pressure cause many headaches. Take, for example, "brain freeze," the excruciating headache you get from a mouthful of ice cream, your favorite snow cone, Slurpee, or milk shake. Apparently a sensor just above the hard palate registers the sudden cold. In an attempt to keep the brain warm, blood vessels to the brain dilate, giving one a sudden headache. Dehydration, infections, fever, or low blood glucose can all cause headaches too. Increased pressure inside the skull or in the sinuses or a hard crack on the head are common triggers, as well as emotional tension and stress.

The Shunammite's son may have suffered from heatstroke or sunstroke. Young children and older people are especially susceptible. As the body grows warmer because of high air temperatures or overexertion, cooling mechanisms normally kick in. The boy was out in the field with the servants. He may have been working way too hard in the sun and may not have been drinking enough. As the body heats up, surface vessels dilate to bring heat to the surface. But when the heat-regulating mechanisms fail, body temperatures continue to rise, resulting in heatstroke, characterized by a sudden splitting headache, dizzyness, weakness, and dry skin. Headaches are warning signals that we may not be taking proper care of the delicate temple that God has entrusted to us. With proper care, headaches can become a thing of the past.

Lord, as I learn better how to care for the body You have given me, may I pay attention and do my part to avoid this most common of all complaints. In full trust and confidence, I'll leave the rest to You.

The Contagious Yawn

You have not given the weary water to drink, and you have withheld bread from the hungry. Job 22:7, NKJV.

No doubt you have seen it happen. Unable to stifle it any longer, someone in a group of people yawns broadly. Then as if on cue, two or three others also succumb to the urge. Just why is a yawn so contagious, anyway? Maybe the answer is as simple as the fact that we smile when others smile and frown when others frown.

Researchers at the Yerkes National Primate Research Center, Emory University, studied 23 adult chimpanzees that belonged to two different groups. Now chimps are extremely social animals but, at the same time, highly conscious of who is in their group and who isn't. They frequently attack outsiders while caring for an insider. The scientists showed nine-second video clips of yawning chimps to the adults. Contagious yawning in the observing chimp happened 50 percent more often when the on-screen chimp belonged to the group compared to non group chimps, leading the scientists to conclude that the contagious yawn was a way of showing empathy for the on-screen chimp—i.e., chimps had much less empathy for non group members.

This data supports previous findings from Drexel University. Its study scanned human brains with MRI during a yawn. The regions known as the posterior cingulate cortex and precuneus showed the most activity. Interestingly, both are areas of the brain involved in self-referential processing and strongly associated with empathetic behavior.

So just why do we yawn, anyway? Several reasons, the first among them sleep deprivation or boredom. Some say that low oxygen levels trigger yawning and it helps correct that. One interesting data set from parakeet research (they yawn, but theirs is not contagious) suggests that yawning is nature's way of keeping the brain cool. Like a computer that works hard, the brain warms up when challenged with problem solving or creativity, and yawning seems to kick the cooling fans on.

Will we yawn in heaven? Will we ever be bored there? sleep-deprived? I look forward to learning the answers to such questions. But in the meantime, contagious yawning is certainly an interesting phenomenon.

Lord, may my empathy for others be far more substantive than contagious yawning. May Your Spirit impress on my heart specific and helpful ways to empathize so that Your love is evident.

June 22

6EQUJ5

For since the creation of the world God's invisible qualities—his eternal power and divine nature—have been clearly seen, being understood from what has been made, so that people are without excuse. Rom. 1:20, NIV.

It was just six characters on the data recorder from the radio telescope. When I look at them—6-E-Q-U-J-5—it is certainly not self-evident what it means. Widely available on the Internet, this is the famous "Wow! signal" recorded by Jerry Ehman on August 15, 1977, while he was at the controls of the Big Ear radio telescope at the Perkins Observatory during the early phases of the Search for Extraterrestrial Intelligence (SETI).

If you take the time to study and decode the Wow! signal you will understand why Ehman wrote "WOW!" in red ink and circled the six characters. Because of the design of the Big Ear radio telescope, scientists were looking for a signal to start out quietly, increase in strength, and then fade away in exactly 72 seconds. Because the scientists reasoned that hydrogen is the most common element in the universe and it resonates at 1,420 MHz and that intelligent life would probably broadcast on this frequency, they were looking for a signal at 1,420 MHz. The six characters above exactly matched the pattern that SETI researchers were looking for. The signal came in on the 1,420 MHz band, started out just above background noise, grew in intensity, then tapered away and died out completely in exactly 72 seconds.

Coming from the constellation Sagittarius, the Wow! signal was detected only the one time. In the long years since 1977 scientists have employed newer and newer technology to search for that same strong radio signal again and again. Nothing. Are there other signals on other bands? The search goes on. Even larger and more sensitive radio telescopes continue to be designed, installed, and come online. Still nothing. If intelligent life does exist out there, many reason, then we should be able to detect its signals. Signals from intelligent life will show patterns, will exhibit organization, and will have meaning.

But wait! Are we looking for signals in the wrong place? Could the telltale signs of intelligence be all around us?

Lord, Your creation is loaded with patterns of precision and order far beyond what I can even comprehend. Are You signaling to me? Are You trying to get my attention and let me know of Your love and Your saving grace? Forgive me, Lord, for the time I spend listening to static.

June 23

Motorcycles

For I am about to fall, and my pain is ever with me. Ps. 38:17, NIV.

Today I was riding my motorcycle behind a friend on his bike. While cruising down the highway at 55 m.p.h. I was looking at him directly from behind. There he was, sitting tall on his bike, one hand on each handlebar, feet on the foot pegs, helmet securely fastened. Then the incongruity of the picture struck me. The motorcycle is a heavy mass of chrome and steel, and my friend adds even more weight. All of it balanced precariously on two tiny patches of rubber-to-road contact. Why didn't the bike just topple over?

One theory suggests that the angular momentum of the wheels resists any tendency to fall over. Even though I don't understand angular momentum fully, I have held a bicycle wheel by the hubs and had someone spin the wheel fast. It takes significant effort to rotate the spinning wheel from a vertical position to a horizontal one. Is that what keeps the biker from falling?

Then I find another theory suggesting that angular momentum plays little if any role in maintaining a motorcycle rider upright. Rather it depends more on the rider's skill at keeping the motorcycle balanced over its tiny center of gravity. When it starts to tilt down on one side or the other, the rider steers the bike or shifts the body weight to reposition the bike over its center of gravity. This works as long as the bike keeps moving and the steering is free. The evidence for the theory has something to do with riding an experimental bike that has gyros spinning in such a way that they cancel out the angular momentum from the wheels. Canceling angular momentum apparently doesn't significantly change the way a bike handles.

For a bike rider it is almost effortless to stay upright while riding down the road. Stop the bike, however, or come up against the slightest groove in the pavement or do something that resists your ability to steer the bike back under the center of gravity, and remaining upright suddenly becomes difficult. You have to put a foot down or crash. Could there be parallels here to my journey with Christ? What is about to make me fall spiritually?

Thank You, Lord, for the sensitive system of balance You have given me that helps keep my bike upright while riding. Please give me equal sensitivity on my spiritual journey so that I can know when I am in danger of falling and can avoid having to stop and put a foot down. My desire is to keep on the move with You.

Countersteering

There is a way that seems right to a man, but its end is the way of death. Prov. 14:12, NKJV.

If you are an experienced motorcycle rider or bicycle rider, then you have probably been fascinated by the concept of countersteering. Chances are you have noticed and experimented with it some, too. Maybe, though, the concept has never entered your head. Not to worry. That is OK, too. Next time you are riding just try it and see how it works.

Countersteering seems counterintuitive. While riding a bike you might think that when you want to turn left, you simply turn left. Or it might make more sense to you that one should point the handlebars to the right when they want to go right. This might work when you are going very slowly and you have lots of jerky handlebar movements just to stay upright, but try riding down the road at a fast pace and analyze what you actually do to turn.

You quickly learn that in order to turn right, you must do one of two things. Either you shift your weight to the right to start a lean or—much more often—you must steer slightly to the left to make your bike start a lean to the right, and then the bike follows through by turning right. This subtle "wrong way" steering becomes so habitual that we are rarely even aware of it. To turn left, steer right. And to turn right, steer left. Countersteering works with all two-wheel vehicles. Add more wheels such as training wheels or a side-car, and it ceases.

At this point nonbicycle riders might think that we are all nuts, but lets go on. To get a bicycle or a motorcycle to change directions, you have to get it to lean, and the easiest way to get it to do so is put the bike off its center of gravity by steering the wrong way. If you are leaning in a curve and need to tighten the curve even more, you push hard the wrong way to get the lean even steeper. The steeper your lean, the tighter your track around a curve.

So how do you stop a turn? The best way again is countersteering. To straighten up a leaning bike, you need to get the wheels back under the bike. You have to get the rider and bike back over the center of gravity. Thus, to stop a tight left turn, you steer more left. I can see you shaking your head. OK, try it. It works—because of the laws of physics. Break the laws, and you will get road rash. Have you ever gotten spiritual road rash? Try following the laws of God. They work every time we apply them. Thank God for laws.

Lord, me? You want me to love my enemies? And do good to them even though they use me? How does that make any sense? OK—I'll do it for You. I'll try it and see how it works.

Humility

He has shown you, O man, what is good; and what does the Lord require of you but to do justly, to love mercy, and to walk humbly with your God? Micah 6:8, NKJV.

When it comes to ranking the importance of texts, I place Micah 6:8 way up there. Look at it again. The text starts out with a statement telling us that God is showing us what is good—what is important. Then it emphasizes it again by asking the question "What does the Lord require of you?" Note that it is not what the Lord might suggest but rather "What does the Lord require?" Then comes an answer that we could not state more succinctly or clearly. Three short commands that we could adopt as our personal mission statement. Act Justly. Love Mercy. Walk Humbly With God.

Today we focus on walking humbly. What is humility? Does nature have any good examples to illustrate it? Most of us are quite familiar with the social structure of a pack of wolves, a herd of wild horses, or a flock of chickens. Each type of animal exhibits what we can describe as a pecking order or hierarchy in which some animals dominate others in the social group. Some schools of fish even have dominance hierarchies, all of which effectively lower the level of destructive aggression and maintain social organization.

If animals are so careful to show due honor and respect, should I not be even more attentive to how I demonstrate respect and honor to God?

A dominant male called the alpha male usually heads a wolf pack. Along with an alpha female, the two work together to keep order. The alpha male or female stands tall, ears erect, tail up. When anywhere near the alpha male, subordinate animals keep their body low to the ground, ears down, and tail down (or even between the legs). When the alpha male approaches, they may even roll over and expose their throat. Occasionally they may test the leader's resolve and position, and a fight breaks out. But usually they display submissive postures.

Where this illustration from nature breaks down badly, however, is the incomprehensibly vast difference between God and me. Though God craves a social relationship with me, He is far above me in power, glory, and honor. Which is why it is foolish for me even to think of Him as my equal. If animals are so careful to show due honor and respect, should I not be even more attentive to how I demonstrate respect and honor to God?

God, I acknowledge You as my Lord and Savior. On my knees I humbly bow before You in worship because You alone are worthy, and You alone are all-knowing, all-powerful, all-wise, and all-loving.

Walnuts

He shall be like a tree planted by the rivers of water, that brings forth its fruit in its season, whose leaf also shall not wither; and whatever he does shall prosper. Ps. 1:3, NKJV.

For a plant, the function of the flower is to attract and reward pollinators so it can get on with the job of making seed. Once the flower is pollinated, various parts of it develop into fruit, the place where the plant carefully forms seeds to begin the next generation.

Identifying fruit types is bewilderingly complex to the point that only professional botanists can really know and appreciate the subtle differences between a drupe, a pome, a legume, a pepo, a nut, a hesperidium, a silique, etc. Then, when everything is nice and tidy, along comes a walnut. Botanists know that a walnut does not qualify as a nut, because it is more like a drupe. But it isn't really a drupe, either. Some botanists call it a drupaceous nut. Others refer to it as a tryma (a nutlike drupe). A walnut must be God's way of letting us know that He doesn't use our definitions. He is not bound by our thinking or our silly classification systems.

Gently crack a walnut open and, if you use great care, you can get the kernel out in one piece. It isn't easy, because one delicate and easily broken connection joins the two halves. What a piece of architectural beauty a walnut is. If you can get it out in one piece, study the complicated curves and lobes of the kernel that look something like a miniature brain. How that got put into a very hard shell with no apparent connections to the shell or the outer husk is a marvel of packaging and engineering that we have yet to figure out.

But the real beauty is the chemistry in the walnut. With high levels of good cholesterol boosting omega-3 fatty acids, antioxidants, and minerals, walnuts are an excellent food. Study after study shows their cardiovascular and immunological health benefits. Besides that, walnut trees are beautiful ornamental shade trees that come in 21 different species. *Juglans regia* makes the best nuts and *Juglans nigra* the best wood, though its heavy musky nut is wonderful too. The wood from black walnut trees is dark and hard with a tight grain. It is easy to tool and takes an amazing shine. Remember to thank God again and again for His awesome walnut creation.

Father, at times I am socially awkward. I don't fit. Remind me that You shaped me for a special purpose. May I always honor You with my best.

Invisible Katydids

Whoever confesses that Jesus is the Son of God, God abides in him, and he in God. 1 John 4:15, NKJV.

I am looking at a close-up photograph of an ordinary tropical tree trunk. Taken in Tingo Maria, Peru, it shows that the bark has normal deep grooves and blotchy patches of lichens. Nothing appears unusual about this picture. It is just a tree trunk covered with lichens, normal in tropical climes. What is puzzling, though, is that the caption under the picture claims that there are two nymphs of a species of katydid called *Acanthosis aquilina* resting on the tree trunk in plain sight. Not one but two. Yeah, right!

After a couple minutes of carefully studying the photograph inch by inch, I am starting to spot some signs of what could be nymphs—the immature form that will eventually become an adult. I see two very round structures that are too round to be pieces of lichen. They must be eyes. OK, now I can pick out legs with wicked sharp spines on them, typical for katydids. They use a powerful kick with those spines to fend off attackers. Finally I notice some long filamentous antennas held close together and straight out front. That confirms it. Katydids are members of the longhorn grasshopper family, meaning that they have antennas that are longer than their total body length. There they are, in plain sight. But they are incredibly well camouflaged. Even their eyes and antennas have blotchy patches in the same colors as the bark and lichen.

Such cryptic coloration is especially common in katydids. Even ordinary katydids are solid leaf green. Some of them have veins in their wings to mimic those in the leaves that they sit on. One genus found in Venezuelan rain forests named *Typophyllum* has wings indistinguishable from a leaf. The wing of this leaf mimic is complete with midvein and major side veins. And wing color in this genus varies from green to yellow to brown, depending on what leaves they spend most time on. The mimicry is so impressive that it takes careful searching to spot even one of the imposters.

Though I am ashamed to admit it, I know that far too often I find myself doing the best I can to mimic the dress, food, drink, music, and behavior of my surrounding culture so that I can escape detection as a Christian. Why do I do that?

Lord, give me the courage I need to proclaim Your name with boldness and confidence.

Aposematism

In the same way, let your light shine before others, that they may see your good deeds and glorify your Father in heaven. Matt. 5:16, NIV.

For those of us who work in the Department of Biology at Andrews University, it isn't at all unusual to see dull-brown crickets scampering around our office or lab. You see, for decades several scientists in our labs have used the cricket nervous system as a model for *investigating* how relatively simple circuits of nerves control the insect's behavior. Crickets often escape from the study colonies, making them frequent visitors in our hallways and rooms.

Most field crickets are black or brown and are experts at hiding in little holes or crevices. They need to be good at hiding and blending in to their background. Their little crunchy bodies provide food for great numbers of animals such as frogs, many kinds of birds, spiders, mice, shrews, raccoons, opossums, etc. Crickets make excellent fish bait, and food for a wide variety of pets. It is a big business raising crickets for this market. Being black or dull brown, being very quiet, or scampering for cover are the only protection such crickets have.

In the rain forests of Kenya entomologists were surprised to find a tiny cricket that they named *Rhicnogryllus lepidus* (pronounced rick-no-grillus leh-pid-us) that doesn't bother to hide. In fact, it hangs out during the day in plain sight. It is particularly easy to see on green leafy surfaces because it has large patches of bright aqua blue on its head, abdomen, and legs. Like bright neon signs, it advertises its presence. What could possibly make it so audacious and bold in showing its bright colors during the day?

To date, very little is known about this cricket, but we do know that it eats green leaves. Most common crickets eat almost anything. Not fussy at all, they consume grass, old fruit, and dead and decaying material of almost any type. The best guess is that their tiny neon blue cricket cousin selects leaves with a toxic brew of alkaloids to which it is immune but which make it taste bad to its predators. Given such potent chemical protection, it pays for the cricket to advertise. The loud colors proclaim, "Don't eat me. Remember how bad I taste? You will be sorry!" Crickets with aposematism (warning coloration) have freedom to be out and about. I wonder why I often fail to raise the bright clear banner of Christ and show my colors.

Lord, why do I sometimes hide my light? Is it because I don't trust You to care for me and protect me? Today may I take refuge in Your flawless Word and experience true freedom.

June 29

Self-discipline

For it is God who works in you to will and to act in order to fulfill his good purpose. Phil. 2:13, NIV.

S am was one of those students. It was the end of his second year in college, yet his grade point average, which should have been soaring, was still flat on the floor, where it had crash-landed after the first shocking semester of reality. What could he do?

Although talented, even gifted, he didn't really know where he was going in life. His day-by-day record was providing yet another example of the proverb of "Aim at nothing, seldom fail." A T-shirt expresses it: "If you aim at nothing, you will hit it every time." So with this understanding and analysis of Sam's situation, my highest goal shifted to helping him find purpose. How could I best encourage him to adjust his focus outward? What social, service, or spiritual gifts had God given him? How could he develop and use them to serve others?

As it turned out, Sam took a break from his studies to be a student missionary teaching English. Discovering the pure joys of simple service, he loved seeing his students blossom. Soon he returned with a burning desire to become a high school science teacher. Careful planning followed to make sure that he could get all his required and recommended courses in the right order. His efforts were now goal-directed. He clearly saw how each course advanced him toward his desired objective. It took hard work and extraordinary perseverance. The smile on his face, his enthusiasm for learning, and his new energy level were positively infectious to all that he interacted with. I could not believe the transformation in his energy level and in his GPA. This was a mantle Sam enjoyed wearing.

One day when I passed Sam in the hallway I asked him what had made the profound difference in his life. Where had he found his new self-discipline? His answer transformed my thinking. He said, "A sleepy driver has to use great self-discipline to stay awake and drive. That often ends in a crash. My own self-discipline is weak, faulty. I have asked Jesus to drive. Now, my self-discipline is totally focused on being a good passenger. I constantly resist the urge to grab at the steering wheel of my life. I have to make moment-by- moment conscious decisions to let Jesus keep driving." For me, it was a powerful word picture. Sam helped me refocus. Now, I realize that my self discipline is the discipline of discipleship—of following my Master.

Lord, on my own I am powerless to discipline my thinking. Please work in me both to will and to do Your good pleasure. I want the mind of Christ.

Mental Focus

You will keep him in perfect peace, whose mind is stayed on You, because he trusts in You. Isa. 26:3, NKJV.

I am confident that you know a toddler or two who demonstrate amazing mental abilities. It isn't unusual to see unusually rapid rates of mental development when a child has good nutrition and a stimulating environment. Then life happens. And far too many people allow their mind to get lazy, and it tends to think along the path of least resistance. It spends too much time wandering, which gets it to worrying, criticizing, and complaining. To solve such mind problems, pop culture articles on mental discipline urge me to memorize and meditate. If I am to believe such experts, the all-too-prevalent human condition of mental laziness is best cured by intentional memorization and the mind is best focused by meditation. The suggestion is memorize anything from the vast storehouse of written works and spend time every day meditating. Memorizing, they say, exercises the lazy mind, and meditation focuses it.

In most cases popular culture suggests that meditation means working hard to think about nothing, or dwell on just one thing in an attempt to still the mind. The idea is to tame the racing, out-of-control mind by focusing on breathing, because that is one body function that we can regulate. When brought under control, the wandering, worrying mind supposedly becomes more responsive and receptive to our present situation, leading to better mental health and greater mental powers.

Is there any better, more uplifting material to memorize than promises of God?

My guess is that in such pop culture observations and injunctions you can see some powerful support for Christian Bible study, meditation, and prayer as methods of focusing and disciplining the mind. Is there any better, more uplifting material to memorize than promises of God? Daily Scripture memorization and rehearsal is, no doubt, the best possible way of exercising the mind and keeping it sharp and ever expanding. Prayerful reading of God's Word and quiet, unhurried meditation on His promises provide multiple benefits. It not only nurtures and grows the all-important life in the Spirit, but also helps the body processes and enhances mental health.

Lord God, Creator of my mind, is this the only channel of communication that I have with You? I pray for clarity of thinking and for a mind dedicated to loving and serving You.

July 1

Weeds

He replied, "Every plant that my heavenly Father has not planted will be pulled up by the roots." Matt. 15:13, NIV.

Throughout his life my father-in-law was regarded as a master gardener. To my knowledge, he never completed any formal courses in horticulture, but his greatest passion was being out in the yard or garden, faithfully tending his plants. Because he spent so much time with them, he had a feel for his beloved plants' every need and recognized every threat to them. The optimal amount of water, fertilizer, and sunlight; additional support; a little less crowding; slimy slugs, thrips, aphids, beetles, moles, fungal or bacterial diseases—his practiced eye would quickly detect problems, and like a good physician, he seemed instinctively to know the best cure. The results were perpetually beautiful gardens and an abundant supply of prizewinning fruits and vegetables. For 40 years he served as groundskeeper at the Fuller Memorial Sanitarium/Hospital in South Attleboro, Massachusetts. His own plantings and vegetable garden received the same loving attention. After his retirement, the neighborhoods where he lived turned into gardens of beauty.

Like every gardener since Adam and Eve were sent out of the Garden of Eden, Dad's biggest battle was with weeds. Late in his retirement, Mom and Dad lived with us, so I had the opportunity to learn much before he died. I remember watching his practiced fingers plucking young weeds from among his bean plants, hearing his well-worn hoe clinking against the occasional pebble, and listening to him describe a weed as simply a plant that was not in its right place. Dad simply didn't give weeds a chance. No matter what his task for the day, whether staking up tomatoes, fertilizing butternut squash, or mulching the roses, if he saw a weed he would grab it then and there. Even while in suit and tie during a casual stroll after church, he would stoop to snatch a weed. Daily he patrolled the entire yard and garden, quickly dispatching any offending weed. He simply didn't ignore them. Once, he observed that "weeds grow all the time. They grow faster than my plants. It is easiest to get them when their roots are little."

Christ used weeds as a metaphor for concepts, ideas, and teachings that were not from His heavenly Father. The fate of such teachings? The Master Gardener, the Father, will pull them up by the roots. How refreshing and beautiful it would be to have a weed-free belief system.

Lord, what extraneous beliefs do I cherish? Please weed the garden of my mind now.

Tree of Heaven

Brothers and sisters, do not slander one another. James 4:11, NIV.

T ree of heaven" is an unlikely name for an exotic tree introduced into the United States around 1750. It smells terrible, and is now prominent on the noxious weeds list for several states and many countries around the world. The scientific name is Ailanthus altissima, which gives us a clue to its common name. The word ailanthus derives from an Indonesian word meaning "tree reaching for the sky," and altissima is Latin for "tallest," not a bad description for a tree that grows very rapidly up to 80 feet or so. Do you see why the name "tree of heaven" fits so well? A native of China where people have used it for centuries in folk medicine to cure various illnesses and to feed certain types of silkworm moths, the tree was introduced into Europe and then the United States as an ornamental tree to line city streets. It grows rapidly and seemed well suited to the rigors and pollution of urban life, as it was resistant to drought, likes full sun, and thrives especially well in polluted soils and air as well as acid rain. In fact, it is one of the most pollution-tolerant trees known. Mining waste, acids, coal tars, even sulfur dioxide and ozone, don't seem to phase the hardy tree.

So why is it such a hated plant? Why do people poison and eradicate it and place it on noxious weed lists the world over? The answer is because the tree of heaven grows too well and actually eliminates many native species. Once the tree of heaven gets rooted, seeds of other species won't germinate nearby. The roots, stems, and leaves of *Ailanthus* make a chemical that kills or prevents the germination of most other plant seeds. The substance is so potent that it even caused the death of other plants in tests when sprayed on seedlings that had already gotten a good start. With its unfair advantage, it can take over in most of its habitats. No wonder it has such a bad reputation.

What about me? Do I take unfair advantage of others? What about the words I speak? Do my words slander others? James 4:11 uses the Greek word *katalaleite*, translated slander in the NIV. Katalaleite simply means "speak against." Do I ever do that to others? Do my words put them down? James lists no conditions, gives no tests to determine if speaking against someone is ever appropriate. He simply states it as God's command. Don't do it. Stop it.

Lord, why do I do it so often, so easily? Forgive me for speaking against any of Your children.

July 3

Cirsium arvense

Cursed is the ground because of you; through painful toil you will eat food from it all the days of your life. It will produce thorns and thistles for you, and you will eat the plants of the field. Gen. 3:17, 18, NIV.

Cursed thistle, creeping thistle, or Canada thistle are three of the 13 common names for what botanists around the world call *Cirsium arvense*. The United Kingdom officially labels the small herbaceous perennial thistle as an "injurious weed." The pesky plant that snakes across the ground till it can get support from another plant to hold it upright is the most commonly listed "noxious weed" on the Montana Department of Agriculture's Invaders Database System. The highly invasive thistle is believed to have originated around the eastern Mediterranean and southeastern Europe, but has spread as far as Australia, New Zealand, northern and southern Africa, Japan, India, and most of South America.

What makes it so successful? Probably the most obvious feature is the sharp spiny leaves that keep everybody from touching or eating the plant. Next, the thistle spends most of its energy in propagating from roots that branch out from its deep taproot and spread out far and wide, creating big patches of pesky plants. It isn't uncommon to have one clone of plants spreading more than 100 feet in diameter. Another survival skill the thistle has is the ability to produce lots of seeds. The up to 100 flower heads per shoot may have as many as 90 seeds per flower head with some counts going much higher. Thus each shoot produces thousands of seeds. Each seed has a tiny parachute, called a pappus, that can carry it in the wind for a mile or more. Seeds generally germinate quickly, but if buried more than eight inches deep, they have been known to stay viable in the soil for more than 20 years. Some researchers claim that the thistle produces chemicals that retard the growth of other plants—an effective competitive process known as allelopathy.

In placing a higher value on their own judgment than on obedience to God's clear instructions, Adam and Eve were the first to experience the curse on the ground resulting in thorns and thistles. Thistles have been successfully spreading to this day—even in my heart as I subject Jesus to public disgrace and crucify Him again through my willful sins.

Lord, keep my heart true to You, constantly drinking in the sweet influence of Your latter rain.

July 4

Polydactyly

In still another battle, which took place at Gath, there was a huge man with six fingers on each hand and six toes on each foot—twenty-four in all. He also was descended from Rapha. 2 Sam. 21:20, NIV.

On the birth of a new baby, one of the first things that parents do is study the face of the tiny new arrival to see who it looks like. "Oh, he has grandpa's nose" or "She has her mother's lips." Then they go on to count fingers and toes and make sure that they have a whole and complete baby. Thankfully, most of the time the miracle of birth results in a "perfect" baby, and we all wonder at how such perfection can happen. From start to finish it is truly a wondrous process that remains well beyond human understanding.

Since Creation is in the distant past, and the enemy of God continues to do his best to cause confusion and mayhem, is it any wonder then that human development has occasional problems? Once in a while parents counting fingers and toes will do a double take and count again. Something is wrong here. They find six fingers on each hand, six toes on each foot. Bewildered, they count again and again to make sure.

Having extra digits (polydactyly) on hands and/or feet occurs in about two out of every 1,000 babies. Most often the extra digit(s) is just one sign of several genetic defects. More than a dozen syndromes exhibit polydactyly as one of their consequences. In many cases, however, the trait is inherited as a dominant trait from one parent who themselves had polydactyly. Parents might not know that they were born with six fingers/toes because it often occurs as just a little fleshy boneless appendage on the side of the hand or foot, and it may have been removed at birth. Less often the extra digit is a fork from the nearest digit and requires surgery. In rare cases the extra digit may be a fully functioning finger or toe. This may have been the case with the giant of Gath.

When David was fighting Philistines, size was an obvious advantage in the close hand-to-hand combat. As you read the context of 1 Chronicles 20 and 2 Samuel 21 you learn how significant those giants were. They were huge guys. But as David knew, giants, even with the extra finger and toe advantage, are no match for an omnipotent God. What giants do you battle today? What seeming advantages might they wave in your face?

Lord, go before me today. Give me courage, faith, and trust in all of today's challenges.

Asparagus

He does not treat us as our sins deserve or repay us according to our iniquities. Ps. 103:10, NIV.

D o you just love eating asparagus, or are you one of those who won't even try the ugly green spears? If you love savoring the amazing shoots, then I have another question. Shortly after eating a few spears of asparagus, have you noticed that your urine has a most disagreeable aroma? The smell is so strong and obnoxious that you may have worried that your kidneys were not functioning properly. Or maybe you failed to link it with the asparagus since the smell is nothing like what you just ate. You might actually be rolling on the floor laughing and wondering what in the world I am talking about, because you simply have not noticed any such fetid odor. What is going on here?

Why is it that I have tendencies for good or evil? Why do I do what I do?

Medical schools have repeatedly used the population differences exhibited by the asparagus phenomenon to illustrate genetic differences in people. Despite the fact that the cause of the smelly urine has been investigated and written about for a few hundred years, mysteries still exist. For example, early researchers asked subjects to eat asparagus and then check their own urine for the smell. Roughly half reported nothing out of the ordinary. The conclusion was that there were differences in how the body metabolically processed it. A later study asked known smellers to check everybody's urine. Those individuals could detect the asparagus metabolite in everybody's urine, which led to the new conclusion that it was a sensory difference rather than a metabolic one. Some could smell it and others couldn't. But that study was flawed because, as often happens, it involved too few samples. So the debate continues: Is it a metabolic variation or a sensory difference? The scientific literature seems to be leaning toward the latter conclusion, but since it isn't a disease, science hasn't checked it out thoroughly.

Why is it that I have tendencies for good or evil? Why do I do what I do? Certainly my genetics and my environment are major players. Choice also plays a huge role. But choose as I might, why I do what I do is often a mystery to me. Paul even expressed exasperation that he found himself doing what he didn't want to do and vice versa. Like Paul, what gives me hope is that God knows every detail of my life, He loves me, and He is merciful beyond knowing.

Lord, is it really true that You made me unique and special? Do You know my every strength and weakness, capability and inability? What peace to rest in Your merciful and loving hands.

July 6

Yeast

Has not my hand made all these things . . . ? Isa. 66:2, NIV.

When anybody says yeast, most people immediately think of *Saccharomyces cerevesia*, the scientific name of the most common and commercially important species of yeast. In actuality, a yeast is just one of a few different growth forms of the kingdom fungi. Most yeasts are fairly large unicellular fungal cells that reproduce by budding. Yeast specialists tell us that scientists have recorded more than 800 species of yeasts but estimate that this represents only 1 percent of the total number of existing types. It makes me wonder how much we really know.

Whether or not we are aware of it, yeast cells, dead or alive, touch our lives every day in important ways. Indeed, life without yeast would be very different. Take breadmaking, for example. Live yeast cells in warm bread dough metabolize sugar, creating bubbles of carbon dioxide that make bread light—one way of leavening bread. The baking industry depends on yeast. The brewing industry also uses yeast cells to ferment malt sugars and grape sugars, creating ethanol as a by-product. Yeast cells make the ethanol used for auto and farm fuels. In a recent development, genetically engineered yeast cells have been put to work in breaking down cellulose in wastepaper, agricultural by-products, and even wood chips to make ethanol as an alternative to gasoline. People often eat deactivated or dead yeast cells as nutritional yeast. Rich in proteins and various B vitamins, low in sodium and fat, nutritional yeast is sprinkled on popcorn or used in place of Parmesan cheese or employed to add a nutty, cheesy, creamy flavor to foods. Yeast extracts such as Vegemite or Marmite add strong flavors. Numerous kinds of yeasts normally inhabit our mucous membranes and skin, contributing to our quality of life. But at times, in those with a weakened immune system, they can grow uncontrolled and cause raging diseases that kill.

Yeast is easy to grow and manipulate in the research laboratory. Because it is a eukaryotic cell, yeast has now become the model system of choice for scientists studying the molecular biology of multicellular organisms— which includes us. In the last couple decades the lowly yeast has taught us much about how DNA replicates, how cells reproduce, how they metabolize their food and produce energy, and so much more. Knowing about yeast was so important that its 12 million base pairs were the first eukaryotic genome that researchers sequenced.

Lord, if yeast cells can be used in so many ways to Your honor and glory, there is hope for me.

Palm Print

You are the Christ, the Son of the living God. Matt. 16:16, NKJV.

Look closely at the pad on your index finger. See the fine texture pattern? You know that as your fingerprint. That textured pattern is typical of your fingers, palms of your hands, toes, and soles of your feet, but nowhere else on your body. The technical name for those minuscule ridges and valleys is friction skin, because it helps you hold on to things and gives your bare feet a bit more traction. Friction ridges are built into the dermis and epidermis of your skin. During the embryonic development, those minute ridges formed in your skin so that by the time you were born, the friction ridge patterns on your hands and your feet were set for life. Except for certain diseases, injury, or death, those friction ridges don't change. And nobody else in the world has the same pattern of handprints or footprints that you do.

Because friction ridge patterns are unique to each person on earth, we can use them as one form of positive identification. Every time you touch something with your bare hands or feet, it leaves prints behind. Those prints show up because each tiny ridge unit in your hands and feet has a sweat gland and constantly puts out water, dissolved salts, and amino acids. Usually our hands and feet aren't 100 percent clean, so any gunk that we have been touching or walking in can get added to the print. Oils from your hair or face, some residue from your last peanut-butter-and-jelly sandwich—any of this works fine. When you are fingerprinted, they roll your finger in ink, the better to make a print with. Fingerprint databases have been growing for decades and now contain millions of records.

With time, law enforcement agencies have learned that most prints at a crime scene are actually palm prints. Both palm prints and footprints have much larger surface areas than fingerprints. Palm-print databases are now expanding rapidly, and soon law authorities will add footprints to the friction ridge databases as well. It is vital that law enforcement agencies always have correct identification of lawbreakers.

Jesus asked His disciples an important question: "Who do people say I am?" (Mark 8:27, NIV). Getting that identification right is crucial to salvation. Following His resurrection, Jesus startled His disciples with His appearance. What was it that He showed as proof of His identity?

Lord, if knowing who You are is so important, then I must know. I long to be taught by You (see John 6:45; Ps. 25:14; 1 Cor. 2:9, 10).

July 8

Foundation

For no one can lay any foundation other than the one already laid, which is Jesus Christ. 1 Cor. 3:11, NIV.

One of the first summer jobs that I had as a teenager was in construction. The contractor that hired me was building a small house on a small lot in a low-budget residential area, which may explain why he was paying new inexperienced help (me) small wages to dig footings rather than renting the power equipment to do the job. So there I was, first day on the job, soft hands, digging a ditch between the yellow nylon twine in the hard red clay with a pickax and a shovel. Hour after hour as the sun beat down, the blisters developed, grew, broke, and got bandaged. The footings had to be about a foot deep and a foot and an half wide with straight sides and a flat bottom. When the foreman returned hours later to inspect and help with his finishing touches and grade stakes, in came a concrete truck to fill in the hard-won space.

Since that first day on the job I have been on many construction sites and helped shape and pour many different kinds of foundations. If a foundation is to be sound, it should rest on firm undisturbed soil or bedrock so that it can provide reliable support for the structure. The type and quality of the foundation required will of course depend on many factors, including the size and weight of the structure to be built as well as the kind and stability of the soil. Foundations for homes are usually no more than one or two feet deep. But if you build a skyscraper, tower, or massive bridge, the foundation will need to be much more substantial. For example, the twin Petronas Towers soaring above Kuala Lampur, Malaysia, were sited on soil that couldn't support the weight of the 1,500-foot skyscrapers, so the foundation had to rest on solid bedrock. Imagine the massive hole that had to be dug for the 394-foot-deep concrete and steel foundation. To date, this is the deepest foundation for any building. For comparison, in January 2010 the world's tallest building, rising 2,717 feet above the desert of Dubai and known as Burj Khalifa, has a nearly half-million-ton concrete and steel foundation that extends down only 164 feet.

Jesus bore my sins and the sin of the world through all time. "He hath borne our griefs, and carried our sorrows. . . . The Lord hath laid on him the iniquity of us all" (Isa. 53:4-6, KJV).

Lord, I simply can't imagine the crushing weight You bore for me. I am grateful. Thank You. With You as my foundation, make me a temple to Your honor and glory (see 1 Cor. 6:19).

July 9
Cornerstone/Capstone

The stone the builders rejected has become the cornerstone. Ps. 118:22, NIV.

On the Fourth of July 1848 the president of the United States of America, James K. Polk, laid the cornerstone for a monument that, during the next four decades, became the 555-foot-tall Washington Monument. Numerous items and important documents of the times are sealed inside that cornerstone. Included in that time capsule treasure trove is an American dollar, a 1783 cent, a copy of the U.S. Constitution and the Declaration of Independence, a Bible, a Farmers' Almanac, maps of all kinds, coast surveys, etc. The list of artifacts preserved in that cornerstone goes on and on. Finally, on December 6, 1884, an aluminum "capstone" was set as the apex of the magnificent obelisk. Three of the four sides of the capstone are inscribed with the names and dates of people and events important in the creation of the monument. The fourth side—the eastern face—bears two Latin words: *Laus Deo*, meaning "Praise be to God."

Cornerstones and capstones are both important architectural elements of buildings or monuments. People choose cornerstones carefully, because they have to withstand great pressure from the weight of the building. They must not crumble from the effects of weathering and time. Cornerstones usually mark the beginning of the building project, and capstones indicate the completion, giving it the finishing touch. For a building they are the alpha and the omega.

In Psalm 118:22 the Hebrew word *lerosh* means "the chief" and *pennah* means "corner." The early editions of the NIV translate this as capstone. Most other versions have "cornerstone" or "chief cornerstone" instead. I can understand the blurred distinction. With its position at the apex, the capstone of the Washington Monument could certainly be thought of as the chief stone, could it not? Before the invention and common use of precision instruments such as digital laser transits, builders needed a solid reference point to establish the orientation of the building or structure and serve as an unmoving reference point for all dimensional measurements. Once set on the foundation, the cornerstone or foundation stone became that solid reference point that the builder based all measurements from. They are also appropriately called chief corners.

The chief corner refers to Jesus who is our standard, who has passed all the tests, a precious cornerstone for a sure foundation for our life (Isa. 28:16).

Lord, I humbly ask You to be the chief cornerstone and capstone of my life. I know that if I can make that daily decision to trust in You, I will never crumble. Make me a holy temple.

July 10

HAPE

And the Lord God formed man of the dust of the ground, and breathed into his nostrils the breath of life; and man became a living being. Gen. 2:7, NKJV.

While on a hiking safari on the slopes of Mount Kilimanjaro, my cousin, Dr. Frank, almost died of HAPE. An acronym for high altitude pulmonary edema (too much fluid in the lungs), HAPE is what happens to some people who spend a day or more at altitudes above 8,200 feet. Rising to more than 19,000 feet, Kilimanjaro is the highest mountain in Africa. Ever since God breathed the breath of life into us, getting oxygen to the cells in the body has been vital to continue living. But above 8,200 feet air molecules are further apart, and oxygen decreases by 40 percent. For reasons still somewhat of a mystery, fluid collects in the lungs, and the susceptible person dies quickly. In fact, HAPE is the most common cause of death of those who venture into high altitudes.

Ever since God breathed the breath of life into us, getting oxygen to the cells in the body has been vital to continue living.

As climbers reach high altitude, they feel their chest tightening, and they have a hard time breathing even when resting. They just can't seem to catch their breath. As a result, they become weak and tired, and may start coughing because of the fluid accumulation in the lungs. If you listen to their breathing you would hear crackling or bubbling sounds and see that their fingernails and lips are turning blue, but not necessarily from being cold. Both their heart rate and breathing rate will be abnormally fast. The condition is dangerous. You must get them to lower altitudes as quickly as possible and seek medical help.

My cousin was most fortunate to survive, because, for him, the only way down was to go up and over the mountain. Before his long ordeal ended, he became conscious of being carried off the mountain by others in his climbing party in order to reach medical help. As a result of his experience, Dr. Frank Artress sold his lucrative anesthesiology business in Modesto, California. Disposing of his homes, his fancy cars, his art collections, and everything that he had, he and his wife moved to Tanzania to provide medical help for those who had saved his life. If you like, read the rest of his story by following the links at fameafrica.org.

Moment by moment, God gives us breath so that we can praise the Lord. Those who have breathed their last have just died. Let us thank God for each breath that He allows us to take.

Lord, may each moment of my life be a praise to You and the power of Your name.

July 11

The High Life

Let everything that has breath praise the Lord. Praise the Lord!
Ps. 150:6, NKJV.

To my surprise, I recently discovered 16 cities, towns, and villages located above 10,000 feet. Two towns are listed as being situated at 16,730 feet. La Rinconada in Peru has 30,000 people eking out a living by mining gold in the high mountains. Another village in Tibet called Wenzhuan lies at the same altitude. Usually altitude sickness sets in as people spend time above 8,000 feet, so how do some people routinely live way above that altitude?

For at least six years I lived in Addis Ababa, Ethiopia, a city positioned at or just below the 8,000-foot mark, so I know the effects of high altitude living. For the first several weeks after arriving I would get out of breath with the least exertion. Because of the lower oxygen level, the body responds by increasing the hemoglobin content in each red blood cell and by producing more red blood cells per unit volume of blood. Once acclimatized, I remember enjoying vacations at the seashore, where it seemed that I could run forever without becoming winded.

Though we don't completely understand all the physiological factors that contribute to altitude sickness, a recent genetics study helped to shed light on the ability of some to live quite well at high altitudes. One human gene dubbed the EPAS1 gene codes for proteins that help regulate how the body responds to low levels of blood oxygen. Research shows that 87 percent of the Tibetans living at very high altitudes have a mutation of their EPAS1 gene that apparently gives them a strong selective advantage in their blood chemistry. It appears that their blood is simply much better at carrying oxygen. By contrast, only 9 percent of the closely related Han Chinese living in Beijing (average elevation 150 feet) carry that same mutation. From historical and archaeological records, it appears that people have lived on the Tibetan Plateau for more than 3,000 years. According to the genetic data the Tibetan population developed this remarkable trait about 2,750 years ago. In contrast to Northern Europeans, who took many more years to acquire lactose intolerance, the Tibetan data stands now as the example of the most rapid adaptive development in a human population known to date.

Through the years I have seen numerous studies expressing wide-eyed surprise at how minor genetic changes happen much more rapidly than ever believed. The more I study the remarkable plasticity and adaptability of populations, the more creative and ingenious my God appears to be.

Lord, every time I learn a new facet about our bodies, I praise You.

By Faith

For in the gospel the righteousness of God is revealed—a righteousness that is by faith from first to last, just as it is written: "The righteous will live by faith." Rom. 1:17, NIV.

D oes God exist? Can we trust His word? Does God mean what He says? Does He even know that I exist? The theme repeated again and again in the faith chapter of Hebrews 11 is assurance while patiently waiting that God means what He says. The book cites individual after individual who lived in trust of God.

Read again the text for today. Romans 1:17 has Paul quoting from Habakkuk 2:4. Then he repeats the same passage in Galatians 3:11, and it appears in Hebrews 10:38. Could there be something here of vital importance? When I read Habakkuk 2, I find God Himself speaking, so let's listen in. "Write down the revelation . . . make it plain . . . the revelation awaits an appointed time; it speaks of the end and will not prove false. Though it linger, wait for it; it will certainly come and will not delay. . . . The righteous person will live by his faithfulness" (verses 2-4, NIV).

Those living words of God comfort and strengthen me. They assure me that the revelation of God is true and in time "it will certainly come and will not delay" (verse 3, NIV). In my own family and in my community, many don't believe for sure that God exists. And if He does, He sure isn't a nice God because He has allowed so much pain and suffering to happen on His watch.

Jesus asked an important question in Luke 18:8: "When the Son of Man comes, will he find faith on the earth" (NIV)? Will there be anybody who is sure that God means what He says? Will there be anybody who is still absolutely certain that God exists and who is patiently waiting for Him?

I have determined that the answer to Luke's question will be a resounding YES. I choose to keep a tight grip on my faith in God—to believe and to wait patiently, knowing that His timing is not mine.

Lord, I simply don't understand Your timing or the way You do things. Nevertheless, I choose to believe, to hold my questions for Your scheduled face-to-face visit. I trust You completely.

Algae Power

Great is our Lord and mighty in power; his understanding has no limit. Ps. 147:5, NIV. Ah, Sovereign Lord, you have made the heavens and the earth by your great power and outstretched arm. Nothing is too hard for you. Jer. 32:17, NIV.

From what I read in the Bible, God never suffers from a brownout, a blackout, or an energy shortage of any type. Recently I attended a talk by New York Times op-ed columnist and Pulitzer Prize-winning author Tom Friedman. The main point of his speech was that the country that first learns to harness or produce inexpensive, nonpolluting, abundant energy will lead the world community in the years to come. Doesn't the good Lord already have a lock on that position (see Matt. 28:18, KJV)?

Today's news describes the search for single-cell creatures that have the ability or potential to be genetically engineered to make biofuels from sunlight and carbon dioxide. Sunlight is abundant and free. And from what we hear, carbon dioxide is much too plentiful in our atmosphere, so removing it to make energy-rich fuels sounds like a good thing. Dozens of companies and more than 100 academic institutions are working to find algae with the capabilities of making hydrocarbons or lipids that we could refine into diesel, ethanol, or gasoline. The microscopic critters reproduce rapidly and use the energy of sunlight to power their chemical reactions that remove carbon dioxide from the environment and string the carbon atoms together to make energy-rich molecules. Screening thousands of strains of algae, scientists select those that appear to be champions in reproduction, growth, efficient use of light, and production of useful substances. Algae are excellent candidates because, in per acre comparisons, they have the potential of being at least 10 times more efficient than corn at producing ethanol or soybeans in making biodiesel, and they can do it in desert or brackish water locations that won't compete with agricultural acreage.

The hope is that we can cultivate the best candidates in large pools or bioreactors in desert locations to satisfy the power needs of the future with renewable energy.

Lord, all power comes from Your hand. Teach us to use the resources that You have provided in ways that care for Your creation as we relieve suffering and tenderly care for those around us.

Clover

Now hope does not disappoint, because the love of God has been poured out in our hearts by the Holy Spirit who was given to us. Rom. 5:5, NKJV.

I s any plant better known or more widespread than clover? Its genus name *Trifolium* simply means "three leaves or leaflets" which is what most clover plants have. Tradition suggests that the three leaflets represent faith, hope, and love. Finding a four-leaf clover is fairly rare, and many consider it a sign of good luck as the fourth leaflet supposedly symbolizes luck.

Some people must be very lucky because they have a knack of finding lots of four-leaf clovers. An old-timer by the name of Edward Martin reportedly had a collection of 160,000 four-leaf clovers, but then he spent several hours each day hunting for them. Some have found five, six, or even seven-leaf clovers. The record is apparently 21 leaflets on one stem. Some people try to eradicate clover from their lawns, because a perfect lawn is supposed to be uniform. The reality is that having it in a lawn means that you don't have to fertilize as often since clover is a legume, and most legumes work together with root bacteria to convert atmospheric nitrogen into ammonia, a form of nitrogen that plants can use.

Making usable nitrogen in root nodules of clover and other legumes is a complicated and beautiful process. It starts with the roots producing complex chemicals called flavonoids. Flavonoids permeate soil around the roots, chemically signaling, "Is anybody out there?" When certain types of bacteria are present in the vicinity, they absorb the flavonoids, which act like a key to the lock of a specific bacterial protein called nodD. With the nodD lock open, the flavonoid-nodD complex turns on a bacterial gene aptly named the nod gene. The job of nod genes is to code for enzymes that produce a bacterial protein called nod factor. Nod factor is the bacteria's chemical answer of "Yes, I am here." Bacterial nod factor seeps into clover root hairs, causing them to radically change their structure in ways that invite the bacteria to live inside root cells, where together they form nodules and work to make usable nitrogen for plants.

The beauty, complexity, and specificity of this process that I have just begun to unpack is yet another evidence of a carefully designed system. Worship Him who made root nodules.

Lord, may I be as sensitive to the calling of the Holy Spirit as the bacteria are to the plant flavonoids. My desire is to work together with You to bring love and peace to my street.

Mighty Men of Valor

How could one chase a thousand, and two put ten thousand to flight . . . ? Deut. 32:30, NKJV.

W ithout doubt the most highly trained warriors on the planet these days are the elite and secretive Tier 1 counterterrorism and Special Missions units. They include SEAL Team 6 (the U.S. Navy unit) and Delta Force (the U.S. Army unit), both modeled after the British Special Air Services (SAS) commandos trained to operate behind enemy lines during World War II. Other elite units include the Australian Special Air Service Regiment, the Canadian Joint Task Force 2, the Israeli Sayeret Matkal, and the German Kommando Spezialkrafte.

Their brutal, intense, training regimen attempts to break them physically and mentally. Only those in peak physical condition, the most experienced and toughened in battle, and the most determined are even allowed to train. Trainees must be mentally sharp, fluent in other languages, highly skilled in munitions, experts in navigation, demolition, and counterterrorism, etc. And though trainees are carefully prescreened, most don't complete the grueling training. Little is known about these highly classified units. But they are good. Certainly they would well represent modern mighty men of valor.

Many references throughout the Old Testament mention David's mighty men of valor with the best descriptions being in 2 Samuel 23:8-38 and 1 Chronicles 11:10-47. You read about Josheb who killed 800 men singlehandedly and Eleazar who fought alone when his comrades retreated. Shammah defended a lentil (or barley) field by himself (or with just a few others). Another unnamed three mighty men broke into the Philistine garrison in Bethlehem to bring David a drink of water from the well of Bethlehem. Abishai killed 300 enemy soldiers at one time. Benaiah slew two heroes of Moab. Another time he killed a lion—in a pit on a snowy day, no less. Then with only his staff, Benaiah wrested a spear from a 7.5-foot-tall Egyptian, killing him with it. Asahel, Elhanan, Shammoth, and a long list of other mighty men of valor follow. In my mind's eye, I can see them standing there, deeply tanned, muscles bulging, grizzled men with sky-high pain tolerances. And they were unbeatable in hand-to-hand combat. But in every case, the victory was theirs, not because of their might and expertise, but because the Lord was on their side. His finger tipped the scales in their favor. For the enemy, it has always been an unfair fight. "With him is an arm of flesh; but with us is the Lord our God, to help us and to fight our battles" (2 Chron. 32:8, NKJV).

Lord, may I be one of Your mighty warriors in this cosmic battle.

July 16

The Vine

I am the vine, you are the branches. He who abides in Me, and I in him, bears much fruit; for without me you can do nothing. John 15:5, NKJV.

The tomato plants in my garden are robust and healthy now. Finally, this year, I purchased a 100-foot roll of steel-welded wire mesh and made five-foot-tall tomato cages. Since I placed a cage over each young seedling, the plants are thanking me now by growing well over my head. With regular training, the vines ended up mostly inside the cages and have adequate support. I am looking forward to a good crop of tomatoes. That will be the bonus.

Just working with tomatoes is a pleasant experience for me, because I love the fragrant musky aroma that surrounds me after lightly brushing past a single vine or leaf. A microscopic look explains the characteristic smell. The surface is extremely hairy. And at the microscopic scale, many of the hairs have the appearance of big round water towers that you see in many towns across America—you know, the kind that look like a golf ball on a tee. The swollen, fluid-filled heads of these glandular trichomes (as they are called) break easily from the lightest touch, releasing the sticky, pungent fluid. Some people don't like the smell at all and think it stinks. That is the reason for the fluid—to help deter insects from eating the leaves.

I find that I have to work very gently with tomato vines, because it is so easy to accidentally break off a fresh young growing tip or branch when trying to insert it back inside the cage. Once separated from the vine, the branch withers within a minute or two. The shape and structure of all soft herbaceous plants such as tomatoes depends entirely on pressurized water cells within. Like air-filled bounce houses, castles, moonwalks, jumpers, dry slides, and other inflatable play structures, some soft-bodied plants rely totally on inner pressures to maintain their form. Breaking the connection to the vine is like turning off the blowers in the play structures. They quickly crumple or wither into an unrecognizable heap.

Breaking the connection to the vine is like turning off the blowers in the play structures.

Inside every plant is a wonderfully complex and delicate system of pipes and conduits that conduct water, dissolved minerals, photosynthetic products, and plant growth regulators to all parts of the plant in a carefully regulated manner. Jesus could not have been more descriptive in calling us branches connected to Him, the vine. Without the connection, we are toast.

Lord, sometimes I wonder why my spiritual life has wilted so badly and isn't producing any fruit. Please forgive me for the many times that I pull away from You and try to go it alone.

The Strongest Insect

The Lord is my strength and my shield; my heart trusted in Him, and I am helped. Therefore my heart greatly rejoices, and with my song I will praise Him. Ps. 28:7, NKJV.

Can you name the strongest insect in the world? Recent experiments on a small beetle discovered that it could pull a weight 1,141 times that of its own body. If you weighed only 100 pounds and were as strong as this beetle, you could move 114,100 pounds. That's more than 57 tons, or more than five large elephants. Can you guess what beetle holds this amazing strength record?

Here is a hint. What kind of beetle reduced the number of pestilent bush flies in Australia by around 90 percent after the beetles were introduced into the country? Not only did the fly population go down, but the soil quality was dramatically improved. So the beetle in question is both a champion weight-lifter as well as a great farmer and fly control expert. Have I given you enough hints yet?

Here is another clue to the same beetle. The people of ancient Egypt considered this beetle sacred because they believed that it carried the sun across the sky every day and buried it each evening, only to bring it up again the next morning. If you are guessing a scarab beetle then you are getting close. The family of scarab beetles has many thousands of species, so to discover the champion weight-lifting beetle you need to zero in on what kind of scarab beetle it is.

What beetle seeks out fresh piles of animal dung, lives exclusively by eating it, and rolls up little balls of dung that it pushes along the ground with its back legs, buries the ball in the ground, mates, and lays eggs in the dung ball, which becomes the brood chamber and only source of food for the developing young? At this point you might be saying yuck or gross and other such words. But dung beetles are critically important in recycling animal dung and keeping it from accumulating. Their hygienic efforts spread and bury tons of animal manure, cutting the number of breeding places for flies, aerating and fertilizing the soil, thus making the world a better place to live. In the United States alone, dung beetles save cattle owners more than $380 million annually. Dung beetles live on every continent except Antarctica. Job 20:7 mentions disappearing dung. We can thank the dung beetle for its role in that process.

Lord, You have given the dung beetle amazing strength and an important task. Be my strength today. Fill me with the Holy Spirit so I can do good works today for You.

Evolution

Of old You laid the foundation of the earth, and the heavens are the work of Your hands. They will perish, but You will endure; Yes, they will all grow old like a garment; like a cloak You will change them, and they will be changed. But You are the same, and Your years will have no end. Ps. 102:25-27, NKJV.

L ike the word "love," the word "evolution" has many meanings. One biological definition of "evolution" is "change in the genetic makeup of a population from generation to generation." A good example of such change is to imagine what Adam and Eve looked like. Then take a careful look at the wide range of appearances in various human populations that exist around the world today. The variation is remarkable. I never cease to be amazed at the extent of plasticity that the Creator must have designed into living systems.

For another example of that wonderful God-given plasticity, look at humanity's best friend. Of all animals, dogs have had the closest association with humans, have had the most selective breeding performed on them, and, as a result, come in all sorts of sizes and shapes. Yet they all probably originated from a basic wolf-type dog in the distant past. Through time, people have worked to develop thin long legs for speed and endurance in greyhounds, to select small size and fearlessness in the Jack Russell terriers, to create a short, compact body with a playful spirit in the pug, and to breed for intelligence and gentleness in Labrador retrievers. They are just a few of many traits that have been artificially manipulated by selective breeding.

Of all the anatomical differences in dogs, perhaps the most notable is the complex shape of the skull. Canine skulls apparently exhibit greater diversity than any other genus. So what has happened to the brain inside that skull? A recent brain-imaging study performed on about a dozen widely different types of dogs show that a dog's brain orientation is most related to snout length. Dogs with short snouts (having a flatter head like the pug) have brains that have rotated forward up to 15 degrees, and their olfactory bulb, the part of the brain that detects smell, has moved from the front of the brain to a position below the brain. The relocation of the olfactory bulb may explain why we don't use short-snouted dogs for drug or bomb sniffing. But let dogs breed randomly for a few generations, and you have a mutt. While the parentage of mutts can be difficult if not impossible to determine, their temperaments may be better than a purebred's.

Lord, You know the many people who contributed to my genetic makeup. May I use the gifts You have given me through them to bring honor to You.

Bats

He has made everything beautiful in its time. He has also set eternity in the human heart; yet no one can fathom what God has done from beginning to end. Eccl. 3:11, NIV.

I wonder why bats are so misunderstood and maligned. Maybe it's because, as a group, ugly is an appropriate descriptor. Check out a few of the thousands of photos posted on batcon.org or simply google Ernst Haeckel's 1904 drawing of bats to discover how grotesque some of their facial features appear. Perhaps it's because we have a hard time understanding how bats can get around so well with such poor eyesight. Or it could be because they have an undeserved reputation for carrying rabies or getting tangled in women's hair. When you take the time to learn about bats, however, you discover what a marvelous creation they really are.

Biologists classify bats as mammals since they have fur and suckle their young. Most people are surprised to learn that fewer than 6,000 species of mammals exist and more than 1,200 of them are bats, the only mammals that can actually fly. Bats are the most abundant mammals too. The smallest bats measure just more than an inch and weigh in at less than 0.1 ounces, while the biggest has a five-foot wingspan and weighs three pounds or so. Bigger bats generally eat fruit, though some consume fish, frogs, and even other mammals. Nearly three out of every four bat species are the small ones that eat insects. Some estimates suggest that the three- to four-inch, half-ounce Mexican free-tail bat consumes about 1,000 insects per hour when they are out feeding. The largest known colony of Mexican free-tail bats numbers about 20 million. Each evening it takes hours for them to exit Bracken Cave near San Antonio, Texas, in large, dark, fast-moving clouds. They return later with an estimated 200 tons or so of insects, saving the surrounding farmers millions of dollars in losses or insecticide expenses.

The small bats are not blind, but they don't see well, and use echolocation to home in on their insect prey. They catch insects such as mosquitoes in the mouth, but for larger insects such as moths, bats cup their wing tips or tails like a catcher's mitt, snag the flying insect, then pass it to their needle-sharp teeth for the death crunch.

Scientists are concerned that many bat colonies are declining. Reasons for bat die-offs include pesticides, habitat destruction, and diseases. But because they are one of God's wonderful creations with important ecological contributions, we need to learn more about bats and care for them.

Lord, is there anything that You made that is really ugly or not needed?

White Nose Syndrome

We know that the whole creation has been groaning as in the pains of childbirth right up to the present time. Rom. 8:22, NIV.

On February 16, 2006, a caver took pictures of bats hibernating in Howe Caverns, a popular commercial tourist cave roughly 35 miles west of Albany, New York. The photographs showed several little brown bats, each with a bright-white nose. Could this be a new species of bat? On closer examination, the white "fur" turned out to be a fungal skin infection on the bat's muzzles. The fungus had also spread to the ears and sometimes even the wings. During the winter of 2006-2007 infected bats appeared in three other nearby caves. The following winter, alarm bells began going off in the community of bat scientists as the infection had spread to a total of 29 caves and abandoned mines in New York, Vermont, Massachusetts, Connecticut, and Pennsylvania. By 2008-2009 infected bats turned up in New Hampshire and West Virginia as well. Bat populations in many of these caves were plummeting. Was the fungus to blame? If so, how?

Researchers identified the fungus as a species related to the well-known *Geomyces* genus. It does not infect people or even non-hibernating bats, because the cold-loving fungus can't grow in temperatures greater than 68 degrees. The little brown bat *Myotis lucifugus* has been hardest hit, but the outbreak has also affected at least five other species. Census figures show that an average of three out of four bats in a colony die. The disease has completely wiped out some colonies. Affected bats lose weight and appear to be starving to death during their winter hibernation. Scientists wonder if the fungus prevents bats from eating enough before hibernation in the fall or are the bats coming to hibernation with adequate fat reserves but somehow the fungus is altering their hibernation physiology? As of this writing, evidence appears to point to the latter hypothesis, as the fungus does not cause inflammation or launch the bat's immune response. The best guess now is that infected bats remain restless during hibernation, preventing them from spending enough time in energy-saving torpor. Thus they consume too much of their body fat and are unable to survive the winter. The search is on now to save some species of bats from total extinction. Will a remedy be found in time?

Lord, all around us we see evidence of sin. All creation is suffering. As we fight the good fight of faith, help us to know how to care for the other creatures that You put here with us.

Sleep Inertia

I lie down and sleep; I wake again, because the Lord sustains me.
Ps. 3:5, NIV.

How long does it take you to clear the sleep cobwebs out of your brain after waking up? Do you wake up alert, chipper, and ready to go, or are you a sleepy grouch for a couple hours after waking up? Researchers are studying sleep inertia—the tendency to stay sleepy, to be unable to function well, and to want to go back to sleep after being awakened suddenly— because some people must perform well quickly after waking. Firefighters rushing to an early-morning alarm and doctors awakened from a nap during a long night shift need to be immediately alert and efficient.

Sleep inertia will naturally be greater if you have been significantly sleep-deprived before falling asleep. And if you have just fallen asleep and have entered the deep non-REM sleep, then when you get awakened, the disorientation and grogginess are particularly pronounced. Yet another factor that may play a role is your circadian rhythm and body temperature. During sleep, body temperature normally drops. If awakened while your temperature is down, you will take much longer to become fully alert.

The brain restores its energy reserves during sleep. Brain levels of adenosine increase during sleep. A common nucleoside consisting of adenine and a ribose sugar and a known inhibitor of the central nervous system, adenosine attaches to cell membrane receptors and enhances sleepiness. Research has shown that caffeine binds to the same receptors that adenosine does, counteracting the effect of adenosine. A study examined sleep inertia in 28 normal healthy adult males between the ages of 21 and 47. All were free of tobacco, alcohol, medications, and caffeine for two weeks prior to the 10-day test. Subjects had three normal days to adapt and do baseline testing. Then began 88 hours of wakefulness broken only by seven two-hour naps every 12 hours. Someone loudly calling their name roused the subjects and immediately began doing neurobehavioral performance tests on them. At regular intervals some of the men swallowed caffeine tablets to keep their blood caffeine levels between three and four milligrams per liter, while others received a placebo. Neither subjects nor researchers knew who was getting what. Results showed clearly that those on a sustained low dose of caffeine did not suffer from sleep inertia nearly as much as those on the placebo.

> *How long does it take you to clear the sleep cobwebs out of your brain after waking up?*

Lord, that I was able to come to full alert without caffeine means that You have other ways of counteracting the nightly tide of adenosine. What a blessing to get a full night's sleep and awake again refreshed.

The Celestial Database

I have blotted out, like a thick cloud, your transgressions, and like a cloud, your sins. Return to Me, for I have redeemed you. Isa. 44:22, NKJV.

From my first dawning of understanding about the book of life, I could see it in my mind's eye. What with all the people, it had to be a big ledger with a beautiful black leather cover stamped in gold. I imagined that the pages were a high-quality vellum or parchment made from the finest leather. And the ink? Why, India ink, of course—that has been in use from antiquity, and it is a fine ink. I could see the names and records written in a fine hand using a quill pen made from the bright-white flight feather of a majestic swan. Daily the heavenly scribes accurately recorded both names and deeds.

But now, with my understanding of how many people there are in the world and the sheer volume of names and deeds to record, and knowing that God must have access to the latest and best database technology (no doubt some device that we have not even thought of yet), I simply sit and wonder what the book of life actually does look like. Does my entry on the "page" have a picture of me, perhaps 3-D movie clips, in color, with seven-speaker surround sound? Or better yet, a full-color, detailed documentary of my life, beginning to end would be more like it. Somehow, whatever the media used, the record is there in the celestial archives— complete, fully backed up, incredibly secure, and safe from power failures or . . . or . . .

But . . . but . . . WAIT! My daily record contains much that I am not proud of. I don't want it to be seen by anyone. The details are ugly, detestable things. I certainly don't want that stuff in my documentary. Please, Lord, is there any way for my documentary to be sanitized? Do You happen to have a celestial delete button that will overwrite the expunged portions? And, Lord, what about the backup disks? Have they been erased too? Oh, slow down, my fast-beating heart. Slow down and listen to what my Savior is saying to me in today's text. Can it be true? I hear Him declaring, "David, my child, don't be afraid. Your sins are forgiven. All of them. They are no more. There is no record of them anywhere in the universe. I have blotted out your transgressions. Return to Me, for I have redeemed you."

O wonder of wonders, here is good news. This is grace. This is love that will not let me go. I don't deserve it. Thank You, Jesus.

Judgment

For God will bring every work into judgment, including every secret thing, whether good or evil. Eccl. 12:14, NKJV.

One of the hardest lessons that I have had to learn in life is that life simply isn't fair. Bad things happen to good people. Good things happen to bad people. And horrible, unspeakable things strike the smallest, the weakest, and the most innocent of children. Now, what did they do to deserve that? It simply isn't fair!

Especially when directed toward babies and young children, outright killing, sexual abuse, physical abuse, and emotional abuse and neglect have to be one of the strongest evidences that evil exists on our planet. What greater demonstration could there be that Satan hates what God loves and is using every means possible to kill, maim, and emotionally scar for life, perpetuating the pain and destruction generation after generation? My father's heart rises up in righteous indignation and cries out, Enough! Stop!

I have known hardworking, kind, honest, God-fearing people who have lived in a community for decades. Unselfishly serving others, they give of their time and resources to build the community. Then disaster strikes. A flood, a tornado, perhaps a landslide. At first they feel blessed to escape with their lives and praise God for watching over them. But they are now destitute and have to start over again. Is this fair?

I have known many families who have lost babies, children, mothers, fathers, to the ravages of fast-growing cancer. Far too young to die. In the prime of life. Snuffed out. Unfair!

I have known too many dedicated workers in institutions, businesses, or other organizations who have been fired by an over-controlling, insecure, incompetent boss. All avenues of grievance were thoroughly checked out and carefully followed to prevent a miscarriage of justice—but to no avail. Such persons lost their job, their dignity, their self-worth, and their pension. Occasionally the bosses get promoted, showing that good things do happen to bad people, too. Life is not fair.

The evil one chuckles with satisfaction. Everywhere there is pain, suffering, and discord. But in the end: the judgment. The playing field will be level. Every work will be judged—fairly.

What a great day for justice that will be, Lord. Remind me again not to take revenge on those who mistreat me. Bless You, my righteous judge and great avenger.

Cape Buffalo

My little children, these things I write to you, so that you may not sin. And if anyone sins, we have an Advocate with the Father, Jesus Christ the righteous. 1 John 2:1, NKJV.

B attle at Kruger," a fascinating home video clip found on the Internet, shows a small herd of Cape buffalo plodding along a riverbank during the heat of the day. From the photographer's vantage point across the river, a small pride of lions, perhaps a half dozen, lie resting on the same side of the river as the buffalo, but 100 yards or so downwind of the advancing herd. A magnificent bull confidently leads the way, his head with its massive boss of horns swinging gently. The lions crouch, watching the oncoming leaders, then inch forward. The buffalo are oblivious to the lions until the bull stops, sniffs the air, tosses his head a few times, and peers intently ahead. He now sees the danger and wheels about, dust flying, and bolts back in the direction he came from. The others follow, perhaps uncertain of the danger.

The lions close the gap in a few bounds. Ignoring all adults, one lion swipes the feet out from under a calf. The two tumble down the bank into the river. Three other lions quickly join the lead attacker and try to pull the calf out of the water and up the steep embankment. The calf struggles to get into the water, its only safety. More lions pounce. But now the drama heightens when a couple large crocodiles join the splashing struggle. In short order it's a tug of war, several lions trying to haul the calf up the steep, slippery bank, two big crocs tugging the other way, aided by gravity and their home turf, the river. About to lose their lunch, the lions mount a huge effort and get the calf up on the bank and continue suffocating and strangling the youngster.

As the video continues, I watch in amazement as the buffalo herd recovers its courage, tightens rank, and returns to help the calf. Heads down, exposing nothing but sharp horns, they challenge the lions. Some of the big cats now lose their courage by being so outnumbered and surrounded, their backs to the river. Others cling to their downed prey. One of the bulls hooks a lion with a head toss, and it goes flying. Little by little, the tide turns. As the buffalo move in closer, the calf struggles to its feet. Buffalo keep pushing the lions back till they have to let go. Breaking the last hold, the calf returns to the safety of the herd, seemingly unhurt. The buffalo stay on the attack till they have chased the lions off into the scrub. All had seemed lost for the helpless calf, but superior strength won in the end.

My Father and my God, thank You for returning to rescue me. You are able to intercede for me no matter how much the odds seem stacked against me.

Brilliant White, Ultra White, Stark White

He who overcomes shall be clothed in white garments, and I will not blot out his name from the Book of Life; but I will confess his name before My Father and before His angels. Rev. 3:5, NKJV.

We like our paper whiter than white. To do that, we've learned to coat it with minerals and clay or add compounds that make it reflect a whiter light. Such coatings, though, are heavy and costly. What about our teeth? Can they ever be too white? We get whiter teeth by bleaching them.

White stands out. Especially when a small white beetle showed up crawling around on white fungi. It was most unusual for a beetle to be white. Most are black, brown, or tan, and a few are even colorful. But this one was white. Named *Cyphochilus*, the tiny insect was not just light but really white. Dazzling white because of tiny scales covering its surface. Scientists were at first curious, then ecstatic, because maybe, just maybe, they could learn a new way to make white. The lead scientist on the project, Peter Vukusic, studied the scales with electron microscopy and other tools and learned that the scales were a photonic solid. What that meant was that incoming light was processed by the ultrathin random pattern of the scale's structure in a way uniquely designed to give off all wavelengths of light. As you may have learned in school, reflecting all wavelengths results in white. Now scientists are working to mimic this photonic solid to make whiter paper that is both lighter and thinner. Numerous other applications are also on the way.

White is of course a symbol of purity. It represents clean and spotless.

White is of course a symbol of purity. It represents clean and spotless, the way we want our clothes. A laundry detergent is often advertised as the one that will get a brighter white. But according to Mark's account of the Transfiguration, Jesus' clothes "became shining, exceedingly white, like snow, such as no launderer on earth can whiten them" (Mark 9:3, NKJV).

Since the fields are already white for harvest (John 4:35) I look forward to seeing my Lord returning for me seated on a white cloud (Rev. 14:14), being handed that white stone with my new name on it (Rev. 2:17), having the robe put around me that was made white in the blood of the lamb (Rev. 7:14), and seeing the One with hair white like wool (Rev. 1:14), who rides on a white horse (Rev. 6:2) and sits on a great white throne (Rev. 20:11).

Lord of whitest whites, purge me with hyssop, wash me so that I can be clean, whiter than snow. I long to be holy and without blemish.

July 26

Incurable Defects

And He said to me, "My grace is sufficient for you, for My strength is made perfect in weakness." Therefore most gladly I will rather boast in my infirmities, that the power of Christ may rest upon me. 2 Cor. 12:9, NKJV.

It's an important family of nearly 20 genes located right in the middle of chromosome 17. And for most of us, thankfully, the genes labeled Wnt work as they are supposed to. What they do is code for signaling proteins that control how cells specialize as they develop and how the cells know which end is which. Many details in the crucial programming of early embryonic development depend on the Wnt genes doing their complex signaling job correctly.

In rare cases, when both copies of one or more of the Wnt genes are defective, a baby might come to full term and be born with tetra-amelia syndrome. The most noticeable defect is that such babies have no arms and no legs—they are the lucky and least-affected ones. Most babies don't survive because of other serious medical defects of malformed body parts.

One survivor of tetra-amelia syndrome is Nick Vujicic, who currently lives in California. Though short of stature, Nick stands tall in my eyes. Perhaps you have heard about "No Arms, No Legs, No Worries" Nick Vujicic (pronounced voy-chich).

As you can only imagine, seeing their firstborn son for the first time without arms and legs devastated Nick's young parents. Growing up in Brisbane, Australia, was especially difficult, because the laws didn't allow him to attend regular schools. When the laws changed, he got what he wanted, but was teased mercilessly and bullied by other children to the point of wanting to take his own life. Thankfully, God pulled him through that dark valley of depression. Nick learned that he wasn't the only one with an incurable defect. He finally stopped begging God to grow him arms and legs and decided to commit what he had to His glory. So with just two toes on the nub of what should be a left foot, he started learning seemingly impossible skills such as answering the phone, shaving, getting a drink of water, or brushing his teeth. Nick went on to graduate from college with a double major in accounting and financial planning and is now a world-famous motivational speaker, writer, and even award-winning movie star. His talks have moved millions of people to stop feeling sorry for themselves. With Nick's inspiration, they now thank God for what they have and get to work, using their gifts for Him.

Lord, forgive me for my self-focus and self-pity. Help me to maximize the gifts You have given me to Your honor and glory.

Mosquitoes

He said to them, "An enemy has done this." Matt. 13:28, NKJV.

The Latin word for fly is *musca*. In Spanish the diminutive form of the word becomes mosquito, literally "small fly." With two wings and a pair of club-shaped halters for aerodynamic balance, the mosquito does qualify as a genuine fly, and a particularly troublesome one. To be fair, only the females of some species feed on warm-blooded animals and only when about to lay eggs. They require certain blood proteins to make viable eggs.

With more than 3,500 species of mosquitoes worldwide and more than 175 different kinds in the United States alone, there is certainly plenty of variety to keep entomologists and parasitologists busy for generations to come. Mosquitoes have attracted much attention because they transmit several serious diseases, including malaria. One genus of mosquito dubbed *Anopheles* includes 460 species, with less than a quarter of them even being able to carry malaria and less than half of those actually involved in transmitting the various species of *Plasmodium*, the disease-causing parasite. Even with relatively few species of *Anopheles* doing the dirty work, approximately 650,000 people die each year of malaria. Besides the deaths, millions more suffer debilitating illness and other complications.

Most mosquitoes, like butterflies, feed on plant nectars.

In addition to malaria, blood-sucking mosquitoes of various species also transmit serious viral diseases such as dengue fever, yellow fever, and West Nile virus. The Centers for Disease Control in Atlanta estimates that as many as 100 million people contract dengue fever each year. So, does the mosquito have any redeeming value? Wouldn't this world be a better place if mosquitos went extinct? To answer this question, it helps to remember that only a tiny fraction of mosquitoes give all the rest a bad name. Most mosquitoes, like butterflies, feed on plant nectars. In fact, one entire genus of large mosquitoes with 95 species is incapable of feeding on blood, and their larvae actually prey on other mosquito larvae. They are allies in our fight against mosquito borne diseases. The constituents of mosquito saliva are proving valuable in medical research. Researcher have isolated more than a dozen proteins from it, including some that depress or block our immune system, prevent blood from clotting, or aid in digesting sugars and proteins. More user-friendly anticoagulants may now be developed based on mosquito saliva models. The mosquito is an amazing insect—a wonderful creation of God. It is unfortunate that one who hates God's people has hijacked a few of them.

Lord, until You come, what would You like me to do to relieve the suffering, sickness, and death from this malicious malarial malware of the devil?

Doubling DNA

How great are His signs, and how mighty His wonders! His kingdom is an everlasting kingdom, and His dominion is from generation to generation. Dan. 4:3, NKJV.

This morning I watched a video clip posted on YouTube called "DNA Replication." A segment from a PBS series entitled "DNA: The Secret of Life," the video shows how one strand of DNA gets precisely copied to make two identical strands of the information storage molecule.

I watch in amazement as the original strand of DNA being copied, a long thin double helix of a molecule, spins or rotates on its axis, as it rapidly feeds in from the left and two new strands materialize out to the right. This structurally accurate animation shows a globular protein (an enzyme) unzipping the double helix, converting the double strand into two single strands much like a zipper separates the two sides of your jacket. Another enzyme called DNA polymerase adds nucleotides, the building blocks of DNA known as bases, onto one of the two strands, carefully matching each base with a specific complimentary base at the rate of about 50 nucleotides per second. The other strand also gets nucleotides matched up to the bases on its strand at the same speed, but because of the orderly way that DNA polymerase works, it constructs this strand in the opposite direction. Several other enzymes also step up to make what scientists call a lagging strand.

Watch this video if you get an opportunity. You too will be fascinated by the machine-like operation of all these tiny enzymes. And the speed! The work they do goes at a frantic pace. But each operation is precise and orderly, producing two identical copies of a DNA double helix.

The circular chromosome of bacterial DNA replicates even faster as about 500 nucleotides per second get matched to their complimentary bases as the sugar phosphate backbone forms. When it is stretched out, the DNA in a bacterium measures only a tiny fraction of an inch in comparison to what we have. Each cell in our body has about two yards of DNA, segmented into 46 chromosomes and tightly packaged to fit comfortably into the tiny sphere of the nucleus only a few micrometers in diameter. That two yards of DNA contains about 3 billion base pairs (6 billion nucleotides), all having to be copied every time a cell divides. Some cells, such as those of our skin, divide every day or so. The immensity of this job and the accuracy with which it gets done encourages me to pay attention to detail and to do my work well.

Lord, how great and marvelous are Your works! I stand in awe with my hand over my mouth. I have nothing to say except to praise You.

July 29

Packaging DNA

He does great things past finding out, yes, wonders without number. Job 9:10, NKJV.

The two yards of double helix thread of DNA found in each cell of your body is carefully organized and tightly packed so that it all fits neatly into an approximate sphere one thousandth the size of the period at the end of this sentence. But not all of it can or should be packed. Significant portions of the DNA need to remain unpacked and available to provide the code for making proteins, ribosomes, transfer RNA, and other structures. So just how is DNA packaged into your 46 chromosomes per cell?

Centuries before we were even aware of DNA we were winding sewing thread on spools to keep it from getting tangled. But long before that, the Creator of life used a variation on this same theme. First, the thin two-nanometer thread of DNA (that's right, only two billionths of a meter in diameter) is wrapped twice and only twice around a "spool" made up of eight globular proteins called histones, actually double sets of four different kinds of histones. At fairly close intervals, the thread of DNA repeats the double wrap around another double set. Again and again this repeats, making the thin thread look more like a tiny beaded chain with a total diameter of 10 nanometers. Scientists call the beads on this chain nucleosomes. What happens next is truly astounding. The beaded chain is coiled neatly, six nucleosomes per turn, making a tightly compact structure referred to as the 30-nanometer fiber.

But we are not done yet. The tightly wrapped 30-nanometer fiber attaches itself at intervals to a sturdy protein scaffolding, leaving many precise loops of the compact fiber that hang from the protein. It is like stapling a very long piece of yarn to a wooden dowel in such a way that six- to eight-inch loops are neatly fastened every one eighth of an inch all around the dowel, making it look like a fuzzy stick. This whole fuzzy structure is almost 10 times wider than the 30-nanometer fiber. The long fuzzy stick analogy breaks down here, however, because the structure is pliable.

The 300-nanometer protein scaffolding now wraps in tight spirals, producing a structure almost three times wider. This is the familiar chromosome replicated before cell division. When an individual DNA molecule was put into a solution with the needed components, the wrapping to the chromosome level took place in seconds. Such order lets me know that God has things under control far more than I know or can understand.

Thank You, Lord. You take care of every little thing so that I can focus my energy on loving others and proclaiming the good news of salvation.

The Blind See

As He went out of Jericho with His disciples and a great multitude, blind Bartimaeus, the son of Timaeus, sat by the road begging. Mark 10:46, NKJV.

What do Corey Haas and blind Bartimaeus have in common? As you might guess, they were both blind, and then, after the miracle, both could see. Corey's blindness resulted from a congenital defect called Leber congenital amaurosis (LCA). We don't know what led to the blindness in the son of Timaeus, but it may have been one of literally dozens of genetic defects similar to Corey's ailment.

A missing gene causes LCA, a form of retinitis pigmentosa. Two parents, each of whom lack that gene in one of their two sets of chromosomes, have a one in four chance of having a child missing the gene too. Even as a baby, Corey was unable to see, so he didn't reach for things in front of his face or track objects as they went by. I can only imagine how hard that must have been for his parents, Nancy and Ethan. Dealing with the pain of having a blind child is a huge challenge. But before Corey turned 10, he participated in a clinical trial on one of his two affected eyes in which researchers injected a virus carrying a working copy of the gene into retinal cells. The virus delivered the gene to the cells. The missing gene was incorporated into Corey's DNA. Within a few days the gene was working to produce a protein with the code name RPE65, a protein that Corey's retina had never made before but which is a vital link in the multistep light-detecting pathway required in order to see properly. To be able to determine the molecular-level cause of blindness, and then figure out an effective treatment to cure the various forms of LCA is truly a miracle of medicine and molecular biology.

When I learned about LCA, one of the dozens of genetic defects that cause blindness (not to mention other causes such as accidents and injury and congenital defects), it made me realize yet again that Jesus wasn't just a poor itinerant preacher wandering through Palestine doing good. Jesus, the God/man, had an intimate minute by minute connection with his Father, a connection available to each of us. Together Jesus and God diagnosed and fixed the problem. I would like to think that He at least touched the beggar's eyes. But the record doesn't say that. "Go your way; your faith has made you well" (verse 52, NKJV).

Lord, I too believe. I too want to see. Open my eyes to perceive You as You really are.

July 31

Aseptic Technique

Whoever touches those things shall be unclean. Lev. 15:27, NKJV.

I t takes a great deal of knowledge and repeated practice for a person to be able to successfully accomplish a task in a sterile field without accidentally introducing contamination. Working aseptically is a skill that I teach students when experimenting with bacteria or when doing animal or plant tissue culture. In any modern operating room aseptic technique is vital to prevent contamination and potential infection following surgery.

You see, bacteria, fungal spores, viruses, and other potential contaminants lurk on surfaces everywhere around us, on our skin, and even in us. New findings on bacteria suggest that each of us is a walking microcosm of organisms with more bacteria on and in each of us than the total number of people that have ever lived on earth. Fortunately, though, God has given us several lines of defense that keep the bacteria in check.

"Sterile" or "asepsis" are words that simply mean the absence of life on a surface or in an operating field.

"Sterile" or "asepsis" are words that simply mean the absence of life on a surface or in an operating field. The presence of living bacteria is called sepsis. With sepsis, bacteria are present, quickly growing, proliferating, secreting toxins, causing destruction and eventually pus and putrefaction. Students quickly discover that there is no such thing as almost sterile or nearly aseptic. Sterility is not a matter of degree. Rather, it is an all-or-none situation. My students must also learn to become hyperaware of all their movements. They must know at all times what is dirty (septic) and what is clean (aseptic) and never let the two touch each other. That strict law of not allowing dirty to touch clean must stay in place, because any time dirty touches clean, the clean becomes dirty. In the tissue culture lab or on the operating table, when clean touches dirty, the dirty never becomes clean—rather the clean almost always becomes dirty.

My favorite exception to this rule is a story that Luke tells near the end of chapter 8. The woman pressing through the crowd was ritually unclean because of constant bleeding that had plagued her for years. Hebrew law was strict. If you bleed or have other stuff running out of you, you're unclean. And you must not touch anybody, because you will make them unclean too. Can you imagine her isolation and loneliness, the absence of human touch? She broke the law by reaching out to touch the hem of Jesus' garment. And in this beautiful story of faith, the purity of Jesus instantly cleanses the woman. The exception happened. The unclean touched the clean and became clean too. Oh, how I long for that to happen to me!

Jesus, I need Your cleansing touch. Purify my heart just now.

August 1

Asparagus

God saw all that he had made, and it was very good. Gen. 1:31, NIV.

I am well aware that not all people enjoy eating asparagus, but I really do. I eagerly look forward to the first asparagus shoots spearing up through the cool spring garden soil at the rate of seven or eight inches per day when air temperatures finally warm up. A native plant of European coastal communities, asparagus plants do well in cool salty soils. In fact, they can tolerate greater salinity than can most other garden plants.

Nutritionists rave about the exceptionally high nutrient values found in "spare grass," as people sometimes call it. Low in saturated fat and very low in both cholesterol and sodium, asparagus is a wonderful source of pantothenic acid, magnesium, calcium, zinc, and selenium. It is an even better source of dietary fiber and protein, especially the amino acid asparagine (notice the similar spelling). Asparagus also has higher than usual levels of vitamins A, C, E, K, thiamin, riboflavin, niacin, vitamin B6, and folate, as well as the minerals iron, phosphorus, potassium, copper, and manganese.

When eaten fresh or lightly steamed or roasted in the oven for four or five minutes after being marinated in olive oil, garlic, and balsamic vinegar, asparagus has a flavor that is to die for. It doesn't taste like anything else. Some say it has a nutty flavor. Others describe it as like artichoke or eggplant. But I still say that nothing comes close.

Unlike any other garden vegetables, asparagus spears are harvested as shoots when they first come out of the ground, before the buds can develop into leaves or branches. I guess the nearest comparison is eating bamboo shoots. Asparagus shoots are much smaller and far more tender than any bamboo shoots, however.

Like garlic and onions, asparagus is a member of the lily family. Jesus may have eaten it, since it has been known and cultivated since antiquity. One Egyptian carving dated to 3000 B.C. shows asparagus. An early Roman recipe that existed hundreds of years before Christ gives a recipe for cooking asparagus.

I thank God for the gift of asparagus. It is a special accent, a love note from the Creator.

Lord, You have created so many amazing plants to give us variety and enjoyment in our diet. Thank You especially for the delights of asparagus.

August 2
Cock-a-doodle-do

Peter replied, "Man, I don't know what you're talking about!" Just as he was speaking, the rooster crowed. Luke 22:60, NIV.

I remember that it was very early in the morning when we awakened to hear three or four roosters each trying to outdo the other in loud raucous cock-a-doodle-do's just outside our bedroom window. The night before when we had arrived on an overnight visit, all the chickens must have been in the coop. Peace and quiet prevailed, but that was then. There was no sleeping through this early-morning cacophony.

Just why does a rooster crow, anyway? The best guess is that, much like other birds, chickens are highly territorial. Males are often the most active in marking and defending territory. The way birds accomplish that is with their calls, displays, and aggressive behavior—in this case, crowing, strutting or waltzing, and cock fighting. Those who keep chickens know that roosters often crow at any time of the day or night. How much and when usually depends on the genetic variety of poultry, its personal temperament, and the quality of its nest box. Roosters that have light-tight and sound-insulated nest boxes reportedly get disturbed less frequently during the night, which contributes to a much quieter nighttime neighborhood and happier neighbors. It is almost impossible to ignore the persistent crowing of a rooster in the wee hours of dawn as it gets into its early-morning routine of proclaiming to the world who's boss. Sound intensities of more than 80 decibels have been reported for a crowing rooster. That is about the same as the traffic sounds you would hear if you lived right beside a busy roadway.

When Peter heard the rooster crow for the third time that early Friday morning so long ago, he wasn't thinking, Territorial birds, or That bird sure is loud. The cock-a-doodle-do loudly announced his greatest failure. Just hours before, he had assured Jesus of his commitment and devotion. But the denials were still on his lips when the rooster's reminder confronted him with the reality of what he had done. Jesus looked directly at him. I simply can't imagine how heartbroken Peter was. Come to think of it, my total failure rate is far higher than Peter's. Does it break my heart when I realize that I have failed to follow through on promises that I have made to my Lord and Savior? When I rely on my own ability, my own strength, my own determination, my own foolish self-confidence, I am sure to fail. But when I accept Jesus' invitation to watch and pray, His strength provides the victory.

Lord, give me the gift of repentance. Assure me with Your look of love. May I be held tightly in Your forgiving embrace.

August 3
Troglodytes troglodytes

Before the rooster crows, you will deny Me three times.
Matt. 26:34, NKJV.

I t is a tiny bird measuring only three or four inches from head to tail and weighing less than a half ounce (about 10 grams). Don't be fooled by its small size, though, because when you hear its voice it sounds as if it comes from a far larger body. In fact, scientists who study birdcalls say that ounce for ounce, the winter wren puts out 10 times the sound of a farmyard rooster at full-throated crow. After yesterday's reading, we know a bit more about the power of the rooster's crow.

The winter wren is the only one of its kind found living energetically on all the continents except for Antarctica and Australia. The word "troglodyte" means "cave dweller," earning the name for the way that the tiny bird pops in and out of small cavities in rocks and trees. Biologists recognized more than 30 subspecies of the winter wren until the American Ornithologists' Union voted (in 2010) to split the winter wren species into three separate species. It might take a little while for all the ornithologists to get onboard with this name change. Meanwhile the diminutive winter wren continues singing its song with unrivaled power and gusto worldwide, unconcerned and uncaring about the controversy swirling about who it really is.

Come to think of it, had the apostle Peter connected himself to a spiritual power source on that darkest of Thursday nights or even early Friday morning, he may well have been able to resist the devil's temptations to raise his voice in disowning Jesus. Hadn't Jesus warned him that he would deny Him? Jesus invited Peter to "watch and pray so that you will not fall into temptation. The spirit is willing, but the flesh is weak" (Mark 14:38, NIV). Without that power, Peter simply didn't have it in him to resist temptation. So as he warmed himself by the fire and those around began asking if he wasn't with Jesus, he failed miserably. "I don't know this man you're talking about." Oh, how we need the power that comes through prayer. With that power we might be able to raise our voice to proclaim our Lord as sovereign.

Lord Jesus, be my strength to resist temptation. Raise Your mighty voice so that the mountains shake and all nature listens. Connect my heart to Yours this moment in prayer.

The Skinny on Fat Mice

Punishing the children for the sin of the parents to the third and fourth generation of those who hate me, but showing love to a thousand generations of those who love me and keep my commandments. Ex. 20:5, 6, NIV.

Though some of us may not know what genes actually are, we do realize that they determine traits such as how tall we will be or what color eyes we will have. The fact is that we have become so used to finding a gene controlling each and every inherited trait that when scientists discovered a trait that lingered for several generations after the gene itself had disappeared, they were astonished.

What is the story? When fed high-fat diets, normal research mice get obese, just as people do. What's more, they develop the same problems overweight people develop—cardiovascular diseases, high blood pressure, and even insulin resistance. But the presence of a single gene that shows up in some mice allows them to eat a high-fat diet and still stay sleek and trim, unlike their pudgy partners. Best of all, they are disease-free. When you put the slim mouse gene into a fat mouse, the fat mouse—you guessed it—gets slim too. Something about that gene helps them metabolize glucose quicker, and they shed the weight and, as a result, are much healthier. The real head-scratcher came about when the fat mice turned slim went on to have pups. Though this next generation were kept on high-fat foods, they stayed slim too even though the gene had disappeared. The gene was not passed on. And for the next few generations the mice, even without the gene, remained thin even on high-fat diets.

This is one example of a phenomenon now known as epigenetics—something that seems hinted at in the first commandment and repeated several more times in the Pentateuch (Ex. 34:7; Num. 14:18; Deut. 5:9), in which God talks about punishing children for the sins of their parents as far out as the fourth generation. But then, He surrounds each statement of punishment with words of love. God assures us that He has mercy and love as far out as a thousand generations of those who "love me and keep my commandments." "The Lord, . . . slow to anger, abounding in love . . . and forgiving wickedness, rebellion, and sin" (Ex. 34:6, 7, NIV).

The way we live has natural consequences that can last for generations through mysterious epigenetic effects. Knowing that what I do can affect my grandchildren and even my great-grandchildren makes me stop and do some careful and deep thinking. Thus I choose to carefully follow principles of healthful living and obedience to God's law.

Lord, I choose to obey Your Word today.

Magnesium

See to it, brothers and sisters, that none of you has a sinful, unbelieving heart that turns away from the living God. Heb. 3:12, NIV.

I am fascinated by magnesium, an element commonly found in the earth's crust and dissolved in seawater. One atom of magnesium forms the central atom in the "head" of a chlorophyll molecule, the beautiful emerald green pigment that absorbs the energy of light to power photosynthesis in plants. Hundreds of biochemical reactions in living cells require magnesium. As one of the most abundant elements in the human body, most of it occurs in bone, with the rest found in other tissues and organs, and a small percentage circulating in the bloodstream. Life as we know it would not exist without it.

Though it is all around us as ions and combined with other elements, magnesium does not exist naturally as a free metal. But when the metal is chemically produced, it's a bright silver substance that burns with an intense white light, which is why it is used in flares, in fireworks, and in the past as a fine tangle of wire in photographic flashbulbs. Even before the invention of flashbulbs in the 1920s, photographers ignited finely divided magnesium metal powder (called flash powder) in a metal pan to light up their subjects. Because flash powder could easily start fires, they had to use it with great care.

Perhaps you have had trick candles on your birthday cake. The stubborn candles refuse to be extinguished. Again and again they resume burning as if by magic. Watch carefully, however, and you will discover

Distrusting God is a sin. Hasn't He proved again and again that He is faithful?

their secret. You will see tiny explosions in the wick as flecks of magnesium powder flare up frequently. Try to blow the candle out, and residual heat in the wick will ignite another fleck of magnesium powder, which reignites the plume of hot wax vapor still rising from the candle.

Come to think of it, unbelief is much like a trick candle in that you have to keep attacking it to extinguish the flame for good. Distrusting God is a sin. Hasn't He proved again and again that He is faithful? The very existence of magnesium and its myriad marvelous functions in living systems as well as its abundance in nuts, soybeans, cereal grains, and other common foods is yet another testament to God's faithfulness to us. Bend every effort to attack unbelief and extinguish it for good.

Lord, may I be overwhelmed by the many evidences of Your faithfulness so that unbelief is uprooted, killed for good, and totally extinguished.

The Plasma Membrane

And this is eternal life, that they may know you, the only true God, and Jesus Christ whom You have sent. John 17:3, NKJV.

I magine a house without walls or a horse without its hide. Could you get along without your skin? Could a bottle of water exist without the container or a package without its box or bag? Right about now you must be asking, "Are you nuts?"

The answer is No, I am just thinking about the critical importance of barriers that keep the insides in and the outsides out. In every case such barriers mark crucial boundaries, separating the inside from the outside, preventing the passage of some things while allowing others to cross. In life we are used to boundaries such as bank vaults, fences, walls, partitions, drawers, organizers, duffel bags, and sandwich bags—well, you get the idea. Containers, packaging, and partitioning are critically important.

So why is it that the gossamer-thin cell membrane (also known as the plasma membrane) gets so little respect or appreciation for its vital structure and function? When one even bothers to give it a passing thought, many regard it as just a simple bag that keeps the good stuff in and the bad stuff out. OK, it does that. But it does so much more. Membrane structure is relatively simple, consisting of two layers of phospholipid with a collection of various proteins embedded or floating in the phospholipid matrix with some of the lipids and proteins decorated with additional glycoproteins, glycolipids, and cell adhesion molecules (simple, huh?). It is rather delicate in that it tears easily. And it is incredibly dynamic in that its component parts are in constant molecular motion. One wonders why it doesn't fly apart or collapse into a gooey mess. In its normal water matrix, with its pumps running and the energy supply of the cell functioning, the integrity of a plasma membrane is really quite good. The important point is that without a functioning cell membrane, no work would be done or energy processed, and thus no photosynthesis or cellular respiration—no life. Life as we know it depends on the integrity of this simple boundary.

While mature mammalian red blood cells get along fine for three or four months without a nucleus, mitochondria, ribosomes, Golgi bodies, or endoplasmic reticulum, they won't last a second without their plasma membrane.

In the spiritual realm, is there anything that rises to the same level of importance?

Lord God, if knowing You is all-important for eternal life, why do I spend so little time truly seeking and getting to know You?

Squeezed Into the Mold

And do not be conformed to this world, but be transformed by the renewing of your mind, that you may prove what is that good and acceptable and perfect will of God. Rom. 12:2, NKJV.

The long steep hike up to the Walcott Quarry on Mount Field isn't for beginners. Once you're there, the breathtaking panorama across Kicking Horse Valley to Mount Stephen with Emerald Lake far below makes it all worth the trip. The unexpected bonus is the millions of fossils under your feet. You can't walk much without stepping on fossils. Visitors must now contract for a guide from the Burgess Shale Geoscience Foundation, and Parks Canada constantly monitors and protects the site since it is in the Yoho National Park. Years ago when I visited, one could pick up a rock and crack it open to reveal a fossil impression. We found trilobites, worms, corals, and marine arthropods in abundance. The most common species in the quarry is *Marrella splendens*, a small arthropod-like critter that has been particularly difficult to pin down because it's not like anything that we know today.

Paleontologists (those who study the remains of ancient life) tell us that a number of different kinds of fossil preservation methods provide us evidence of life in the past. Some animals left footprints, burrows, or impressions of their bodies in the mud or sand. In those cases, we have no remains of the organism itself, just marks in the sediment showing that they have been there. Another type of fossil is the actual remains of the animal or plant. It may consist of bones or teeth. Sometimes individual molecules of the animal or plant have been replaced, one by one, until the entire specimen is mineralized (turned to rock), such as happened to petrified forest trees and many nautiloids. Occasionally we find a hollow cavity or impression where the critter lay in the sediment over time before disappearing. If the organism-shaped cavity then fills with sediment, it becomes a cast. Casts always take the shape of the mold. Their detail naturally depends on the quality of the external mold that they were made in and the grain size of the casting material.

Paul uses this mold and casting imagery in Romans 12:2, in which he gives us a strong negative command. Do not be conformed to this world, he tells us. Don't allow the world to squeeze you into its mold. Stop letting the world system shape you. Instead, he says, be transformed.

Lord, renew my mind so that I can know Your good and perfect will for my life.

Christ Is Divine

The Word became flesh and made his dwelling among us. We have seen his glory, the glory of the one and only Son, who came from the Father, full of grace and truth. John 1:14, NIV.

Just how divinity became human flesh and blood so that He could live among us as a human and yet show us the Father's glory is such a huge mystery that I have a hard time getting my mind around it. But here is what I know for sure. Without question He surely is divine because:

- only God could heal and soften my stony, stubborn, prideful, selfish heart.
- only God could break my chains of slavery to sin, fear, and selfishness.
- only God could lift me out of the confusion of my sins and give me clarity.
- only God could continue to draw me with love even as I struggle to distance myself from Him.
- only God could quiet my struggles with His assurance of acceptance and love.
- only God could say, "Your sins are forgiven, be of good cheer, enter into my joy."
- only God could turn my pain and deep sorrow into laughter.
- only God could enter my desolate heart and bring me indescribable joy.
- only God could account for the created magnificence of this universe.
- only God could keep all the promises that He has made.
- only God could satisfy the deep hunger of my soul with the banquet of His grace.
- only God could be such a kind and gentle master to this grateful servant.
- only God could be such a good friend, brother, and constant companion to me.
- only God could be such a loving husband to my lonely soul—no spouse could be as true.
- only God could be a loving and tender Savior to this wretched sinner.
- only God could be a soothing comforter to this mourner.
- only God could surround my grinding poverty with His extravagant wealth.
- only God could heal my feverish sickness with vibrant health.
- only God could light the oppressive darkness with His shining brilliance.
- only God could enter the chaos of my life and give it order and beauty.
- only God could be so devoid of retribution and wrath in light of my perpetual disobedience.
- only God could be so full of grace throughout my lifetime of spurning His love.

Glory to God in the highest. Great things He hath done.

August 9

Catbird

Everyone who is called by my name, whom I created for my glory, whom I formed and made Isa. 43:7, NIV.

How would you like to wear the name of your most feared enemy? It seems rather odd, doesn't it—to be given the name of what eats you?

At the sound of a bird strike, our two cats instantly come to full alert. With many well-occupied bird feeders just outside our picture windows, an occasional bird mistakes the reflection of the sky in the glass for a clear flying lane and will crash into the window. Sometimes the collision is lethal, but more often the bird veers at the last second, hitting the sheet glass in a glancing blow that leaves the bird woozy on the deck for a few minutes. Our cats' senses are particularly well tuned to that sound announcing an easy snack if they happen to be outside. Which brings me to this question: "Since most cats will eat any bird they can get a claw into, why would anyone name some 'catbirds'?"

Around the world there live at least seven different species called catbirds, and they all get their name from the catlike mewing sounds that are part of their vocal repertoire. On the African continent one catbird is closely related to warblers, while on the Australian and Asian continents the catbirds are more like bowerbirds. The catbirds of the Americas resemble mockingbirds and are closely related to the Caribbean thrasher. The only common element the seven songbirds share is their plaintive mewing call evocative of a lost cat, thus earning the creatures the name of their nemesis, the cat.

Birds, chipmunks, snails, liverworts—none of them have a choice of names, because, from the first, we humans, *Homo sapiens*, have been the designated namers. Plants and animals are what we call them, and many go by multiple regional names, which is why scientists have agreed upon written conventions that they follow carefully to establish a Latin scientific name for each organism.

Come to think of it, I didn't get any say in what my name was going to be either. The family I was born into determined my surname, and my parents decided my given names. But what gives me great joy and fills my heart with wonder and awe is that my Creator and Lord is willing to call me by His name. So today, proudly wearing the name of my most ardent friend, I will choose to live up to my new given name.

Lord Jesus, do I dare put Your name tag on today? I need Your moment-by-moment help so that I won't dishonor Your name.

Light Bearer

How you are fallen from heaven, O Lucifer, son of the morning!
Isa. 14:12, NKJV.

M y family and I were weekend camping with friends in the Great Smoky Mountains along the border of North Carolina and Tennessee. The sun had gone down in a glorious display of color, and it was now well into the Sabbath hours on a dark Friday night. I left the cheery flickering of the campfire to locate more downed wood for our dying fire when I saw them: small, perfectly shaped mushroom caps with delicate straight gills on the underside, slender stalks, and all glowing a relatively bright fluorescent green in the darkness of a moist woods. I had never seen this phenomenon before. What beautiful and unexpected light bearers.

Returning to camp, I got the others to come see the glow-in-the-dark mushrooms. The campfire forgotten, with flashlights off, we began to explore a bit more and came up with many more glow-in-the-dark critters—more mushrooms, bits of decaying wood permeated with bioluminescent fungal mycelia as well as glowworms, and even an occasional firefly. With eyes adapted to the dark, we even found fungal hyphae glowing down in the leaf litter.

Many life-forms emit light in a range of wavelengths that we can see. Most notable of course are the fireflies and glowworms that we are all familiar with. Other insects and their larval forms, some spider types, and some segmented worms produce visible light too. Then there are the fungi that we found that dark Friday night. Botanists say about 25 phyla or divisions of fungi are bioluminescent. If you venture deep into the constant pitch-black darkness of the ocean, most of its inhabitants make their own light.

Colors of light produced by living creatures include the yellow-green of fireflies and glowworms to a more bluish green of some of the fungi and lots of marine forms. Some fungi and some marine fish put out a reddish light. Others actually do infrared. Various light-bearing life-forms turn their lights on to locate, attract, and catch food, to confuse predators, to lure predators that will in turn eat something that is just about to eat the light bearer, to find mates, to light the way, and to communicate with other light bearers. Some actually turn their light on to hide. In the ocean a critter looks dark from below, so some squid apparently illuminate their underside to match the brightness above so that they can't be seen as easily.

I had never seen this phenomenon before. What beautiful and unexpected light bearers.

Lucifer must have been a magnificent light bearer until his fall.

Lord, Lucifer's fall suggests that I must stay connected to You, the light of the world, if I am to live in the light.

August 11

Gecko's Feet

Hold me up, and I shall be safe. Ps. 119:117, NKJV.

A side from the little bright-eyed, green, smart-talking model on Geico Insurance advertisements, have you ever seen a real live gecko? If you have spent much time in the tropics, you probably have. Geckos are small lizards known for their ability to scamper up a glass surface and run at top speed across a smooth ceiling. Until recently it was a mystery how they could do that.

Many of the couple thousand species of geckos live in houses, and their occupants often welcome them because the lizards are experts at catching and eating insects, even mosquitoes. If you watch a Geico Insurance ad, besides talking with an Australian accent, one of the really cute things the model does is blink its eyes. Most real geckos don't have movable eyelids—just a clear membrane coving their eyes. So you will occasionally see a real gecko licking its own eyes to get them clean. But then that wouldn't look good on TV, would it?

Several scientific experiments have focused on the interesting ridged design of the gecko's foot pads in an attempt to learn how they get such sure footing on smooth surfaces. The feet are not sticky. They don't have hooks on them. Experimental results show that each gecko foot has nearly 500,000 tiny hair-like structures called setae, a Latin word for bristle or fine hair. Each gecko setae is only one tenth the diameter of a human hair. But here is where it really gets interesting, for each seta terminates in 100 to 1,000 even smaller flattened hairs called spatulae, which are only .2 to .5 micrometers wide. When ultrasmall structures such as this come close to any other structure, weak attractive forces called van der Waals interactions draw them together. Scientists have now isolated a single seta and have determined that it holds 10 times the weight that they had previously estimated based on whole animal studies, and that van der Waals forces are indeed the secret to the gecko's excellent footing. With five toes on each of its four feet, geckos have 20 toes. Calculations show that, with just one toe in contact with a surface, a gecko can support eight times its own body weight.

Material scientists have now devised nanofibers that mimic the ultrafine hairs on the gecko's foot. Using such nanofibers, robots are climbing glass walls, and high-tech Band-Aids coated with such fibers now hold wounds together for healing. They are not sticky, so they don't hurt when they come off.

Masterful Designer, because You created systems such as gecko toes, surely You have ways to hold me and never let me go. Enfold Your arms around me so that I cannot fall.

Shark Skin

And the fish of the sea will explain to you. Job 12:8, NKJV.

J udging from the popularity of Shark Week on the Discovery Channel, everybody must love sharks—especially the great white sharks that patrol the coastal areas of every major ocean. Since its debut in 1988, Shark Week has been an annual summer highlight of the Discovery Channel programming, and great whites seem to attract the major attention since they are so big (about 20 feet long) and so quick. As of this writing, the channel has aired 161 episodes. Shark Week gets Discovery Channel's highest ratings, with more than 20 million viewers.

Sharks are just one of several types of cartilaginous fish, with more than 400 species ranging from dwarf six-inch sharks up to the whale shark that measures about 40 feet long. What impresses me most overall is their exceptionally streamlined bodies, which allow them to slip through the water with the greatest of ease. Look at the beauty and symmetry of a gray reef shark, for example. The snout starts out with a slim flattened appearance, like the tip end of a wedge that widens as you move back toward the eyes and wider yet where the pectoral fins connect to the body. Pectoral fins look like the sweptback wings of a jet fighter. The widest top-to-bottom thickness is at the first dorsal fin. As you keep going front to back, the body now slims down but is flattened side to side rather than top to bottom, as at the front end. As you pass the second dorsal fin, the body is now clearly flattened side to side.

More important, for ease of swimming through water, shark skin is covered with near-microscopic dermal denticles that give the skin the feeling of rough sandpaper. When seen in the electron microscope, each denticle or scale looks like a miniature stealth bomber on a short stalk. Denticles give the shark a huge advantage in swimming, because the denticles prevent water turbulence and drag, allowing sharks to swim much faster with less energy compared to animals their size with smooth skin. An added advantage of this rough, microscopically complex surface is that barnacles can't attach. Neither can bacteria nor algae. As a result, shark skin remains free of parasites. The shark stays clean and goes fast in the water.

Bioengineers have learned to mimic the microscopic winged denticles making up the rough shark skin. Speedo now offers what they call the fastskin swimsuits, used by most swimmers in recent Olympics. An added bonus is the bacteria-resistant surfaces based on this design and now used in hospitals.

Lord of all sharks, we have learned so much by studying these amazing creatures. Indeed, their grandeur clearly illustrates Your creative genius.

Flamboyant Cuttlefish

Who is like You, O Lord, among the gods? Who is like You, glorious in holiness, fearful in praises, doing wonders? Ex. 15:11, NKJV.

The first time I saw a movie clip of a flamboyant cuttlefish I could not believe my eyes. First, a cuttlefish isn't really a fish at all—it's more like an octopus with really short tentacles. Octopi, squid, nautilus, and cuttlefish are all a type of mollusk in the class Cephalopoda (meaning head foot, because they have feet on their head). It gets better. Cephalopods have a powerful water jet that they power up when they need to escape quickly. When they blast off, they leave behind a cloud of black ink to make it appear as if their body just went poof and disappeared. But wait, it gets even more weird. The flamboyant cuttlefish is only three inches (eight centimeters) long, and its name is what it is: flamboyant.

This little guy looks like a neon sign competition in Las Vegas. YouTube archives several good video clips. The best as of this writing are "Underwater Studios" and "Cuttlefish Catching Dinner." What you will see are clips of this small critter looking—at times—very dull and camouflaged and "walking" along the sandy seafloor using two of its eight tentacles and two underbelly skin flaps. Two tentacles extend straight ahead, two feel the sand for food, and two wave above the body. When the flamboyant catches dinner, it looks almost as if a slow-motion frog tongue comes out (actually a modified tentacle with suckers on the end) and suddenly grabs shrimp, small fish, worms, and other crustaceans. Because this small cuttlefish is extremely poisonous, it advertises that fact so that it will not be mistaken for some tasty morsel by a hungry fish or other cephalopod. And what an advertisement. Here is where the "flamboyant" part of the cuttlefish name comes in. Within seconds the dull-brown, mottled, sandy color turns to a pale white with a bright-yellow fringe or skirt pulsating and waving around the edge of the underbelly. The upper tentacles turn white, with a brilliant pink on the ends. The lower tentacles can go to black and yellow. The most amazing part is a rhythmic flow of dark diagonal chevron stripes that seem to sweep the cuttlefish body from front to back. Pink, yellow, and red stripes show up frequently too. The best analogy that I can come up with would be a gaudy Las Vegas sign with moving lights and changing colors.

Creator of the flamboyant cuttlefish, yes, I know that it is just one of Your many wonders. You are a truly amazing Creator God. There is none like You.

August 14

Goodpasture

Their tongue is a deadly arrow; it speaks deceitfully. With their mouths they all speak cordially to their neighbors, but in their hearts they set traps for them. Jer. 9:8, NIV.

Ernest William Goodpasture was a young pathologist serving the United States Navy during World War I when he treated a young soldier suspected of having the flu but was coughing up blood and had an inflammation of the small blood vessels in the kidney, causing him to have blood in the urine, too. His condition turned out to be much more than the flu and is now known as Goodpasture's syndrome, a disease in which the body's immune system is overactive, attacking its own cells and tissues.

Medical science now classifies nearly 30 conditions as autoimmune diseases, including such common examples as type 1 diabetes, multiple sclerosis, psoriasis, and rheumatoid arthritis, as well as the rarely encountered Goodpasture's syndrome and Wegener's granulomatosis. Whatever the case, the more we learn about some diseases, the more of them get recognized as autoimmune disorders.

Autoimmune diseases have to be considered as one of the world's worst forms of high treason. When something designed to protect the body goes on the rampage and starts attacking perfectly good and well-operating systems, what can be done? When your foot hurts because you have a rock in your shoe and neither the doctor nor you know about the rock, solutions might include bandages and ointments and staying off the sore foot. Similarly, first lines of treatment for autoimmune diseases usually focus on relieving symptoms. When those treatments don't produce lasting results, good pathologists such as Goodpasture seek the actual cause and try to get the rock out of the shoe, so to speak. For really severe cases, immunosuppressive drugs such as cyclosporine or tacrolimus (another product of a fungus) might help for a little while, but they are not selective in their target. The whole immune system gets suppressed, so that the whole body is susceptible to real infections and cancers that the immune system would normally deal with. The point is that there is no "cure" for autoimmune diseases. Gene therapy is still undergoing clinical trials. At the moment all we can do is seek relief through stopgap measures.

Fortunately, there is a cure for sin. We must invite the Holy Spirit and allow Him to heal our heart of selfishness, filling it with God's love.

Lord, please, create in me a clean heart and renew a right spirit within me. Come in and dwell within my mind.

The Nitrogen Cycle

Return to the Lord your God, for He is gracious and merciful, slow to anger, and of great kindness; and He relents from doing harm.
Joel 2:13, NKJV.

Those of you who grow plants know that they need lots of nitrogen. The most common component of plant fertilizers is, in fact, nitrate (NO_3^-) or ammonium (NH_4^+) ions—both usable forms of nitrogen for plants. The bag of fertilizer in your garage will have three numbers on it. The first number represents how much nitrogen is in the bag. The other two numbers report the phosphorus and potassium contents, respectively. Since nitrogen is an important part of all amino acids (building blocks of proteins), all nucleic acids (which provide energy and genetic information), and most plant pigments involved in photosynthesis, plants need lots of nitrogen.

With a concentration of about 78 percent, nitrogen gas comprises the largest component of earth's atmosphere. It has at least a million times more nitrogen than found in all living systems combined. The bad news is that all of this atmospheric nitrogen consists of molecules of N_2—that is, two atoms of nitrogen bound tightly together by three strong covalent bonds. Unfortunately, it takes a great deal of energy to break the triple bond. Because plants can't use molecular nitrogen, it has to be transformed into one of the two absorbable ions.

In His wisdom the Creator provided several ways to convert atmospheric molecular nitrogen into usable forms that will dissolve in water so that plant roots can absorb it. The immense energy of lightning easily breaks nitrogen's triple bond, turning it into nitrates and washing it down in the rain of a good thunderstorm. Have you noticed how green your lawn is after a noisy one rolls through? Even more important, many types of bacteria convert nitrogen from one form to another. Nitrogen-fixing bacteria convert atmospheric nitrogen to the more plant-friendly ammonium ion (though it is toxic in large concentrations). Ammonifying bacteria also create the ammonium ion, but they do it by decomposition of plant and animal matter. Check out the smell of your compost pile. It reeks of ammonia. Fortunately, another family of bacteria called nitrifying bacteria transforms the ammonium ion to the safer nitrates. (As you might guess, the cycles are actually more complicated than what I am describing.) Finally, denitrifying bacteria close the loop by returning nitrates back to the enormous pool of nitrogen in the atmosphere. What a brilliant Creator we serve.

Lord of magnificent cycles, there are times I leave You. Don't ever let me go. Please bring me around again and again for more instruction.

Two-edged Sword

The sword of the Spirit, which is the word of God. Eph. 6:17, NIV.

The superbly crafted sword felt smooth and solid in my hands as I slowly drew it out of its protective scabbard. Wow! Whoever made this beauty certainly knew what they were doing. Perfection of heft and balance, flawless artisanship down to the smallest detail. Bright reflections of morning light danced off the highly polished steel, dazzling my eyes. It was an exceptional work of art. With great care I gingerly fingered the razor-sharp edges, imagining how easily they would slice through bone and gristle. But being a man of peace, I can't imagine actually using it to do harm, though I can easily see why it's a weapon of choice for hand-to-hand combat. Fortunately, it's just a showpiece now, for ceremony and display.

But wait, there is a war going on—an intense and deadly serious one. The struggle is for my allegiance and yours. Will you turn your back on Jesus? Unless you maintain a fine sword and keep honing that edge daily, you are in mortal danger of compromising faith. Your personal sword of truth is your most important weapon for fighting this spiritual warfare. Knowing and living the truth found in God's Word is crucial. To survive the conflict, we must treasure truth.

> *But wait, there is a war going on—an intense and deadly serious one. The struggle is for my allegiance and yours.*

Does anybody really care about truth anymore? In a study by Common Sense Media, nearly a quarter of middle and high school students surveyed didn't think that having notes on their cell phone was really cheating. One third had actually used them during tests and quizzes. Cheating on marriage vows, tax returns, government contracts, and the like seems to be the norm. Scientists falsify data. Employees steal from their employers. Shoplifting is epidemic and raises the cost of goods for all of us. The theft of music and software attracts much media attention. This world is awash in lies, deceit, and dishonesty—all started by that first lie in the garden: "You will not certainly die" (Gen. 3:4, NIV).

Jesus came to liberate us from the tyranny of lies and the distrust and broken relationships that result. God's Word, the sword of the spirit, is truth. He said, "I am the way, the truth, and the life. No one comes to the Father except through Me" (John 14:6, NKJV). Christians should love the truth, study the truth, memorize the truth, and live the truth. Without a sharp sword, we won't be able to separate truth from error.

Lord, has my sword lost its edge from inattention? Help me to keep it sharp through spending time in Your Word.

August 17

Constant Companion

And surely I am with you always, to the very end of the age.
Matt. 28:20, NIV.

Wait a minute. Did Jesus really mean what He said? "I am with you always." Could He have possibly said it more clearly? The simple declarative sentence tells who ("I" = Jesus speaking), when ("am" = a statement of fact, right now), what ("with you"), and for how long ("always"—there is never a time that isn't part of always). Read it again. This isn't a promise of "I will be with you always" sometime in the future. Nor is it a conditional promise: If you do this, then I will be with you always. It is simply a statement of fact now. "I am with you always." And if you read the rest of what Jesus said in that same breath, you learn that He reemphasizes or clarifies just how long His promise lasts. "I am with you always, to the very end of the age." Did you get that—to the very end. But wait, there is more. The preface to the statement is an assurance of the reality of the words that follow: "And surely." It is as if Jesus is saying, "You can believe this. Don't forget this. Pay attention now." The opening lets you know that what is to follow is important.

So the question I have to ask myself is: "Why don't I live my life, 24/7, as if I actually believe this?" Every day I do things that show my wife, my family, my community, that I simply don't believe.

For example, there was the time—lots of times, actually—that I was rude to my wife. I wouldn't have done that if my neighbor had been with me. And my Constant Companion has specifically asked me to love this woman—for Him. So why was I rude while He was there watching? What about the time I watched a movie on TV that I wouldn't want my own children seeing? Would I have kept watching knowing that Jesus was there at my side? Or when I didn't respond to the obvious need of the ashen-faced homeless guy who crossed my path? Would Jesus have made eye contact with him, looking on him with compassion, and at least touched him tenderly instead of avoiding eye contact and passing him by, as I did? One time I went out to eat with friends and simply ate way too much and spent all the time talking about my latest vacation and all the features of my next dream purchase. I can't believe that I didn't even introduce the Constant Companion at my side and talk about what He has done in my life. See what I mean? My life is evidence that I don't believe that simplest of declarative statements: "I am with you always."

Constant Companion, forgive me for my unbelief. I choose now to believe. Help my unbelief.

War

Fight the good fight of the faith. 1 Tim. 6:12, NIV.

L et's watch a column of army ants for a few minutes. We are in the jungles of Panama in Central America. It's early morning, and the ants are already on the move. Fanning out from an enormous mass of ants, almost a million of them camped at the base of a tree, columns of ants head out in different directions, searching for breakfast. Looks like rush hour on a busy freeway, with no lanes and no right side to drive on. Ants run back and forth along the column. Looking closer, we see a weird collection of several different kinds of ants. Tiny harmless-looking ants and huge wicked-looking ones with long curved sword-like pincers, as well as midsize ants. Not only different sizes, but even different colors. Some are tan. Others are darker brown. All scurrying along as if they had no time to lose.

At the head of the column, ants spread across the ground. An ant bumps into a grasshopper as if blind. Truth is, these ants have no eyes, so they are totally blind, navigating only by feel and chemical trails laid down by scouts. The surprised hopper springs up into the air but accidentally drops right into the center of the fan. Other ants attack it in a second, swarming over its body. The smallest in the swarm grab on, stinging it to death. Larger ants use scissor-like mandibles to cut pieces of legs and wings off even before it stops struggling. The biggest ants with sword-like pincers are guards, watching out for the safety of others. Workers gather around to pick up the dismembered grasshopper pieces. Working together, they haul fragments many times larger than they are. It looks like hard work, but they manage to get their loads back to feed the ant mass that is already on the move.

Army ants are always alert and aggressively attack any creature that isn't a member of their colony—size doesn't matter. Biting and stinging, they will not give up. Every day the colony clears all the insects, spiders, scorpions, and other arthropods and animals out of about 200 yards of forest. An army with a mission, they resolutely stay on task.

Do we take a casual attitude in spiritual warfare? Perhaps we need to go to the army ants of Central and South America and consider their ways.

Lord of the highest heaven, thank You for equipping me for this spiritual warfare. Tune my heart to the intensity of the battle.

The Magical Setup

Walk as children of light (for the fruit of the Spirit is in all goodness, righteousness, and truth). Eph. 5:8, 9, NKJV.

It was a rare event. I have seen it happen only a few times in the decades that I have been teaching biology and setting up lab experiments to explore the miracle of photosynthesis. What my students and I were looking at with such amazement was a fine stream of tiny bubbles pouring out of the razor cut end of a water plant stem. The plant was totally immersed in water with the cut end of the stem pointing up, the leaves down. The bubbles poured out of the cut stem in a single file—about three or four of them per second. Of course, since it was an experiment involving photosynthesis, we had a bright light shining on the plant, making it easy to see the bubbles. When we snapped the light off, the bubbles stopped instantly. When we switched the light back on, the bubbles instantly resumed. By turning the light on and off several times in rapid succession, we could shape little pulses of bubbles to trace the form of a dashed line from the end of the stem to the surface. By flipping the light on and off with the right rhythm, a creative student could spell out the dot-dash-dot of Morse code. It was much like firing tracers out of a machine gun, except that the bubble bullets traveled slower.

The only connection between the thought-controlled finger on the light switch and the highly responsive plant pouring out tiny uniform units of oxygen (the bubbles) was the bright light that flowed between. By moving the light back just a few inches, the bubbles emerged slightly slower. Moving a hand across the light would produce a visible pulse of slower emerging bubbles. As I said, it was one of those magical lab setups that happen only once in a while. Presumably, the razor sliced the stem in such a way that all the oxygen production of the plant got funneled to one point on the stem. More often, we see the submerged piece of plant exuding little bubbles of oxygen all over, like sweat beading up all over the entire shoot.

In case you are interested, Google "photosynthesis elodea" to get instructions and pictures so that you can arrange your own experiment. Maybe your setup will duplicate this if you are lucky. Photosynthesis is carbon dioxide and water reacting in the presence of chlorophyll and light to make sugar and oxygen. As you can tell from the description of this experiment, photosynthesis is highly responsive to light.

Lord, today may I be as responsive to Your gospel light in welcoming the Spirit to produce His fruit in me.

Stuff

By faith we understand that the worlds were framed by the word of God, so that the things which are seen were not made of things which are visible. Heb. 11:3, NKJV.

Could it be that stuff loves me? Or maybe it's the other way around. Whatever the case, stuff has a tendency to accumulate in my living spaces. Must be that way with others too. Recent tornadoes ripped open homes in Tuscaloosa, Birmingham, Pratt City, Ringgold, Apison, and hundreds of other large cities and small quiet communities, exposing people's stuff for all to see. Photos in the news and on the Internet show unbelievable and bizarre jumbles of stuff. One house that wasn't blown completely away had portions of the roof and walls neatly removed, exposing a spiral staircase leading to the sky. In the dining room, now with a view, a vase of flowers sat undisturbed on an heirloom table under a cloudless sky, a wrecked washing machine from down the street at the head of the table. One op-ed piece in the New York Times said: "When I think of tornadoes, I think of the winds, how ruthlessly they break apart our homes, get at what's inside, what we touch and think we have hold of, scattering it across the sky, 60 miles, 100 miles, until it floats down like harmless snow, rain, shooting stars unrecognizable to the ones who find it."

"When I think of tornadoes, I think of the winds, how ruthlessly they break apart our homes, get at what's inside, what we touch and think we have hold of, scattering it across the sky, 60 miles, 100 miles, until it floats down like harmless snow, rain, shooting stars unrecognizable to the ones who find it."

Physicists with a passion for peering inside the atom use a somewhat similar strategy. Instead of waiting for ferocious winds to expose what's inside, they smash small particles of stuff into each other, sometimes blowing them apart, to learn what's inside. To do this, they first have to build an enormous ring of magnetic and electronic equipment. Designed to get particles (electrons, protons, or their antiparticles) moving unbelievably fast, the equipment produces two tightly confined and controlled streams aimed right at each other. It is somewhat analogous to shooting bullets at each other to see what happens when they collide head-on. The laboratory is filled with particle and energy detectors carefully positioned where the two streams of particles intersect, and capable of reporting the debris coming out of the collisions. By producing enormous numbers of atomic smashups and carefully analyzing the stuff that results, physicists are getting some idea about what atomic particles consist of. Somewhat akin to analyzing trash strewn about by a tornado, their task perhaps involves more predictability.

Lord, when I consider the stuff that You made, the work of Your fingers, who am I that You even care about me? Teach me how much You care. Teach me how to love.

August 21

Myrrh

Then they gave Him wine mingled with myrrh to drink, but He did not take it. Mark 15:23. NKJV.

Plants that live in hot dry areas are known as xerophytes ("xero" = dry, "phyte" = plant). In order to survive with very little water, xerophytes have numerous adaptations, including tiny, light-colored, either hairy or waxy leaves that they may drop frequently to avoid water loss, well-developed root systems to mine the water deep in the rocky soil, succulent stems to store what little water there is, plenty of armor in the form of spines, thorns, or prickles to prevent animals from eating them, and finally a variety of potent chemicals to make them taste bad.

So if I were to take you to the arid Arabian peninsula or just across the Red Sea to Somalia or the desert scrub lowlands of neighboring Ethiopia, we would not be surprised to find a low scraggly, thorny tree eking out an existence on the thin rocky soils. Technically, the tree we seek is placed in the genus *Commiphora*. *Commiphora* trees have short, fat, succulent trunks with a flaky, papery bark exceptionally good at retaining water. When the tree does have leaves, they are very small and covered with dense waxy scales well suited for reducing wind flow across the stomata and subsequent evaporation of water from leaf surfaces. And the tree is incredibly thorny. For centuries, people who live in the area take advantage of the fact that when they cut the tree bark, a lightly scented, translucent, gummy resin will ooze out and congeal on the surface. As that resin dries, it hardens into little amorphous blobs with a delightful spicy scent. People have highly prized the resin of the *Commiphora myrrha* tree and its related species for making incense, embalming products, perfumes, and medications. At times myrrh has cost more than its weight in gold. God gave Moses a recipe for the holy anointing oil that included myrrh (Ex. 30:23).

From the tortured existence of desert living comes this precious product of *Commiphora myrrha* as a preservative, an aromatic perfume for lovers, a sacred incense, or a crucial ingredient in anointing oil. This gives me hope as I go through my dark nights of private pain. When life feels shriveled and dry, devoid of meaning, or when I am slashed and cut by critics, I think of the myrrh tree and remember the beauty that it exudes in its distress. God is the one who makes everything beautiful in its time.

Lord, I submit my life to Your care and keeping, knowing that through Your intervention the greatest beauty emerges from the greatest suffering. May Your will be done.

239

August 22

Fruit of the Vine

I will not drink of this fruit of the vine from now on until that day when I drink it new with you in My Father's kingdom. Matt. 26:29, NKJV.

E ach year about this time we enjoy going to a local vineyard to pick fresh, vine-ripened grapes. The enormous clusters of colorful berries with their grayish frosty coating of wax are gorgeous. On a warm summer day the aroma of ripe grapes is heady. The neat rows of well-dressed vines marching up and over the hill are each heavy with their own kind and color of grapes. The many hundreds of varieties have beautiful-sounding names: Concord, Jupiter, Valencia, Steuben, Marquis, Venus, Seneca, Sultana, Catawba—the list goes on and on. Each summer when we come into the vineyard, we sample grapes here and there to see what we like best. Maybe our taste has changed from last year. Perhaps they have some new varieties. For several summers now we have returned to Steuben grapes as our favorite. We enjoy the color and the rich, sweet flavor that has a spicy and fruity twang to it.

With sturdy scissors supplied by the grower, it takes us only a few minutes to snip off the long heavy clusters, enough to fill several grocery bags full of grapes. Now we have time to dawdle and sample some more and enjoy the view across the rich farmland.

Our practice is to store the grapes just as picked in the fridge until ready to fix and eat. What we do then is take just enough for that one meal, wash, pick the clusters over to remove any spoiled grapes, then press them through a conical strainer into glasses and ahhhhh, enjoy.

The taste and aroma of fresh-pressed juice has no comparison. Before we learned what happens to fresh-pressed grape juice after just a few hours in the fridge, we used to set the extra juice aside for later use. But what a disappointment. After just a few hours the color and flavor goes flat. To be sure, it is still good juice. But after you have experienced the fresh-squeezed variety, there simply is no comparison.

I wonder. Could simple "fresh made" have been the major factor in the quality of the drink that came out of the six stone jars at the wedding feast in Cana? But probably the big difference was the fact that the Creator made Edenic-quality juice, unspoiled by centuries of blight, disease, and genetic weakness. Now, that is a glass of grape juice that I want to try.

Matchless Creator, are You really waiting till we get home before You will drink another glass of grape juice? Oh, how I long to celebrate with You at the marriage banquet.

Connections

But the fruit of the Spirit is love, joy, peace, forbearance, kindness, goodness, faithfulness, gentleness and self-control. Against such there is no law. Gal. 5:22, 23, NIV.

H ow does every photosynthetic cell in every leaf get supplied so it can do photosynthesis and help the plant bear fruit? The beauty is in the details of connectivity.

Choose a leaf and look closely at its veins. Big primary veins are easy to spot as they divide into smaller secondary veins that continue to branch into smaller and smaller ones until the network is so extensive that every single microscopic leaf cell is very close to, if not right next to, at least one microscopic vein. Veins consist of long pipe-like conducting cells of various types. One family of hollow pipe-like cells called tracheids and vessels primarily function as conduits bringing water and minerals from distant roots to the photosynthetic cells. Without such raw materials, photosynthesis won't happen. Another conduit cell type called sieve tubes carry away the products of photosynthesis, most often sugars, amino acids, and the like. Without free-flowing outbound routes, photosynthesis would be an exercise in futility. So having both inbound and outbound conduits is crucial to a leaf.

But wait. Think how the plant has to create those inbound and outbound routes from scratch every season. The entire factory layout of every leaf from photosynthetic cells to inbound and outbound routes develops in miniature in the winter bud sometime during late summer or fall. Carefully dissect a winter bud to find all the leaves for next spring neatly but very tightly packaged. Give a winter bud appropriate resources and conditions, and it will break dormancy, expand, and open into a full flush of leaves.

But how do all the pipes in the short-lived transient leaf join the more enduring vascular network of the stem and the branches? Making those connections is crucial. It works this way. Big bundles of vascular tissue in the main stem branch out into each smaller division of the stems. And at each leaf, an even smaller bundle (or group of bundles) of vascular tissue leaves the stem and branches, entering the leaf itself. This is the all-important leaf trace. All the leaf's primary veins originate from it and split out to supply the factory cells and gather products from them. Break that leaf trace, or sever the pathway at any point, and the in and out traffic stops. The leaf or the branch dies. Details of connectivity are all-important in the Christian life, too. Broken connections yield fruitless lives.

Lord, remind me again that fruit doesn't come from me or my effort. You are the vine.

My Jesus, I Love You

Do you love me? John 21:16, NKJV.

My Jesus, have I told You yet today that I love You? I do indeed love You very much. Though I have never seen the kindness in Your twinkling eyes or Your nail-scarred hands; though I have never heard the melodious timber of Your voice; and though I have never felt the soft warmth of Your touch, I still love You. I am certain that You already know why, but do You mind if I tell You anyway?

First and foremost, I love You because each moment of every day You give me the awesome gift of life. The magical, mysterious, meaningful gift of life. Every beat of my heart, every breath I inhale, every blink of my eye and step in my walk, is a special gift from You. Every thought in my head, song in my heart, and word on my lips wells up as a blessing from You. Oh, unfathomable Creator, because of You, I am—and I love You for that reason.

Another reason I love You is that You voluntarily removed Your royal robes, took off Your crown, laid down Your scepter, and left the command center of the universe to come to our dark sin-sick world as a helpless baby. You showed us how to live life in the Spirit, under the guidance of our Father. Then You suffered a death You did not deserve, in order to pay the penalty for my sins, giving me life that I don't deserve. There is no way to repay You for this. The magnitude of the gift takes my breath away. I can only bow in humility and say Thank You and I love You, and I will obey You and follow You.

I love You because You have freed me from slavery. Your greatest enemy once held me captive. It was as though I was in a dark and cold prison of fear, doubt, and pain: fearful about what my future would hold, fearful that I could never be good enough, fearful that I would never amount to anything, fearful because, when I tried to be "good," I kept failing again and again. Sometimes it was hard to see what the point was. Occasionally I got around to a casual reading of Your Word, but would question whether or not You even existed. Where were You? Did You care about me? The grinding pain of broken relationships was a constant tormentor. Little by little my feet turned toward You. Now I feed daily on Your words of encouragement, instruction, comfort, and love.

My Jesus, I love You more every day. Teach me to love the people around me as You want me to love them—for You.

Vile, Unclean, Wretched, Despicable, and Detestable

(Job) Behold, I am vile. Job 40:4, NKJV. (Isaiah) Woe is me, for I am undone! Because I am a man of unclean lips. Isa. 6:5, NKJV. (Paul) O wretched man that I am! Who will deliver me from this body of death? Rom. 7:24, NKJV.

D o I hear you saying that you have to clean up your life before you can come to Jesus? That He surely won't like you because of the filth that clings to you? Because the nauseating stench of death is on you, you have to scrub yourself clean first? Then you will come to Jesus? Is that what I hear you saying?

Listen closely, my friend. The reaction is always the same. Job, Isaiah, Paul—they all had the same feeling. You can hear it in their choking sobs. "I am so vile, so wretched, so unclean." Each, in his own way, had an encounter with the Holy. Awesome and glorious, it let them recognize their true state. If those Bible greats saw themselves as unclean and wretched, doesn't it put us all in the same boat? So if you are seeing your own condition as vile beyond description, that is good news indeed. Because, now, at last, you can come to Jesus just as you are. Jesus longs for you to turn to Him just as you are. In fact, He is the shower that we step into for cleansing. Jesus is the physician that heals our blindness with His healing touch, the one who puts His robe of righteousness around our shoulders. He is the one that looks lovingly into our eyes and says, "Welcome home. I am glad that you have come. It is good that you have returned to Me."

All that we do to try to make ourselves presentable to the Holy is utterly useless—it simply doesn't work?

Don't you see that all that we do to try to make ourselves presentable to the Holy is utterly useless—it simply doesn't work? Every saint who has ever lived had the same terrible realization of just how despicable they really were. Shame wrung confession from their lips. With your realization you also join them in seeing the light of this good news. Jesus did not come to call the righteous, but the vile, unclean, despicable sinners like you and me. He did not die for the righteous but for sinners.

O Jesus, I confess my sins. I am a sinner. I am vile. Wash me, that I may be clean.

Job's Hedge

Have you not put a hedge around him and his household and everything he has? You have blessed the work of his hands, so that his flocks and herds are spread throughout the land. Job 1:10, NIV.

After surviving the bloody landing on the beaches of Normandy on D-Day, Allied troops worked their way inland only to find themselves fighting their way through Norman hedgerows dating back to the Roman Empire. To keep livestock penned in, the Normans had built mounds of earth and planted dense hedges on top. Branches of the developing hawthorn and blackthorn trees interlaced to make impenetrable walls of vegetation. Other trees and plants grew up through these rows, strengthening them. With overarching trees, the roads between the fields seemed like tunnels. The hedgerows became death traps for many an Allied platoon. Besides getting lost in the maze of hedges, troops had great difficulty communicating with their units. Even the Sherman tanks were vulnerable as their unarmored underbellies became exposed to antitank fire as they tried to go up and over the earthworks.

While visiting in the United Kingdom a few years back, I did some rambling on footpaths through the British countryside. I found the trails between neighboring hedgerows to be places of great beauty and wonderful ecological diversity. Here, too, hawthorns with their long sharp spines and English holly with their prickly leaves provided wonderful security and privacy for small plots of land. Originally planted to mark property lines and keep cattle restricted, these hedges are now succumbing to development and larger agricultural operations.

If you need privacy or security, a green living hedge might work much better than a fence. First research the kinds of plants that grow best locally. Determine if they keep their leaves year-round. Depending on your needs, check out shade and drought-tolerant varieties.

Hedges are effective. Which is why God put a hedge around Job and his family and why, even today, He places a hedge around those that He loves to shield them from the forces of evil. Have you experienced the blessings of the hedge? Have you prayed for that kind of divine protection?

Lord, I know that the prickly hedge that effectively protects my property is only a metaphor of the ring of angels that excel in strength and surround us at Your command. You sent angels to encircle Lot and Elisha. I too pray for that kind of divine protection. Hedge me in today.

Pop Culture

For all that is in the world—the lust of the flesh, the lust of the eyes, and the pride of life—is not of the Father but is of the world. 1 John 2:16, NKJV.

What is the essence of pop culture, anyway? How should we best define it, and how should we relate to it as disciples of Christ? Is it best for me to ignore it, to try to change it, or to join it if I decide that I can't beat it? Isn't pop culture what's hot in contrast to what's not? But doesn't that change from day to day, if not from moment to moment? What effect is pop culture having on me, on my children, on my church, and on my community?

Pop culture exists in all societies and through all time. It is the concepts and values that most of the people consider good and acceptable. Without the media and Hollywood, ideas of the past were diffuse, were localized, and tended to ebb and flow through society slowly. But now modern digital media effectively unifies, concentrates, and focuses the furious ebb and flow in both time and space, giving pop culture great national if not global impact. Like shooting stars, cultural icons explode on the screen for their 15 minutes of fame before fading from view. Mainstream media hype the worry of the day while endlessly parading and glamorizing should-be shame. In collusion with so-called news outlets, the entertainment industries mission is to establish pop culture at the level of the lowest common denominator, trivializing all that is great about spirituality, sexuality, history, art, science, tragedy, and death. Pop culture now idolizes things, people, activities, and ideas. Changing from week to week, any idea or belief can become somebody's truth and equivalent to all other truths.

So, to get back to answering the opening question, the essence of pop culture is who or what gets center stage. In postmodern America and those portions of the world that emulate it, center stage is occupied by things, people, activities, and ideas. We worship things we buy or want to buy, superstars or cultural idols, exotic vacations or extreme sports, and our own concepts and ideas. Such worship is idolatry and detestable to God. After King Manasseh led his people into the deepest idolatry, his son Josiah ruled, repented, and brought his people back to worship of the one and only true God. Read in 2 Chronicles 34 how Josiah discouraged idolatry and encouraged worship of the true God. Like Elijah, he placed a clear choice before the people.

Lord, You gave Yourself to deliver me from this present evil age. Let Your gift not be in vain.

Trumpet

Praise Him with the sound of the trumpet; praise Him with the lute and harp! Ps. 150:3, NKJV.

I used to play a trumpet. Sadly, I was never very good at it. But I still love listening to those who can make music on the trumpet. Some trumpet greats include Louis Armstrong, Al Hirt, Miles Davis, Dizzy Gillespie, Wynton Marsalis, Maurice André, Herb Alpert, Carolyn Jackson, Maynard Ferguson, Doc Severinsen, Harry James, and Dave Tasa. When one uses a trumpet to praise God, the music is especially glorious.

A ram's horn with the small end drilled and shaped to a shallow cup works as a simple "trumpet" known as a shofar. Used for centuries as a call to assemble for sacrifice and worship, to signify special high days, or even at times to panic the enemy during war, the shofar has a long and colorful history. Later the shofar seems to have been used to make music. The Hebrew word sho-v-far designates the ram's horn instrument and is often translated into the English word "trumpet." Another Hebrew word also translated as "trumpets" (plural) is cha-tzo-vtz-rot. These trumpets are first mentioned in Numbers 10, in which God commanded Moses to make two silver trumpets for summoning the congregation and setting the camp in motion. Scholars debate what the instruments may have looked like. Certainly they were not like the trumpets we have today. In all likelihood, they were perhaps more similar to the ram's horn shofar.

Today, thanks to a long history of technological development, much better quality music comes from a brass or silver trumpet. The physics of sounds made by buzzing the lips with the correct embouchure (mouth/lip and muscle position) and then putting the buzz to the mouthpiece so that it can be amplified, sweetened, and controlled by the pipes, valves, and bell is a complicated process indeed. Musicians have written volumes trying to explain it in order to refine the music. But as always, the quality of the music is a marriage of carefully designed and crafted instruments to highly trained and skilled musicians. For example, I still have a fine trumpet. But little of what one could describe as music ever emerges from its silver bell.

The word "trumpet" appears in 111 New King James Version passages. What I long to hear is that sound of the seventh angel (Rev. 11:15) sounding the trumpet along with the loud voice announcing that the kingdoms of this world have become those of Christ. That will be the sweetest music imaginable.

Lord, even the dead will respond to Your trumpet call and Your loud voice. Maybe I will have more time to practice music in the new earth.

The Cube

The city is laid out as a square; its length is as great as its breadth. And he measured the city with the reed: twelve thousand furlongs. Its length, breadth, and height are equal. Rev. 21:16, NKJV.

As a three-dimensional solid object with six sides, the cube is one of the five so-called Platonic solids. To qualify as a Platonic solid, the convex solid structure must have every side or face looking just alike, and at every corner or vertex it must have exactly the same number of faces meeting at exactly the same angles. Only five solid shapes qualify as Platonic solids. Just in case you wanted to know, they are the tetrahedron, with four triangular faces, six edges, and four corners; the cube or hexahedron, with six square faces, 12 edges, and eight corners; the octahedron, with eight triangular faces, 12 edges, and six corners; the dodecahedron, with 12 pentagonal faces, 30 edges, and 20 corners; and finally the icosahedron, with 20 triangular faces, 30 edges, and 12 corners. Though humanity has known such structures from antiquity, the Greek mathematician and contemporary of Plato, Theaetetus, provided the first proof that no other solids fit the criteria detailed above.

I enjoy holding each of these solid objects in my hands, feeling their corners, edges, and smooth faces, and marveling at their beauty and symmetry. The cube especially fascinates me, because of its biblical significance and its repeated appearance in nature. I say repeated, because every grain of common table salt (a crystal of sodium chloride) is a beautiful cube. When I see them in the electron microscope, their perfection is stunning. To be sure, some cubes have little bits missing here and there, but the smaller the crystal, the more likely it is to be cubic.

Also, the Fibonacci numbers, in which every additional number is the sum of the previous two numbers can be plotted as squares (the face of the cube) that ultimately form a spiral. The numbers 1, 2, 3, 5, 8, 13, and so on, as well as the spirals, repeatedly appear in nature.

The biblical significance of the cube is this: the Most Holy Place in Solomon's Temple was a perfect cube, as is the Holy City in heaven. It is hard for us to imagine a city that is 1,367 miles long, wide, and high. Yes, cities do have high-rise buildings, but 1,367 miles high? For all we know there may be more than three dimensions to space in that celestial city, the New Jerusalem. We will just have to be there to see it for ourselves.

King of kings and Lord of lords, how long until we can be reunited with You and explore the beautiful dimensions of Your celestial city and the greater beauty of Your love?

Wrap Rage

He who loves his life will lose it, and he who hates his life in this world will keep it for eternal life. John 12:25, NKJV.

A report out of Great Britain claims that more than 60,000 people injure themselves each year trying to get into packages of food, and here in the United States the Consumer Products Safety Commission pegged the 2004 number of plastic packaging-related emergency room visits at 6,500. Getting into modern plastic packaging is not only frustrating—it can be dangerous to your health if you use an inappropriate tool.

One yarn I heard about recently had a rough-and-tumble cowboy trying to open one of those plastic bubble packs to get at the electric toothbrush inside. He couldn't rip it open by hand, so he went at it with—you guessed it—his teeth. That didn't work either. Surprisingly, his big Bowie knife wasn't up to the task, so in desperation he pulled out his single-action Smith and Wesson and shot his way into the package. Definitely a case of wrap rage. Just yesterday I was trying to get into a package of delicate crackers. The very tightly sealed plastic wrap resisted tearing, and the heat sealing was so tight that I couldn't pull it open at the seams. Without scissors or a knife, I would have reduced the crackers to crumbs before successfully opening the package.

> *Getting into modern plastic packaging is not only frustrating—it can be dangerous to your health if you use an inappropriate tool.*

Many high-priced small electronics are packaged in heavy-duty clear plastic blister wrappers known in the industry as oyster packs. Purposefully designed to be difficult to open in order to reduce or prevent pilfering of the product, it takes special tools to get your purchase out so that you can use it. Yes, the package makers have been highly successful at protecting the product.

Come to think of it, God Himself has designed some food packaging that is difficult or nearly impossible to open. Brazil nuts, black walnuts, and coconuts all require special tools to get to the good stuff inside (even if the tools are just a couple good-sized rocks). Wrap rage, a new disease? Really? Isn't wrap rage and any rage (such as road rage, computer rage, or work rage) really a symptom of selfishness—wanting what I want when I want it and going "postal" if I can't have it my way? "To follow Jesus is to disown self-centeredness" (note on John 12:25 in the Andrews Study Bible).

Teach me Your way, O Lord. I too want to be content with what I have. Assure me with Your words again, "I will never leave you nor forsake you." Thank You, Jesus.

Rest on Every Side

Asa did what was good and right in the eyes of the Lord his God.
2 Chron. 14:2, NIV.

A repeating theme in the experience of God's chosen people, as described in many stories throughout the Old Testament, is an account of decades of turmoil, chaos, famine, poverty, pressure from foreign aggression, and captivity, interspersed with decades of peace, rest, abundance, and wealth. In every case, what made the difference was their attitude toward the one and only true God who had brought them out of Egypt.

When His people focused wholeheartedly on finding God, listened to His Word and obeyed His instructions, worshipped Him only, and depended on Him to fight their battles and provide for their needs, they prospered. The rains came, or they were victorious in battle. But above all, they had long periods of rest, peace, and safety. Life was good—even very good. They got respect from others, because their God was more powerful, more communicative, and infinitely more awesome than any other deities.

The contrast is striking. How could the lessons have been more obvious? When they ignored God—or worse, when they worshipped other gods and did detestable things, fought their own battles, and thought they knew better how to conduct their life—things didn't go so well for them. They suffered terrible defeat when warring neighbors would attack. Those who did not get killed found themselves taken captive and forced into slave labor. Their conquerors robbed them of their national and religious treasures. The rains stopped coming, which made them suffer terribly from famine and disease. For decades at a time or even for generations on end, life was downright miserable.

Does God do the same today? Numerous passages have Him encouraging us to put Him to the test. "Oh, taste and see that the Lord is good; blessed is the man who trusts in Him!" (Ps. 34:8, NKJV). "'And try Me now in this,' says the Lord of hosts, 'If I will not open for you the windows of heaven and pour out for you such blessing that there will not be room enough to receive it'" (Mal. 3:10, NKJV).

Make your single purpose in life to search for Him with all your heart. When you find Him, experience His love, and bask in His bountiful blessings, your heart will respond to His. As you develop a daily relationship, you will fall in step and walk with the Lord.

Lord, I believe. Help my unbelief!

Cinnamon

Then the Lord said to Moses, "Take the following fine spices: 500 shekels of liquid myrrh, half as much (that is, 250 shekels) of fragrant cinnamon, 250 shekels of fragrant Calamus, 500 shekels of cassia—all according to the sanctuary shekel—and a hin of olive oil. Make these into a sacred anointing oil, a fragrant blend, the work of a perfumer. It will be the sacred anointing oil." Ex. 30:22-25, NIV.

Today let us worship Him who made cinnamon, that amazing spice we love in warm, just-out-of-the-oven cinnamon rolls or in Oriental curries. Fresh cinnamon tastes sweet, warm, and spicy primarily because of three essential oils made by the inner bark of scores of species of tropical shrubs and trees in the laurel family. The one plant that seems to do it best bears the scientific name *Cinnamomum zeylanicum*, meaning "cinnamon from the island of Ceylon [now known as Sri Lanka]." Second-best is the closely related *Cinnamomum cassia*, which produces a slightly lower grade of cinnamon. The essential oils in cinnamon bark give it the wonderful flavors and aromas that gourmet cooks and perfumers exploit to tease and please taste buds and noses the world around.

But cinnamon isn't just for flavoring food and drink or providing a long-lasting base for perfumes. From time immemorial people have used it as a preservative. For example, Egyptians employed cinnamon and other spices to embalm their dead. Recent research shows that cinnamon oils and other included phytochemicals also have many medicinal qualities.

The Bible mentions cinnamon only four times. The first appears in Exodus 30:23, in which God gives Moses a recipe for making a sacred anointing oil. Moses was to use it for anointing the tent of meetings and its furniture and utensils. Once anointed, those items and places were sacred and "most holy." Anything that touched them thereafter became holy. God also commanded Moses to anoint Aaron and his sons to do their sacred work. Come to think of it, I too crave anointing that would mark me as holy: "For he chose us in him before the creation of the world to be holy and blameless in his sight" (Eph. 1:4, NIV).

Lord, every time I taste or smell cinnamon, may it remind me that You have chosen me to be holy and that my life can be a pleasing aroma to You.

Red Blood Cell

In Him we have redemption through His blood, the forgiveness of sins, according to the riches of His grace. Eph. 1:7, NKJV.

About one fourth of the cells in our body are red blood cells, gorgeous biconcave disks measuring only 0.00027 inches (7 micrometers) in diameter. Normally blood has 4 or 5 million red blood cells in each cubic millimeter of blood. A little less than 50 percent of our blood is actually cells. The rest is a fluid called plasma. When you cut yourself and the blood stops flowing, the clear yellow stuff is serum (plasma minus the clotting components).

Physiologists who track functions in the body estimate that we make about 2 million new red blood cells every second of every day. We need those new cells because red blood cells last only three or four months at best. Just think, every red cell makes about three complete circuits through your body every minute. It involves going from heart to lungs first to pick up oxygen, then back to the heart, where it gets pumped out to some capillary bed in an organ before it returns to the heart again. That is one circuit. With more than 4,300 round trips per day, you can see that a red blood cell can log a lot of miles in its three- or four-month life span.

Keep in mind, too, that red blood cells are extremely flexible. They have to be, because the capillary beds that they squeeze through are often not big enough for them to just flow along. They jostle into traffic jams and then single file and even squish out like a hot dog to make it through some tight spots. Let them have more room, however, and they spring back into a flattened disk with both flat sides concave inward. This unique shape gives them a huge surface to volume ratio so gas exchange can take place rapidly.

Circulating red blood cells have lost their nucleus before entering service, and it doesn't take them long to discard their mitochondria, their endoplasmic reticulum, and their ribosomes as well. This maximizes room for hemoglobin, that precious oxygen-carrying protein.

Red blood cells transport oxygen and some carbon dioxide. Plasma transports nutrients, metabolic waste, and important regulatory hormones. The white cells in blood provide important defenses against disease, constantly patrolling every nook and cranny to spot danger and deal with it quickly. These important functions are what make blood loss so serious. When uncontrolled, it can quickly lead to death. But Christ's spilled blood through His death on the cross is the basis of eternal life for those who accept His sacrificial gift.

Lord, You gave Your life so that I can have life. Out of gratitude I choose to accept Your precious gift and live a life of obedience and service to You.

Keep It Simple

Do this and you will live. Luke 10:28, NIV.

I f you have ever had a science course that involved technical laboratory experiments, then you know how frustrating it is when an experiment just doesn't work. The data all comes out screwy. To add insult to injury, your teacher will tell you that every experiment actually works. The data you get is always good data. You just didn't do the experiment carefully enough and control all the variables, thus making it look as if you have crazy data.

For example, one common and actually simple experiment involves measuring the effect of solute concentration on osmotic pressure, or the strength of osmosis in a solution. Water moves through a membrane into regions that have a greater solute concentration, such as that inside a cell, causing the cell to swell because of the so-called osmotic pressure. It is an important concept for all biologists to test and understand. The apparatus used to measure osmotic pressure is called an osmometer. Typically a glass tube flared out at one end (called a thistle tube) serves as the osmometer. After tightly fastening a semipermeable membrane with rubber bands over the flared end, you syringe a sugar solution into the thistle tube. Hopefully the membrane is intact and doesn't have any holes in it. When all is ready to go, you mark the sugar water level inside the glass tube, insert the tube into clean water, and start the timing.

What students (and teachers) expect is that the clean water will diffuse through the membrane into the sugar solution, raising the level of the sugar water in the tube of the osmometer. The height to which the fluid will rise is directly proportional to the concentration of the sugar solution that you start with—the more sugar, the higher it should go.

More often than not, nothing happens, or if the height of the sugar solution is well above that of the pure water outside, it may actually go down. Students recording it will complain that the experiment isn't working. Oh, it actually is, but it is showing that the membrane is leaking. Because of this common problem, I designed a novel system made from common plumbing parts available at any hardware store. When you screw a flange down tightly, it creates a seal. It is simple and works. Now we rarely get the anomalous results of a leaky system.

I like simple systems that work and get results. That is why I like the simplicity of Jesus' exchange with the young lawyer detailed in Luke 10:25-37.

Without Your help, Lord, I don't have it in me to love You and the people You love.

The Undivided Heart

Neither before nor after Josiah was there a king like him who turned to the Lord as he did—with all his heart and with all his soul and with all his strength, in accordance with all the Law of Moses. 2 Kings 23:25, NIV.

The need to breathe was getting more and more urgent with each passing second. I was attempting to swim underwater the length of a rather long pool, but it was obvious that I am not the swimmer I used to be. After covering little more than half the distance, my personal physiology and lack of conditioning was forcing me to surface well before I had reached my objective. Why my sudden change in priorities? My body was screaming for air. My life depended on stopping this trial.

Survival literature suggests that one can live only four or five minutes without air, two to 10 days without water (depending on the ambient temperature), and three to six weeks without food. For those deprived of these basic human needs, the imperative to breathe, drink, or eat grows until it becomes the highest priority. I have been interested in observing how priorities can suddenly change, as for example when there is a fire, accident, or catastrophic illness.

Does one priority supersede all others? Is there one commitment that should be my highest? Staying married for better or worse, a commendable priority, requires commitment. Running a successful business or completing a marathon—both take a commitment to training and hard work over the long haul. Maintaining the present life requires air, water, and food. What about the life to come—eternal life? Should I be paying attention to that ultimate priority?

A search of text strings in the 2011 NIV turned up 23 texts bluntly pointing out that God wants service "with all your heart," seven texts say "with all their heart," six "with all his heart," one "with all her heart," two with "undivided heart," and three "with all your mind." Scripture has numerous other ways to describe total commitment, such as Proverbs 4:26: "Give careful thought to the paths for your feet and be steadfast in all your ways" (NIV). The Bible is unambiguous that Jesus asks total commitment from us. Halfhearted attempts to serve God fall short. Both of the references above are examples of the total commitment that Jesus longs for us to have.

My Lord, I live in a world of so many changing priorities. Many of them are good ones. But please help me focus on the single most important priority of serving You only.

Antinutrients

And do not set your heart on what you will eat or drink; do not worry about it. Luke 12:29, NIV.

Science is learning that phytic acid, or phytate (the salt of the acid), found in fiber-rich grains and beans, is the agent responsible for stopping colon cancer. Though it is popping up more and more on food blogs, I suppose most people have not heard much about phytic acid, or phytate. It may help to know that it is the main storage form of phosphates in plants, usually found in the skins or hulls of nuts and seeds, which includes many cereal grains. And what an effective way of storing phosphate it turns out to be. Phosphate is an atom of phosphorus surrounded by four atoms of oxygen with a couple hydrogens coming along for the ride, which is what makes it acidic. Phytic acid is nothing more than a beautiful ring of six carbons (hexane), with each carbon decorated with a single phosphate group.

How phytic acid prevents cancer is by effectively binding to metal atoms such as iron, zinc, copper, magnesium, and calcium and preventing them from being available. Chemists call phytic acid a chelating agent because of the way it ties up these nutrients. Making them unavailable for cancer cells means that cancer cells will get less nutrition.

"But wait!" you may say. "My good non-cancerous cells need those nutrients too. Does phytic acid deny nutrition to my good cells as well as the cancerous cells?" The simple answer is yes. In this sense, phytic acid is an antinutrient—a molecule that reduces absorption of nutrients in our small intestines. Some nutritionists, writing alarming articles about how phytic acid robs us of our nutrients, have caused undue worry in the general public. Granted, getting the right nutrients is important, and phytic acid can be a major problem in developing countries, where most of the nutrition comes from beans or cereal grains.

The secret to separating phosphate from phytate or phytic acid is having the enzyme phytase. Some seeds such as wheat, rye, and barley have phytase in them. So soaking these seeds before cooking reduces the phytic acid levels to nearly zero. Oats and corn, however, lack the enzyme, so it helps to soak them with a tablespoon of freshly ground wheat, rye, or barley. Sprouting grain seeds (changing seeds into seedlings) also drops the phytic acid levels, turning antinutrients into nutrients.

Thank You, Lord, for my daily bread and for assuring me that I don't need to worry about it.

The Miracle of Hemostasis

Therefore confess your sins to each other and pray for each other so that you may be healed. The prayer of a righteous person is powerful and effective. James 5:16, NIV.

W hile gathering some fresh-cut roses you accidentally prick your finger on a thorn. A tiny drop of bright-red blood wells up. "Ah, it's nothing," you say, so you ignore it and continue gathering the fragrant blossoms. Would you care to follow me in a description of what you so casually call "nothing"?

At the microscopic level, as the sharp thorn entered your soft flesh it tore through cells, ripping open a dozen or more capillaries and a venule or two. Puncturing the closed plumbing system and creating breaks in delicate pipes produces leaks. Any leak in the system is serious. While you may refer to it as nothing, the body knows differently, and immediately goes to work.

Endothelial cells are flat pancake wraparound cells forming the tubes of capillaries and the inner lining of arterioles and venules. Tearing open the cells releases chemicals that immediately cause vasoconstriction in the area of the leak. The pipes actually close down. Muscles around the pipe constrict to minimize the leak. It doesn't stop the flow entirely, but the rate of loss slows. And if the leak looks serious to you, likely you will put a finger on it to halt the bleeding too. Plugging the leak and repair of the pipes comes next.

Constantly circulating in each cubic millimeter of blood are thousands of delicate platelets with gossamer-thin membranes. The ragged cell fragments are smaller than red blood cells. And, as long as the hypersmooth endothelium of the pipe is intact, the platelets continue to fly by without incident. But break the smooth endothelium and expose the raw collagen of the connective tissue outside the capillaries, and platelets stick to the collagen, rip open, and spill their contents. The chemicals signal other platelets to gather and stick. They also cause more vasoconstriction so that the vessels squeeze down tighter. In short order, cells that were flowing through the open pipes are now clumping together, beginning to plug up the leak.

While you may refer to it as nothing, the body knows differently, and immediately goes to work.

Finally, the liquid portion of blood has hundreds of proteins. Several of them are liquid clotting factors with names such as XII, XI, IX, X, prothrombin, VIII, VII, XIII, and fibrinogen. Substances released from the damaged tissue initiate steps that change prothrombin to thrombin, which in turn converts the liquid fibrinogen into fibrin, a stringy protein net that blocks the leakage of any more cells. Does that sound like nothing to you?

Lord, if stopping blood leaks is so important to You, what systems do You have in place to repair broken channels of communication?

September 7

Meditation on Delight

And his heart took delight in the ways of the Lord. 2 Chron. 17:6, NKJV.

Delight" is a such a happy word, evoking lightness, satisfaction, gladness, and pure unadulterated enjoyment. It's a mother looking lovingly into the face of her newborn, a father teaching his son to ride a bicycle without training wheels, a husband enjoying the wife of his youth (Prov. 5:18), or a wife sitting in the shade of her husband and tasting his sweet fruit (S. of Sol. 2:3).

Thus delight is finding great pleasure in a place, an activity, or the company of another. God created us for His glory (Isa. 43:7). He takes great delight in us (Ps. 18:19; Zeph. 3:17). Seeking joy or pleasure is good if we seek delights that are God-ordained long-term pleasures. They are far preferable to the deceiver's counterfeit "delights" that quickly turn to bitterness and sorrow.

Read the following carefully, because it is a statement stamped with the seal of God at the end, i.e, "The mouth of the Lord has spoken": "If you turn away your foot from the Sabbath, from doing your pleasure on My holy day, and call the Sabbath a delight, the holy day of the Lord honorable, and shall honor Him, not doing your own ways, nor finding your own pleasure, nor speaking your own words, then you shall delight yourself in the Lord; and I will cause you to ride on the high hills of the earth, and feed you with the heritage of Jacob your father. The mouth of the Lord has spoken" (Isa. 58:13, 14, NKJV).

It is clearly important that I try to figure out exactly what brings the most delight to my Lord and then make sure that I pay attention to it. Fortunately, His Word doesn't beat around the bush or put it in hard-to-understand language. Found in Jeremiah 9:23, 24, it is bookended front and back with His seal of approval. Here it is: "Thus says the Lord: 'Let not the wise man glory in his wisdom, let not the mighty man glory in his might, nor let the rich man glory in his riches; but let him who glories glory in this, that he understands and knows Me, that I am the Lord, exercising lovingkindness, judgment, and righteousness in the earth. For in these I delight,' says the Lord" (NKJV).

Lord of lovingkindness, judgment, and righteousness in the earth, may I too delight in Your beautiful and glorious character. Indeed, that is Your glory.

September 8

Seek the Lord

Now set your heart and your soul to seek the Lord your God.
1 Chron. 22:19, NKJV.

Bloodhounds have a huge reputation for being excellent trailing dogs. That is, they can pick up and follow the scent of a particular person days after the individual has passed through an area. Though all dogs have the ability to detect scent incredibly well, bloodhounds, by far, have the best nose. They are big dogs, up to 150 pounds, but also gentle ones—they simply won't get aggressive or hurt anybody. In fact, when a bloodhound is tracking a criminal, both the dog and its handler must be protected by law enforcement officers, because the dog will not attack or defend itself or its handler. The bloodhound is an animal that just loves to track.

When I read the story of Yogi, I was astonished that Yogi, the bloodhound, could track Alie, a missing little girl, three days after her abduction. Hundreds of friends, neighbors, and police had been searching the neighborhood to no avail. Alie had simply vanished into thin air. And though the crime scene had been totally contaminated by the hundreds of searchers, Yogi quickly picked up the trail and headed off down the street. As Yogi strained at the leash, he pulled his handler out onto the freeway as he followed his nose to Alie. She had been taken by car, down the freeway more than 10 miles, and off into a canyon. During the next two days Yogi followed the trail and found the missing girl. As I read the account, I learned that the bloodhound is so focused on following the scent trail that it pays no attention to anything else. The dog is oblivious to its own health and safety.

This story had two important lessons for me. First, the dog's abilities to lock onto a particular scent and follow it is phenomenal. When I think of how scent, over time, gets diluted down to fractions of one part per trillion yet the dog is able to detect it and strain at the leash to follow it, that just has to be a God thing. The physical and physiological apparatus to accomplish that feat needs more research, and we certainly should thank God for giving some of our best friends that truly amazing ability. Read the story and learn of Yogi's many excellent contributions to society before he died of old age. Second, I learned that I need to have the attitude that bloodhounds have when they are on a scent. I am certain that my search for my Maker and Friend is far too casual, i.e., when I have free time on the weekends—maybe. Or perhaps when I am in serious trouble.

Lord, do You really want me to expend that much effort searching for You? Help me to prepare my mind to do that just now and every day.

Sniff, Sniff—What Is That Smell?

If the whole body were an eye, where would be the hearing? If the whole were hearing, where would be the smelling? 1 Cor. 12:17, NKJV.

What is that odor that I'm smelling? And why am I sniffing it to follow it to its source? Olfaction means smelling, having a sense of smell. In order to detect odors, we have two olfactory bulbs, projections from the brain that extend forward, one across the top of each nasal cavity. Extending from them, specialized nerve cells penetrate through the floor of the skull and through the nasal epithelium so that dendrites (nerve endings) hang from the roof of the nasal cavity. Mucous and antibodies coat the dendrites to protect them from infection. We smell chemicals called odorants. Sniffing brings in lots of odorants and forces them against the roof of the nasal cavity, where they quickly dissolve into the mucous coating. Researchers have identified about 1,000 genes that code for odor receptors, though we use only a fraction of them. Each specialized nerve cell expresses the gene for only one kind of receptor. So when a specific odorant (key) fits into a specific receptor (lock) in the dendritic membrane of the nerve cell, that nerve cell will respond somewhat like an alarm going off. Forgive me for skipping the details of the multistep signal transduction pathway between the odorant/receptor complex and the action potential. A summary of that description alone would require a full page.

God has given us a separate system in each nostril (the two bulbs) so that we smell in stereo. We can actually tell what direction the smell is coming from, because it is stronger on one side than the other. Most of us have less than one square inch of olfactory epithelium servicing each olfactory bulb. Dogs have about 13 square inches per bulb. And they have about 100 times more nerve endings per square inch of epithelium than we do, which is why they can detect smells so much better than we can. Those who run the numbers suggest that dogs can smell odors 100,000 to 1 million times better than we can. Bloodhounds get even higher ratings at 10 to 100 million times better. But the grizzly bear has a nose seven times more sensitive than the bloodhound. They use that keen sense of smell for finding food.

When it comes to detecting odors, our capabilities pale in comparison to some of God's other creatures. But He has given us the ability to figure these things out, to think about them, and to stand in awe of the ingenious Creator—something that the others have no way of doing.

Lord, I thank You for the senses that You have given to me. I am grateful that the study of these marvelous sensory abilities leads me back to You.

Hyperspectral Imaging

Hear this now, O foolish people, without understanding, who have eyes and see not, and who have ears and hear not. Jer. 5:21, NKJV.

Seeing the invisible is the essence of hyperspectral imaging. The special forces who found and killed Osama bin Laden during the dark of night used hyperspectral imaging technology, developed just the year before, in order to see clearly without light. So how does it work?

The rods and cones in our eyes respond to electromagnetic radiation with wavelengths between 400 and 700 nanometers. Considering the very broad range of the electromagnetic spectrum, 400 to 700 nanometers is a very narrow band that we call visible, or light, because we can see it. Get outside that narrow spectral window, and we call it dark, though there is still plenty of radiation to detect. For example, objects radiating heat, whether from body heat or from heat built up during the day, emit infrared radiation. That is radiation in a different part of the spectrum of electromagnetic radiation. Hyperspectral imaging employs detectors for as many windows of the broad spectrum as possible.

Of course, infrared detectors have been around for a long time. But a person can hide behind or beside a hot rock and become invisible to infrared detectors. Then oil and mining companies figured out that different minerals emit characteristic spectral signatures. So by flying over an area and taking pictures with detectors tuned to what they were looking for, prospectors could see the invisible.

Before long, researchers began putting similar technology to agricultural uses. Plants absorb and reflect radiation with minute differences in their signatures so that now we can identify specific types of plants from aircraft or from space. In fact, the radiation spectrum from each and every object has slight differences in their emission signatures. So by precisely tuning detectors, we can spot animal protein contaminants, for example, in grain feeds, which will allow us to attempt to stop the spread of the so-called mad cow disease. The technology has literally thousands of uses. Even a common scanning electron microscope can be fitted with detectors to pick up characteristic X-ray signatures that emerge from elements after absorption of the electron beam. Thus, even at the smallest scale, the invisible becomes visible. Submission and obedience upon seeing the invisible is the essence of godliness, too.

Lord, give me, I pray, hyperspiritual imaging so that I can see and know You as the only true God and Savior.

Walking

And they heard the sound of the Lord God walking in the garden in the cool of the day. Gen. 3:8, NKJV.

I had never thought of it this way before: God was out on His daily walk in the cool of the day. He must enjoy walking too! Did you know that walking is one of the best exercises possible? It doesn't require any expensive equipment or health club memberships. Weight bearing, it involves all the muscle groups and is relatively easy on the joints. If you make it a brisk walk that is long and frequent enough, it can aid your fitness, strength, and mood. You will also improve your blood chemistry (such as cholesterol and sugar) and help manage your weight. Taking a brisk walk every day is just a good habit to develop.

Be sure to have good walking shoes that fit well and give good support and shock protection. Dress in loose-fitting clothes appropriate to the weather and layered so that, as you warm up during the walk or chill because of turning into the wind, you can make the appropriate adjustments and stay comfortable. It helps if you start slowly every day to warm up, stop and stretch the warmed muscles, and then cool down slowly with some more stretching. In addition to a regular time to walk, having a walking partner will keep you accountable to the routine, but more important, you can deepen a friendship as you improve your level of health. I do believe Enoch had the best of all walking partners (Gen. 5:22).

God was out on His daily walk in the cool of the day. He must enjoy walking too!

My wife and I have developed the habit of walking and talking and have been at it for years, so we can recommend it from personal experience. Our walk time is one of our favorite occasions to communicate deeply on a wide variety of topics. We do it rain or shine, wind or snow. Even on ice, though you do need special equipment, and the risk of falls increases.

Walking with God is a rich metaphor for a relationship with God. Enoch and Noah walked with God. I wonder where the line between metaphor and reality blurs? Did they actually walk together shoulder to shoulder? David and Hezekiah walked in God's ways. Many of the bad kings walked in the ways of Jeroboam or Ahab, both models of a wicked king. Good kings walked in the ways of David, Asa, or Jehosophat, models of good kings. Walking after other gods, walking according to the dictates of their own heart, or even walking by human precepts are the opposite of walking in God's laws or in His statutes. Walking in peace and equity suggests agreement. In another blurring of the metaphor, Amos asks if it is even possible for two to walk together unless they agree (Amos 3:3).

Lord, do You still walk in the cool of the day? May I walk with You today?

Light of the Lamb

Then Jesus spoke to them again, saying, "I am the light of the world. He who follows Me shall not walk in darkness, but have the light of life." John 8:12, NKJV.

What happens when you walk in darkness? Now, I have in mind real darkness, not when the lights go out and you still have some illumination from glowing clocks or streetlights or maybe a sliver of moon. I suppose it depends somewhat on how well you know the terrain. If you are in your own house when it turns pitch-black, you might stand a chance. But if you are in unfamiliar territory and the lights go out, leaving you in total darkness—you are in trouble. Few places have such a complete absence of light, but deep inside a cave is one. I have done some caving, and I know from experience that when your light suddenly goes out, whether on purpose or by accident, you have a profound sense of vulnerability. That is why every caver has multiple forms of light. Redundancy is a must in such situations. Turning one of them on, you can then figure out what went wrong with your primary source of light as well as have the ability to move and to do. Without light we are powerless.

Estimates are that 1.6 billion people live in countries or regions without electricity. Kerosene lamps work well to light up the night, but they can start fires or cause burns, and they contribute to carbon emissions—same with candles. Traditional batteries are much too expensive and are not recyclable. Enter Light Up the World (lutw.org), BarefootPower.com, SuryaBijlee.com, and a number of other organizations working to defeat darkness by providing solar-powered LED lights at affordable prices in developing countries. Citizens of Zambia, Sri Lanka, South Africa, Afghanistan, Honduras, India, and many other countries rejoice to get such affordable, reliable lighting systems. Whereas they previously paid at least a dollar per month for kerosene, they now have the sun providing the energy for light at night. Those who get such lights describe how life now continues after dark. They are no longer afraid of the darkness or the animals of the night, because, within their protective sphere of light, they feel empowered and safe.

This type of Light Up the World project is a wonderful metaphor for the safety and power that the Light of the world brings into peoples' lives. The tiny LEDs are but a dim symbol of what the light of the good news can do to illuminate and empower lives.

Lord, may I be as excited about bringing the Light of the world to the unenlightened as some of the organizations promoting solar-powered LEDs.

The Syllabus

*I will delight myself in Your statutes; I will not forget Your word.
Ps. 119:16, NKJV.*

One of the perks of being a teacher is that I get to write a syllabus for each course that I teach. Now a syllabus is a simple document, usually only a few pages. Though brief, it's important. Besides providing the teacher's name, contact information, course name, and hours of credit, it always includes a course description, letting students know what text and lab manuals we will be using. It notifies them whether or not we have online material and how we expect them to employ it. The syllabus details what the teacher requires the students to do to earn a grade, and it even gives a breakdown of grades, i.e., what grade they will get for various levels of performance. The syllabus includes course policy concerning attendance, academic dishonesty, use of electronic equipment, safety, etc. In short, the syllabus is my contract with the students, letting them know exactly what I look for from them. In a very real sense, I am the lawgiver and the judge, since my job includes assigning a letter grade at the end.

Suppose a student signs up for my course but has a conflict and can't attend class very often. Perhaps they have a different textbook, one they got from a cousin at a different school. Textbooks are expensive, and they don't want to pay for the latest edition the course is using. Lab times are inconvenient for them so they want to come in later. They don't have a computer, so how can I expect them to utilize the online helps for the course? I bet you think I am just making these up, right? I wish that were the case. These are just a few examples of issues that regularly come up. And when I have a course with more than 100 students, the potential for chaos grows exponentially.

What I find is that students who pass the course with flying colors usually share a common characteristic. Some of you might have already guessed what that might be. Those who do well, carefully read and understand the syllabus.

I have been teaching such courses for years, so I know what it takes for students to learn the material. Time-tested methods work well. My desire is for them to be successful. God has been running the universe for much longer. His syllabus is shorter than mine, just 10 clearly written statements. He wants my joy to be full and knows what it takes to make that happen. Might it be important for me to pay attention?

Lord, thank You for the clarity of Your laws. May they truly be my delight.

Truth

Very truly I tell you, we speak of what we know, and we testify to what we have seen, but still you people do not accept our testimony. John 3:11, NIV.

Some days I am certain that I am being inundated by a tsunami of information. As the water recedes, however, it is apparent that much of it was disinformation or misinformation. How can one know what is true and what is honest? Take, for example, a long-running battle concerning a possible link between childhood immunizations and autism.

Though the story is much too lengthy to recount here, it centers on a gastroenterologist in the United Kingdom named Andrew Wakefield. Dr. Wakefield published the results of a small "study" in the British medical journal Lancet in 1998, claiming a link between measles, mumps, and rubella (MMR) vaccine and autism. His conclusion was that the three vaccines given together caused autism and that they should be separated. What was not revealed at the time was that he had applied for a patent on a competing measles vaccine.

About the same time concerns began growing in the United States about three other childhood vaccines all containing an ethylmercury preservative, thimerosal. When that hit the news, it didn't take long for some to begin claiming that mercury poisoning was the cause of autism. So the Centers for Disease Control and Prevention (CDC) got right on it by asking the Institute of Medicine (part of the National Academy of Sciences) to check out both the MMR link and the thimerosal concern. A high level panel of experts carefully reviewed many hundreds of studies done on hundreds of thousands of children for almost a decade. Early interim reports were typically cautious in concluding no danger from either problem. Later reports, based on more data, came out with greater certainty. But throughout this time activists, parent groups, and the media were piling on, crying conspiracy, and even threatening to kill scientists or defenders of vaccination. The debate was ugly on both sides of the Atlantic. Many children began dying because they had not been vaccinated. At the same time thousands of parents of autistic children were suing for damages.

Little by little the truth emerged. Wakefield, called an outright fraud, faced charges of serious professional misconduct. Lancet withdrew his 1998 publication.

Lover of all the little children, how the great deceiver desires such fights, and how he enjoys seeing those You love get hurt. Lord, may the truth always emerge.

One

There is one body and one Spirit, just as you were called in one hope of your calling; one Lord, one faith, one baptism; one God and Father of all, who is above all, and through all, and in you all. Eph. 4:4-6, NKJV.

O h, the power of 1! Without a single unit of it, what you have is noth-ing— zero. Once you get a single unit, you go from having none to having one (1). When you work with probabilities, a 1, by definition, means that there is no chance that it won't happen. It is certain to occur. So we can say that the probability that Jesus will come again is 1. It is an absolute certainty (John 14:3). Other interesting facts: 1 is the only number that is its own square and its own square root. Not only that, 1 is the first whole number in the sequence, and many say that it is the first natural number in its sequence. Computers all use the binary system, a base-2 number system using just 0 and 1. Digital electronic circuitry employs logic gates that are either open or closed, a 0 or a 1. There is nothing in between.

One is unity, defined as the state of being undivided, whole, or complete. The Middle English word "unite" comes from Old French. In Latin it is unitas. From it we get singing in "unison" and the words "unite" and "union."

On June 16, 1858, Abraham Lincoln gave his now-famous "House Divided" speech based on Jesus' words quoted in Matthew 12:25 and Luke 11:17. Lincoln said: "'A house divided against itself cannot stand.' I believe this government can-not endure, permanently, half slave and half free. I do not expect the Union to be dissolved—I do not expect the house to fall— but I do expect it will cease to be divided. It will become all one thing or all the other. Either the opponents of slavery will arrest the further spread of it, and place it where the public mind shall rest in the belief that it is in the course of ultimate extinction; or its advocates will push it forward, till it shall become alike lawful in all the States, old as well as new—North as well as South." Given before he became president, the speech went against the popular thought of the day, but was the star that guided his presidency in pulling the country back together again.

After Jesus' resurrection, He told the disciples not to leave Jerusalem, but to wait there to be "baptized with the Holy Ghost" (Acts 1:5, KJV). So, following those instructions, all 11 of the disciples "continued with one accord in prayer and sup-plication" (verse 14, KJV) until they were filled with the Holy Spirit (Acts 2:2). Oh, the power of 1. A united nation. A united church.

My one Lord and one God, bring us together in unity as one body filled with one spirit under Your leadership because we have one faith.

The Checkerboard of Salt

Salt is good, but if the salt loses its flavor, how will you season it?
Mark 9:50, NKJV.

I was sitting at the console of our new electron microscope. As the beam scanned the small crystal of salt on the Peltier stage, a small perfectly shaped cube came into focus on the flat panel screen. A cursor allowed me to control the humidity in the chamber. As I adjusted it, small droplets of water gathered on the cube and within seconds the crystal dissolved. Then, when I slid the cursor to lower the humidity, the water droplets shrank and many small cubes of salt formed as the ions found their place in a new crystal lattice. How did water make the salt disappear? And then as the water evaporated, how did the salt reappear?

Sodium ions have a positive charge and chloride ions carry a negative charge. So in a crystal lattice the two sit side by side. When thousands of the ions get together, you never see two sodium ions together or two chloride ions together (remember that similar charges repel each other). So think of making a big stack of boxes of two different colors. As you stack the boxes you have to alternate colors so that no two of the same color ever sit beside or on top of each other. Think of a big stack of colored boxes in a checkerboard pattern.

In my mind's eye, I see water molecules looking like the well-known Mickey Mouse logo (a simple black circle for the face and two smaller circles for the ears). The big face circle represents the lone oxygen atom. Each of the ears symbolizes a hydrogen atom. The beauty of the salt-water interaction is in the details of how the Mickey Mouse water molecules gather around the neat stack of sodium chloride boxes.

The beauty of the salt-water interactionis in the details of how the Mickey Mouse water molecules gather around the neat stack of sodium chloride boxes.

Because both the ions in the stack and the water molecules are charged, they are attracted to each other. Watch now as the positively charged ears of dozens of tiny water molecules surround a single relatively large negatively charged chloride ion. They separate it from the stack, and off they go together. Similarly a swarm of the negatively charged faces of the Mickey Mouse water molecules cluster around a positively charged sodium ion, isolating it from the stack. In short order, every sodium ion and every chloride ion is separated from the others by spheres of water molecules, not letting them reform their stack. But it's easy to see how, when water evaporates, the stack rebuilds, ion by ion, to form the perfect cube again. Being made in God's image, I too enjoy seeing order and organization.

Lord, I pray for simplicity and order in my life. Bring me into harmony with Your will.

Most Assuredly

Jesus said to them, "Most assuredly, I say to you, before Abraham was, I AM." John 8:58, NKJV.

C ameron Diaz on marriage: "I think we have to make our own rules. I don't think we should live our lives in relationships based off old traditions that don't suit our world any longer."

Jesus on marriage: "Have you not read that He who made them at the beginning 'made them male and female,' and said, 'For this reason a man shall leave his father and mother and be joined to his wife, and the two shall become one flesh'? So then, they are no longer two but one flesh. Therefore what God has joined together, let not man separate" (Matt. 19:4-6, NKJV).

Ask Richard Dawkins about God. "The existence of God is a scientific hypothesis like any other." (Dawkins supported an advertising campaign putting large banners on London buses reading: "There's probably no God. Now stop worrying and enjoy your life.")

Ask Jesus about God. "Most assuredly, I say to you, before Abraham was, I AM" (John 8:58, NKJV). "You call Me Teacher and Lord, and you say well, for so I am" (John 13:13, NKJV).

Relativism—the idea that there is no absolute truth and that our ideas about truth depend on what we think is true—marches under many different banners. Truth relativism and moral relativism are just a couple of many examples. Doesn't it make sense, though, that if all the different variations of truth or morality are just as good as any other, then all are just as bad as any other? And if a nuance I believe on any given day is actually true, then I can never be mistaken or change my mind as that would invalidate the truth that I first believed.

The Bible could not be more emphatic or clearer in its claim to be the standard of truth. "Your word is truth" (John 17:17, NKJV). "God, who cannot lie" (Titus 1:2, NKJV). Avoid being "tossed to and fro and carried about with every wind of doctrine, by the trickery of men, in the cunning craftiness of deceitful plotting" (Eph. 4:14, NKJV). What is the source of relativism anyway? "Now the Spirit expressly says that in latter times some will depart from the faith, giving heed to deceiving spirits and doctrines of demons" (1 Tim. 4:1, NKJV).

Lord, You have said again and again that the just will live by faith and that without faith, I can't please You. My desire is to honor You and glorify Your name. Lord, I believe.

September 18

Meditation on Prosperity

Hear me, O Judah and you inhabitants of Jerusalem: Believe in the Lord your God, and you shall be established; believe His prophets, and you shall prosper. 2 Chron. 20:20, NKJV.

Prosperity, success, achievement—who wouldn't want it? Is that because we believe that happiness comes with prosperity?

But what is my goal or your goal of prosperity? By what standard should we measure it, and how do we define it? If you have "acquisitionitis" and subscribe to the concept of "He who wins has the most toys," then you need to do a toy count, or if it's wealth, then a money count or a summary of total investments. What about beauty or power? How many people report to you or depend on you for their living? How many people jump when you say "Jump!"? Talent, skills, or abilities that lead to fame and renown in music, art, acting, sports, collecting, public speaking, medicine, or scientific achievement—one or more of them is the goal for some, probably even many. But in every one of these areas, how much is enough? How do I know when I have arrived? Is there ever enough?

History strongly suggests that getting more and more success of the types listed above only whets the appetite for more. Few are the examples and fortunate are the few who, after becoming wildly successful, truly agree with Paul when he said: "I have learned to be content whatever the circumstances" (Phil. 4:11, NIV). The devil's lie is that happiness comes from more. If I just had more _____ (fill in the blank).

Haman was certainly prosperous. He had wealth and power. Everybody bowed to him except one—Mordecai. Unfortunately, Haman couldn't be happy until just one more person bowed to him (Esther 3:5). The story is a powerful example of how the obsession to get more always backfires and ends in great unhappiness and destruction.

History's flip side story is that if people do believe in the Lord and in His messages sent through His prophets, God does take care of His own. They enjoy times of peace, of rest, and of great financial prosperity. The "seek ye the kingdom of God; and all these things shall be added unto you" rule applies (Luke 12:31, KJV).

Through Jeremiah, the Lord said: "Let not the wise man glory in his wisdom, let not the mighty man glory in his might, nor let the rich man glory in his riches; but let him who glories glory in this, that he understands and knows Me, that I am the Lord" (Jer. 9:23, 24, NKJV).

Lord, let my delight be to know You by studying Your Word.

September 19

Power

The Son is the radiance of God's glory and the exact representation of his being, sustaining all things by his powerful word. Heb. 1:3, NIV.

Those who survive a close lightning strike speak of its amazing power as do those after an F5 tornado or a 9.0-magnitude earthquake. All these release large amounts of energy. Potential energy becomes kinetic energy, hurting people and destroying property—stuff gets dramatically rearranged. Stuff is matter, and matter has mass.

Until Albert Einstein convincingly persuaded us about the validity of his most famous but perhaps little understood equation $E = mc^2$, summarizing the special theory of relativity, most people who worked with and thought about energy and mass sincerely believed that they were different and separate entities. Einstein's special theory inextricably linked the two, showing how a very tiny bit of mass (m) can be converted into a huge amount of energy (E). Or the equation quantifies the enormous amounts of energy it takes to produce a tiny bit of mass. The one factor in the equation that results in the unimaginably huge amount of energy is that small c representing the speed of light—a very big number: a little more than 186,000 miles per second (nearly 300 million meters per second). But then, to make that big number really big, the equation squares it. So mass (m) times the speed of light multiplied by itself (c^2) is the amount of energy that you get. Obviously a very tiny bit of mass can be lost or destroyed while creating an enormous amount of kinetic energy (one of the lessons we learned firsthand with atomic bombs).

Experiments with particle accelerators that smash subatomic particles together have taught us that, indeed, Einstein's equation works the other way, too. When we use enormous amounts of energy to accelerate incredibly tiny particles (small mass) and they collide, more mass can be "created" at the expense of kinetic energy. Thus particle physics supports Einstein's special theory and shows how matter (mass) can be created if we have enough energy to put into the system. According to the first law of thermodynamics, energy can't be created or destroyed, but it can be changed from one form to another (the law of conservation of energy). But where in the world do you get enough energy to create enough mass to make even a pinhead? A thousand tornadoes converging on one point isn't sufficient. Neither are a thousand earthquakes. Only God's word has the energy, the power, needed to create our universe. What a magnificent and awesome God!

Omnipotent Lord, when You speak, the power is terrifying. I bow with my face to the ground and worship You who made everything that has been made.

Glory

That you may with one mind and one mouth glorify the God and Father of our Lord Jesus Christ. Rom. 15:6, NKJV.

I do believe that one of my favorite places to be to welcome the Sabbath as the sun drops near the horizon late on a Friday afternoon is at the top of Mount Erie on Fidalgo Island, near the town of Anacortes, Washington. I have been there for several sunsets, sitting on a rock looking west out over the San Juan Islands out toward the Juan de Fuca Strait. As I sit there on the rock in cathedral quiet, Lake Erie is just below me, beyond that Langly Bay and Burrows Bay, then Burrows Island. More distant Lopez Island has a tiny ferryboat silently cutting a path toward it through Puget Sound. When the air is crisp and dry, I can even see Victoria on Vancouver Island and the beginnings of the Juan de Fuca Strait leading out to the Pacific Ocean. Off to the left are the majestic snowcapped peaks of the Olympic Mountains. As the sun nears the horizon, the colors, hues, and textures of sea, sky, islands, forested hills, and snowcapped mountains is glorious. Words and music start playing silently in my mind.

As I watch the glorious display of my Creator-God, I feel like David sitting before the Lord there in the Temple (1 Chron. 17:16), or Elijah when he was on the mountain and told to go out of his cave and stand before the Lord (1 Kings 19:11). Interactions with God are always grand and thoughtful times. I think of my own life and how frequently I miss the point of what life is all about. My to-do list is endless—more added each day than crossed off. It isn't possible to get it all done—and to what end? To look good or really to be good just doesn't get any traction under this sunset sky interaction with Deity. To make money, to have things, to get to "easy street" doesn't work either. When confronting the God of the universe, the point of life is crystal clear. My one and only mission is to reflect God's glory. Jesus' glory first broke through at the wedding in Cana (John 2:11) at which He first exhibited His divine character. The record of both Isaiah 42:8 and 48:11 are clear that God will not allow His glory to go to another. Which is why this life is not about me. It is about how I glorify my Father as Jesus both modeled and commanded me to do (Matt. 5:16). That for me is the lesson of every welcome-Sabbath sunset.

Glory to God in the highest. Give to the Lord the glory due His name. For Yours is the kingdom, and the power, and the glory forever. Amen.

> *Interactions with God are always grand and thoughtful times. I think of my own life and how frequently I miss the point of what life is all about.*

September 21

Wonderful Water

Give us water that we may drink. Ex. 17:2, NKJV.

Water—H_2O, two atoms of hydrogen bonded to one atom of oxygen, also called dihydrogen monoxide or oxidane—is, I believe, a miracle molecule. Designed by a loving Creator to be the solvent for all life forms, serving as the pressurized structure of most herbaceous plants, and stabilizing the temperature of the earth, water does so many good things for us. But most of us just take it for granted. We turn on the tap and don't give it a second thought.

Water has a molecular mass of 18 grams per mole. Most molecules that are that light exist naturally only as a gas, or if a liquid, they have a high vapor pressure and will quickly evaporate. Take methanol, for example. Its molecular mass is 32, nearly twice as much as water, but it vaporizes quickly. Carbon dioxide has a molecular mass of 44 and must be highly pressurized to make it behave as a liquid. So for water to exist naturally in all three states (gas, liquid, and solid) on earth is pretty awesome.

Well, you say, there must be a reason. Right you are. It is rooted in the unique shape of a water molecule. Oxygen takes center stage in the molecule with each hydrogen atom connected to it by a polar covalent bond. If the two hydrogen atoms were on the same line with each other, water wouldn't behave like . . . well, like water. It would act more like carbon dioxide and be a gas all the time. But because the two hydrogen atoms are bonded at an angle to each other, the molecule becomes a highly polar molecule, and that is where the magic is. The 104.5-degree angle makes each water molecule and its orbiting electrons fill the space of a tetrahedron with its four corners spaced as far apart as possible. Two of the corners of the tetrahedron have a slightly negative charge, and two have a slightly positive charge. Because of that, water molecules attract each other and bring their oppositely charged corners together. The resulting bonds are called hydrogen bonds. Because of intermolecular hydrogen bonding, water molecules just "like" to be together. Try pouring the smallest quantity of water out of a bottle. It comes out in drops because molecules stick together. Molecules that don't stick together pour out more like salt or sand.

The polarity of the water molecule and its hydrogen bonds are the secret to water's magical powers of cleaning, dissolving, hydrating, and stabilizing temperature. Truly, water is a wonderful gift of an all-wise and loving Creator.

Lord of all water, wash me, and I shall be clean. Lord, I long to drink of the water of life coming from Your throne.

Water: Cold, Light, and Hard

The waters harden like stone, and the surface of the deep is frozen. Job 38:30, NKJV.

Hot and thirsty, you get a big glass, drop in several ice cubes, fill it with water, and sit back to enjoy. Most of us never think about or appreciate the way solid and liquid water interact. The solid water always floats at the top of the liquid water! What is so astonishing about that?

Well, think this through for just a minute. Cooling a liquid means that molecular motion slows down. Molecules that are going slower take up less room so you have more molecules per unit of volume, making cool liquids more dense than warm liquids. More dense means the slow moving molecules sink to the bottom. Which is why it is always cooler deep in a lake and really cold down in the ocean. Cool always sinks because of greater density. So why does water get less dense when it gets cold enough to become ice?

The secret has to do with the tetrahedral shape of the water molecule and its charged corners. Water molecules, even at room temperature, bounce around so vigorously that their positive corners only interact momentarily with the negative corners of other molecules. They may have only two or three of their corners interacting at any given time, but they still have enough to make it hard for a molecule of water to leap out of the glass of water and become a gas. Only the molecules with the greatest energy can do that—thus the high heat of vaporization. But cool the water down, and, as the molecules slow, they come into more contact, allowing their corners to interact more and for longer periods. The greatest density of water is just a few degrees above freezing.

Continue to cool water and the molecules move so slowly that they start setting up hydrogen bonds that can even become permanent. Then as water freezes, the water molecules get locked into a crystalline structure with most molecules hydrogen-bonded to four other molecules. To enter this stable crystalline arrangement, the molecules have to move apart from each other, taking up almost 10 percent more volume than liquid water. That arrangement makes it less dense. It floats. And the expansion of water when it freezes in a tiny crack of a rock or inside a water pipe causes breaks.

If water froze from the bottom up, life would not exist on earth. Most water would be locked in ice deep down where the sun doesn't shine. But ice floats, and quickly thaws each spring. A tiny design detail, so vital to life.

Lord, I worship You for thinking of every design detail required for the gift of life.

Eating Together

Here I am! I stand at the door and knock. If anyone hears my voice and opens the door, I will come in and eat with that person, and they with me. Rev. 3:20, NIV.

It happens every day, in every culture, and in every city, town, and village. To establish or deepen relationships, we humans sit down and eat together. The habit is in our genes.

Go into any restaurant at lunchtime or dinnertime or visit any sidewalk cafe and quietly observe. You are sure to see business being transacted over a meal, or it could be a reunion of friends from way back. Look around, and you will certainly see several couples, some at the earliest stages of getting to know each other, others perhaps embarrassingly giddy in love (maybe even on their honeymoon), and yet other older couples celebrating life together. Perhaps you will see a family enjoying eating out, or several tables pulled together for a party—for a birthday or maybe a retirement. It is human nature to eat together.

This is the door to my heart, my mind. I am always home. He knows that.

Important relationships may progress to the point of inviting someone into your home for a meal. First you set a time and date. You carefully plan the menu, shop for ingredients, and start preparations well ahead, making sure that the setting is right—lighting, music, flowers, the best china, crystal, polished silver, and freshly laundered linen. And the food—everything done to perfection, ready at the same time so that you can sit down to eat together. In spite of all the preparation and attention to detail, it's not about the meal—it is all about the relationship. Hearts knit together over food and drink. It is what we do.

So when the one and only Creator-God, Sovereign of the universe, Lord of lords and King of kings, walks up to my door and knocks, waits patiently, and knocks again, and waits again . . . maybe I'm not home. Oh, I am home, all right. This is the door to my heart, my mind. I am always home. He knows that. So He calls to me. He isn't a bill collector or a loan shark, but a Father longing for a relationship with me. Hear the cry in His voice: "If anyone hears my voice and opens the door, I will come in and eat with that person, and they with me." It isn't about the meal, mind you—it's about the relationship.

Lord, please come in. Let's eat. But more important, let's talk. Let's be friends.

Scale Wings

If I take the wings of the morning, and dwell in the uttermost parts of the sea, even there Your hand shall lead me, and Your right hand shall hold me. Ps. 139:9, 10, NKJV.

Is that butterfly drunk? Just look at the erratic flight pattern. How does it land without crashing? Seems to me its flight control system needs a major overhaul. But then it lands lightly on a flower and sips nectar before accurately zigzagging to another nearby blossom.

Butterflies and moths belong to the order of insects called Lepidoptera, a name meaning "scale wing." Look at a butterfly wing with a hand lens, and the view is much like a shingled roof. Neat rows of overlapping scales come into view with about one third to half of the end of each scale showing in a particular row. The rest of the scale is hidden back under the overlapping scales in the next higher row. Now glance at your roof. That's what a butterfly wing looks like under a hand lens. Handle a butterfly or moth, and dusty material comes off on your fingers. Find physical damage on the wing, and chances are that you will see where the scales were rubbed or knocked off, making the small cloud of dust.

Study that same damaged area with the electron microscope, however, and you will see that each scale is plugged into a miniature socket on the wing. Rows of tubular sockets, with slightly constricted openings, line a naked wing. Each scale has a stem with a swelling or knuckle in the middle of it. Scales plugged into their socket have the swelling in the stem gripped by the constricted end of the socket. So just a light touch can unplug the scale and make dust. Apparently that damage is permanent.

Increase the magnification, and you will see that each scale is really a lacy structure made by ridges running lengthwise down it. Thin areas between ridges actually have numerous crossbars connecting the ridges together, but the holes between the crossbars makes it look lacy. Even more magnification reveals that the ridges consist of overlapping fingers of material fused together with spot welds. Like a long straight row of standing dominoes that have been pushed over, each finger rests on top of the neighboring one.

With the exception of melanin pigments that make dark colors, the elaborate structure of those tiny scales is actually what gives a butterfly its bright distinctive colors.

Lord of highest heaven, if You have put that much thought and detail into making a beautiful butterfly-wing scale, why is it that I ever wonder if You care about the details of my life?

Shining Butterfly Wings

And behold, I am coming quickly, and My reward is with Me, to give to every one according to his work. I am the Alpha and the Omega, the Beginning and the End, the First and the Last. . . . I, Jesus, have sent My angel to testify to you these things in the churches. I am the Root and the Offspring of David, the Bright and Morning Star. Rev. 22:12-16, NKJV.

The Andrews University Museum of Natural History is blessed to have a beautiful collection of tropical butterflies from South America of sizes and colors just not found in our temperate climes. As I pull out drawers of neatly arranged insects to show museum visitors the wealth of color and form of these tropical flyers, the reaction is always the same. Appreciative oooohs and ahh-hhs interspersed with lots of wows or "That's awesome!" The bright-blue metallic morphos and huge owl butterflies with the big "eyes" always get rave reviews, as do the clearwing butterflies with the transparent windows in their wings.

Scientists at the Georgia Institute of Technology work with butterfly wings. Zhong Lin Wang and his colleagues were attempting to construct a photonic waveguide. Now, a waveguide is something that has incredibly small repeating structures such that the geometry of the structure confines or directs light in ways determined by the structure. In other words, very small structures will precisely control the way light is given off. After much work they finally succeeded in using a novel technique to impregnate the fine structure of butterfly scales with angstrom thick layers of aluminum oxide. By controlling the number of treatment cycles, Wang could regulate the thickness of deposition on the butterfly scales.

After the coating, he heated the samples to drive off all original wing material and to crystallize the aluminum, creating tiny metal replicas of the wing's fine structure. "We can never come close to the richness of the structures that nature can make," Wang observes, so by using the butterfly wing as a template he could make fine structure copies in aluminum oxide.

The aluminum replicas, all without dye, exhibited characteristic colors depending on their thickness. The thinnest samples looked green. Thicker samples appeared yellow, pink, and purple. Non pigment-based colors won't fade or change color over time. Many butterflies derive their color from the fine structure of their scales. What a concept!

Clearly, Lord, You are the God of order and structure, of beauty and color. Everywhere I look I see evidence of Your creative genius.

Afterimage

Let no one deceive himself. If anyone among you seems to be wise in this age, let him become a fool that he may become wise. For the wisdom of this world is foolishness with God. 1 Cor. 3:18, 19, NKJV.

Imagine 50 black stars arranged in nine horizontal rows on a yellow field. Starting at the top, the odd-numbered rows each have six stars and the even numbered rows have five each. The yellow field is set in the upper corner of 13 horizontal green and black stripes. When projected on the screen, my students recognize what it is, but because of its color, it looks wrong. I ask them simply to stare at the lower center corner of the yellow field for about 30 seconds. Then, after 30 seconds, we go either to a plain black or plain white slide. What emerges in their head is a beautifully correct red, white, and blue flag.

By focusing both eyes steadily on one point, the image on the retina stays in one spot. Where the green stripes fall on the retina, the green-detecting cones repeatedly fire messages off to the brain reporting green. But it doesn't take them long to deplete their chemicals. We call such cones bleached or fatigued. Neighboring red- and blue-detecting cones in the green stripe areas, however, get to build up their supply of reporting chemicals. Where the yellow field image falls on the retina, cones that detect red and green both signal the yellow color and also become bleached.

So now when we switch to a completely plain white or plain black background, we get the same visual effect. A white background stimulates all cones equally, because white is a combination of all colors. In the regions where the green stripe was, the red- and blue-reporting cones now fire more effectively so that the brain detects red. Where the yellow was, the brain is now detecting blue, because the blue-reporting cones are so much stronger than any others. Where the black was before now looks light, giving the appearance of white. Switching to an all-black background suppresses the firing of all rods and cones. But since these photoreceptors never totally quit functioning, the bleached receptors do not respond as much, so now you see the red, white, and blue image quite clearly. And it lasts for 30 to 60 seconds until the bleached cones get their supplies of messenger chemicals restored again.

Perhaps a good point to remember here is that things are not always as they seem. Because our senses are so complex, they can be fooled.

Lord, keep me humbly focused on You so that I don't deceive myself or become misled by others. I do want to be true to You always.

Taking Pictures

When He is revealed, we shall be like Him, for we shall see Him as He is. 1 John 3:2, NKJV.

T hey are everywhere. And so small, too. Chances are you are in pixels several times every day. Walk into a store, go through an intersection or into a parking lot, or attend an event, and you find yourself recorded in pixels. Digital cameras are everywhere. Most cell phones double as a camera. All create pixels at the touch of a button.

Once you activate the camera, an image focuses on a silicone sensor consisting of a grid of tiny solar cells. Each position on the grid (i.e., each solar cell) corresponds to a position on the final picture called a pixel. Solar cells convert the energy of light into electricity according to the intensity of the light that strikes it. Much light makes more current. More current from the solar cell will make a brighter pixel in the final picture. So when all the information is gathered from each solar cell and the brightness of each pixel of the picture determined, we now see a nice black-and-white photo. The more solar cells that gather information and the smaller they are, the greater the resolution of the final image.

But what about color? Camera manufacturers accomplish this by putting an even smaller grid of filters (green, blue, and red) in front of each solar cell. Measuring how much colored light from each of those three colors that gets through the filters determines what color each pixel should be. A four-megapixel camera keeps track of the data from 4 million pixels that combine to make one picture.

Somewhat like a digital camera, our eyes have solar collectors called rods and cones that convert light into electrochemical signals Each eye has about 125 million rods so sensitive to low light that they can report as little as a single photon. Each eye has about 6 or 7 million cones for detecting color. Cones come in three different models. One kind detects red light best, another green, and yet another blue. But because their detection ranges overlap, we can distinguish millions of different colors. Most cones are concentrated in the central fovea of the retina (the area of sharpest vision), with far fewer out on the periphery. In contrast, most low-light-detecting rods are outside the central fovea, which is why dim points of light, like distant stars, disappear when you look directly at them and reappear when you glance away.

Lord, how much longer until we get to see the bright full-color image of Your face? I long to study every detail of Your kindness and Your love.

Meditation on the Name Joel

Return to the Lord your God, for he is gracious and merciful, slow to anger, and of great kindness. Joel 2:13, NKJV.

We named our son Joel. About a dozen people in the Bible share it, most notably a prophet, son of Pethuel, who wrote the book of Joel.

Joel is a simple name with just four letters. The first two letters stand for Jehovah, one of God's proper names. Jehovah is actually the anglicized form of the Hebrew YHWH, or Yahweh, a word that orthodox or observant Jews hold as so sacred that they dare not say it. Every time the word YHWH occurs in writing, they substitute "Adoni" ("My Lord"). The last two letters of Joel are another Hebrew name for God. El means God, as in Elohim, a word appearing more than 2,000 times in the Hebrew Bible. Another example is "Immanuel" (El = God, immanu = with us) used in reference to the Messiah.

Simply saying the name Joel is a one-word declarative statement affirming "Jehovah is God." Throughout history, the Creator-God has been so misrepresented, ignored, and maligned that whenever someone says the name Joel with meaning and understanding, it must bring joy to His heart. Just read a little from Isaiah 53 and think how you would feel if you were Jesus. "He is despised and rejected by men. . . . And we hid, as it were, our faces from Him; He was despised, and we did not esteem Him. . . . He was oppressed and He was afflicted, . . . He was led as a lamb to the slaughter" (verses 3-7, NKJV).

How do you feel when you go to your best friends' house? You are eager to see them. The lights are on, and both of their cars are in the driveway. Expectantly you walk up to the door as you hear sounds of merriment inside. Ringing the doorbell, you wait a while, then ring again. After another wait, you use the knocker on the front door. One of your friends walks by the door, glancing out the side glass. Although you know that he sees you, he still walks back into the house. I think anger would boil up in my heart. Why should I even try to be friends if he doesn't care about me? I have had it with this friendship. "Behold, I stand at the door and knock. If anyone hears My voice and opens the door, I will come in to him and dine with him, and he with Me" (Rev. 3:20, NKJV). Joel—Jehovah is God.

God's greatest desire is to be friends with us. Our first step in developing that friendship is to say with meaning and understanding, "Jehovah is God, and He is knocking on my door."

Come in, my Lord. I am truly sorry that I ignored You so long. Can we still be friends?

Harbor Seal Whiskers

And the fish of the sea will explain to you. Job 12:8, NKJV.

Just look at those big doleful eyes on a sleek, tan-furred, slightly spotted head. On either side of the black triangular nose and just above the mouth—would you look at those whiskers? A harbor seal has an amazing set of long vibrissae (that's what biologists call them) on each side of the upper lip and just a few over the eyes where an eyebrow should be.

For more than a decade a group of researchers have been training one harbor seal named Henry to teach them how he uses those amazing whiskers. We have always assumed that whiskers were sensitive to touch and might be really good for zeroing in for the last few inches of a fish kill— what harbor seals typically eat. But before Henry's lessons, we really didn't have a clue as to all they did. Wolf Hanke and his graduate students at the University of Rostock blindfolded and put headphones on the seal so that he couldn't see or hear what the scientists were doing. They ran a little toy propeller-driven submarine through the water of a small penned-in area. After sending their sub in random directions for a few seconds, they would turn it off and at the same time remove Henry's headphones, his signal to find the sub's trail in the water. Still blindfolded and using just his sensitive whiskers, Henry could find the path of disturbed water (a hydrodynamic trail) and accurately follow it to the sub 256 out of 326 trials (79 percent). The researchers tried more experiments, making Henry wait for a bit before locating the trail. The seal could follow aged hydrodynamic trails 10, 15, or 20 seconds old with the same ease and accuracy as before. It astonished the scientists. How could his whiskers be that sensitive? They knew he was using them because a sock over his muzzle that smoothed and held his whiskers down totally disabled his trailing abilities.

Later experiments, moving a fin through the water instead of a sub, showed that Henry could accurately follow trails up to 35 seconds old. After that he lost them easily. The most recent experiments have him following the hydrodynamic trail (the path in the sea) of different shaped paddles to see if he can distinguish the difference in shapes. For the most part, he can. Remember he is doing all these experiments blindfolded.

Since harbor seals don't have sonar and often hunt in murky water with poor visibility, being able to follow a hydrodynamic trail to a fish is an extremely useful ability.

Lord, Your creative genius continues to astonish us at every turn. How great You are. We worship You as our Creator and Redeemer.

Refining Gold

I indeed baptize you with water unto repentance, but He who is coming after me is mightier than I, whose sandals I am not worthy to carry. He will baptize you with the Holy Spirit and fire. Matt. 3:11, NKJV.

With gold and silver prices climbing out of sight, would-be prospectors seek ways to strike it rich. Mining river bottoms and sedimentary deposits often produce small quantities of gold and silver that one can then turn into small buttons or ingots of metal—primary refining. Secondary refining refers to collecting the gold or silver in old jewelry, electronics, gold fillings, and other stuff that accumulates in people's junk drawers.

Refining is a complex art with far too many steps to detail here. Most, however, involve purifying and concentrating the precious metals with acid baths and high-temperature flames that eradicate the base metals, leaving the gold and silver behind.

Very similar to the way that base metals and impurities cannot coexist with precious metals when heated to high temperatures, sin cannot coexist in the presence of God. His brightness—His fire—consumes sin instantly. Malachi 3:2 says that He is like a refiner's fire, i.e., a very hot fire. Silver melts at 1,763.2°F (961.8°C) and gold at 1,947.5°F (1,064.2°C). Zechariah 13:9 declares: "I . . . will refine them as silver is refined, and test them as gold is tested" (NKJV). And Hebrews 12:29 reminds us that "our God is a consuming fire" (NKJV). Now, that makes me wonder. Was it in any way symbolic that Shadrach, Meshach, and Abednego went into the fire, joined by God, and yet the three were not burned? They were there in the presence of God and were not consumed. Nebuchadnezzar's fire may have been just incidental. Because the three were true to Him, they could go through the fire and come out as pure gold. Is there a connection here?

Very similar to the way that base metals and impurities cannot coexist with precious metals when heated to high temperatures, sin cannot coexist in the presence of God.

I have to ask myself why I cling to sin so tenaciously. If sin is going to be automatically destroyed by the presence of God, then it stands to reason that whatever is stuck to sin will be eradicated too. Which is why Jesus warned: "If your hand or foot causes you to sin, cut it off and cast it from you. It is better for you to enter into life lame or maimed, rather than having two hands or two feet, to be cast into the everlasting fire" (Matt. 18:8, NKJV). Jesus was not, of course, recommending amputation, but was using imagery to emphasize the importance of separation from sin.

My Lord and Refiner, put me through the acid bath of daily trials and the flame of adversity if that is needed to purify me. Whatever it takes, prepare me for the fiery trials ahead.

Heart of Steel

A new heart also will I give you, and a new spirit will I put within you. Eze. 36:26, KJV.

In 2005 a glass and steel sculpture by German artist Julian Voss-Andreae was installed near the corner of 1st Street and A Avenue in the city of Lake Oswego, near Portland, Oregon. Entitled Heart of Steel, it is a giant replica of a hemoglobin molecule. At first the silvery steel facets reflected light in all directions. Within 10 days, though, iron in the steel had bound enough oxygen to turn the sculpture tan. After a month oxidation had worked its magic, producing a rich dark rusty-red surface. True to the function of an actual hemoglobin molecule, the steel model of hemoglobin also latched on to oxygen. Thus, in the artist's plan, the rusting was intentional, an attempt to model hemoglobin's important role in the body.

In our body the reaction between hemoglobin and oxygen happens in fractions of a second. Every single one of our many trillion red blood cells contains approximately 300 million molecules of this wondrous four-part protein called hemoglobin. Hemoglobin consists of four subunits, each a polypeptide of about 145 amino acids and a nonprotein heme group tightly holding an atom of iron at its center. Oxygen binds to iron, so it follows that each hemoglobin molecule carries four molecules of O_2 from the lungs to the tissues.

Hemoglobin thus has a natural affinity for oxygen, especially so when the CO_2 levels are low and pH is high—conditions typical in the lungs. But the really cool thing is that when one molecule of O_2 binds to the iron in one subunit there in the lungs, the other three subunits change shape slightly, greatly increasing their affinity for oxygen even more, so O_2 loads onto the hemoglobin molecule quickly. In contrast, in the tissues, where CO_2 levels are high and pH is low, the reverse happens—oxygen gets unloaded. Also, when one oxygen unloads, the shape-change thing happens again, making all unload quickly.

Blood in the lungs picks up the oxygen, and in less than 10 seconds that oxygen is passing through the capillaries, where it is in high demand. Within the next 10 seconds the red blood cells are back in the lungs, collecting another load.

It is the "heart of steel" in the hemoglobin molecule—that single atom of iron in each of the four heme groups—that gives hemoglobin its crucial ability. What is the crucial heart component that gives my heart great affinity for the Lord of the highest heavens?

Lord, I want a heart of flesh that quickly responds to Your Spirit.

Purple Loosestrife

Remember this: Whoever sows sparingly will also reap sparingly, and whoever sows generously will also reap generously. 2 Cor. 9:6, NIV.

Purple loosestrife is a colorful aquatic perennial plant native to Eurasia. Introduced into North America in the early 1800s, the plant known to botanists as *Lythrum salicaria* has proved that it is well able to establish robust populations and crowd out most native plant species, thus causing significant changes to normal plant and animal life in wetland areas. By the mid- to late-1900s botanists in the United States and Canada had become extremely concerned that the aggressive plant would simply take over, because it seems that it can outcompete other wetland plants, specifically grasses, sedges, and cattails. In Europe and Asia, where it is a native, the plant lives with insects that depend on it for food, and as such, the insects keep the plant in check so that it doesn't overgrow. But in North America the plant didn't have much of anything eating it.

Possibly its small seeds accidentally arrived as hitchhikers in raw wool or even in the wool of sheep brought over as stock animals. Sometimes it's purposefully introduced as a garden or medicinal plant because it has a beautiful stalk of purple flowers and is used in herbal medicine. Purple loosestrife, as its species name implies, contains salicarin, an astringent useful in reducing diarrhea and inflammation. People have also treated bacterial infections with it. The plant proliferates especially well when its seeds end up in disturbed wetland habitats. In addition, it can spread from plant parts and roots. I don't know of any plant that produces more seeds per plant per year. One plant can yield 2 to 3 million seeds in one year, with each flower on the stalk bearing literally dozens of tiny seeds that remain viable in the soil for years.

In Asia and Europe purple loosestrife is the only food of two species of leaf beetle called *Galerucella*. The *Galerucella* beetles consume its leaves and new tender buds. So when biologists started releasing the beetles in heavily infested areas, they began to see a reduction in loosestrife and a gradual return of cattails, sedges, and grasses as populations came back into balance. Is the loosestrife totally eradicated? No, but it no longer dominates. The beetles overwinter in the ground or in the stems of the loosestrife plants. Beetle females lay up to 500 eggs apiece each season, so the potential for population growth is strong.

Lord of prodigious productivity, You give us so many examples of abundance in nature. May I be as generous in donating my time and talents.

Hairy-winged Bats

The Lord will keep you from all harm—he will watch over your life.
Ps. 121:7, NIV.

Ever wonder how bats can fly with such great precision? After spending some time watching slow-motion video of bat flight, I am in awe. As the only mammals capable of sustained powered flight, bats lack feathers or a long stabilizing tail like birds. Rather, their wings consist of a thin membrane stretched from shoulder to shoulder by way of their tail. From the shoulder, the membrane goes out along the arm bones, around and between long delicate finger bones, then down to the tail. The weak hind legs provide the rear attachment for the wing membrane that is continuous, connecting both back legs and enclosing the tiny tail. As I watch bats fly, most of the movement is in the slender fingers. Forearm movement is slight compared to the fluid hand movements that generate the most lift and thrust. Slow-motion video of a bat maneuvering in a tight space demonstrates unbelievably aerobatic feats involving tight turns, climbs, dives, and controlled stalls and recoveries. And then there is the incredible landing that involves flipping upside down and gripping the ceiling with hind feet. The complexities of bat flight controls all seem to be built in (hardwired mechanisms) because very young bats don't spend time practicing flight—they just take off from their upside-down hanging position.

Susanne Sterbing-D'Angelo is a neuroscientist at the University of Maryland in College Park with strong interests in studying bat flight-control systems. In the June 21, 2011, online edition of the Proceedings of the National Academy of Sciences she confirmed suspicions that a previously discovered array of microscopic domed hairs on the otherwise hairless gossamer-thin membranous wings of bats provide them with flight control information. Her experiments involved finding the flight-control regions of the brain connected to these hairs, gently puffing air onto their wings, and watching the brain regions light up, then removing the hairs and recording how that affected flight behavior. All evidence points to the conclusion that bats get air-pressure data from each microscopic wing sensor. The bat's fly-by-wire control system apparently uses this data to micromanipulate yaw, pitch, and roll by slight changes in wing position and the strength and angle of downstroke to prevent stalls during tight turns.

Lord, why do I sometimes fret and worry because things don't seem to be turning out the way I would like them to be? If only I could remember that You have every detail all figured out.

Feral Cats

No temptation has overtaken you except such as is common to man; but God is faithful, who will not allow you to be tempted beyond what you are able, but with the temptation will also make the way of escape, that you may be able to bear it. Therefore, my beloved, flee from idolatry. 1 Cor. 10:13, 14, NKJV.

Since she always looks as dirty as a chimney sweep after cleaning a chimney, we named her Sooty. Better known to all as a tortoiseshell calico cat, she showed up on our doorstep as a feral cat one day many summers ago. To qualify as feral, a normally domesticated animal either returns to the wild or is born there and has not learned yet to trust humans. I have little doubt that Sooty was born in the wild, because, even after more than a decade of tender human care and affection, she still approaches us only on her own terms.

When she first started hanging around our isolated rural home, it was obvious that she was hungry. Suspecting that she may have belonged to one of our neighbors, we resisted the urge to feed her. But after more than a month of constantly showing up and slinking along the edges of our woods and life, we broke down and fed her. She has stayed around ever since.

Though there is simply no way to know for sure, estimates peg the United States feral cat population at somewhere between 30 and 60 million. In Australia, New Zealand, and other islands, feral cat populations have now been documented as the cause of species extinctions, particularly of birds and small mammals. Island populations of birds and small mammals are particularly vulnerable because they just don't have it in their DNA to be savvy in protecting themselves from new types of predators.

Their behavior is a good model for me to follow in escaping the wiles of the devil. Why is it I flirt with danger in my reading, my entertainment, my music, my Web browsing, and my friendships?

Feral cats tend to be top predators in many environments. Around our home, however, cats are vulnerable to hawks, owls, eagles, foxes, coyotes, and feral dogs. In other areas, wolves, bears, cougars, and other big cats might prey on them. So feral cats must become good at escape and evasion. Perhaps the reason that they do fend for themselves so successfully in the wild is that they are ever alert.

Their behavior is a good model for me to follow in escaping the wiles of the devil. Why is it I flirt with danger in my reading, my entertainment, my music, my Web browsing, and my friendships? What do I have in my home that needs to go out in the trash if I am to escape?

Lord, search me and know my heart. Strengthen my resolve for spiritual housecleaning.

Do Not Be Afraid

The seventh day shall be a holy day for you, a Sabbath of rest to the Lord. Ex. 35:2, NKJV.

Sabbath is a good day to remind myself that God is in control. I can relax and worship Him as my Lord and Savior. In Ecclesiastes 12:13 the wisest man who ever lived said: "Let us hear the conclusion of the whole matter: Fear God and keep His commandments, for this is man's all" (NKJV). In this context, "Fear God" does not mean to be afraid of Him but rather revere and adore God, have faith in Him, and with all humility submit to His will for your life.

Whenever angels or the Lord Himself appeared to humanity with a message or when God communicated through His prophets, their first words were usually "Do not be afraid" or "Fear not." Some examples:

- Genesis 26:24: "Do not fear [Abraham], for I am with you" (NKJV).
- Genesis 21:17: "Fear not [Hagar], for God has heard the voice of the lad" (NKJV).
- Genesis 46:3: "Do not fear [Jacob] . . . for I will make of you a great nation" (NKJV).
- Joshua 11:6: "Do not be afraid because of them [Joshua], for . . . I will deliver all of them slain" (NKJV).
- Isaiah 44:2: "Fear not" (NKJV).
- Isaiah 41:10 and 43:5: "Fear not, for I am with you" (NKJV).
- Isaiah 41:13: "Fear not, I will help you" (NKJV).
- Isaiah 43:1: "Fear not, for I have redeemed you" (NKJV).
- Daniel 10:19: "Fear not! [Daniel] Peace be to you; be strong, yes, be strong!" (NKJV).
- Joel 2:21: "Fear not . . . for the Lord has done marvelous things" (NKJV).
- Luke 1:13: "Do not be afraid, Zacharias for your prayer is heard" (NKJV).
- Luke 1:30: "Do not be afraid, Mary, for you have found favor with God" (NKJV).
- Luke 2:10: "Do not be afraid, for . . . I bring you good tidings of great joy" (NKJV).
- Revelation 1:17: "Do not be afraid [John]; I am the First and the Last" (NKJV).
- Revelation 2:10: "Do not be afraid of what you are about to suffer" (NIV).

So you see, Sabbath is a day of rest and gladness, because the Lord our God reigns and is in control of His creation, and we need not be afraid.

Lord, but what about . . . , but will I have enough . . . , but there are so many . . . , but—OK, my Jesus. In total faith I will trust in You. Your strength is sufficient.

October 6

The Harp

Praise Him with the sound of the trumpet; praise him with the lute and harp! Ps. 150:3, NKJV.

Is there any sound sweeter or gentler on the psyche than a well-played harp? With its variety of ornately carved and inlayed woods, its gold leaf accents, and its beautiful curves, is there any instrument more beautiful to look at than a modern concert harp? The word "harp" has negative connotations however. Take, for example, this phrase: "You keep harping on the fact that I need more sleep." "Harp" simply means to dwell on an idea tediously.

Harps are undoubtedly the oldest stringed instruments in existence. Images of them show up on prehistoric pictographs in French caves and in the tombs of ancient Egyptian pharaohs and even on a vase in an ancient Babylonian temple. To be sure, their shape, number of strings, and musicality have changed much through the years, probably starting out with the lyre, the bow harp, then the angle harp and post harp, and ending up with today's pedal harps.

With 53 references to the harp in the Bible from Genesis 4 to Revelation 18, the instrument has enjoyed a long history of service in praise to God. Jubal shows up just a few generations after Adam and is said to be the father of all those who play the harp (some translations use "lyre" here). First Samuel 16:16 describes David as acquiring his first royal palace experience because he was "a skillful player on the harp" (NKJV). Saul had been advised to get a musician to calm his nerves. So David was employed to soothe King Saul by playing the harp, an experience that almost cost him his life. David's psalms include 16 references to the harp. Most are along the lines of Psalm 33:2: "Praise the Lord with the harp" (NKJV).

Harpists were among the musicians that regularly gave praise to God during the Temple services. I understand that there were whole groups of Levites assigned to sing and to play harps and other instruments. At the dedication of Solomon's Temple hundreds of musicians came together to perform.

Certainly, Lord, You must have recordings of David's songs accompanied with harp and stringed instruments and cymbals. I can't wait to visit Your music archives and listen. Praise the Lord!

My Brethren

Then King David rose to his feet and said, "Hear me, my brethren and my people." 1 Chron. 28:2, NKJV.

I am blessed to have three brothers. I know that, of all my brothers, I am the favorite son. But then, I know that my older brother, and younger brother, and baby brother (now a grandpa himself) all feel the same way. Each of us knows that and can say it with conviction: "I am a favorite son." Thus when we get together as family, as we so often do, we enjoy great times together. The camaraderie and love are genuine. If we had beards, the oil would be dripping all over Mother's kitchen floor (Ps. 133:1, 2).

Whenever I consider King David, I think of an exceedingly successful servant leader. What made him a "man after God's own heart" was the fact that he was submissive to God and His leadership. Yes, at times he ran ahead of God, but he always came back under His headship. But then David aged, and it became time for him to step down.

As I read the story of the transition of power from David to Solomon as recorded in 1 Chronicles 28 and 29, I am awed by the power and majesty of David's rulership. He had conquered all of the surrounding kingdoms and was receiving tribute from them. As far as we can tell, his people loved him. He had been king for 40 years—that's two or perhaps three generations of his people. Yet when he rose to his feet to give his farewell speech, he didn't call his people subjects or peons or vassals. He addressed them as brothers, placing himself on their level. And his language showed that he had not forgotten God's instructions in Deuteronomy 17 when He had agreed to let His people have their own king. The Lord had directed them to choose one from among their "brethren" (verse 15, NKJV) and that the king should observe all of His laws and statutes so that his heart "be not lifted up above his brethren" (verse 20, NKJV).

David's humility reminds me that pride is what causes most Christians to run ahead of God and eventually lose their faith. Pride caused the fall of Lucifer. C. S. Lewis, in his book Mere Christianity, observed that pride "has been the chief cause of misery in every nation and family since the world began. . . . As long as you are proud, you cannot know God. A proud man is always looking down on things and people" (p. 96). King David, though he had great power and glory, ascribed it all to God and called his people "brothers."

Lord, again and again, as long as it takes, teach me to come under Your headship, to be submissive in every facet of life, and to give You all the glory and honor.

The Wonders of Wood

"Go up to the mountains and bring wood and build the temple, that I may take pleasure in it and be glorified," says the Lord. Haggai 1:8, NKJV.

C an there be a more enjoyable hobby or profession than woodworking? Jesus must have been good at it. I can see Him now, chiseling the perfect dovetail joint for something He was making for His father. Wood is a marvelous medium for making so many things besides cabinets.

Remove the bark from a twig and feel the slippery smooth surface. What you feel is a single microscopic layer of cells called the vascular cambium that makes wood—cell by cell, day by day during the growing season. As the long, slender cells divide lengthwise down the middle, they add another layer of long tubular cells known as tracheids or vessels to the hard outer surface of the existing wood. The newest cells mature by thickening their walls of cellulose, depositing hard lignin in the cell wall, and then they die, leaving behind just the empty lignified cell wall to be a new conduit for water flowing from root to shoot.

A mature well-watered tree may evaporate 300 to 400 gallons of water from pores in its leaves on a warm summer day. Flowing water brings with it a dilute solution of minerals that leaves use in photosynthesis. By combining atmospheric carbon dioxide, water, and minerals, a huge list of organic compounds called phytochemicals materialize. The tree transports and uses them as building blocks to make new cells or stores it in the wood. Saw into fresh wood, and you will smell the aroma of those stored chemicals being released.

Black walnut is a hard close-grained wood with a nutty aroma. With its large vessels red oak is amazingly porous and smells a bit sour. Who doesn't like the scent of butter-soft white pine with its resinous smell? Each wood has its unique look, its characteristic scent, and its most useful function. For example, baseball bats are made of ash. Black cherry, black walnut, mahogany, and oak are wonderful furniture woods. Tool handles employ hickory. Redwood and cedar are great for outdoor projects, because of their resistance to rot. Think of all the exotic woods such as spalted maple and beech, bubinga and wenge, ebony, zebrawood, purpleheart, and rosewood. Their beauty and functionality is breathtaking. We find endless variety in grain and figuring. No two pieces are alike. Can you tell that I love wood? Jesus must love wood, too, because He made it with so much beauty and functionality.

O Master Designer, use me in the way that You planned for my life.

Morse Code

—• ——— —••   •• •••   •—•• ——— •••—   • 1 John 4:8.

I f you didn't understand the code above telling you that "God is love", maybe you will recognize this: ••• ——— •••. Oh, yes. Most of us understand the sign SOS of distress.

Before computers, before ascii text, before UHF radio, or any voice radio for that matter, there was Morse code. It actually got started in 1836 when three men started collaborating together on what would become an electrical telegraph machine. Physicist Joseph Henry, machinist and inventor Alfred Vail, and a well-recognized portrait artist and painter named Samuel F. B. Morse worked together to design and build a contraption that would open and close an electromagnet at some remote location to make clicking sounds. By 1844, about when the system was first used, a stylus made dots and dashes on a strip of moving paper that one could decode as letters. Later, the operators simply learned to listen to the clicking and tell what letter was coming—they didn't have to look at the paper.

The code itself started out with just numbers, but Vail later expanded it to include letters and also special characters such as periods and commas. Though it is hard to believe now, when Charles Lindbergh flew the Spirit of St. Louis across the Atlantic in 1927, he had no radio, no form of communication with anybody. He was totally alone. Only later did airplanes get equipped with radios, and they employed only Morse code.

A story tells about a man who responded to a newspaper ad for Morse code operators. On finding the right address, he walked into a noisy office with clicking telegraph machines. Only a sign at the front desk instructed applicants to fill out a form and be seated until called. After completing the form, the man joined seven other individuals waiting patiently to be called. In short order, the newcomer got up and boldly entered the office door, closing it behind him. The seven other men raised their eyebrows, wondering about his impudence.

Within minutes the prospective employer emerged, thanking and dismissing them with the information that the position had been filled. More than a bit nonplussed, the seven jobseekers complained that they had been there first and hadn't been given a chance. Smiling kindly, the interviewer stated that he had been in his office tapping out the message "If you understand this message, then come on in, the job is yours."

Lord, teach me to hear Your voice amid the cacophony of life. Tune my ear to Your message for me. Give me clarity of understanding.

October 10

Teacher Ant

Show me Your ways, O Lord; teach me Your paths. Ps. 25:4, NKJV.

His body language spoke volumes. It took all the self-control and discipline he could muster just to take a seat in the back corner of my classroom on that opening day of class. Chin close to chest and glowering, narrowed eyes peering out through tensioned eyebrows telegraphed that he didn't want to be here and was not interested in biology. Taking note of the negative vibes, I greeted him warmly. Somehow he managed to make it through the first class period . . . and the second . . . and the third. But the going wasn't easy. Poor reading skills usually translate into poor academic achievement, but at least he was staying with the class and starting to connect with me and the content of the course.

My job as teacher is like connecting a big fat invisible rubber band to each of my students. Some are raring to go, and the rubber band just keeps them close to me. Others I have to start pulling. The rubber band stretches and applies tension, but they aren't moving yet. The summertime inertia is too great. At last, I feel a slight movement. They are starting to learn. Applying more tension can get them going faster or break the rubber band. Sensitive to the fragility of each band, I pull harder. We are both moving now and picking up speed. Uh, ohhh, we hit a hard spot. One or more of my students comes to a screeching halt. The bands break, and I have to back up and hook up again before we are all on the move once more.

Adjusting the teaching to the pace of the learner, keeping teacher and student connected with constant feedback from both parties, used to be thought of as a uniquely human situation. But now researchers at the University of Bristol, studying ants, have concluded that they find teaching/learning behavior in at least one species of ant. Ants who have been to a food source and learned the route home regularly teach it to other

My job as teacher is like connecting a big fat invisible rubber band to each of my students.

ants. An ant will run in tandem with a teacher ant leading the way. Without a "student" ant following, the teacher could get to the food source and back twice in the time it takes with the other ant tagging along. The student ant wanders in little loopy detours, getting the "lay of the land." So the teacher ant slows up, waiting for the other ant to tap it on the leg before it moves on. After one trip, student ants hurry right along or become tandem-running teachers themselves. Occasionally, when a student is simply "piggybacked" to the food source, it still doesn't know the way home.

Lord, how many detours have I been on? I know that You are teaching me to stay on a level and smooth path. Be my tandem runner.

October 11

No Fear

So do not fear, for I am with you; do not be dismayed, for I am your God. I will strengthen you and help you; I will uphold you with my righteous right hand. Isa. 41:10, NIV.

Nighttime is the best time to hunt for krill and fish in Antarctic waters, the main food of penguins. So it makes sense that penguins should fish at night. But penguins hunt for food only during the day, when it is actually harder to catch their food. David Ainley and Grant Ballard published a June 2011 report in the journal Polar Biology concluding that the danger of predators prevents penguins from entering the water at night. Leopard seals, their main enemies, sleep during the day.

It seems that most animals have a fear of one type or another, though silverback gorillas, elephants, and hippos may show no fear, and such top predators as lions and tigers will appear fearless. Perhaps they exhibit less fear because they have more control. Fear is most often associated with the loss of control—one reason that people become especially fearful after earthquakes or tornadoes or terrorist attacks. Big animals and top predators seem to have more mastery over their lives. Prey species, being weaker, have to use their wits and develop strategies (such as hunting during the day) to survive.

One experimental psychologist tested the concept of fear and control in rats this way. She sounded a tone and then shocked the feet of rats. Half of the rats had a ledge they could step on that turned off the shock in one second—a way of controlling the situation. The others didn't. Later, just playing the tone would elicit fear in the rats without control much more than in those who had the control.

Therapists who work with fear and phobias in humans have learned that exposure therapy or systematic desensitization, a form of cognitive behavioral therapy, is quite effective in calming fears. Clients start off by talking about their fears in the safety of the office. Later they visit frightening situations accompanied by the therapist who can help them realize their fears are unfounded and irrational. My God is big enough, powerful enough, and wise enough to control each and every situation. By staying close to Him and trusting Him fully, I need not fear.

Lord, You are my light and my salvation—whom shall I fear? You are the stronghold of my life—of whom shall I be afraid?

A Beautiful Crash

He has made everything beautiful in its time. Also He has put eternity in their hearts, except that no one can find out the work that God does from beginning to end. Eccl. 3:11, NKJV.

When I tried it, it took the Google search engine only 0.19 seconds to come up with 33,500 hits on the two words "trifid nebula" when in images mode (five times more hits in Web mode). And what a beautiful montage of images shows up on my screen. In terms of cosmic beauty, I have always been partial to the Trifid Nebula located about 7,600 light-years away from us in the constellation Sagittarius. Nebulas get that name from being, well, nebulous (a Latin word meaning cloud or haze—we also use the word to mean unclear, vague, or ill-defined). Classified as an H II region, astronomers know it as M20. Enormous amorphous clouds of ionized atomic hydrogen glowing beautifully receive H II status in contrast to H I, which contains neutral hydrogen atoms and molecular hydrogen. OK, enough of the technical stuff.

The Trifid Nebula is simply gorgeous. What I see in the photos is a large bright-white star in the center. Moving out from that glorious brightness, the bright white fades to pinks, blues, yellows, and finally oranges. It is somewhat like a big spherical fuzzy rainbow of colors. Colors vary from picture to picture depending on what emissions astronomers were sampling. In all pictures, however, the bright glowing regions have either big cracks across them, letting dark space show through from behind, or seen another way, you can imagine the dark as masses of stuff blocking the glow from behind.

Of course, the Trifid Nebula is only one of many H II regions in the cosmos. For example, the middle star in the sword of Orion, known as the great nebula of Orion, was the first H II region recognized as a cloud of glowing gas rather than a single star. Other beautiful nebulas include the Horsehead Nebula and Flame Nebula (both in Orion) and the Eagle Nebula in the constellation Serpens.

Japanese astronomers, using telescopes in Chile, are now carefully analyzing Doppler shifts in the red regions of the Trifid Nebula, giving them data on the velocities of their gases. They conclude that the gases are glowing because of two different clouds crashing into each other. What a God to bring so much beauty from cosmic collisions.

How often have You done it in my life, Lord? You seem to specialize in turning tragedy into triumph, tears into diamonds, and anguish into joy and jubilation. To God be the glory.

October 13

Gopherwood and Bitumen

Make yourself an ark of gopherwood; make rooms in the ark, and cover it inside and outside with pitch. Gen. 6:14, NKJV.

God is an amazing material scientist. He excels too as an architectural engineer. The text above is a mere snippet of God's instructions for Noah on what to use to make the ark so that he and his family (and hopefully additional passengers) and animals could escape the Flood. Let's consider for a minute about what God provided for the construction.

Gopherwood—what is that? Good question. No tree called gopherwood exists today. Since we don't know where Noah originally lived, we can't go and see what grows there now. And even if we knew where Noah did the construction, we don't know where the wood might have come from or how the ecology of the construction zone may have changed since the Flood. Clarke's Commentary on the Bible suggests that the wood may have been cypress since that tree was abundant around a likely Mount Ararat site. But that too is just a guess. What we do know is that specifications for the wood would have had to have been spectacular. Think of a wooden boat making it through a catastrophic flood without having the sides caved in by the extreme forces.

We have examples of tough and durable woods with high breaking strength. Hickory is excellent. Tool handles are made of hickory because it is so tough. Teakwood is exceedingly tough as well as rot and water resistant, making an excellent candidate for ark building. Acacia wood and locust woods are also possibilities because of their strength and durability. Wood is an amazing construction material because it is light and strong. Whatever wood the 450-foot-long ark consisted of, it must have been durable and well crafted to survive the beating of what must have been the perfect storm.

Pitch is one of several biblical words used to signify asphalt or more properly, bitumen. It is a black, highly viscous hydrocarbon goo that oozes out of the ground in various places. Around the Dead Sea, outcrops of the black rock are common, and cracks in the rock underlying the Dead Sea allow bitumen to periodically produce masses of floating asphalt. When heated, bitumen liquefies, then cools hard as rock. Because of its adhesive qualities, people in Bible times used it as a mortar for brick. The little basket of bulrushes that floated baby Moses was coated with pitch to make it waterproof. Noah's ark had a layer of pitch outside and inside to seal joints and prevent leaks. What a God to provide the needed materials.

Creator of strong wood and protective pitch, strengthen me for the storms ahead and seal my commitment to obeying Your Word.

Bats and Wind Turbines

Concerning the works of men, by the word of Your lips, I have kept away from the paths of the destroyer. Ps. 17:4, NKJV.

Bats are important insect-control agents, saving farmers millions of dollars on insecticides. Have you tried catching a flying insect? Its erratic movements make it terribly hard to intercept. But the bat is an expert at catching insects while in flight, homing in on them in the dark with their elaborated echolocation system. The twists and turns of its flight path to catch insects are awesome to watch.

So why are some using bats as an excuse to halt construction of giant wind turbines employed to generate clean electricity? Why do wind turbines get shut down during light wind conditions at night and during periods of known bat migration? The short answer is that a lot of dead bats are being found around the base of wind turbines after a night of light wind conditions, times when most bats are out hunting insects. Many dead bats also show up there during bat migration. Are they being attracted to and colliding with the rapidly moving giant turbine blades that sometimes travel several hundred miles per hour? Since several species of bats face possible extinction, as environmental stewards we should find out what is going on.

At first people attributed the dead bats and birds around wind turbines with collisions with the blades. It only makes sense. But now, after careful study and dozens of autopsies, we are beginning to understand the problem. Compared to the number of dead birds, there are far more dead bats. Most if not all birds show signs of impact damage. On the other hand, almost half the bats have not been hit by anything. They just fell out of the sky dead. Autopsies show extensive internal hemorrhage—specifically, burst capillaries in the lungs and lungs filled with fluid. Bird lungs are quite different than those of the bats. They are tougher, more resistant to sudden pressure changes. Scientists conclude that spinning blades cause large air pressure drops behind the blade. Experiments show that a pressure drop of as little as 4.4 kilopascals can kill a lab rat. Pressure drops behind the spinning blades have been measured at 5 to 10 kilopascals. A bat flying through this space would suffer rapid expansion of lung tissue, causing blood vessels to burst quickly. Even getting close to a blade can kill a bat.

Lord, how does proximity to sin affect me? Is this yet another lesson for me to stay as far away from it as possible? Teach me that Your Word is my only protection from spiritual violence.

October 15

Strong Repellent

Therefore submit to God. Resist the devil and he will flee from you. Draw near to God and He will draw near to you. James 4:7, 8, NKJV.

It was supposed to be one of those fun summer afternoon parties—a picnic with friends. The Frisbees are flying, badminton net is up, food on the grill, soft drinks on ice, watermelon cut, colorful strawberry and spinach salad dressed in zesty vinaigrette. Friends bring lawn chairs and blankets to sit on. As the badminton game gets going, uninvited guests begin arriving too. Slap. Scratch. Slap. Slap. Bare legs bloom with bloody spots from direct hits on mosquitoes caught in the act. Necks, cheeks, and shoulders now show welts too. But only for some people. Why am I slapping and scratching while others are unfazed? It isn't fair. Do mosquitoes actually pick and choose whom to bite? Are some people's clothes, skin, or blood more attractive to them than others?

Yes, some people do get targeted much more than others. With some factors we have no control. For example, our genetics might make our natural body odors unusually attractive to mosquitoes. How we metabolize cholesterol and the composition of organic acids on our skin may affect how mosquitoes respond. But some things we can control, such as wearing light-colored clothing and avoiding shady areas. Leaving off the sweet-smelling shampoo, deodorant, and perfumes sometimes helps a little. Slathering nasty-smelling DEET or odorless Picaridin has proven to be protective, because mosquitoes don't like those chemicals. One thing I haven't tried yet is to stop moving and to stop breathing. The word is that movement attracts mosquitoes, and they have excellent CO_2 detectors that can zero in on you from up to 50 feet away. Do the last precaution, however, and you won't be the life of the party—at least not for long!

> *Do mosquitoes actually pick and choose whom to bite? Are some people's clothes, skin, or blood more attractive to them than others?*

In Alaska, where mosquitoes can be serious threats, the recommendation is to keep all your skin covered with tight cotton fabrics, not loosely woven polyesters. Head nets, good clothing, at least 30 percent DEET, and smoldering pyrethroid impregnated coils offer your best protection against dark swarms of mosquitoes.

The lesson is clear. Stay close to fresh DEET and smoldering coils. The mosquitoes will actually turn and fly the other way. Keeping close to the protection is the key.

Lord, is that the way it is with You and the devil? Give me a heart totally submissive to You and totally resistive to the devil. Keep me close to You, my protector and shield.

Random Acts of Kindness

What is desired in a man is kindness. Prov. 19:22, NKJV.

Recently my wife and I hopped on the motorcycle to take a warm summer evening spin out to celebrate what for us is a special day. It wasn't a big deal, really, but in a way it was—just taking time to be together and enjoying our friendship. A short drive out through beautiful orchards and aromatic vineyards sits one of our favorite little country restaurants. In the back corner near the register are a couple glassed-in freezer cabinets with a great selection of flavors of . . . you guessed it . . . ice cream. This time when we stepped in, a crowd had gathered around the freezer cabinets— most unusual for this small restaurant. The tables were empty—not at all uncommon when it's not a regular mealtime.

One man in the crowd saw us enter and boldly asked if we were coming in for ice cream. I replied yes, but that we were in no hurry. We could come back later. He must have been their leader, because he insisted that we go ahead. So, after more insisting, we did step through, made our selections quickly, and headed for the register to pay for our treats. But then he ordered the clerk not to take our money. Again he insisted that she put our selections on his tab. Who was he, anyway? A total stranger. Thanking him profusely, we went out to sit in the breezy shade to visit and attempt to finish our ice cream before it melted. It was a random act of kindness when we could at least thank the giver.

Another time we were in a distant city with family, enjoying a meal in a restaurant. Someone must have heard and enjoyed our animated conversation, because when we asked for the check, the waiter informed us that another patron had already paid our entire bill while expressing joy in our interactions. We were free to go. "Well, who was it?" I asked. "Are they still here? Can we thank them?" All we got was a shrug and a side-to-side shake of the head. Another random act of kindness from an unknown benefactor.

Being the recipient of such a thing is an unexpected blessing, a pleasant reminder that many good people do live in our world. But, as Scripture says, it is more blessed to give than to receive. And because I joy in the blessing, I make a practice of doing random acts of kindness. Plowing the snow from a neighbor's (or better yet, a distant neighbor's) driveway while they are still sleeping, mowing someone's yard without their knowledge, raking their leaves while they are away for the weekend . . . there are thousands of ways to bless and be blessed. Try it today.

My kind and loving Jesus, give me an idea today of a way I can bless another.

Cause and Effect

And you, my son Solomon, acknowledge the God of your father, and serve him with wholehearted devotion and with a willing mind, for the Lord searches every heart and understands every desire and every thought. If you seek him, he will be found by you; but if you forsake him, he will reject you forever. 1 Chron. 28:9, NIV.

T wo things happen in short succession. One is a loud crash followed by tin- kling as the plate glass shatters into a million pieces. Another is a session of batting practice in the front yard going well until . . . the misdirected line drive heads straight toward the big bay window. It doesn't take long to figure out which happened first, does it?

Take any two connected events. The first to happen is always the cause, while the next is the effect. It is that simple. Pull the tail of a cat (the cause), and you hear a yowl (the effect). Punch a hole in the bottom of your sailboat (the cause), and it fills with water (first effect) and sinks (second effect), then you have to swim to shore (third effect) and call a taxi to get home (fourth effect). Some causes set off a chain of events.

Does a certain cause always have exactly the same effect? Golfers certainly hope so. That is why they practice so much. They figure that if you hit the ball exactly the same way, it will go to the same place. The challenge of golf is controlling the many variables of the swing, the weather, and the course to get the little dimpled ball in the hole. Scientists also depend on certain causes always giving the same effects. Controlling all the variables is the challenge of scientific experimentation. Most scientists would abandon their pursuits if they thought that nature was capricious.

The story of Job lets us know that at times factors (causes) we don't know about produce effects that we may not understand. Job was doing (causes) everything right, but because of a little cosmic experiment, all of his effects suddenly went south. His friends blamed him for wrong actions. And though Job didn't under- stand what was going on and certainly wasn't enjoying the effects, his unshakable trust in God pulled him through. Most of the time, though, cause and effect are predictable and understandable.

Lord, I am ready to serve You now. What is Your wish for me? I will "cause" what is Your will today, following Your written and oral instructions. However, the effects, Lord, are Your department entirely, and I won't worry about them at all. I trust You completely.

Egg to Egg

Sing to Him, sing psalms to Him; talk of all His wondrous works. 1 Chron. 16:9, NKJV.

Like a colorful stained-glass window with brilliant orange panes edged in black, the female monarch butterfly daubs her abdomen several times on the underside of a milkweed leaf. She will lay as many as 500 eggs.

Within three or four days the tiny yellowish eggs, looking like miniature Japanese lanterns, turn slightly transparent. Inside, darks spots move around. As we watch, a hole develops near the top end of one egg. We see a tiny light yellow- green caterpillar with monstrous black eyes and some dark transverse banding struggle to get out of the hole it just made. As soon as it extricates itself from the close confines of the egg, it turns right around and eats the egg case.

The larva starts chewing holes in the leaf. Gripping the edge of the leaf with its peg-like anal and abdominal prolegs, the larva eats and eats, growing larger every day. It stops briefly to shed its skin for a larger size, then consumes the old skin. For a couple weeks it eats and molts and grows about 30,000 times larger than what it started out in the egg.

The last larval instar (the biggest and last of the caterpillars) is a handsome yellow to green with black transverse stripes bordered by white. Because it feeds on milkweed, the larva is full of cardiac glycosides, chemicals poisonous to birds and mammals and thus why it is such a colorful caterpillar. When you don't taste good and can poison who eats you, it pays to advertise that fact with bright, gaudy colors. Two long black fleshy "horns" on the front end and two shorter ones on the tail end help make the big fat caterpillar look dangerous. Now comes the truly miraculous part. The caterpillar attaches its anal prolegs to the underside of a twig or branch by spinning a mass of strong silk threads. Then it just relaxes, hanging head down. At this point it looks dead except it wiggles every once in a while. Soon you see its striped skin split down the back. After more wriggling and squirming, the skin falls off, leaving a green segmented pupa. Time passes, and the pupa loses the segmentations, becoming a green chrysalis. After first getting darker and darker, it then becomes semitransparent so that you can see inside. Soon the chrysalis splits open along the butterfly's back, and it pushes itself out, stretching long delicate legs, antennae, and a long coiled mouthpiece, and spends a couple hours pumping out its short stubby wings till they are full and beautiful.

Lord, watching You change the big fat caterpillar into a delicate flier assures me that You can change me from a selfish sinner into a kindhearted, generous soul. I am ready.

Friends

Then King David went in and sat before the Lord.
1 Chron. 17:16, NKJV.

A deeply suntanned man with kind eyes walks heavily down the hallway. Pausing at the door of his small private chapel, he removes his crown and lays it on the small table beside the flickering oil lamp. Reverently entering the cedar-paneled room, he bows low before sitting gently on a cushion. His mind races back over the past few months. The big conference of leaders had agreed with him and unanimously voted to bring the ark of God from Abinadab's home at Kirjathjearim to Jerusalem. Music, praising, singing. All had been going well, the ark riding high, in full view of all, on a new cart pulled by a matched pair of oxen. That is, all went well until one of the oxen stumbled, the ark teetered, and Uzza reached out to steady the load.

King David shakes his grizzled head in dismay, remembering his anger, mostly at himself, for not following the Lord's instructions, thus making him responsible for Uzza's death. Celebration had turned to mourning as they had parked the ark temporarily in the home of Obededom. God had certainly blessed that home. Now, three months later, and this time, with everything done right—ritually clean priests carried the ark by its poles as per instructions. A pause for sacrifices accompanied the singing, instrumental music, and dancing. David smiled, remembering the resumption of tabernacle services. Joy bubbled up in his heart as he reviewed the psalm of thanksgiving composed for the grand occasion (1 Chron. 16:8-36).

As he returned to the palace, David replayed in his mind the high he had felt. Walking through the carved cedar doors held wide by the mighty men of his guard detail, he continued down the hall to his private chambers paneled in the finest cedar and trimmed in gold. He remembered the nagging question "How can I live in splendor while my God lives in a tent?" Quickly he had consulted with the prophet Nathan, who had supported his idea. And then Nathan had returned the next day, bringing a message from God to David. Oh, what disappointment. David was not the one to build the Temple. It would be his son that would get that privilege.

So now David sits before the Lord and talks as to a friend. It's OK, Lord. You know best, and I will do just as you say. Thank You for Your blessing.

O Lord, my God, give me a heart that longs to sit down and chat, a heart that seeks to do Your will. Give me a heart instantly submissive, constantly tuned to Your commands.

Probability

Most assuredly, I say to you, he who believes in Me has everlasting life. John 6:47, NKJV.

C ontrary to what you may have heard in advertising or political debate or what you may believe about science, real scientists don't "prove" anything. Rather they hypothesize and test and develop theories and models that best explain the data. And throughout all this activity, they work with probabilities, demonstrating that, given the conditions X, there is a high probability that Y is likely to happen (or little probability, whatever the case may be). OK, if nothing else, perhaps scientists have "proved" that everything in science is open for debate. Take gravity for example. All of us experience it every day. Isaac Newton presented the universal law of gravitation to the Royal Society in 1686, a model that has worked wonderfully to describe attractions between bodies, so much so that we use his laws to calculate the orbits of space objects even today. So it's settled . . . right? Wrong. Physicists are still trying to figure out exactly how gravitation works. So even the universal law of gravitation is still being debated.

A French mathematician and philosopher who did much to refine and mature probability theory was Blaise Pascal, a child prodigy and inventor of the mechanical calculator. In his Pensées, a collection of notes published after his death, Pascal wrote about the existence of God and how to think about it. He believed that God is incomprehensible—that we simply can't know much about Him. Reason, he wrote, was not adequate to determine whether God does or does not exist. So in note 233 of his Pensées he suggested the following logic to make a decision.

> *Real scientists don't "prove" anything. Rather they hypothesize and test and develop theories and models that best explain the data.*

There are only two possibilities. God either exists or He does not. You must make a choice to believe or not believe—you don't have an option. If you choose to believe in Him, that leads to only two outcomes. If He does exist, then you have won it all. But if He doesn't exist, you have lost nothing. Think of the alternative now. Say you choose not to believe in God. Again there are two—and only two—outcomes. If God does exist, you lose it all, but if He does not, you lose nothing. Given the possibility then of losing all if you don't believe and gaining all if you do believe, Pascal decided that it was a philosophical no-brainer. One should choose to believe in God. This logic about the existence of God is known as Pascal's Wager.

Fortunately, we have words from Jesus Himself. "Most assuredly" means "without doubt." It is not a gamble or a game of probability, but a sure thing.

Lord, I choose to believe in You as my God.

Caddisfly

So in Christ Jesus you are all children of God through faith, for all of you who were baptized into Christ have clothed yourselves with Christ. Gal. 3:26, 27, NIV.

Perhaps he didn't look strange walking the streets of fifteenth- and sixteenth-century English villages. But to us, the bits of cloth and ribbon almost obscuring the coat of the Cadice-man would certainly catch our attention today. Had we been there, our incredulous stare would no doubt be taken as an invitation by the Cadice-man to approach and attempt to sell fabric or ribbon similar to the samples advertised on his coat.

Perhaps entomologists named the caddis fly in honor of Cadice-men, traveling fabric salespeople of the time. For you see, caddis fly larvae or nymphs living on stream bottoms or lake beds spin little silken tubes to live in. And like the Cadice-man, the nymph decorates its home tube with sand, gravel, or vegetation of various types to camouflage its home, making it a safe refuge. I remember watching the first caddis fly nymph that I had ever seen crawling in a quiet pool. The back half of its body was inside a nifty sand tube, and when I touched it, the whole body retracted into the tube instantly. Then I found similar tubes of fine gravel cemented with silk, making a wonderful home for an extremely homely insect larva.

After weeks of feeding on detritus on stream bottoms, the nymph seals up both ends of the tube and pupates. When the water temperature gets to the right (cold) temperature, all caddis fly pupa, in synchrony, chew out of their cases and get to the surface, where they emerge as adults. Many different species, each emerging at different times, produce several blooms of adults or imagos, an important source of food for fish. So many adults can emerge at one time that they can clog air-conditioners or make a mess of your car as you drive through the swarms.

Caddis fly nymphs have learned the secret of dressing properly. Without their tube, it is easy for fish to recognize them as a tasty morsel. But when inside their decorated tubes, their predators do not see their grub-like or caterpillar-like body. Likewise, we are instructed to clothe ourselves in Christ, to be hid in Christ, to put on the body of Christ. When properly clothed, then others will see Christ and His righteousness when they look at us.

Lord, I do want to dress for success in Your kingdom. Cover me with Your robe of righteousness, because all of my garments are as filthy rags.

October 22

Humus

He also had farmers and vinedressers in the mountains and in Carmel, for he loved the soil. 2 Chron. 26:10, NKJV.

The Creator-God is concerned with every detail of His creation. You might think that dirt or soil is just what everything eventually turns into—sort of the refuse pile of the world—and God wouldn't have to bother Himself much with that. Just think, when anything dies, even a car, it eventually gets recycled, returned to the earth as small particles that mix in with the soil. It might take a while, but even solid rock breaks down to become sand, then silt, finally clay. When living things decompose, smaller and smaller critters eat and recycle. Eventually the organic matter becomes special stuff called natural organic matter (soil scientists or geochemists call it NOM). Most NOM consists of humic substances. So what are they and why are they so important?

The International Humic Substances Society (yes, there is such an organization, with members from most developed countries of the world) even has difficulty defining exactly what humic substances are. They describe it as consisting of very large, exceedingly complex, highly stable organic molecules resulting from biological decomposition. The large molecules tend to be brown to black, their atomic mass varying from 200 to 20,000 atomic mass units, and they generally result from the breakdown of animal and plant products such as lignin, cutin, waxes, tannin, resins, cellulose, and other sugars as well as proteins and fats. Their molecular components combine in different ways to make a wildly creative array of complex NOM. To date, the molecules have resisted all attempts to crystallize them, so we cannot determine their molecular structure by X-ray crystallography, the normal method of analyzing a compound. So what good are these brown compounds that constitute much of compost?

Much uncertainty remains, but they are important for holding water, buffering the pH of the soil, grabbing soil minerals to keep them from leaching to deeper layers, enhancing soil quality in terms of its workability, and providing "food" for some soil bacteria. Like good king Uzziah (verses 9, 10), farmers know the look and feel of good soil even if only God knows the chemical makeup and how He has designed it to work.

Lord and designer of miraculous mega-molecule humic substances, teach us to be better stewards of the soil even as we learn about the gifts You have given to us.

Be Ready

Therefore you also be ready, for the Son of Man is coming at an hour you do not expect. Matt. 24:44, NKJV.

Have you ever checked the Web site www.ready.gov? Called "Ready America," it is part of a public-service advertising campaign started in 2003 to enhance citizen preparedness for disasters that might happen. The earth seems to be convulsing with major earthquakes, volcanic eruptions, flooding, tsunamis, tornadoes, forest fires, winter storms, civil unrest, and wars. If there ever was a need for "Ready America," it is now.

The main message for all is: 1. Have a kit with water, food, first aid, and other important emergency supplies. Get it together and ready to go because once disaster strikes, there is no time to gather your supplies. 2. Make a plan for whom to contact out of town and how you will get in touch with each other. Gather the important phone numbers and plan ways for regrouping after a disaster. 3. Be informed on the types of disasters most likely to impact you and be especially ready for them.

As important as it is to be ready for the life-changing occurrences that happen every day to someone, somewhere, it is far more vital to be prepared for the event of all events. When God returns to earth in His great rescue mission at the end of time, no kit or list of phone numbers or spot of safety on this planet will suffice. Let's listen in as Jesus gives His disciples pertinent information as recorded in Mark 13: "Watch out that no one deceives you. . . . When you hear of wars and rumors of wars, do not be alarmed. Such things must happen, but the end is still to come. Nation will rise against nation, and kingdom against kingdom. There will be earthquakes in various places, and famines. These are the beginning of birth pains. You must be on your guard. . . . Everyone will hate you because of me, but the one who stands firm to the end will be saved. . . . Let no one on the housetop go down or enter the house to take anything out. . . . At that time people will see the Son of Man coming in clouds with great power and glory. And he will send his angels and gather his elect" (verses 5-27, NIV).

Ellen White says: "See the storms and tempests. . . . Here we are dependent upon God for our lives—our present and eternal life. And being in the position that we are, we need to be wide awake, wholly devoted, wholly converted, wholly consecrated to God. But we seem to sit as though we were paralyzed. God of heaven, wake us up!" (Selected Messages, book 2, p. 52).

God of heaven, wake us up. May we be ready to meet You in the air.

Before You Were Born

Before I formed you in the womb I knew you, before you were born I set you apart; I appointed you as a prophet to the nations. Jer. 1:5, NIV.

D oes it give you a good feeling to realize that God knew every detail about you long before you were born? Does it provide you a sense of satisfaction and security to know that He has a plan for you? If that is true—and I believe that it is—my being here on this earth is not an accident. You and I are part of a big plan. Here is just some of the basis for my belief.

God told Abraham that his descendants would be slaves for more than 400 years (Gen. 15:13). It came to pass just as He said (Ex. 1; 12).

Josiah's birth is predicted, even what he would do as king (1 Kings 13:2). Three hundred years later he came on the scene and burned human bones on the altar exactly as predicted (2 Kings 23:16).

Isaiah predicted that a Persian king by the name of Cyrus would rebuild Jerusalem (Isa. 44:28; 45:1). A hundred years later it took place (Ezra 1; 3; 4; 5).

Micah predicted that Jesus would be born in Bethlehem (Micah 5:2). Seven centuries later it was fulfilled (Matt. 2:1).

David predicted that Jesus' hands and feet would be pierced (Ps. 22:16), and about 1,000 years later it occurred (Matt. 27; John 19). David also foretold that Jesus' bones would not be broken (Ps. 34:20), which also happened (John 19:33). And one more of many: David predicted that they would cast lots for Jesus' garments (Ps. 22:18). That too came to pass (John 19:23, 24).

Hundreds of detailed messianic prophecies from the Old Testament all proved to be true much later in the New Testament. These prophecies and those in Daniel and Revelation let me know what will take place in the future. Only a God of love is going to allay my fears and concerns by letting me know what is about to happen. As Amos said: "Surely the Sovereign Lord does nothing without revealing his plan to his servants the prophets" (Amos 3:7, NIV). And on a personal level, the Lord Himself declares: "'I know the plans I have for you,' . . . 'plans to prosper you and not to harm you, plans to give you hope and a future'" (Jer. 29:11, NIV).

O Lord, You know everything about me. Strengthen my decision to submit to Your plan for me.

Giraffe

Who is like You, O Lord, among the gods? Who is like You, glorious in holiness, fearful in praises, doing wonders? Ex. 15:11, NKJV.

Have you ever tried hanging in an inversion table (or an inversion rack as it is sometimes called)? Generally, it is an A-frame structure with a short canvas or metal "table" pivoting on it—somewhat reminiscent of a tee-ter-totter. To get on board, you rotate the frame down so you can lock your ankles securely at one end of the table while standing on the floor. Then slowly swing the foot end up till your head is tilted down. Increase the angle for more intensive inversion therapy. Go all the way, and you are hanging upside down, held by your ankles, blood rushing to your head, face turning red, and eyes bulging. How can this be good for you?

The idea is that by hanging from your feet, you take the pressure of gravity off the spine and send lots of good blood to the head. Some claim that it is good for the back and joints. And since your brain needs lots of blood—well, it gets plenty this way. Blood to the skin of your face, scalp, and brain is invigorating. Those that practice regular inversion therapy believe in its therapeutic effects. When you return to upright, the blood rushes back out of your head and can make you feel woozy—like standing suddenly after sitting for some time.

If you think that you got woozy doing this, consider the problem a giraffe has. Its head is usually about 12 feet above its heart (ours is maybe 1 foot above). Then when it drinks at the water hole, its head goes down, seven feet below the heart. The giraffe head has to make an elevation difference of almost 20 feet without passing out. What keeps it from having major dizzy spells?

For starters the giraffe has a heavy-duty G-suit type skin. The skin is an inch thick and very tough and strong. Second, though a full-grown male giraffe weighs about 10 to 12 times what a person does, the giraffe heart weighs 40 times that of a human heart. Third, the long arteries and veins in the neck of the giraffe dwarf a standard garden hose. And unlike our jugular vein, the giraffe's has special muscles and intricate valves to control blood pressure in the head and neck. Some of the first crude measurements of blood pressure in the giraffe head showed that whether the head was up or down, the pressure remained at or near 200 mm Hg (compared to ours at 120 mm Hg). When we take the time to put our finger on the pulse of God's creation, His creative wonders abound.

Lord, no matter what problem we explore, You have provided solutions that astound and amaze. Thank You for Your attention to every detail.

October 26

Bacterial Sonar

Yet the Lord longs to be gracious to you; therefore he will rise up to show you compassion. For the Lord is a God of justice. Blessed are all who wait for him. Isa. 30:18, NIV.

Let's turn our attention to a common probiotic bacterium to see what we can learn from it today. Formerly known as *Streptococcus faecalis* because it forms long chains of tiny spheres and lives in the lower gut of humans and other mammals, biologists have moved it to the genus *Enterococcus*. Probiotic means "for life," a moniker for the live bacteria-laden food supplements that you can buy in most health food stores. *Enterococcus faecalis* isn't always the good probiotic guy, however. Some strains can be deadly, and more often than not they are highly resistant to antibiotics.

For decades science has known that *E. faecalis* produces a protein called cytolysin, meaning "cell destroyer." The bacterium kills cells as a way to release cell nutrients for its own consumption and growth. The organism normally produces cytolysin in small quantities. There is no use spewing out the substance if there are no cells in the vicinity. It would be a waste of energy. Then when there are cells around, the bacteria ramps up production of cytolysin, making it a potent killer. Scientists have long wondered how the bacterium knows when to increase cytolysin production. Without eyes or ears, how would it detect the presence of cells?

Researchers discovered that cytolysin is actually a complex of two proteins, one large and one small subunit that stay coupled together while out on patrol so to speak. When it encounters a target cell, the large subunit lets go of the small one and begins the attack. The liberated small subunit scampers back to report cells in the area. Free small subunits turn on the production of more cytolysin. As long as the large and small subunits stay coupled, the small one can't report. But as soon as the encounter with another cell happens, the small protein rings the alarm bells.

Probiotic means "for life," a moniker for the live bacteria-laden food supplements that you can buy in most health food stores.

This system is remarkably similar to a sonar or radar system that generates a signal. When the signal encounters an object, a weaker signal gets reflected back to the sender, giving information about the encounter. The Lord longs for us to hear His voice. He is constantly patrolling for hearts that will respond to Him. His Word, His life on earth, the Holy Spirit, His marvelous creation are strong signals of His love and His longing for us to respond. "Here, Lord, is my responsive heart."

Lord, don't give up on me. You are patient and kind. Hear now the cry of my heart.

Carpenter Ants

There are four things which are little on the earth, but they are exceedingly wise: The ants are a people not strong, yet they prepare their food in the summer. Prov. 30:24, 25, NKJV.

Suppose you find some big black or red ants in your home. Could they be the dreaded carpenter ants taking your home apart? How do you know if you have a carpenter ant or not? Many ants look alike, but carpenter ants in the genus *Camponotus* are mostly big scary-looking creatures that can do lots of damage to a house, so it helps to be able to identify them. I have studied a lot of carpenter ants, from big to little, and they all have two things in common. Look at their profile from the side. The easiest way to do that is to put the ant into a sandwich bag or an envelope and pop it in the freezer for a bit. That will slow it down. Now examine its profile. If you see one little tooth-like structure sticking straight up at the waist joint and if the curve of the top outline of their middle section is smooth, with no dips in it, then bingo, you got one.

Carpenter ants don't eat wood, as termites do, but they still make tunnels in soft, wet wood to create places for their nests and raising their young. So if you have leaky gutters, faucets, drains, or a roof or other places on your house that stay wet much of the time, that's where carpenter ants like to nest, and they will do lots of damage. Besides, as they forage for food at night, you could have them scampering across your face while you sleep.

So when you see these big critters in your home, it is time to start looking for their nest. Find out how they are getting in, seal any cracks, repair leaks, and get some ant spray from your local hardware store. But take note that the big ants may be living outside in a nearby rotting stump or tree, and the workers may be coming in at night just to get food. Eating almost anything, they like sweets, fats, plants, animals, even other insects. So just because you see them in your home doesn't necessarily mean that they are living with you. They might be neighbors coming in for a midnight snack.

Are such ants good for anything? Yes. They recycle downed trees and limbs. As soon as the wood gets soft enough for them to start tunneling, they go to work. We can also learn important lessons from them. In the wisdom literature of Proverbs the wise man Solomon wrote about the ants teaching us first to be industrious, and second how we should plan ahead and prepare for the future. The insects work together, sharing tasks and food. No doubt they can teach us so much more if we take time to listen.

Lord of the ants, teach me the lessons You want me to learn from Your creatures.

The Apoptosome

But fire came down from heaven and devoured them. And the devil, who deceived them, was thrown into the lake of burning sulfur. Rev. 20:9, 10, NIV.

When I study the biological process of apoptosis, I never cease to be amazed. If you know anything about the delicate and complex life of a cell, you would assume that every activity of the cell is intended to enable it to live. Most cells are either reproducing rapidly or are performing their mature function—whatever it is they were designed to do.

On the other hand, apoptosis, something that takes place in multicellular organisms such as humans, is a cell-killing process. Known as programmed cell death, apoptosis is a bewilderingly complex system that eliminates cells and all traces of them. Activation doesn't happen unless a cell needs to be removed for normal development, such as those from between a baby's fingers. Another reason to kill a cell would be after it is infected by a virus or has become cancerous and is dividing uncontrollably. As you might guess, removing rogue cells to prevent their spread is vital. When apoptosis isn't working well enough, cancer or even rheumatoid arthritis can result. But when it works too well, it can take out normal cells, and Parkinson's, Alzheimer's, preeclampsia, or other degenerative diseases may result. So in order to have normal function, apoptosis needs to work just right—thus the elaborate system.

Apoptosis involves literally dozens of proteins, including a whole family of caspases, DNases, death receptors, and even a granzyme, to name a few. One of the many pathways that particularly interests me is the one that constructs a multiprotein complex called an apoptosome. When completed, the apoptosome looks somewhat like a seven-armed throwing star, and its job is to activate procaspase-9, which in turn triggers other caspases, which initiate the cascade of events leading to successful apoptosis. Whew!

The elaborate system required to eradicate a single microscopic cell gives me assurance that God has an equally well-designed system to eliminate sin along with its author in order to keep this terrible cancer from spreading to other inhabited planets.

Lord, thank You for designing and instituting these elaborate cleanup systems. Truly You are a God of love and order.

October 29

Gardenia

And the other lamb you shall offer at twilight; and you shall offer with it the grain offering and the drink offering, as in the morning, for a sweet aroma, an offering made by fire to the Lord. Ex. 29:41, NKJV.

D oes your nose have a favorite flower? Or do you pick it by touch? Most of us, I would think, select our flowers by sight. Who doesn't respond with great pleasure to the riot of color in a well-designed flower garden? The gardenia, however, is a flower whose greatest attraction is its powerfully pleasing aroma. The two most important mothers in my life are particularly attracted to gardenias and enjoy growing these acid-loving plants in their gardens. The intoxicating fragrance of gardenia enchants both my mother and my wife's mother.

Gardenias honor Alexander Garden, a surgeon who lived in Charlestown, South Carolina, before the Revolutionary War. A naturalist with wide interests in both plants and animals, Dr. Garden regularly collected specimens of various types and sent them to his friend Carolus Linnaeus, the most famous of taxonomists (biologists who specialize in classifying and naming organisms). In gratitude, Linnaeus named the sweet-smelling member of the coffee family after Garden. The dark-green gardenia leaves are leathery and evergreen, giving a pleasant background to the bright-white blossoms with five or more petals. The genus Gardenia has 142 species. Some flowers have a slight yellow color in the center, but most are pure white and deliciously fragrant, which is why they often appear in bridal bouquets.

The wonder is that my recognition of this measureless gift, my gratitude, and my acceptance of it is the pleasing aroma to God.

Speaking of delicious smells, Scripture repeatedly describes God as being drawn to the "sweet aroma" of His people burning sacrificial animals on the altar. I can understand the sweet aroma of incense that was part of this service. But burning animals? Sweet-smelling? When properly practiced, Old Testament sacrificial services graphically portrayed the horror of death, particularly death of the innocent that is the natural consequence of sin. Sacrificial services required the sinner to slay an innocent animal as a type of what was to come—a graphic portrayal of Christ's death on the cross. Today my sin drives the cruel spikes afresh into innocent hands and trembling feet. The wonder is that my recognition of this measureless gift, my gratitude, and my acceptance of it is the pleasing aroma to God. In contrast, my rejection, indifference, and ingratitude of His indescribable gift of love and life is what stinks in His nostrils.

Lord, may the odor of my deep gratitude and acceptance of Your gift of life be a pleasing aroma to You.

Two Great Projects

As you do not know the path of the wind, or how the body is formed in a mother's womb, so you cannot understand the work of God, the Maker of all things. Eccl. 11:5, NIV.

C hances are that most of you have heard about the Human Genome Project supposedly completed in 2003. The 14-year multibillion-dollar project to sequence the 6 billion nucleotides organized into 20,000 to 25,000 genes of a human cell is said to be complete, but much remains to be done even a decade later. As you can tell, we don't yet know how many genes were actually sequenced. That's because of gene overlap and the interesting way that various splicing strategies can make multiple proteins from a sequence of DNA. Also, large regions of each of the 46 human chromosomes resist sequencing because of endlessly repeating sequences.

So what have we learned? First and foremost, the human genome (the sum total of all of our genes) is exceedingly complex yet highly ordered. Again, we must admit that we don't really know how many genes we actually have. Once we thought we knew how genes work, but now we realize it isn't as simple as we thought. Further research has revealed that most of our DNA (nearly 99 percent) is not genes. Much of that non-gene DNA is repetitive sequences and DNA control sequences. In addition, we are finding out that we share a lot of DNA with other organisms.

The large community of neuroscientists kicked off the Human Connectome Project in 2009. A connectome is a map or diagram of all the neurons and synapses in an organism's nervous system. The project is a five-year collaboration by 16 divisions of the National Institutes of Health, with a two-pronged attempt to map the brain to enhance our understanding of how it works. One consortium of two research universities is currently mapping connectomes of 1,200 people, including many sets of twins, to determine how brain structure relates to function, as well as possible effects of environment on brain structure. Another consortium of two big research universities plus a research hospital is using new MRI techniques to track the movement of water through brain cells to develop high-resolution maps of brain pathways. Putting all this data together will help in treating mental illness and common brain disorders.

I can just see the Creator and Designer of all standing in the shadows watching and smiling broadly as science reveals His handiwork.

Since I am fearfully and wonderfully made, I gladly dedicate my life to Your service, Lord. Now what would You like me to do for Your kingdom today?

Goats

And He will set the sheep on His right hand, but the goats on the left. Matt. 25:33, NKJV.

Most tree climbers rely on sharp claws for grip, short muscular legs, and long tails for balance. Or, like me, they may use ropes and harness. So to see long-legged, short-tailed, hoofed goats climbing around in trees is unusual, but I have witnessed it with my own eyes. On the African continent where acacia trees branch near the ground and where ground forage is scarce, one often see goats browsing even in the top branches. From a distance you would think it's a flock of big squirrels the way they jump from branch to branch. Believe it or not, I remember observing one goat even using two trees side by side. Like a rock climber between two rocks doing a chimney climb, the goat used his front legs on one tree and hind legs on the other to climb 10 to 15 feet up to reach a food source. No doubt you have spotted them on steep rocky cliffs, nimbly jumping from one tiny toehold to another.

One of the earliest domesticated animals, goats can be trained to carry loads, and they provide milk and meat for people to eat. Their manure can serve for fuel and fertilizer, and their hair weaves excellent textiles and fabrics. The animals' hides make good water-skins or wineskins, leather straps, and other leather articles. Surgeons use thin strips of their intestines for suturing. Called catgut, it never comes from cats but rather domesticated livestock. Goat horns can be made into musical instruments and spoons. And because they are curious and highly intelligent animals that train easily, and can forage on very poor soils, goats are easy to keep. Aid programs for poverty-stricken peoples frequently include goats, because they are so useful and productive.

As even-toed ungulates, goats have a four-chambered stomach with a rumen. They are classed as browsers rather than grazers. As such, they prefer nibbling on shrubby vegetation and on weeds rather than grazing on grass. Their reputation for eating almost anything stems from the fact that, like human babies, they explore things with their mouth. Whatever is edible they will consume. Otherwise, it might look as if they are eating it when they aren't.

Goats appear frequently in the Bible as herd animals, as food, as providers of fabric, as sacrificial sin offerings, as a prophetic symbol of a nation, and as a symbol of those that Jesus doesn't know when He divides the saved from the lost.

Creator of multifunctional goats, thank You for Your gift of creatures who serve so generously. May I learn to serve others as well as they do.

Dic Dic

Having then gifts differing according to the grace that is given to us, let us use them. Rom. 12:6, NKJV.

One of the first pets that I remember having as a child growing up in Ethiopia was a dic dic. At least that is what we called it. While living in western Ethiopia in the little village of Gimbie, some local villagers brought us a fawn about the size of a small dog. Part of the reason I remember so well is because of a picture of me sitting on the grass feeding the tiny antelope from a bottle. The smallest of all antelope, dic dics, also known as the bush duiker or common duiker, weigh a little more than 20 pounds and stand about 20 inches tall when fully grown. Named *Sylvicapra grimmia* in 1758 by Carolus Linnaeus, the species now has almost 20 subspecies because of its wide range of habitats and the fact that it is so small and doesn't travel widely like some of the other antelope.

A 2008 assessment of common duiker population levels by the International Union for Conservation of Nature and Natural Resources placed their numbers in the millions. That they do so well probably results from several factors. First, with their small size, they stay below the radar of the big cats and other hunters. While the small males will spend considerably more time on a rise where it can watch for danger, the larger females prefer to stay in the thickets with more cover. The diminutive antelope don't mind living near villages or around people. Duikers and people enjoy a peaceful coexistence. Finally, duikers have the ability to eat almost anything and go for long periods without drinking, something the other antelopes simply can't do. The creatures will browse on almost any vegetation—shoot, stem, root, and fruit. They also consume insects, small mammals, birds, frogs, and lizards, and can even eat carrion when necessary. Moisture from plants in their diet provides most of their water needs.

Except for their ability to disappear into the scenery, dic dics don't have much protection from predation. They are too small to run fast, and their tiny horns are only a few inches long, providing rather poor protection at best. But they don't worry about being the smallest and the weakest. Instead, they just use the many skills and adaptations that God has given them. In fact, they do so well that they have the widest distribution of any African antelope.

Lord of all gifts and abilities, help me to use the spiritual gifts You have given me to extend Your kingdom throughout the world.

David's Psalm of 1 Chronicles 16

For great is the Lord and most worthy of praise. 1 Chron. 16:25, NIV.

I don't know of a more beautiful and heartfelt praise to God than David's psalm recorded in 1 Chronicles 16:8-36. He sang it when the ark of God was finally installed in the tent that he had prepared for it in Jerusalem. It was a time of high national achievement accompanied by celebration, pageantry, and praise to God.

"Oh, give thanks to the Lord! Call upon His name; make known His deeds among the peoples! Sing to Him, sing psalms to Him; talk of all His wondrous works! Glory in His holy name; let the hearts of those rejoice who seek the Lord! Seek the Lord and His strength; seek His face evermore! Remember His marvelous works which He has done, His wonders, and the judgments of His mouth, O seed of Israel His servant, you children of Jacob, His chosen ones! He is the Lord our God; His judgments are in all the earth. Remember His covenant forever, the word which He commanded, for a thousand generations, the covenant which He made with Abraham, and His oath to Isaac, and confirmed it to Jacob for a statute, to Israel for an everlasting covenant, saying, 'To you I will give the land of Canaan as the allotment of your inheritance,' when you were few in number, indeed very few, and strangers in it. When they went from one nation to another, and from one kingdom to another people, He permitted no man to do them wrong; yes, He rebuked kings for their sakes, saying, 'Do not touch My anointed ones, and do My prophets no harm.'

"Sing to the Lord, all the earth; proclaim the good news of His salvation from day to day. Declare His glory among the nations, His wonders among all peoples. For the Lord is great and greatly to be praised; He is also to be feared above all gods. For all the gods of the peoples are idols, but the Lord made the heavens. Honor and majesty are before Him; strength and gladness are in His place. Give to the Lord, O families of the peoples, give to the Lord glory and strength. Give to the Lord the glory due His name; bring an offering, and come before Him. . . .

"Oh, give thanks to the Lord, for He is good! For His mercy endures forever. And say, 'Save us, O God of our salvation; gather us together, and deliver us from the Gentiles, to give thanks to Your holy name, to triumph in Your praise.' Blessed be the Lord God of Israel from everlasting to everlasting!" (1 Chron. 16:8-36, NKJV).

O Lord, hear my prayer of praise and thanksgiving to You today. I honor You as my sovereign Lord.

Quick

For as the Father raises the dead and gives life to them, even so the Son gives life to whom He will. John 5:21, NKJV.

The word "quick" (and its variations) appears 60 times in the New King James Version versus 74 times in the King James Version. That difference results because of a change in the way that we use the word. Compare the wording of today's text from the King James Version: "For as the Father raiseth up the dead, and quickeneth them; even so the Son quickeneth whom he will." Other texts refer to God judging the quick and the dead (Acts 10:42) or quickening the dead (Rom. 4:17 and 8:11). So the word "quick" used to mean "living" or "alive." Makes sense, doesn't it? The dead are quite slow compared to the living.

So how quick is quick? Well, how fast is your reaction time? You can easily check it. Just google "reaction time" to find some fun online tests of how fast you react. It took me 231 milliseconds to respond to a change in the light. Take the test when you first get up to see how much slower you are first thing in the morning. A brisk walk outdoors might shave a few milliseconds off your average reaction time. Reaction time is critically important when you are driving. At 55 m.p.h. you travel almost 81 feet every second. If it takes a half second to respond, you have traveled at least two car lengths before you even start to take your foot off the accelerator. People with a blood alcohol concentration of as little as .02 percent exhibit increased response times, which is why they shouldn't be driving or doing things that require fast responses. By the time one reaches the legal blood alcohol limit of .08 percent, the response time is totally shot, as is judgment. Far too often, alcohol increases response time to infinity—the dead do not respond, at least not until they are quickened by God again.

What did Jesus mean by all the urgency of language in Matthew 24 ("immediately" [verse 29], "near," "at the doors" [verse 33], "this generation" [verse 34], "be . . . ready" [verse 44])? The sense is even greater in Revelation 3:11 and Revelation 22 ("quickly," or "coming soon" [NIV]). Obviously, quickly or soon are relative terms. Telling my boss that I'll get the report in soon may mean later today, later this week, or even later this year depending on the extent of the work remaining to be done. Think about it. Quickly means "today" for some people. If today is a normal day on Planet Earth, about 155,000 people will die. For them, Jesus' coming is just an eyeblink away. Now, that's quick.

Lord, just how quickly will You come for me? Will it be today? I am ready now or whenever You say, because I trust You completely.

November 4

Scarlet and Crimson

They stripped Him and put a scarlet robe on Him. Matt. 27:28, NKJV.

M ake it with blue, purple, and scarlet yarn with finely twisted linen" is a common element of God's instructions for making the curtains at the entrance to the tabernacle courtyard, the entrance to the tabernacle itself, the ephod, the waistband, and the breast piece. But where would people out in the desert obtain dyestuff to make blue, purple, and scarlet? In ancient times these were expensive, hard-to-get colors that only royalty could afford.

Apparently the blue and purple dyes came from marine mollusks thriving along the Mediterranean Sea. But the scarlet or deep red of crimson derived instead from a lowly scale insect. With 7,500 or more species in about two dozen families and half as many more in the fossil record, scale insects are an army of plant-juice-sucking pests. All have tubular mouth parts that they jab into plants to obtain the sweet plant sap. Sucking plants dry to make babies is what they do. Our most infamous miscreants are mealy bugs, closely allied with aphids and white flies. Besides causing billions of dollars in crop losses, these insects transmit plant diseases through dirty mouth parts. They are tiny pests of the highest order.

Since the time of the Aztecs, one species of scale insect that sucks the life out of *Opuntia* cactus has produced the rich scarlet color for royalty. Known by the common name cochineal, these scale insects make carminic acid to keep other insects from eating them. Nearly one fourth of their dry weight consists of the bright-red dye we call carmine and still use in food coloring, textile dyes, even lipstick. Since most synthetic red dyes have turned out to be carcinogenic, we have again turned to natural dyes from cochineal.

But carmine was a Western discovery of the fourteenth or fifteenth century. What produced red during the Exodus and the time of Christ? Considerable sleuthing by scientists and Biblical scholars has uncovered evidence suggesting that *Kermes echinatus*, another species of scale insect drawing life from a species of scrub oak around the Mediterranean, was the source of the shani (meaning "red" in Hebrew) dye described in Exodus and Isaiah. In this case, bright-red eggs of *Kermes* produced a deeper red than any plant-based red dye. Even the word "crimson" is apparently derived from *Kermes*. If only the Roman soldiers had known who it was that they mockingly dressed in royal crimson, they would have bowed in earnest. One day they will. One day soon every knee will bow.

Creator of blue, purple, and scarlet, though my sins be as scarlet, Your crimson bloodstained cross can make me white as snow.

Trig Point

I have set the Lord always before me; because He is at my right hand I shall not be moved. Ps. 16:8, NKJV.

I have seen them many times while out hiking or visiting national historic sites or other places of historical interest. No doubt you have too. In the United States it is a small bronze disk about three or four inches across set in concrete called a triangulation station or trig point. Factory stamped into the disk around the outside edge are these words: "U.S. COAST & GEODETIC SURVEY TRIANGULATION STATION." The next inner ring of words reads: "FOR INFORMATION WRITE TO THE DIRECTOR, WASHINGTON, D.C." The innermost circle of words continues: "$250 FINE OR IMPRISONMENT FOR DISTURBING THIS MARK." At the very center of the disk is a dot within an equilateral triangle. Before embedding this disk in concrete, the surveyor who set the trig point stamped the name of the station and the year it was installed—for example, "Meades Ranch 1891." The Meades Ranch trig point is fairly near the geographic center of the United States. But more important, it served as the reference point for nearly all United States land surveying from 1927 until the establishment of a more accurate reference point in 1984. The normal practice is to have trig point disks set so they read properly when you face north. What you may not know is that the disk is just the tip of a concrete column extending about four feet down with another identical disk in the lower few inches of the column. It preserves the mark if something should disturb the surface one.

Various government jurisdictions place triangulation stations all over the world. Trig points give surveyors stable reference points. Continents are actually drifting slowly—just a small fraction of an inch per year—so trig points lack the accuracy needed in this modern age. In 2007 the American government established the U.S. National Spatial Reference System using extremely accurate GPS measurements.

The Meades Ranch trig point is fairly near the geographic center of the United States.

In The Desire of Ages Ellen White describes how John the Baptist had to be rock-solid. "John was to go forth as Jehovah's messenger. . . . Such a messenger must be holy. . . . He must have a sound physical constitution, and mental and spiritual strength. Therefore it would be necessary for him to control the appetites and passions. He must be able so to control all his powers that he could stand among men as unmoved by surrounding circumstances as the rocks and mountains of the wilderness" (p. 100).

Lord, make me an immovable trig point for You. May I stand firm for You in my community.

November 6

Mystery of Sleep

In peace I will lie down and sleep, for you alone, Lord, make me dwell in safety. Ps. 4:8, NIV.

With so much to do and so little time for it, why do we spend six to 10 hours out of every day in a state of inactivity and unconsciousness? It seems that my cats sleep at least 20 hours each day. It's a mystery to evolutionists, who think in terms of survival and fitness. Yet animals display so much downtime not being alert to predators, not searching for food, not competing for mates or space, not mating, and not taking care of their young. Sleep doesn't seem logical, but it must be adaptive and important. Almost all critters spend time either sleeping or dormant. So what about us?

Though literally hundreds of sleep research centers exist around the world, with thousands of highly trained people intensely studying sleep, the consensus is that the physiology of sleep is still largely a mystery. We do know that during sleep the brain stays incredibly active while our muscles go dormant. Scientists have recorded five phases of sleep, with different types of electrical brain activity. The body makes growth hormones during sleep, which is why babies, children, and teenagers need more sleep than adults. But growth hormones are involved in cell maintenance, too, explaining why adults also require sleep. The consensus is that while we are asleep, the brain processes things that we have done or thought about while awake, something akin to organizing data files and doing routine maintenance on your computer's hard drive. Called memory consolidation, it is a form of brain maintenance. We also recognize that stress damage gets repaired during sleep. The mystery of sleep is an area that provides many ongoing challenges.

Furthermore, we know some of the serious problems that happen if we don't get enough sleep. As little as one hour of sleep deprivation slows response time, making it more difficult to think clearly and focus on problems. It explains why students usually do worse on tests after pulling an all-nighter. My students who include sleep and exercise in their daily discipline perform better academically. Compared to those who do get adequate sleep, those who are sleep-deprived make more bad decisions and poor choices, have lower job performance, take more risks, have more accidents on the highway, in the home, and on the job, gain more weight, are more irritable, have higher blood pressure and more heart disease, and have less resistance to disease to name just a few. We honor God by sleeping well.

Lord, I sleep so much better knowing that all my cares are in Your hands.

Sleep Disorders

Sleep fled from my eyes. Gen. 31:40, NIV.

D oes it bother you when you go to bed and lie there for hours unable to go to sleep? It happens to all of us at times. But when sleeplessness becomes the rule rather than the exception, perhaps the sleep disorder called insomnia has set in. Insomnia means nothing more than not being able to sleep. But sleeplessness may have a variety of descriptors and causes.

Some people have a chronic problem with falling asleep. They feel tired and go to bed early enough, but then toss and turn for hours. Another form of insomnia happens when you go right to sleep only to awaken and lie there for hours. It could result from any number of reasons, such as a spouse who snores, a cat that jumps on the bed, lights in the room, or noise. And if it happens on a regular basis, you can certainly suffer from insomnia.

Others fall asleep and remain that way all night. But in the morning they do not feel rested. They have not enjoyed the sweet sleep described in Jeremiah 31:26. Their exhaustion may indicate sleep apnea, another potentially serious sleep disorder that prevents deep sleep during the night. Those with classical sleep apnea have a breathing disorder in which they just stop breathing for 10 to 20 seconds or so. And when breathing pauses happen 20 to 30 times each hour, it is a major cause for concern. In central apnea the brain is slow to signal the body to take another breath. More often, the sleep apnea is called obstructive sleep apnea and is associated with carrying too much weight and not being in good physical shape, so that when you lie down to sleep, loose soft tissue collapses and pinches the breathing tubes closed.

Insomnia may also result from restless leg syndrome (RLS), a disorder in which you constantly move the legs because of unpleasant sensations in them. RLS is often the result of various other disease conditions, and one form has a genetic origin.

Narcolepsy, a chronic, lifelong condition, is a sleep disorder in which an affected individual has frequent sleep attacks during the day. It is not a mental illness, but it does qualify as a nervous system disorder, because, for unknown reasons, the brain produces too little of a family of important brain neuropeptides called hypocretins or orexins. The hypocretin/orexin proteins, identified in all major groups of vertebrates, cause wakefulness when bound to hypocretin/orexin receptors. Lacking either the protein or the receptors causes narcolepsy.

Lord, I thank You for the gift of sleep and for the knowledge of medical specialists who can help minimize the effects of sleep disorders.

November 8

Pillow

Taking one of the stones there, he put it under his head and lay down to sleep. Gen. 28:11, NIV.

I must admit, I have often wondered about this story in Genesis 28. It has never occurred to me that using a rock for a pillow might be a way of getting a better night's sleep. For Jacob it must have worked, because the story goes on to describe the beautiful dream that God gave him that night. What does it take for you to get a good night's rest?

Research has identified what factors contribute to better sleep. First and foremost is developing a sleep schedule that you stick to—weekends included. Without a schedule or with a chaotic disorganized life, sleep gets disrupted at both ends of the night. The sleep environment is important too. If you are either too hot or too cold, it is harder to fall asleep. Temperature changes can awaken you from a good sleep, so do your best to control them. Too much or too little noise can also make a difference. A ticking clock or dripping faucet can keep you awake or put you to sleep depending on what you are used to. So adjust the noise level to suit your needs and habits. Make your bed and pillow clean and comfortable and move the TV or computer out of the bedroom. Darken the bedroom by getting rid of nightlights or brightly lit clocks.

Research shows that taking a late or long nap can make it hard to fall asleep at night. Also a late or heavy meal before bedtime can prevent sleep. Substances such as caffeine, nicotine, and alcohol disrupt sleep as do certain prescription and over-the-counter medications and supplements. Daytime activities that contribute to good sleep include getting some bright-light therapy every day—best done by being outside in the sunshine for at least 30 minutes. Dedicating time for regular vigorous exercise outdoors in the sunshine—provided it ends several hours before bedtime—also helps.

Then as your regular bedtime approaches, consciously relax and unwind from the day's activities. Develop a ritual of reading or listening to good music. Take a warm bath. Though the scientific literature is silent on worship and sleep, spending time in the Word, meditating, and thanking God for the blessings of the day work wonders in preparing for a good night's sleep. It helps to turn all your cares over to Him who is our burden bearer. How often we are robbed of sleep by being fearful or mulling over problems, broken relationships, and the stresses of life. Proverbs 3:24-26 assures us that our sleep will be sweet, for the Lord will be at our side.

Lord, I thank You for restful sleep. Truly it is a gift from You.

The Sabbath Rest

Today is a Sabbath to the Lord. Ex. 16:25, NIV.

The CNN headline reads: "In a Tough Economy, Working Seven Days Becomes Norm for Some." It's true that in the present age a sizable portion of the population works constantly. Some who hold multiple jobs rarely get a day off. Stress-related illnesses rise, marriages and children suffer, and leisure time evaporates, injuring individuals, families, and communities.

I am so thankful to God for setting aside a special rest day for me. But wait, is it really a day for me? Yes, without a doubt. Jesus Himself said that the Sabbath existed for humanity, not the other way around. So yes, it is for me and for you. It is a day when we don't have to go to work. We can forget about shopping, paying bills, planning schedules, weeding the garden, or mowing the lawn. I like to think of every Sabbath as a weekly 24-hour date with One who loves me more than anybody else. During Sabbath I can focus on my Savior and practice the unselfish and loving service that He modeled.

My wife and I have been dating for many decades now. We both enjoy a weekly night when we take time off from the other pressures of life to simply enjoy time together. Sometimes we work together on a project. Or we might go grocery shopping together, walk at a mall, eat at a favorite restaurant, or hike or cross-country ski in the woods near our home. It doesn't matter much what we do together as long as we are not pressured, as long as we have time to visit, problem-solve, and communicate openly and honestly about what is on our minds. Part of this relationship-building strategy also involves spending regular time each day reading to each other. Last year we went through all five books of the Conflict of the Ages Series. This year we are enjoying working our way through the new Andrews Study Bible. Time together is critical for building and maintaining relationships.

Just think, the Creator of the universe is asking me to set aside one day each week to be with Him, working on that relationship. He is asking me to use this time each week to honor the incredible genius, the awesome energy, and the unbelievable organization that happened during that Creation week, which resulted in . . . well . . . everything—this earth and all life-forms and all their life-support systems. So this eternal God, Creator of all, supreme sovereign of the universe, asks me to meet with Him because He wants a relationship with me. Seems a little disrespectful if I turn Him down and trundle off to work so that I can earn a few more bucks.

Supreme sovereign God, forgive me for the times that I have disrespected You. May I always stay focused on improving our relationship.

November 10

Resurrection

He has risen from the dead. Matt. 28:7, NIV.

Francesco Redi first announced in 1668 the most unbreakable rule in biology—"*Omni vivum ex ovo*" ("life only from the egg")—following a series of famous experiments with meat and maggots. With the experiments Redi began to refute popular Aristotelian concepts that life could arise spontaneously. Not long after the great disappointment of 1844, experiments by the eminent French microbiologist Louis Pasteur and the great German pathologist Rudolph Virchow led to the amending of Redi's earlier pronouncement to read: "Life only from life." And modern science has since done nothing but confirm this concept so that now we can say with certainty that the dead are truly dead and cannot come to life despite even the most intense efforts of modern science.

But what about J. Craig Venter and his May 21, 2010, announcement that his research group had created synthetic life? The reality is that Venter's group synthesized the genetic code, the DNA sequence, of *Mycoplasma mycoides* (a type of bacteria with the shortest known genetic code) using its known DNA sequence from computer records. Then they removed the genetic code of another species of bacteria, *Mycoplasma capricolum* (a cousin, if you will). Finally they inserted that synthesized copy of DNA into the gutted *Mycoplasma capricolum*. After all the painstaking work, they were successful in getting the modified bacterium to replicate to a population of billions of organisms. It is telling that even a spokesperson for the Venter group would not claim that their work was a breakthrough, producing life from nonlife. After all, synthesizing DNA and moving it from organism to organism is a routine practice in molecular biology laboratories and has been so for years.

> *Christ arose from the dead. It proves His divinity and His supremacy and is the beautiful basis of all Christianity.*

The only real exception to this rule remains that Christ arose from the dead. It proves His divinity and His supremacy and is the beautiful basis of all Christianity. The Author of life, Jesus, designed all the genetic codes. More than that, He created the cells in which the genetic codes can function. His victory over death and the grave gives us the hope of eternal life. "And if the Spirit of him who raised Jesus from the dead is living in you, he who raised Christ from the dead will also give life to your mortal bodies because of his Spirit who lives in you" (Rom. 8:11, NIV).

Thank You, Jesus. Thank You for life. Thank You for paying the terrible price for my sins.

DEET

Therefore, my dear friends, flee from idolatry. 1 Cor. 10:14, NIV.

Study the label on most insect and tick repellents these days and you are sure to find DEET listed as an active ingredient. In use now for more than 60 years, DEET is a light-yellow oil developed by the United States Army to protect troops who have to spend time in mosquito-infested tropical jungles. DEET (N, N-diethyl-meta-toluamide) appears at various percentages in most commercial repellents because it works. You put it on your skin or your clothes to keep mosquitoes and ticks from biting and passing on one or more of the numerous serious diseases that they transmit, such as malaria, yellow fever, encephalitis, dengue fever, and West Nile virus. But how does DEET work? Finding the answer to that question has been difficult.

Some studies suggested that DEET inhibits the mosquito's ability to smell us. Other results seemed to show that mosquitoes simply don't like the smell of DEET. Research indicates that the plume of carbon dioxide emanating from an animal's body attracts the insects. If you are outside in a mosquito-infested environment, you can watch mosquitoes pick up the scent downwind of where you are standing, and they simply follow the growing concentration of CO_2 till they get close enough to land. The first studies suggested that DEET blocked the ability of mosquitoes to detect CO_2, but that doesn't seem to be the case now.

In addition to CO_2, several other volatile body-odor chemicals boil off of our skin. They include 1-octen-3-ol, lactic acid, and other compounds produced by sweat and skin bacteria. Mosquitoes have lots of specialized chemical detectors on their antennae tuned to these chemicals so that they can home in and get their next blood meal.

The latest research by entomologists at the University of California and University of Arizona working together have discovered another chemical receptor, a short hairlike structure on mosquitoes' antennae, that is extremely sensitive to DEET at very low levels and signals more rapidly as DEET levels increase. Results from these careful studies have ruled out the masking effect that DEET was thought to have had. The report makes a good case that mosquitoes have the neurological equipment to smell DEET and simply avoid it if possible.

Wouldn't it be nice to have an ample supply of sin DEET? With that, sin would be both detectable and detestable. The good news is that it exists. It is called the mind of Christ.

Lord Jesus, give me, I pray, a sharply tuned sin detector (conscience).

November 12

Stiff-necked

What shall I return to the Lord for all his goodness to me?
Ps. 116:12, NIV.

Stiff-necked: it feels terrible when you have one, but I must admit, it is an amusing description that occurs 13 times in the Old Testament and once in the New Testament. The New Testament reference in Acts 7:51 uses the Greek term sklero ("hardened") tracheloi ("neck") to describe the condition of people. Using Hebrew terminology, a few of the references in the Pentateuch describe the stiff-necked condition. Surprisingly, most of the remaining references refer to the people stiffening or hardening their own necks. A self-imposed condition, it is certainly an apt metaphor of being stubborn, hard-hearted, rebellious, churlish, and unresponsive to discipline.

Come to think of it, of the many stiff necks that I have had to put up with during my lifetime, some may have been accidentally acquired by being in an auto accident in which my head was whipped around or by a sudden twisting movement during gymnastics or other sports activities. Others may have been caused by bacterial or viral infections, spasms in the neck muscles, or by sleeping in an awkward position. But some of my wry necks I have probably imposed on myself by straining my neck needlessly. Holding an awkward position too long while studying or focusing on some activity, reading a book for too long with my head propped on my arm—these and other sorts of activities can cause the painful neck symptoms. Fortunately, the pain does go away, usually without needing muscle relaxants or other treatments.

While growing up in the mission field, I had ample opportunity to watch indigenous people carrying extraordinarily heavy loads on their heads. With amazement I observed how, despite neck muscles straining, the sweat pouring, and the face contorted in a grimace, a human being could carry those heavy loads for so many miles. No doubt, in order to do it, they had to stiffen their necks and harden those neck muscles to resist the stresses of the load. It makes me wonder. How often do I stiffen my neck under my load of sin? How often does my stubborn resistance mean that I have to carry my own burdens longer?

Lord, I choose to put my burdens down at the foot of Your cross. I choose to love and obey, not as an attempt to earn salvation, but out of gratitude for all Your goodness to me.

November 13

Branding

I will praise You, O Lord my God, with all my heart, and I will glorify Your name forevermore. Ps. 86:12, NKJV.

Since 1986 I have been employed by Andrews University, one of many universities in the educational system of the Seventh-day Adventist Church. Both the university and the church are alert to any misuse of their name, their logo—their brand, if you will. Distortion of the logo in terms of color or shape, misappropriation of the name by others, or misrepresenting the name in any way will get immediate and vigorous attention that escalates to legal action if needed.

Of course the word "brand" comes from the practice of cowboys burning their marks into the hides of their animals for identification purposes. So today, every major organization has their brand consisting of their name, logotype, logo, or mark that identifies who they are. When legally protected, a brand becomes a trademark. Corporations hire a raft of lawyers and researchers to protect their trademarked names or logos.

Names have always had great meaning. The third commandment, inscribed in hard rock by God's own finger, reads: "You shall not take the name of the Lord your God in vain, for the Lord will not hold him guiltless who takes His name in vain" (Ex. 20:7, NKJV). That sounds serious. If you ask people to explain it, most will tell you that you shouldn't use God's name in swearwords. OK, that would be a good start. Perhaps more important, it means that you shouldn't claim to be one of His people when you don't really know who He is or obey His commandments. The dictionary definition of "in vain" is "to no avail" or "without success." In other words, failure to use the name properly or to represent it fairly would be taking the name in vain. When we got married, my bride took my name. Thankfully, Mrs. Steen, my wife, represents my name well.

When I read God's own description of His name in Exodus 34:6, 7, I am overwhelmed by His kindness, goodness, and love. Let's listen in: "The Lord, the Lord, the compassionate and gracious God, slow to anger, abounding in love and faithfulness, maintaining love to thousands, and forgiving wickedness, rebellion and sin" (NIV). And then in Numbers 6:27 God says: "So they shall put My name on the children of Israel, and I will bless them" (NKJV). God places His name on me to bless me. I struggle to grasp how awesome that is.

Your name is precious to me, O Lord. May I always protect Your brand.

The Prayer of Jabez—Oh, That You Would Bless Me Indeed

I will not let You go unless You bless me! Gen. 32:26, NKJV.

B uried in a mind-numbing list of impossibly difficult to pronounce old Jewish family names, lineages, and ancestries, the biblical author pauses to transcribe the prayer of Jabez, a godly man that we know very little about. Only the context—plunked down in the middle of a dry and mechanical listing of the clans of Judah—and just two sentences of a single verse (1 Chron. 4:9) compose the sum and substance of the biography of Jabez. What we know about him is enhanced by one additional verse (verse 10) detailing his two-sentence prayer followed by the statement that God granted his request. We can imply from the brief prayer that Jabez was a pious man. It appears that he knew God, had faith in Him, and was totally committed to Him.

After stating that he was from the tribe of Judah, the text tells us that "Jabez was more honorable than his brothers. His mother named him Jabez" (verse 9, NKJV). Why did she pick that name? Because, she said, "I bore him in pain" (verse 9, NKJV). Isn't childbirth painful? Especially when you have to do it without spinal blocks or modern-day analgesics? Some biblical commentators suggest that Jabez may have been illegitimate. So his mother may have been thinking emotional pain more than physical. Whatever the case, his name means "sorrow." I can tell you right now that every time I was called a "sorry _____" (you fill in the blank), it didn't feel good. No wonder Jabez poured his heart out to God for a blessing. It wasn't just a simple "Please bless me" request. Notice the angst at the beginning ("Oh, that You would" [verse 10, NKJV]) and the emphasis at the end ("indeed") of his request. Maybe this was a painful groaning from deep in his soul.

The point is that Jabez was blunt enough with God to ask for a blessing. Like Jacob who wrestled with God all night, screaming in pain and desperation, we, too, must level with God and make our requests known. Leveling with God means being honest with Him, accepting Him as our sovereign Lord, having a heart totally committed to knowing Him. Psalm 66:18 is clear on the importance of leveling with God so that He will hear our prayer. God wants to bless us. "This is the confidence that we have in Him, that if we ask anything according to His will, He hears us" (1 John 5:14, NKJV). James 4:2 says that "you do not have because you do not ask" (NKJV).

OK, Lord, I am leveling with You, and I am asking. Search my heart and hear my voice. Oh, that You would bless me, too.

The Prayer of Jabez—Enlarge My Territory

"Oh, that You would bless me indeed, and enlarge my territory, that Your hand would be with me, and that You would keep me from evil, that I may not cause pain!" So God granted him what he requested. 1 Chron. 4:10, NKJV.

To control cane beetle infestations in northeastern Australian sugarcane fields, growers transported a few thousand marine toads, *Bufo marinus*, from Hawaii and introduced them into the beetle ravaged cane fields during the 1930s. Appropriately dubbed cane toads because of their success in controlling cane beetles, the very large terrestrial toads, which happen to be highly toxic and exceptionally good at producing young, have been fanning out south and west across the island continent at alarming rates. For the first couple decades the toads moved into new areas at the rate of more than six miles per year. Now, 70 years later, their invasion front is advancing at almost 45 miles per year. The giant toads (one record individual kept as a pet weighed nearly six pounds and measured 21 inches head to toe) are known to travel fastest along roads or cleared fence lines at night. And the most surprising thing is that scientists gathering data at various checkpoints discovered that the toads leading the way had longer legs than those that came later. Cane toads may be the most studied animal in terms of its invasive characteristics. Originally from Central and South America, it has been successfully introduced to a number of tropical islands in both the Caribbean and Pacific to control insects. Unfortunately, the toad has been so successful that it has turned into a pest in many areas.

One specific thing that Jabez asked for was for God to enlarge his territory, blessing him as he moved into new areas of life. If indeed Jabez was an illegitimate son, he would not have had an inheritance of property as a legitimate son would, so it would have been an appropriate prayer—asking God for a niche to live in. More likely, his was a request to expand the borders of his ministry. Should not each of us invite God to push back the margins of our envelope? Staying in our comfort zone means that we think we can do it ourselves, without God's help. It is only when we attempt to do the impossible that God can reveal His power.

Staying in our comfort zone means that we think we can do it ourselves, without God's help. It is only when we attempt to do the impossible that God can reveal His power.

Lord, do I dare step out in faith to do that task You are asking me to do? You know how terrified I am of that. Only with Your help can I sincerely pray for You to expand my borders. Make that my sincere prayer now.

The Prayer of Jabez—Your Hand Would Be With Me

"Oh, that You would bless me indeed, and enlarge my territory, that Your hand would be with me, and that You would keep me from evil, that I may not cause pain!" So God granted him what he requested. 1 Chron. 4:10, NKJV.

The second specific blessing that Jabez asks God for is that His hand would be with him. Let's spend a few moments meditating on God's hands. Handcrafted, handmade, hand-rubbed, hand-carved, hand-finished, and handiwork are all terms suggesting high quality. Handmade items have received special attention. Most work that we do requires hands at one point or another. Even the hands of public speakers actively participate in getting the message across. Hands shape pottery and wood, craft fabrics, write papers, sow seeds, reap the harvest, and make the bread. They do thousands of things both good and bad.

As you read the Bible, perhaps the first allusion to God's hands is in the creation of Adam. We can imagine the Lord shaping and forming him from the dust of the ground. But this is by inference only. The first explicit statement about God's hands appears in Genesis 49. Jacob is very old, nearing death, and under the inspiration of the Holy Spirit he blesses his sons and tells them what their future will be. In verse 22 Jacob finally gets to Joseph who had been badly mistreated by his brothers. Then in verse 24, Jacob says that the arms of Joseph's hands were "made strong by the hands of the Mighty God of Jacob" (NKJV). I find it interesting that the strength of the hand comes from the strength of arm that it is attached to. Moses repeatedly refers to the mighty hand and outstretched arm in Exodus and Deuteronomy. David describes it in Psalm 136 in which he connects the hand power to mercy that endures forever. Solomon mentions it in his prayer of dedication for the Temple. The author of 2 Kings 17 as well as the prophets Jeremiah and Ezekiel repeatedly refer to God's strong hand and outstretched arm. Most of the references are to the great deliverance from Egyptian bondage, but Jeremiah 32:17 links the power of God's hand and outstretched arm to the creation of the heavens and earth. Ezekiel ties the hand and arm power to returning captives back to their homes and a knowledge of God. All of these references seek to let us know that God is supreme and that we should return to Him.

Lord, I pray that Your hand will cover me and hold me close.

The Prayer of Jabez—Keep Me From Evil

"Oh, that You would bless me indeed, and enlarge my territory, that Your hand would be with me, and that You would keep me from evil, that I may not cause pain!" So God granted him what he requested. 1 Chron, 4:10, NKJV.

The Lord's prayer as recorded in Matthew 6 asks for deliverance from evil or from the evil one. So this same request of Jabez for a very specific blessing of keeping him away from evil is highly significant. Scripture, of course, clearly identifies evil as originating with the devil, that great deceiver, Satan (Acts 13:10; Rev. 12:9). Powerless against the powers of darkness, we don't stand a chance when confronted with evil.

We have two cats. They spend significant time out on our back deck acting as if they are sleeping, just lazing in the sun. Stretched out to full length on their side or coiled up in a tight ball, head tucked in out of sight, either way they look as if as they are snoozing without a care in the world and quite harmless. When a titmouse gets momentarily distracted, however, and flies into the picture window, the strike instantly alerts the cats, and they are on it. The small bird doesn't stand a chance. Its only safety is if one of us cat "owners" can get there first to protect the titmouse from certain doom.

The inequality of the matchup between the alert cats and an addled bird somewhat approximates the unequal odds that I face when confronted with evil. What is the probability that I can escape? Zero. Jabez must have realized that. The devil has a highly organized army of agents who know my every weakness and artfully allure me in. My only safety is the prayer of Jabez: "Keep me from evil."

Perhaps that is why Psalm 1 points out how blessed the person is who avoids counsel from the ungodly. Notice the progression of the psalm: walking, stopping, standing in the way of sinners, and then sitting down in the seat of the scornful. The magnetism of evil has a way of drawing me in as I walk by, getting me to stop and look, and then leading me to sit down to enjoy. When Jesus was tempted following His 40 days in the wilderness, He didn't depend on His own strength. Rather He met the temptation with the power of Scripture and commanded Satan to get behind Him—another way to say, "Get outta my sight!"

Lord, I am powerless against the evil one. Keep me from evil. But when evil does get to me, my resolve is to let You fight the battle for me.

The Prayer of Jabez—That I May Not Cause Pain

"Oh, that You would bless me indeed, and enlarge my territory, that Your hand would be with me, and that You would keep me from evil, that I may not cause pain!" So God granted him what he requested. 1 Chron. 4:10, NKJV.

I t is when we give in to evil that we cause pain for others. Notice the cause and effect in the text above. So if the Lord chooses to keep me from evil, then I should not be the source of another's pain. I simply can't imagine the pain that King Saul caused for his harpist David. Like bending a wire back and forth until it breaks, Saul's alternating affection and hatred of David must have strained the relationship terribly.

What about Saul and the early Christian church? Did he cause physical and emotional pain for the believers in Jerusalem and surrounding towns? Sure he did. His persecution and killing drove the Christians underground. Without question that evil in his life delivered pain. It is Satan's highest objective—to bring pain to God by hurting His children.

This final request Jabez presented for a specific blessing is one that I can relate to. I have experienced enough pain in life to know that most of it comes from broken relationships with those closest around me. The last thing I want to do is bring pain to my loved ones. But in reality, I am the one most likely to do exactly that.

Two young adults become friends, are attracted to each other, and then fall in love. The relationship grows. It deepens with the intensity of young love. Then, for one reason or another, fearing that she may not have chosen wisely, she rejects further advances, instead choosing the company and affections of another. The suitor is devastated.

The fact is that we are made in the image of God, although with many of His characteristics imperfectly expressed. One of those qualities is that we were given the ability to love others deeply. But profound love has profound risk. What if that love gets rejected or spurned? The more we love, the greater the risk of pain.

Lord, I now understand. As the greatest lover ever, You have the potential of experiencing the greatest pain ever from broken relationships. Lord, keep me from evil, I pray, that I may not cause pain for You.

The Prayer of Jabez—God Granted Him What He Requested

"Oh, that You would bless me indeed, and enlarge my territory, that Your hand would be with me, and that You would keep me from evil, that I may not cause pain!" So God granted him what he requested. 1 Chron. 4:10, NKJV.

One thing I have learned in my brief life is that God is standing by, eager to grant the requests of the penitent, obedient, faithful, humble servant. Rich, magnanimous, generous, and abounding in love, He knows how to give good gifts and longs to bless.

For a few moments let us meditate on just a few testimonies from the past: "You will eat all the food you want and live in safety in your land" (Lev. 26:5, NIV). "Now you have been pleased to bless the house of your servant, that it may continue forever in your sight; for you, Lord, have blessed it, and it will be blessed forever" (1 Chron. 17:27, NIV). "You make known to me the path of life; you will fill me with joy in your presence, with eternal pleasures at your right hand" (Ps. 16:11, NIV). "You came to greet him with rich blessings and placed a crown of pure gold on his head. . . . Surely you have granted him unending blessings and made him glad with the joy of your presence" (Ps. 21:3-6, NIV). "How abundant are the good things that you have stored up for those who fear you, that you bestow in the sight of all, on those who take refuge in you" (Ps. 31:19, NIV). "Give thanks to him and praise his name. For the Lord is good and his love endures forever; his faithfulness continues through all generations" (Ps. 100:4, 5, NIV). "The eyes of all look to you, and you give them their food at the proper time. You open your hand and satisfy the desires of every living thing" (Ps. 145:15, 16, NIV). "Listen, listen to me, and eat what is good, and you will delight in the richest of fare. . . . Surely you will summon nations you know not, and nations you do not know will come running to you, because of the Lord your God, the Holy One of Israel, for he has endowed you with splendor" (Isa. 55:2-5, NIV). "Then you will look and be radiant, your heart will throb and swell with joy; the wealth on the seas will be brought to you, to you the riches of the nations will come" (Isa. 60:5, NIV).

Lord, since You are so generous with me, why am I so stingy with others? Forgive me for my sin of greed. Let me be an open channel of Your love and blessings to others.

Gaze Awareness

Turn your eyes away from me, for they have overcome me. S. of Sol. 6:5, NKJV.

E ye contact. Looking straight into someone else's eyes is powerful, powerful stuff! Lovers do it regularly, for it is an important factor in bonding. Parents look into baby's eyes, and baby looks back. Gazing deeply into another's eyes, searching for meaning and context of what is being said, is an important component of nonverbal communication. What I just heard—was that said with love or with disrespect? The eyes tell the story, and they don't lie.

Depending on your culture, holding steady eye contact can be a sign of strength, solidity, and honesty (Western cultures), or it could be a sign of aggression or considered rude or arrogant (Eastern cultures). Holding eye contact between men may be part of a power struggle, while between women it can mean lots of things. As for between the genders, it is often a sign of extraordinary interest. Eye contact (making eyes) is often one component of flirting.

Closely related to eye contact is gaze awareness, the ability to correctly tell where someone is looking. Not only can you accurately detect if someone is paying attention to you or something just past you, you can tell if they are focused on your eyes or a smudge on your nose or the broccoli in your teeth. We are acutely aware of another's eye position, and research shows that our judgments have a high degree of accuracy.

> **What I just heard—was that said with love or with disrespect? The eyes tell the story, and they don't lie.**

Many teachers nowadays, myself included, no longer struggle with whether or not a student is cheating. If one student gazes for any length of time at another student's paper during a test or quiz, they are subject to corrective action. When my students spend more time watching me, their teacher, than they do writing answers to questions, they are usually seeking opportunities to cheat when I am momentarily distracted. I have seen it happen far too many times.

The psalmist David is clear: "The eyes of the Lord are on the righteous" (Ps. 34:15, NKJV). He never stops looking. Like loving parents who can't keep their eyes off of their new baby, the Lord is deeply in love with each of us. Do we show any indication that we are aware of His gaze? Do we respond to His loving looks? Do we lock eyes with Him through daily meditation and prayerful communion? Chances are that my God has better gaze awareness than I do. Which makes me wonder why I act worshipful at times when my heart is not in it.

Lord, as I turn my eyes to You and look full into Your wonderful face, may everything else grow strangely dim in the light of Your glory and grace.

Sweet Cane

You have bought Me no sweet cane with money, nor have you satisfied Me with the fat of your sacrifices; but you have burdened Me with your sins, you have wearied Me with your iniquities. Isa. 43:24, NKJV.

T he wetland plant commonly known as sweet flag, sweet sedge, sweet rush, sweet root, sweet cane, sweet myrtle, or cinnamon sedge, is neither a rush nor a sedge but rather a monocot with the scientific name *Acorus calamus*. Through the inspiration of the Holy Spirit, the prophet Isaiah has God decrying the fact that His people have failed to bring him gifts of "fragrant *calamus*" (in the NIV) but have instead worn Him out with their sins. So just what is this fragrant plant that we should be presenting to God?

Sweet flag consists of a few species found native to the northern climes of North America, the Himalayas, China, Japan, Myanmar, and Thailand. It is common and widespread. A well-known plant and widely traded for its many medicinal and aromatic uses, *calamus* has been in use for thousands of years. A small piece of the fragrant stem and even more fragrant root make a pleasant chew for calming toothaches, to ease nausea, to decrease bloating, and to stimulate the digestive system. One can increase the dosage to safely induce vomiting, because it isn't toxic. Since *calamus* contains an organic ether called asarone, it is good for killing insects and bacteria. It is a strong antioxidant, and its essential oils with a pleasant citrus-like smell contribute to its value in the perfume industry.

The Song of Solomon includes *calamus* along with cinnamon, nard, saffron, and other sense-pleasing spices. So the question for me is How have I treated my Lover—my Lord—today? He loves me with an everlasting, unconditional love. His heart is always turning toward me. What is my response to His longing for a personal relationship? Am I willfully sinning against Him or just ignoring Him as I go about my day? Or do I turn back to Him often, gifting Him with my best, my most fragrant, my most costly, my sweetest? Am I regularly asking for His advice, thanking Him for His gifts, including Him in the ongoing conversation in my head? Perhaps now, when I hear the wind rustling through these reeds of sweet cane, I will hear His voice and answer back with love and adoration.

Lord of all, You have given me so much. What can I give to You other than what You have given to me—my time, my attention, my obedience?

My People

I will be their God, and they shall be My people. 2 Cor. 6:16, NKJV.

I was watching home-recorded tornado video of the massive storm that ravaged Tuscaloosa, Alabama, on April 27, 2011. The voice behind the camera kept repeating, "Oh, My God." The repeated phrase didn't sound like a prayer or an invocation to the Deity, but rather an expression of amazement and awe at the size and ferocity of the maelstrom wreaking havoc on the city. These few moments of audio impressed on me again how casually people use the "OMG" phrase or abbreviation these days. OMGs are far too common in text messages and social Web sites. Many are unmindful of the depth of meaning carried by the words "my God." Oh, how I want to know the majesty and supremacy of my God.

Bible writers regularly use that possessive phrase "my God." It appears in approximately 130 to 150 texts (nearly half from the Psalms), depending on the Bible translation that you choose. Here are just three examples of how the Bible employs it. "I thank my God, making mention of thee always in my prayers" (Philemon 4, KJV). "Therefore I will look unto the Lord; I will wait for the God of my salvation: my God will hear me" (Micah 7:7, KJV). "You are my God, and I will praise you; you are my God, and I will exalt you" (Ps. 118:28, NIV). In nearly every case "my God" appears in thanksgiving, praise, and prayer. The term is to exalt God and show a personal relationship. Is it significant then that "Oh, my God" does not appear a single time in the sacred record? Could it be because it trivializes and profanes the holy name of God?

On the flip side, the New King James Version has 218 usages of the expression "my people." According to my count, 185 instances quote God as He takes "joy in my people" (Isa. 65:19, KJV), or moaning "for the hurt of the daughter of my people I am hurt. I am mourning; astonishment has taken hold of me" (Jer. 8:21, NKJV). Reading such "my people" texts impresses me with just how much God longs for a relationship with us. Thirty two of the "my people" passages included the concept of the two-way relationship: "I will be their God and they will be my people" (2 Cor. 6:16, NKJV). The crown jewel of that type of relationship text showing God's longing is Jeremiah 24:7, in which He says: "Then I will give them a heart to know Me, that I am the Lord; and they shall be My people, and I will be their God, for they shall return to Me with their whole heart" (NKJV).

O Lord, You are my God indeed. Let me never deny You or even take Your name in vain.

November 23

Roll the Credits

Father, I desire that they also whom You gave Me may be with Me where I am, that they may behold My glory which You have given Me; for You loved Me before the foundation of the world. John 17:24, NKJV.

In 1956 a man by the name of J. T. Haley donated 6.3 acres of his land on Whispering Pines Road in the northwest corner of Albany, Georgia, to a newly established Sherwood Baptist Church. With about 300 members meeting each Sunday in an Army Reserve building, the company of believers needed a permanent home. The church has grown steadily through the years, and today the Sherwood Baptist Church is a small megachurch of a couple thousand members, with numerous buildings and scores of outreach ministries. Perhaps their best-known ministries outside of Georgia are the film productions written, acted, produced, and marketed largely by church members. With one camera and a budget of $20,000, the church released its first film, Flywheel, on April 9, 2003. Their second film, the 2006 Facing the Giants, had a budget of $100,000 and has grossed more than $10 million to date. Fireproof came out two years later. It had a million-dollar budget and supporting cast of 1,200 volunteers from Sherwood Baptist Church. Fireproof grossed more than $33 million in the United States alone. As of this writing, Courageous, their fourth film, was a cooperative effort of Sherwood and Mount Zion Baptist churches. The production budget for Courageous was in excess of $1 million. All of these Christian movies teach solid lessons about God and His grace, portraying people learning important spiritual lessons as they confront real issues of life. The creators of the films want God to get all the glory. To make sure that happens, they spend much time in prayer, pleading for divine guidance.

I enjoy staying after everybody else walks out to watch the credits roll. Credits always start with names written big so you can read them: lead actors, producers, directors, etc. Then the font size gets smaller and packed closer and closer together until barely legible: those who did makeup, arranged flowers, painted sets, served food, drove vans, baked cookies, managed child care, and did a thousand other tasks. All are listed, and most are members of Sherwood Baptist Church wanting to give glory to God. And He should get all the credit. He is the one who provided all the resources, all the inspiration, all the talent—everything. Without Him, nothing.

Lord, forgive us when we try to grab credit for ourselves. Without You, we can do nothing.

Nethinim

Jesus replied, "Very truly I tell you, everyone who sins is a slave to sin. Now a slave has no permanent place in the family, but a son belongs to it forever. So if the Son sets you free, you will be free indeed." John 8:34-36, NIV.

My heart breaks when I see them or read about them. It seems that every country has them in one form or another. In India, where the caste system is complex and highly organized, they are called "Dalit," or "untouchables," while in Japan they are the Burakumin. The island of Okinawa has Ryukyuans, Bali has Shudras, and Sri-Lanka has Kinnaraya, Rodiya, and Demala Gattara, depending on which part of the country you are visiting—but all are outcasts. Many countries in Africa have caste systems with the lowest levels occupied by Osus in Nigeria, Jonow in some West African countries, Jaam in Senegal, Hutus in Rwanda, Watta in Ethiopia, and Madhiban in Somalia. The list includes slaves of different types in every country of the world.

According to Anti-Slavery International, an international nongovernmental organization and lobby fighting slavery for almost two centuries, slaves include any people who are sold like objects, forced to work for almost nothing, and are totally at the mercy of their so-called employers. Though most countries of the world have outlawed slavery, it still exists in every jurisdiction in various forms such as child labor; bonded laborers working to pay off loans; early and forced marriages; trafficking in men, women, and children; and slavery by descent, to name a few. Some estimates of slavery range from 12 to 27 million worldwide, probably the most slaves ever, though perhaps the smallest percentage of world population.

As the Israelites conquered Canaan, the people of Gibeon put together an elaborate drama complete with props consisting of worn and patched clothing and sandals, cracked wineskins, and stale bread. For the Gibeonites, it was a life-or-death act, so they played their parts magnificently, pulling a fast one on Joshua. He should have consulted the Lord. But he didn't and got snookered into signing a treaty. When the truth came out (as it always does), the Gibeonites were assigned as woodcutters and water carriers for the house of God. The lowest of the low on the societal scale in Canaan, set apart to serving (nethinim) the Levites in their care of the Temple, they were in fact slaves. Now, aren't these the people that Jesus came to set free?

Lord, during Your life here on earth You treated the outcasts of society with love and tenderness. Teach my broken heart to respond to human suffering as You demonstrated.

Information Overload

And further, my son, be admonished by these. Of making many books there is no end, and much study is wearisome to the flesh. Eccl. 12:12, NKJV.

W e are flooded with e-mail, text messages, and RSS feeds, not to mention the excellent books, journals, and magazines that enter our space every day. Add to that the e-books, video downloads, DVDs, and advertisements that we get. The rate of increase in information is most certainly logarithmic. A 1989 book by Richard Saul Wurman called Information Anxiety claimed that one daily issue of the New York Times has more information than a person would get in a lifetime during the seventeenth century. What about today?

The smartest man that ever lived said that the constant torrent of new books was "wearisome to the flesh." That's what stress feels like to me. Wouldn't you agree? And Solomon wrote this long before Gutenberg's 1439 invention of movable type. Once printing presses started stamping and rolling, there soon were more books than one could read in a lifetime. When I was in graduate school in the early 1970s, conventional wisdom suggested that the scientific literature increased by 1,000 articles each and every day. For a young graduate student facing comprehensive exams, that was incredibly stressful. I could read only a few papers each day on a good day. As always, the numbers looking back appear tranquil compared to the ever-steepening slope of information expansion ahead. So now that we are well into the age of the Internet, in which anyone with a computer can publish, making tons of additional information available, the problem that Solomon described is really just more of the same, isn't it? We can get stressed if we really want to. But we can also do the daily work of tuning our filters to carefully select what we will peruse with our limited time.

One daily issue of the New York Times has more information than a person would get in a lifetime during the seventeenth century. What about today?

In the past, when publishers, music companies, and movie studios handled all the decisions about what to publish or not, they made choices based on the economics of whether or not it would sell. Production costs were high. Risk was great. But now that everybody can digitally publish in all formats for little or no expense, I am the one who must now decide where to look for information in appropriate quantity and quality to carry out my personal mission. My filter needs daily divine adjustments to keep me stress-free and mission-centered.

O Lord, adjust my filter to hear Your voice and instantly respond to Your commands.

November 26

Vision of the Night

I was not disobedient to the vision from heaven. Acts 26:19, NIV.

No doubt it happens to all of us. Numerous times, while in the middle of doing a major auto repair, or while working on resolving a difficult personnel issue, or while deeply involved in research, or while inventing a widget to do a much needed task . . . many are the times I have come up against a dead end. I could see no solution. There is no way to get a wrench on that nut. Irreconcilable differences have led to that office dispute. That research variable simply can't be controlled. I didn't see a way to get past this engineering dilemma. It was late. I was tired. I fell into bed exhausted and simply gave the matter to God. "Lord, I know You have a universe to run. But if You know a way to _____, would You mind letting me know about it? It's no big deal, really. But if I don't find a solution, my car will never run again. I'll be forced to fire that guy at work. Research along this track will be over—forever. I won't be able to make the all-important widget."

Then it happens. During the night, halfway between deep sleep and wakefulness, the solution is there in my head. It seems so simple. Eureka. The big aha moment just happened. Where did that come from? I can't wait till morning so that I can put the bright idea to the test. And it works. Meanwhile, the God of the universe stands on the sidelines with His own question: You want to know where it came from?

This type of scenario has happened too many times to be just coincidence. I am a big believer in an all-knowing God that loves to surprise His children. Finding the lost keys, providing a solution to the calculus problem, arranging events that put people together at exactly the right time and place, bringing a man and a woman together at the start of a lifelong relationship—God works in mysterious and wonderful ways.

The prophet Amos assures us that "surely the Sovereign Lord does nothing without revealing his plan to his servants the prophets" (Amos 3:7, NIV). Most of those revelations occurred during a night vision. In virtually every case the vision was troubling. True prophets often felt reluctant to give the message, while eager self-promoting false prophets sought the "vision." What has God revealed to you lately? Be instantly obedient to right a wrong, to put away a secret sin, to ask forgiveness. It may not be a full-color picture show, but God's visions come to all of us in impressions or a quiet voice that tells us, "This is the way."

My Lord and Master, thank You for speaking to me in the quiet of the night. Teach me to tune my heart to listen more carefully.

November 27

Shoes

And with your feet fitted with the readiness that comes from the gospel of peace. Eph. 6:15, NIV.

Protecting feet while walking or running has resulted in a broad range of solutions. Many decades ago in Africa I used to watch shoe shoppers stand barefoot on a piece of rubber tire. The sales person/shoe manufacturer would draw around the foot, cut out the piece of rubber, then attach that improvised sandal sole to the shopper's foot with leather or plant fibers. That was it. It may have been a slight improvement over sandals worn in Bible times.

In Holland I observed craftspeople carve shoes called klompen out of solid chunks of wood. Though reportedly not uncomfortable for wearing, the noise they make while walking means that you can't sneak up on anybody. Wood was more durable than leather in the wet marshy lowland Dutch farms. Elsewhere in Europe people have worn for centuries leather uppers nailed to wooden soles called clogs.

These days, the protective function of shoes may have diminished. Some wear shoes primarily to make a fashion statement. As I observe their wearers hobbling along, I can't imagine that the footwear is either comfortable or safe, or contributes to good body mechanics. The science of body mechanics has improved so much that most shoes now work to blend both comfort and protection. Just think of their many functions: steel-toed boots for working; tight, thin rock climbing shoes; lightweight shoes for running; bicycle shoes; golf shoes with pegs; football and baseball shoes with cleats; and shoes with crampons for ice climbing.

On one recent exercise walk I somehow managed to get a very tiny pebble flipped into my shoe. Before long it was right under the ball of my foot and seemed trapped there. As much as I tried I couldn't get it moved to where I wouldn't be stepping on it. The only solution was to stop, take the shoe off, and get the thing out. Until the rock was out, I was crippled. I find it highly significant that putting on the whole armor of God involves fitting our feet with the gospel of peace. Putting on boots for fighting takes longer than strapping on a sword or a helmet. But your feet are important in battle. How else will you stand and fight or pursue or flee? Foot damage takes you down quickly.

Lord, do I need yet more preparation to stand firm in the gospel? Teach me how to wear Your whole armor and to fight the good fight of faith.

In Everything? Are You Kidding?

In everything give thanks; for this is the will of God in Christ Jesus for you. 1 Thess. 5:18, NKJV.

How can I give thanks when I just came back from the doctor's office with a diagnosis including the dreaded "C" word and only three months to live? Is there any way to give thanks just after burying a soul mate of 23 years? How can one even think of giving thanks after accidentally running over your own toddler while backing out of the garage? Yes, these are real-life situations. Yet Paul said that we should be thankful in everything. Can he be serious?

My heart breaks when I read about the inhumane hardships endured during the Thirty Years' War during the early to middle 1600s. First swirling through Germany, it eventually involved much of Europe. Apparently it had no clear cause, though political and religious differences contributed to it. Reading descriptions of what happened sounds more like anarchy, as unpaid soldiers roamed in bands, killing, looting, raping, and wantonly collecting their pay from the enemy. With the countryside totally devastated, citizens died of disease and famine.

In the small German walled city of Eilenburg, northeast of Leipzig, the war took a terrible toll. Country people from miles around sought refuge there. The enemy besieged the town, cutting off all supplies. Too many people and too little food exacerbated famine and plague. People died constantly. Martin Rinkart and three other clergymen conducted dozens of funerals every day. When two of the three clergy died and the other managed to escape, Rinkart was left alone to do it all—40 to 50 funerals daily. Before it was over the townspeople buried people in trenches without any service. A total of 4,480 people perished in Eilenburg. At one point, Rinkart's wife sickened and died. After a particularly trying day, one account has Rinkart writing a prayer for his children. Another account says that he composed it for a celebration immediately following the end of the war. In any case, his words are a beautiful statement of total trust in God and certainly an example of being thankful under all circumstances: "Now thank we all our God, with heart and hands and voices, who wondrous things has done, in whom this world rejoices. . . . O may this bounteous God through all our life be near us."

Lord, thank You for teaching me that, no matter what, I can always stay in tune with Your heart and give You thanks—in everything.

Tomato Fruitworm, Cotton Bollworm, or Corn Earworm

But as morning dawned the next day God prepared a worm, and it so damaged the plant that it withered. Jonah 4:7, NKJV.

Believe it or not, all three names—the tomato fruitworm, the cotton bollworm, and the corn earworm—refer to the same type of critter! What you call the worm just depends on where you happen to find it.

This eat-anything destructive worm is the aggressive larval form of a moth called *Helicoverpa* (pronounced hee-lee-co-vur-pah). The larvae has yellow, tan, brown, and yellow/orange lengthwise stripes with a darker dotted line down the center of the back and black spots on the side. Sometimes the lines have green or even pink hues. Its head is dark orange. When the worm pupates, the adult emerges as a nondescript fat-bodied, fuzzy tan moth with darker spots merging into stripes toward the outside edge of the wings.

Fortunately for us, a small, non-people-stinging wasp, dubbed *Microplitis*, is good at following its nose (or, rather, its sensitive, chemical-detecting antennae) to the worm's dung. Finding a *Helicoverpa* worm, it will first sting and then inject a single egg into its now-paralyzed body. The wasp egg quickly hatches into a wasp larvae that burrows throughout the earworm larvae's insides, eating it alive and killing it before it can become another egg-laying adult moth.

Recent research with this small worm-hunting wasp shows that it can quickly be trained to go to any odor, and it can detect those odors at unbelievably low concentrations—only a few parts per billion. Just as Pavlov conditioned his dogs to salivate when he rang the bell, *Microplitis* wasps can be taught to respond to specific odors by repeatedly giving them a drop of sugar water as a reward whenever the odor is presented. After this brief and simple training period, the wasps can detect ulcers or they can be trained to respond to specific cancers by checking a person's breath. Another training, and they can identity plant fungal diseases, bombs, or drugs, etc. With their phenomenal odor-detecting mechanism, these half inch-long wasps work almost for free and are far easier to train than dogs.

Some worms destroy; others prevent that destruction. God has given His creatures truly amazing talents. Am I using my talents to advance God's peaceable kingdom?

Lord, sharpen my senses today to detect discouragement, pain, or anger. Lead me to one who needs a listening ear or a helping hand. Use my Spirit-filled talents to bring You glory and honor.

Secrets

The secret things belong to the Lord our God, but the things revealed belong to us and to our children forever, that we may follow all the words of this law. Deut. 29:29, NIV.

Ask the Holy Spirit to reveal the bright light of truth as you compare it to these statements.

"Biology is the study of complicated things that give the appearance of having been designed for a purpose" (Richard Dawkins, in The Blind Watchmaker: Why the Evidence of Evolution Reveals a Universe Without Design, p. 1). And then later on page 3, after he describes the long and purposeful process of constructing an airplane, he writes: "The systematic putting together of parts to a purposeful design is something we know and understand, for we have experienced it at firsthand.... Each one of us is a machine, like an airliner only much more complicated. Were we designed on a drawing board too, and were our parts assembled by a skilled engineer? The answer is no."

"Biologists must constantly keep in mind that what they see was not designed but rather evolved" (Nobel Laureate Francis Crick, in What Mad Pursuit, p. 138).

"It is not that the methods and institutions of science somehow compel us to accept a material explanation of the phenomenal world, but, on the contrary, that we are forced by our *a priori* adherence to material causes to create an apparatus of investigation and a set of concepts that produce material explanations, no matter how counterintuitive, no matter how mystifying to the uninitiated. Moreover, that materialism is absolute, for we cannot allow a Divine Foot in the door" (Richard Lewontin, professor of biology, Harvard University, in The New York Review of Books, Jan. 9, 1997, p. 6).

"No educated person any longer questions the validity of the so-called theory of evolution, which we now know to be a simple fact" (Ernst Mayr, emeritus professor of zoology, Harvard University, in What Evolution Is, p. 141).

These examples remind me of Paul's statement in Ephesians 4:17, 18: "So I tell you this, and insist on it in the Lord, that you must no longer live as the Gentiles do, in the futility of their thinking. They are darkened in their understanding and separated from the life of God because of the ignorance that is in them due to the hardening of their hearts" (NIV).

Lord, I pray that I will listen attentively to Your still small voice.

December 1
Roundup-ready

One fine spring morning my wife and I were out for our regular morning walk, wending past recently planted fields, orchards, and vineyards. Passing one field of corn we commented about the lush weeds shouldering aside the orderly rows of corn. We thought of how much work it would be to hoe the weeds from those miles of rows or how much fuel it would take to till between the rows several more times. We noted how the farmer needed to get on it before the corn got overwhelmed. Then, just a few days later, we noticed all of the weeds turning yellow at their tips of their leaves while the corn appeared totally unfazed.

Roundup is the most commonly used herbicide in the world. Discovered in 1970 by John Franz, Roundup's main active ingredient is glyphosate. Glyphosate sounds ominous, but in fact it is a slightly modified form of the simplest of all amino acids, glycine. All living organisms require glycine, and all make their own. The name glyphosate is just a shortened form of the chemical's name: glycine phosphonate—glycine with a methyl phosphate on one end. Glyphosate kills plants by inhibiting a single plant enzyme with a huge name and an even more important function. The enzyme 5-enolpyruvylshikimate-3-phosphate synthase (EPSPS) catalyzes a biochemical reaction in which plant cells make three important amino acids having an aromatic ring, namely phenylalanine, tryptophan, and tyrosine. Like glycine, all living cells require those three amino acids. But animal cells do not make them. Animals get them from their plant-based foods. Since plants must manufacture them, the EPSPS mechanism is crucial.

Like a broken-off piece of key in a lock, the herbicide glyphosate blocks the ingredients from entering the active site of EPSPS, and the plants die. Animals are unaffected, which is why nearly 50,000 tons of glyphosate can be used each year in the United States alone. Worldwide it has tremendously reduced applications of truly toxic herbicides. But what about the cornfield that we passed? Why isn't the corn killed? Monsanto thoughtfully developed soybeans, cotton, alfalfa, canola, sorghum, and corn all having a different version of EPSPS, one unaffected by glyphosate.

Lord, like Roundup on plants, sin is killing people everywhere. How can I be resistant to sin and ready when You come to gather Your harvest? Deepen my faith and trust that I might have immunity to the deadly scourge of selfishness. Teach me to love as You love.

Navigation

Their hearts are always going astray, and they have not known my ways. Heb. 3:10, NIV.

I was deep in the Amazonian rain forest with a group of students, following a guide down a trail. An hour or so into the hike a few students lagged behind to get photographs of tiny poisonous frogs. In short order we separated into two groups, one with a guide and one without. I opted to stay with the slowpokes to make sure they didn't get lost. But my problem was that I had never been down this trail before either. We were all novices in this jungle. So when the trail split, it was anybody's guess as to which way to go. And we were deep in the jungle. Backtracking the right trail would require considerable amounts of lucky guessing. What to do? Layer upon layer of foliage blocked any view of the sun. Dim light came from everywhere, erasing clues as to solar position. If you have ever lost your sense of direction for even a few minutes, then you know what a helpless feeling sweeps over you.

If you have ever lost your sense of direction for even a few minutes, then you know what a helpless feeling sweeps over you.

Ancient explorers out on the trackless sea in their balsa wood rafts sailed accurately from one Pacific island to another. In his epic Kon-Tiki, Thor Heyerdahl fancifully described early mariners navigating by feeling the rhythm of the ocean through their feet, sensing barely perceptible reflected waves from unseen islands beyond the horizon. He suggested that they were experts at navigation because their senses were tuned to receive important cues. With only the stars and their feeling for the winds and waves, they could pinpoint an island in the vast expanse of ocean.

The same was said for caravans crossing the great deserts in their camel trains. Without chart or compass or GPS, they knew the stars, and it mattered little when sand dunes shifted, because they were tuned to pick up useful navigational cues.

Before GPS, I remember being able to find my way through a strange city by paying attention to maps and landmarks. Then, having been there once or twice, I could return without a map. But today with dependable and ubiquitous GPS units, I am realizing that, like many others, I am losing an overall sense of direction, because I now depend on different cues.

What navigational aids guide my spiritual journey? Am I even paying attention, or am I drifting? Just as in life, I must pay attention to reliable cues, or I will soon be lost.

Lord Jesus, lead me home. I love the reliability of Your Word, the power and companionship of Your Comforter, and the dependability of Your still small voice within. Thank You, my Jesus.

Bird Migration

Does the hawk fly by your wisdom, and spread its wings toward the south? Job 39:26, NKJV.

Just how do birds return to the same nest year after year after doing their long distance seasonal migration? Do they have a built-in map in their head? Perhaps they have magnetic compasses in their brains. Or maybe they can accurately detect sun angles by being able to see polarized light. For those that fly during the night, do they have a star map in their brains? Or maybe they can hear or smell navigational cues.

With so many different types of birds and wintering grounds, it is likely that they employ various methods. But just for fun, consider this data:

- When moved a significant distance from their nest site first-year fledgling birds couldn't find their way to their wintering grounds. It suggests that birds either inherit a compass heading or direction to go or maybe accompany their parents or relatives on that first trip.
- Researchers who temporarily disrupted a group of catbirds' sense of smell discovered that they lost their ability to navigate. Other catbirds that kept their smell but wore magnets on their heads navigated fine, implying that smell was more important than magnetic cues.
- On cloudy days starlings have difficulty deciding which way to fly. But when the sun is visible, they orient perfectly. Perhaps they depend on a sun compass for navigation.
- Since most birds migrate at night, researchers put birds in a planetarium in cages designed with sloped sides to constantly force the birds to the middle. The birds oriented properly depending on the positions of the projected constellations, rather than any single star. When the sky was black, they became disoriented, strongly suggesting they use a star compass.
- German scientists placed caged birds in a room with no star or sun cues. They still hopped in appropriate directions. When wire coils changed the direction of the earth's weak magnetic field, it produced a statistically significant and appropriate adjustment in hopping direction, leading researchers to conclude that some birds may orient using a magnetic compass.

After decades of research, science has no definitive answers as to how birds acquire their map and their compass so that they can find their way so precisely. That is a delightful problem to keep working on throughout eternity.

Lord, You are glorified by the order in time and space exhibited in the seasonal migration of birds. May I also glorify You by the way that I order my life according to Your will.

Smelly Feet

How beautiful on the mountains are the feet of him who brings good news, who proclaims peace, who brings glad tidings of good things, who proclaims salvation, who says to Zion, "Your God reigns!" Isa. 52:7, NKJV.

T he female African malarial mosquito "prefers" getting its blood meal from the feet of its sleeping victim. Could the reason be because the buzzing of a mosquito around the head might alert the victim and doom the mosquito with a well-aimed death slap? Yet how does a tiny mosquito find the tender area between the toes during the dark of night?

In an attempt to eradicate malaria, one of the world's biggest killers, the Bill and Melinda Gates Foundation has sponsored a great deal of research on malaria and its carrier, the African malarial mosquito *Anopheles gambiae*. The female mosquito requires blood proteins to make eggs that she deposits as rafts on the surface of quiet water, so technically she is the only one that requires a blood meal. And to find that blood, we now know that she is fantastically well equipped with a huge array of chemical sensors on and under special hairs covering her antennae, her maxillary palps, and various parts of her proboscis, the elaborately wicked probe that she pokes into a capillary to get the blood.

As it turns out, she has CO_2 detectors to locate the ever-expanding cloud of gas exhaled with each breath of the sleeping person. So, at full alert, she follows the ever-increasing concentrations of CO_2. Since most CO_2 comes from the mouth and nostrils, the head of the sleeper, the dangerous end of the body for her, the mosquito has a problem. But as the insect gets within a couple yards of the victim, it turns out that other odors distract the mosquito and effectively block the CO_2 detectors. The mosquito's navigation actually switches to another set of sensors that detect bacterial odors, the kind of bacteria that colonize the skin of sweaty feet and toes. Scientists have identified 10 different foot odors, nine of which are incredibly attractive to mosquitoes and five of which effectively block CO_2 detection. This research has confirmed that repellents based on blocking CO_2 detection are clearly not the answer. What may be much more effective in mosquito control would be traps baited with the delicious scent of smelly feet. With a few such traps in the house, many of the bloodthirsty female *Anopheles gambiae* would meet their end, thus preventing much human misery and death. How beautiful are the feet of those with that good news.

Lord, use me in some creative way to help relieve human suffering and to spread the good news that You are on Your throne.

Ant Trails

Whether you turn to the right or to the left, your ears will hear a voice behind you, saying, "This is the way; walk in it." Isa. 30:21, NIV.

"**H**oney, there are ants in my kitchen again! Just look at them!" The anguished wail from my wife brings me running from my study.

Sure enough, an occasional ant hurries along the countertop, around the sink, and over the edge, meeting, stopping, and touching antennae with another ant going the other way before continuing on, eventually vanishing into a pinprick hole between the tile and the baseboard. There aren't a lot of them. But my wife's kitchen is her domain, and to her the only good ant is a dead ant. She has no tolerance for those tiny biblical teachers of wisdom scurrying through her kitchen.

But for her biologist husband, her invitation to "just look at them" is a welcome opportunity for an experiment. So, on my belly on the tile floor, I watch in wonder as the ants hurry back and forth along an invis-

> **But my wife's kitchen is her domain, and to her the only good ant is a dead ant.**

ible trail. Wetting my finger with my tongue, I wipe it across the trail as if it were a grease pencil mark. A few seconds later the next little traveler along the trail runs into my invisible swipe as if it were a block wall. It stops, turns around, and runs back to where it came from as if checking to see if it was on the right trail. Then it returns to the swiped area and halts. Ants approaching the other side of the swipe do the same thing. In moments, ants on both sides of the gap mill around in confusion, just a half inch apart from each other. They get bolder in their casting around for the trail. Soon they are on it again, rapidly establishing an invisible detour around an invisible gap.

The invisible trail is, for the ants with their excellent chemical detecting antennae, a very real trail of pheromones. The ants I am watching must be trail marking with their abdomen, because I don't see them doing anything else but running. Using a bit of detergent on a kitchen sponge, I can wipe out great lengths of the trail—that really confuses the poor ants. But when I come back in an hour they have reestablished an alternative route.

By now my sweetheart has had enough of the experiments and wants the ants out of her kitchen. Time to move into exterminating mode.

Lord, I choose to be as true to following the guidance of Your Holy Spirit as the ant is to the pheromone trail. Help me to stay tuned to Your voice and obedient to follow.

December 6
Extermination

The great day of the Lord is near—near and coming quickly. The cry on the day of the Lord is bitter; the Mighty Warrior shouts his battle cry. Zeph. 1:14, NIV.

When ants heard the Lord's command to be fruitful and multiply, they took it to heart. Myrmecologists (those who study ants) estimate that there are far more ants than any other kind of insect. So far they have named 11,000 species, with possibly another 9,000 yet undiscovered. What makes ants so important is the sheer number of them in each colony. The ant biomass in the rain forests of Brazil is four times the biomass of all other jungle amphibians, reptiles, birds, and mammals combined! The only places you won't find ants are the poles and high up on freezing mountaintops.

For the most part, ants mind their own business, which is finding food and making babies. But too often they cross paths with us, and we take exception to fire ants expanding their colonies into our yards, or harvester ants excavating our gardens, or pharaoh ants taking up residence in our homes or offices, or sugar or grease ants foraging for food in our kitchens. Where they have food and appropriate housing, their colonies will expand, and we all see them swarming, then landing, losing their wings, and going quietly underground again.

When ants invade our spaces, some choose to call an exterminator. If entirely professional, they will know the type of pests in your area and will poke around the house before positioning ant traps and/or spraying toxic chemicals. Although effective, such toxic products lack specificity, thus killing beneficial insects and potentially harming or sickening pets and people. Is there a safe, nontoxic alternative?

When I find a trail of ants in the home, I mix a couple spoonfuls of water with a quarter spoonful of borax (shelved with laundry detergents in any store) and half a spoonful of granular sugar. I stir till the sugar and borax have dissolved. By studying the ant trail, I try to find which end is closest to their home and then present a few drops of this brew to them on a small square of aluminum foil. If the ants are sugar eaters, they will quickly discover it. Gathering around the drop, they will fill their little bellies and take it back to the colony to feed all the members, including the all-important queen. In a day or two, problem solved. Mix the borax with butter if they are grease ants. Either way, borax dehydrates and exterminates completely.

Lord, I thank You for the natural products that You have provided to keep some of Your critters in check. I long for the day when all the evil in the cosmos will be exterminated and Your peaceable kingdom will flourish.

December 7

Skin

And as many as touched Him were made well. Mark 6:56, NKJV.

Once you see it, it's hard to take your eyes off of it. It's just a black-and-white etching and engraving attributed to the sixteenth-century Spanish artist Gaspar Becerra now in the Royal Academy of Arts, London. Dated 1556, it is accurately entitled "A flayed man holding his own skin." And there he is, knife in his left hand, all his muscles distinct and labeled as in any good illustration of human anatomy, the largest organ of his body—his skin—held head high, draped over his right hand, and hanging to below the knees. The man's gaze is riveted on what used to cover him and what all of us care for passionately—our own skin. Becerra's flayed man appears to have been the inspiration (if not the model to copy) for one of the exhibits on display at Body Worlds, the traveling exhibit of plasticized human bodies.

Our nine pounds of skin provides a study in contrasts and wondrous construction. Gently feel the soft suppleness of cheek, neck, or shoulder, contrasting their texture to the hard cornified resistance of heel, ball of foot, or elbow. Look how the skin between your thumb and index finger is wrinkled and folded compared to how it's stretched tightly over the nose, hip, or bicep. Note the relative insensitivity of skin to touch on the thigh or inside the arm as opposed to the extreme sensitivity of finger tips, lips, or around the eyes. Hairy places and hairless places, oily places and dry places, thick and thin, darkly pigmented and nonpigmented, places that can't sweat, places that won't stop sweating—the list goes on and on.

Our skin has so many crucial functions that losing even a small percentage of it is life-threatening. It gives us protection from drying out, giving control of body temperature, acts as a barrier to bacteria and pathogens that would consume us, and has a vast array of sensors for touch, pressure, hot, cold, and injury. Another important function of this marvelous organ, I believe, is communion with others, especially those nearest and dearest. Whether cruel or loving, skin-to-skin contact communicates powerfully. The hateful slap to the face or punch in the stomach is the same in every language. Skin-to-skin contact is the first meaningful communication that a baby experiences, the medium for the strongest of human interactions and bonding, as well as the last hand squeeze or soothing touch for the dying. How does my skin communicate to those around me?

Lord, how I long to feel Your loving embrace and to touch Your scars. My Savior, use my skin, my fingertips, and my gentle touch to communicate Your love to others.

Belgian Malinois

Now the purpose of the commandment is love from a pure heart, from a good conscience, and from sincere faith. 1 Tim. 1:5, NKJV.

I was waiting in line to clear security at Ontario International Airport on an outbound flight to Chicago when I saw him coming down the line of passengers, nose low, head casting back and forth, working quickly. His partner was a stocky, bulletproof-vest-clad police officer with a tight haircut typical of law enforcement. He held the leash high with one hand and low with the other, talking quietly to his K-9 partner that I later learned was a Belgian Malinois, a breed of working dogs preferred by law enforcement because of their optimal size and their coat color. Also known as a Belgian shepherd dog, it is slightly smaller than a German shepherd so it is easier to handle, and it has a fawn to mahogany coat color, many shades lighter than its German cousin, making it less susceptible to heat stress.

And as I found out standing there in line, the Belgian Malinois is a master at bomb sniffing. Thankfully the dog kept moving all the way down the line and never sat down once. In fact, the pair moved up to the upper level of the airport and continued working the hundreds of passengers in the terminal. Fortunately, the dog didn't sit down a single time during that shift. The animals are rigorously trained to sit immediately if they smell gunpowder or any type of commercial or military explosive. As long as the dog keeps walking and working, all is well. When they do sit, the area is cleared immediately, and the bomb squad comes in with their robots to investigate. Since the dogs are carefully trained to recognize a wide range of explosives and since they undergo weekly practice and recertification, they get really good at finding bombs of all types. During practice sessions it generally takes them only a few minutes to locate multiple bombs planted on or in a jumbo jet. Having a high energy level, they just love to work.

Maintaining public safety takes vigilance, training, and a clear and certain mission. Doesn't spiritual safety require something similar? God has given each of us a conscience that alerts us to right and wrong, protecting us from danger. But it takes vigilance, discipline of faith, and training in God's Word to keep our conscience alert and properly tuned.

Lord, lead me in Your way everlasting. Give me a will to flee from evil instead of stopping to investigate.

Flute

> And all the people went up after him and the people played the flutes and rejoiced with great joy, so that the earth seemed to split with their sound. 1 Kings 1:40, NKJV.

Flutes are one of the simplest instruments and certainly the oldest known musical instrument, dating far back into unrecorded prehistory. Even children quickly discover that blowing across a hollow grass stem (or bottle) can make a hauntingly beautiful tone. In less time than it takes to tell, they learn that different sizes of grass stems (or bottles) produce different pitches. Smaller volumes produce higher notes, and larger volumes, lower ones. Closed grass stems (or bottles) are simple Helmholtz resonators that produce resonate sound as the air blown across the top creates pulses of pressure in the chamber.

To understand how it works, think about how to create a single pulse. Some of the air going across the top hits the lip and goes into the chamber, causing an increase in pressure. The pressure inside builds and pushes back till it overcomes the pressure coming in. Because the pushback has inertia, it produces an overcompensation in the pressure, making lower pressure in the chamber. Low pressure inside causes air to rush back in, starting another pulse. Like a weight bouncing on a spring, the air pulses go in and out of the chamber. To prevent the pulses from dying out, the airstream blowing across the top keeps adding a little energy. The pressure pulses generate the sound that resonates in the chamber.

The flute is an acoustic cavity resonator. Air in the pipe of the flute is set in harmonic motion by pressure pulses generated by air being blown across the top of the mouthpiece. The flute cavity is an open cavity. Its size (and resonant frequency) is determined by which valve is open. The larger the cavity, the lower the note. Blowing more air across the mouthpiece puts more energy in, making the sound louder.

To generate sound in a flute, you must blow air across the top at just the right angle and velocity to get the pulses started. That takes lots of skill and practice. Ducted or fipple flutes are much easier to play. Blowing air into the duct directs it across the lip at just the right angle to get the pulses started. Police whistles, recorders, ocarinas, and pipe organs are examples of fipple flutes.

Lord, though I don't really understand the physics of music, I will raise my voice to You in praise and adoration. The music of flute and pipe organ connect my heart to Yours.

The Gift

All who are gifted artisans among you shall come and make all that the Lord has commanded. Ex. 35:10, NKJV.

He was a student in one of the first courses that I ever taught in college. I was fresh out of graduate school with a bright new degree that still had the ink drying on the signatures. As it turned out, he may not have learned much from me, but I gained much of great value from him. I am grateful for his lesson that, forever after, profoundly shaped my career as a college professor.

His rounded shoulders, long, unkempt hair, big thick glasses, crooked teeth, and pimply face may have contributed to his socially awkward, mouse-in-the-corner demeanor. He rarely spoke. When he did, it was a raspy voice, uncertain, overly cautious. His clothing, though clean, was badly dated and ill-fitting. Much like a camel's gait as it nears retirement, his walk was a galumphing-along, head-bobbing routine. Throughout the course we had but few interactions. Like many students taking biology, he found the material difficult if not overwhelming. Even though it was one of those bonehead courses to fulfill general education requirements, he was in over his head. Both of us knew it. But we both did our best. He ended the semester with a low grade but at least passed the course and wouldn't have to do it again. At that point I would have struggled to find much positive to say if I had had to write a recommendation for him.

As it turned out, he may not have learned much from me, but I gained much of great value from him.

Then it happened. I don't remember what brought me to a different church. But there he was, perched on the bench of the enormous pipe organ, peering through his thick glasses at the music, hands and feet moving up and down the keyboard and pedals with astonishing fluidity. The expression on his face, the total focus on making music, showed that he was feeling it, body, mind, and spirit. Heavenly music emanated from the ranks of pipes that lifted me to the courts of heaven itself. After the service I had a chance to visit with my former student. In this setting his poise and confidence was so obvious that I wondered if it was the same person.

During the course of the conversation I learned that this gangly, socially awkward student not only made music but actually built, installed, and tuned pipe organs when he was not in school working toward a degree. Whereas I was honing my gift of simply teaching about the structure and function of trees, he could take their wood, craft it into pipes, keys, pedals, and blowers, and give it a voice to praise its Creator.

Lord, forgive me for being so quick to pigeonhole and categorize others. May I see others as You do and celebrate the gifts that You have given.

December 11

Performance Anxiety

But when they arrest you and deliver you up, do not worry before-hand, or premeditate what you will speak. But whatever is given you in that hour, speak that; for it is not you who speak, but the Holy Spirit. Mark 13:11, NKJV.

Public speaking. Just saying the words makes my mouth go dry, my heart start racing, and my stomach begin knotting up. Or put me in front of important people, and my mind goes blank. Good ideas that I had carefully thought through and meticulously organized for the big presentation skitter away like a nicely raked pile of leaves in an autumn wind. From professional speaker, musician, or performer to novice, we all get stage fright now and again. We start breathing hard, the sweat pops out, and the blood pressure rises.

My guess is that it won't really help to explain what is going on in your body. Those reflexes are automatic (actually autonomic) and most difficult to control through rational thought processes. The sympathetic nervous system is firing all out, putting you in top shape for the fight or flight response, and at this point flight appears to be the preferable option. But there is too much at stake. You have to get up and make your speech, sing your song, or nail the landing of your full twisting triple backflip.

Is there a remedy for performance anxiety? The good news is that several things do help. Perhaps the first thing to do is practice. Compose the speech well ahead, learn the music, get all the fine points down carefully, then rehearse and practice again and again. Fear derived from not being ready is normal and actually a good thing. Respond to that fear with careful preparation. Next, I like to think of the presentation as a fun opportunity. Imagine drawing energy from the eager faces of those in the audience. Good presentations are exhilarating, enjoyable events. Another strategy is to put the presentation in its proper context. How important is it, really? What would happen if you really blow it? Would your mother still love you? Would God still love you? Yes, you want to do well, to put your best foot forward. But this one thing won't make or break you. Finally, for me, the clincher is that this life is not about me anyway. My days here will be measured, not by my success, but by how I bring honor and glory to God. He has given me the talents and the skills. How am I using them to honor Him?

Lord Jesus, You even said that the words You spoke while here on earth were not Yours but that they came from the Father. May I connect so that I can bring You glory also.

A Hideous Flower

For He shall grow up before Him as a tender plant, and as a root out of dry ground. He has no form or comeliness; and when we see Him, there is no beauty that we should desire Him. Isa. 53:2, NKJV.

I find it interesting that some of our holidays are closely linked with characteristic plants. Easter lilies, Christmas trees, St. Patrick's Day shamrocks and four-leaf clovers, and of course Valentine's Day roses. Christmas actually has several characteristic plants connected with the year-end celebration. Mistletoe and holly are beautiful in their own way, but have you seen the deep-green foliage and brilliant reds of the poinsettias this Christmas season? These striking plants are a real favorite because of their bright Christmas colors. Nothing comes close to matching the beauty of a big cluster of poinsettias. One of our local greenhouses is a virtual sea of red and green in early December when their poinsettias start developing their color.

But if you look at the poinsettia bloom closely, you will discover that the flower is really rather plain. The descriptors "ugly," "simple," and "unattractive" also come to mind. If you have noted how the bright-red "petals" look much like leaves, you are right. They aren't petals at all. Botanists call them bracts. Bracts are modified leaves that surround a cluster of unimpressive yellow flowers. And in poinsettias these hideous flowers called cyathia do their flower thing of making pollen and seed but in a very low-key way.

Various legends of poinsettias and Christmas originate in Mexico, where the plant grows as a native weed up to 15 feet tall. According to one such legend, poor Mexican children gave their best love gift that they had to the Christ child lying in the manger, part of the village nativity scene. Other children laughed and ridiculed the collection of weeds placed in the manger by the poor urchins. But then the miracle happened. The brilliant red star-shaped color developed, showing that a gift of love from the heart is of surpassing value.

Like poinsettia flowers, Jesus is described as unattractive and plain. But the reality of His birth, death, and resurrection, born of unquenchable love, surrounds Him in indescribable beauty and splendor. Why not give Jesus your best and watch how He turns it into beauty?

Lord, today I give You my heart, my life, my all. Though it isn't pretty, it is my best and most precious gift that I can give. Through the miracle of Your grace, may it be a thing of beauty to glorify Your name today.

Cuetlaxochitl (pronounced cute-el-axo-chit-el)

He has made everything beautiful in its time. Also He has put eternity in their hearts, except that no one can find out the work that God does from beginning to end. Eccl. 3:11, NKJV.

The beautiful poinsettias that grace our homes, churches, and businesses around Christmas time are a legacy of Joel Roberts Poinsett (1779-1851). Highly educated and from South Carolina, he was fluent in five languages and served in his state legislature, then in the United States Congress, before being appointed as the first minister to Mexico in 1825. Poinsett was an accomplished botanist who became enamored with *Euphorbia pulcherrima* (the scientific name for poinsettias that means "the most beautiful euphorb") that grew abundantly in southern Mexico. Like most Aztec monikers, the Aztec name for this plant is a real tongue twister—slow down and sound it out phonetically: cuetlaxochitl. Other names for poinsettias include Christmas star, star of Bethlehem, lobster flower, Atatürk flower, and flame leaf flower. No wonder scientists opt for scientific names.

During the time since Poinsett introduced this plant to North America, poinsettias have become a best seller for plant growers, and much research has gone into learning their habits. How can we keep the shrubby plants small enough to be potted plants? What conditions turn the bracts red, pink, or white? Growers learned that plants bloom only during the winter when days are short and nights are long. In fact, to get plants to bloom in time for Christmas, growers have to "put the plant to sleep" early each night starting in October. Even a brief exposure to light during their required 14- to 14.5-hour night will prevent them from flowering. For two months the plants have to be treated with long nights if they are to develop their characteristically colorful bracts.

For Moses, his "long night" of character development in the wilderness may have been hard to endure. What night of private pain are you going through this Christmas season? I heard Wintley Phipps say: "It is in the quiet crucible of your personal private sufferings that your noblest dreams are born and God's greatest gifts are given in compensation for what you've been through." Cling to the promise that God makes everything beautiful in its time.

Lord, You knit me together in the darkness of my mother's womb. All the days ordained for me were written in Your book before one of them came to be. May I trust You completely, no matter how dark my nights of pain.

Bitter Herbs

And the earth brought forth grass, the herb that yields seed
according to its kind, and the tree that yields fruit, whose seed
is in itself according to its kind. And God saw that it was good.
Gen. 1:12, NKJV.

P oinsettias are members of a large and diverse family of flowering plants
called Euphorbiaceae, which has more than 7,500 species. The largest genus
in that family, Euphorbia, has more than 2,100 species. Most euphorbs have
a white or occasionally yellowish milky sap that is under pressure and will quickly
well up or even spurt out. Sometimes a gentle touch is enough to break the skin
of a euphorb, causing the sap to appear immediately. On contact with air the sap
quickly congeals and seals the break. What's more, the milky sap contains a rub-
bery latex plus a rich cocktail of organic chemicals with varying degrees of toxicity
that can kill insects, snails, or even mammals that try to feed on euphorbs. Many
types of milky sap can cause severe skin or eye irritation. The sap of some plants is
10,000 to 100,000 times more irritating than capsaicin, the stinging bite in hot chili
peppers. Getting euphorb sap in the eye will be painful and will affect vision for a
few days, but it won't last long. Eating the plant parts of some euphorbs can cause
vomiting or digestive upset, but nothing more unless you have a severe sensitivity
to latex. Other euphorbs can be highly toxic.

So what good are the plants from the genus Euphorbia? Because the genus is
so large and each plant produces a wide variety of organic chemicals, euphorbs
have played an important role in medical therapy. Some concoctions from various Euphorbia have been part of folk medicine for hundreds of years. One can
quickly find reports of extracts from euphorbs with the power to calm digestive
upset, cure colic and cancer, rid the body of intestinal parasites, and treat skin diseases, migraines, etc. Some of the most interesting recent testing I have discovered
involved culturing cancer cell with euphorb extracts added to the growth medium.
Cancer cells failed to grow, while normal cells remained unaffected. That is good
news to pharmacologists searching for a plant-based drug that will attack cancer
cells selectively and without side effects. Researchers have also developed compounds to kill snails and insects. Certainly our Creator knew what He was doing,
and with our new analytical machines and knowledge of bioactive molecules, we
better understand the phrase: "And God saw that it was good."

Lord, use the bitter experiences of my life as a healing balm for others.

December 15

Bucket List

I never knew you; depart from Me. Matt. 7:23, NKJV.

How many items have you crossed off your bucket list? What is the most important item on it? Do you even have a bucket list? Some of you may be asking, "What's a bucket list?" The quick and easy answer is that your bucket list is the list of things you want to do or accomplish before you "kick the bucket," so to speak. At bucketlist.org you can see what others have put on theirs. The items are many and varied. Some are as simple as riding a train or passionately kissing in the rain. Others are more difficult, such as: visit Stonehenge, drive a race car on a racetrack, visit all 50 states, see the Great Wall of China, take a picture in front of the Taj Mahal, climb Mount Everest, visit Disneyland, or float in the Dead Sea.

Wish lists or to-do lists have been around since the beginning of time. Such lists keep us on track from day to day as we go about the business of life. In contrast, the bucket list is the big one. The phrase became *Seems to me there is just one item that needs to be on our list: Be known by Christ.* popular after the movie by the same name appeared in 2008. The film tells the story of two very different terminally ill lung cancer patients who became good friends while sharing a room in the hospital. One, a mechanic and family man, makes a list of things that he would like to do before he dies. But when told that he has only a year to live, he realizes that he can never fulfill it. The other, a wealthy tycoon, likes the list and insists that the two go together and do it all. He will pay all expenses. The unlikely couple go skydiving, take a safari, and visit some of the Seven Wonders of the World. From the top of the Great Pyramid they talk about the importance of their family relationships and relational successes and failures. The story illustrates that relationships are most important.

Yes, it is good to have plans, to work toward long-term goals, to make wish lists—even bucket lists. Without these kinds of targets, we will very likely hit exactly what we are aiming at—nothing. The world, the spirit of this age, urges the biggest adrenaline rush, the distraction for the moment, or food for selfish passions. I was interested to find this entry in bucketlist.org: "Stand at the feet of Christ the Redeemer." Yes, definitely. But as I think about it, won't we all stand at the feet of Jesus? Doing good or bad doesn't seem to be the issue at that point. Seems to me there is just one item that needs to be on our list: Be known by Christ.

Lord, do You know me yet? Am I seeking You with that all-important undivided heart? Have I crossed everything else off my list in order to seek You first, last, and only?

Heartwood

O Lord God, remember me, I pray! Strengthen me, I pray.
Judges 16:28, NKJV.

For the most part, trees mind their own business and just stand there in the same spot year after year. About the only way you can tell they are growing is if you have photographs from the past. But comparisons will surprise you with how much the tree has matured.

Most of the cells in trees are the dead water-conducting cells of xylem—that's what wood largely is. As the tree develops, cells in the center of the stem cease to function, because the continuous stream of water will have been broken. Only the last several annual rings of xylem preserve an unbroken stream of water to conduct nutrients up the trunk. After any break in the water pathway (be it from insect damage, air embolism, or winter freezing) the cells are unable to reestablish the continuous water pathway. The problem is that retired xylem cells are hollow cavities. Moist and dark are preferred conditions for fungi, bacteria, carpenter ants, millipedes, and other things looking for food and housing. Growing trees produce a large number of products. Many manufacture resins, waxes, and terpenes. Some of them are waste products of photosynthesis, and some are even highly toxic to other life-forms. Many are water-resistant, hard, and durable. In any case, some trees will routinely send such products to the center of the tree, where they get deposited in the empty cavities of the xylem cells. As axial tissue in the center of the tree fills up with them, the color changes along with the density of the wood, both of which help us to see the difference between heartwood and sapwood. Sapwood actively conducts while heartwood can strengthen a tree. That heartwood isn't always protected from decay is shown by the fact that the center of a tree may rot out completely with no evidence on the outside. From all appearances, it is still a healthy tree.

When storm-tested, however, a hollow tree will generally break first, since it simply isn't as strong as the one with a solid heartwood core. It makes me wonder what the core of my walk with Jesus is like. Do I have a prayer life that draws strength from my source of life? Do I spend time in the Word storing up protective scriptures?

Lord of the highest heavens, protect my heart from the rot and decay of this world. Strengthen me to withstand the storms of life.

Cymbals

Then David and all Israel played music before God with all their might, with singing, on harps, on stringed instruments, on tambourines, on cymbals, and with trumpets. 1 Chron. 13:8, NKJV.

To get emphasis and attention for a particular note in music, nothing beats the "crash-bang" of a good pair of cymbals played with energy and flair. I like the way David puts it in Psalm 150:5: "Praise Him with loud cymbals; praise him with clashing cymbals!" (NKJV). Wow, there is nothing somber or reserved about this method of praising God. Clearly the cymbals mentioned in this passage are not the tiny finger cymbals or zills originating in Turkey. They must be the big brassy noisy cymbals that we find and love in major symphony orchestras today. "Praise God in His sanctuary. Praise Him in His mighty firmament!" (verse 1, NKJV). But then, maybe that was one reason God picked David out as a "man after His own heart" (1 Sam. 13:14, NKJV). David had a history of praising God "with all his might."

With many originating in Turkey, the major cymbal manufacturers such as Paiste, Zildjian, Sabian, and Meinl Percussion carefully design their cymbals to have a wide range of sounds rather than always being bright and sassy. The best are cast from various formulations of bell bronze (the bronze that bells and gongs are made from) generally consisting of 80 percent copper and 20 percent tin and sometimes with traces of other additives. Then after casting, some are hammered and/or lathed to get the right thickness and tone. Less-expensive cymbals are easily pressed from sheets of malleable bronze with less than 10 percent tin. Even with hammering and lathing, they don't have the depth of sound of the cast cymbals.

An expert percussionist uses cymbals in many ways. The clashing cymbals of Psalm 150 can easily be heard over the sound of a full orchestra at fff ("fortissimo possible"), meaning as loud or as strong as possible. Some lovingly refer to this dynamic as "blastissimo." Besides loud "clashing," cymbals can also be made to "tap-clash" by tapping an edge of one against the body of another, to "scrape" by scraping the edge of one from the inside out on another, to "sizzle" by rubbing their thin edges together, or to "hi-hat chick" by bringing two cymbals together strongly and holding them tightly together to choke off the sound.

Incredible levels of technology and hard work come together to make a good pair of cymbals, resulting in a particularly appropriate instrument for praising God.

Lord, search me and know the depth and honesty of my praise.

Rinderpest

Then He who sat on the throne said, "Behold, I make all things new." And He said to me, "Write, for these words are true and faithful." Rev. 21:5, NKJV.

The New York Times trumpeted the news: "Rinderpest, Scourge of Cattle, Is Vanquished." So what is rinderpest, and why should I care?

Any German speaker will tell you that rinderpest means "cattle plague," but what they may not know is that this disease of cattle and other animals with cloven hooves is a viral infection closely related to distemper in dogs or to measles in humans. Though rinderpest doesn't affect humans directly, millions have died from starvation or suffered major disruptions after their cattle died. Soon after infection, animals spike a fever, their eyes run, sores appear in their nose and mouth, and their entire gut, beginning to end, is red and inflamed, and they die quickly from dehydration and protein imbalance. It can completely wipe out herds that lack immunity. For cultures dependent on cattle, goats, sheep, or water buffalo, the disease is life-changing. It may also affect such wild animals as antelope, kudu, and giraffe.

Though some at first blamed rinderpest for decimating Pharaoh's cattle during the fifth plague of Egypt (Ex. 9:3-7), recent genetic analysis from Japan suggests the virus more likely originated in central Asia sometime during the thirteenth century. Since its first wave of destruction, rinderpest epidemics broke out repeatedly through the centuries in Europe, India, the Mediterranean, Africa, and Britain, sparing few if any Eastern countries. In 1761 the first ever school of veterinary medicine organized to combat the disease, and the World Organization for Animal Health started in 1924 as an international continuation of that effort. Immense efforts to quarantine, immunize against, and monitor the disease eventually isolated it to islands of nomadic herds in Africa. Victory celebrations in 1979 proved premature when additional outbreaks occurred. Continued improvements in vaccines, education, and protocols again reduced contamination to isolated regions so that a final assault in 1998 was eventually successful. The last known animal to have the disease died in 2001. For 10 years veterinarians, research scientists, and cattle raisers held their collective breath. Finally, it was time to celebrate.

Even so, come Lord Jesus. With Your return to claim Your faithful followers, all sickness and disease will be eradicated in a moment.

December 19

Peaceable Fruit: Meditation on Hebrews 12:11

Now no chastening seems to be joyful for the present, but painful; nevertheless, afterward it yields the peaceable fruit of righteousness to those who have been trained by it. Heb. 12:11, NKJV.

The lesson of life is no pain, no gain. Long years of painful rigorous schooling and residency programs always come before the career of a famous neurosurgeon—just ask Ben Carson. Training for a marathon takes years, and the marathon itself is brutal. A startup business requires years of exhaustive work before one can move from the business plan to the mature business. For Lynn Hill to free-climb the nose of El Capitan in a day takes years of discipline and dedicated practice and training. To forge a free republic, a people must have a vision and fight for it, giving it all that they have.

After sailors battle winds and waves for days, keeping their vessel afloat during a raging storm, then comes the calm. Pain first—reward later. Samson first killed the lion, then found the honey. Only after David drove out the Canaanites did the land have rest. First the Hebrew worthies went through the fire, then the proclamation that all must worship the God of heaven. The Great Disappointment preceded the renewed hope of the three angels' messages. We must clear the land, prepare the soil, and sow the seed before we can have the harvest.

So why would we expect Christian life to be any different? Whatever trials and tribulations we are going through now, can any be too great considering what we are looking forward to? Just think of the great shout and loud trumpet blast on resurrection morning. Consider all the reunions you will have with loved ones on that glad morning. From there we rise to meet Jesus face to face in the clouds. Imagine the journey to the Holy City. As you approach the city, you will see its brightness. You will explore those streets, walk beside the sea of glass, and stroll in parks where there is no litter, no crime, no frigid blasts or beastly hot humid air. Finding your new home, you will walk from room to room, taking in the view from the balcony. No trouble here on this dark earth can come close to being so great that I am going to give up. But best of all, I will see Jesus, face to face.

Lord, when I get discouraged and depressed, remind me of the pain and suffering that You went through because You counted it as nothing compared to the joy of bringing me home.

The Attitude of Gratitude

Enter his gates with thanksgiving and his courts with praise; give thanks to him and praise his name. Ps. 100:4, NIV.

In the rich garden of virtues, gratitude is not only the soil but the sunshine and the rain—it is that vital. Gratitude is thankfulness no matter what. It is the ability to take a status report and then make a list of blessings. While not blind to problems, concerns, and deficits, it is the gift of being thankful for what we have rather than complaining about what we don't.

In the rich garden of virtues, gratitude is not only the soil but the sunshine and the rain—it is that vital. Gratitude is thankfulness no matter what.

Chester W. Nimitz was selected as commander of the United States Pacific Fleet just 10 days after the attack on Pearl Harbor on December 7, 1941. On Christmas Day 1941 Nimitz toured the terrible destruction in the harbor. Eight battleships, three cruisers, four destroyers, and five additional ships and one dry dock of the Pacific Fleet had been sunk or badly damaged. Aircraft damage included 188 destroyed and 159 damaged. The raid had killed 2,403 people (including 68 civilians) and wounded 1,178. U.S. forces had been whipped badly. Dejection, despondency, despair, and defeat filled every face. Afterward someone asked Nimitz for his thoughts. His reply was optimistic and upbeat, pointing out that the enemy had made three huge mistakes: 1. The attack on Sunday morning meant most of the military personnel were ashore, so casualties were comparatively light. 2. All the fuel for the Pacific theater was still available, because they hadn't thought to include fuel storage tanks in the attack. 3. All but one of the dry docks for ship repair were unscathed. Most of the sunk or damaged ships were repairable, and, sitting close in shallow water, they could be back in business quickly.

Scientific research studies focusing on gratitude and reports of wellbeing are getting definitive and consistent results. In one study by Emmons and McCullough (Journal of Personality and Social Psychology 84, no. 2 [2003]: 377-389), those who wrote down their gratitude experiences daily enjoyed "higher levels of positive effect" and were more likely to help others or offer emotional support than those who journaled problems or neutral issues. The gratitude group also accomplished more of their personal goals. They also reported higher "levels of positive states," such as enthusiasm, determination, and energy.

Lord, my heart bursts with gratitude to You. First You gave me life, then You let me know about Your love and gift of salvation and protection from evil; and to top it off, You have given me friends, family, and food to make the heart glad. What more could I ask for?

Man's Best Friend

"Lord," she replied, "even the dogs under that table eat the children's crumbs." Mark 7:28, NIV.

W ho or what comes to mind when you hear the phrase "man's best friend"? If your mind is programmed like mine, you may be thinking of your favorite dog, perhaps a pet you have now or one you used to have. You may know a dog that wants to be near you, running on ahead of you when you take a walk, constantly coming back to check on your progress, sitting beside you when you pause for a rest, picking up a stick or a rock and wanting you to toss it out so that it can fetch. Such a dog will protect you from suspicious people or fight to the death for you.

A dog named Delta appears in a story printed in the November 1878 issue of "Our Dumb Animals," a newsletter of the Massachusetts Society for the Prevention of Cruelty to Animals. Delta and his master, Severinus, lived in Herculaneum some time before the eruption of Mount Vesuvius. Not only did Delta save his master from drowning in the sea once, but he protected him from a band of robbers, and another time from a she-wolf robbed of her cubs. The story goes on to describe how the animal became the best friend and protector of Severinus' only son. When the mountain erupted and buried the city, Delta covered the child with his body, but to no avail. They were entombed together.

Though dogs serve us exceedingly well in this day and age (working dogs of all types, i.e., police, guard, herding, rescue, Seeing Eye, and companion dogs, and pets), the Bible has little good to say about dogs in its 47 references to them. Job 30:1 mentions a sheepdog in a deprecating way. Jesus' interchange with the Canaanite woman suggests that dogs may have been pets living in the house and picking up crumbs from the table even as they do today. By inference we can guess that dogs may have served as guard dogs (cf. Ex. 11:7). Most biblical passages, though, refer to them in negative ways: as scavengers (Ex. 22:31; 1 Kings 14:11; 16:4; 21:19), creatures with nasty habits (Judges 7:5, 6; Ps. 22:20; 59:14; Prov. 26:11), and outcasts (1 Sam. 17:43; 24:14; 2 Kings 8:13; Phil. 3:2; Rev. 22:15). Nowhere does the Bible lovingly describe a dog's devotion and service to humanity. It makes me wonder why that is when dogs are so loved now. Could it be that God Himself wants to be man's best friend?

Lord, Your loving care, attention, provisioning, healing, protection, and saving are infinitely more important to me. Give me a heart true to You only.

Mango

He does great things past finding out, yes, wonders without number. Job 9:10, NKJV.

S ince our paths first crossed early in 2001, Nida and Placido Roquiz have become dear friends who bless our lives periodically with a box of fruit from trees in south Florida. They are the most exquisite mangoes imaginable. First, they are huge. Even with big hands, you can't possibly surround one with both hands with all your fingers touching. The skin is smooth and green with shades of orange and red blushes. The pit is slender, taking up very little space. The pulp or fruit is butter soft and juicy with little if any fiber. And the flavor . . . ahhh, the flavor must be something akin to fruit from the tree of life itself. It is sweet and aromatic, with some spicy notes. Indescribably delicious, so I'll stop trying.

Unfortunately some people can't eat mangoes without breaking out in a rash around their mouth and on their face. Mango, poison ivy, poison oak, and poison sumac are members of the plant family Anacardiaceae. Their sap contains a chemical called urushiol, the cause of severe contact dermatitis in certain people. Another member of the same family is the lacquer tree, also known as the varnish tree or Japanese sumac, the source of urushi, lacquer made from the sap of the lacquer tree. As you might guess, lacquer can cause severe rashes and needs to be handled with care too. Cashews also belong to this interesting family.

Mangoes grow on trees that usually become rather large (up to 100 feet tall). Because of excellent root systems and the mild weather where they grow, they can also produce fruit for a very long time. Being one of the few tropical tree fruits, mangoes have been selected and cross-pollinated for centuries, so that more than 1,000 varieties now exist, primarily in frost-free areas of the world, since their flowers and fruit don't do well when it gets cold (below 40°F). When it comes to fruit popularity worldwide, three mangoes are eaten for every banana, and 10 mangoes for every apple, making the mango the "king of fruit."

John the revelator describes the tree of life. That we don't understand it well is an understatement, because it grows on both sides of the river. Sounds like one tree with two trunks. The tree of life bears 12 crops of fruit, yielding its fruit every month. Is that 12 different types? Could any of those be anything like a mango? What marvelous growth factors are in those leaves?

Lord, creator of the most amazing mango, You are the one who gives access to the tree of life.

December 23

Today

God again set a certain day, calling it "Today." . . . "Today, if you hear his voice, do not harden your hearts." Heb. 4:7, NIV.

en Franklin may have said it best: "One today is worth two tomorrows." That is because today is the only day we have. Yesterday is gone. We can't call yesterday back to do what we failed to do. Nor can we reuse yesterday to undo what we may have messed up really bad or to repeat what we may have done well. All we have is today. Tomorrow is not here yet, and we aren't even promised a tomorrow. So what are we going to do today? How will I spend its precious gift of time?

What is time, anyway? Clearly it isn't a thing that you can touch, save up, or store. You can measure it and mark it off as it passes, but, as long as you keep your feet on mother earth, you can't speed it up or stop it, because it just keeps marching on, second by second. Some describe it as being a dimension of the universe, a way to characterize things or events. Others prefer to think of time as an abstract, nothing more than an intellectual way to compare and sequence events. Of course, navigators and astronomers must measure time with extreme accuracy in order to practice their craft. For them, time flows steadily like the grains of sand through a tiny hole in an hourglass—or to be more precise, like the resonance frequency of atoms in ammonia or cesium 133, the element used by the National Institute of Standards and Technology as well as the U.S. Naval Observatory and the International Bureau of Weights and Measures. Most atomic clocks employ cesium 133, because its atoms oscillate at a constant frequency. All you need is a method of counting off exactly 9 billion, 192 million, 631 thousand, 770 oscillations (9,192,631,770) of this remarkable element, and there you have it. One second has passed and is now lost forever. As you can guess, we need a very fast counting device as each second ticks by.

As your time passes today, will you use it to build up or to tear down? Will you employ it to promote yourself and your cause or God and His kingdom? Each moment in time is a gift from God. The psalmist said: "This is the day the Lord has made; we will rejoice and be glad in it" (Ps. 118:24, NKJV). And the Lord Himself declared: "I must work the works of Him who sent Me while it is day; the night is coming when no one can work" (John 9:4, NKJV).

Lord, my commitment is to follow Your example in doing the work of Your Father today. Let my every decision instantly turn toward You now. Keep my heart open to the Holy Spirit.

Fresh Every Day

But some of them left part of it until morning, and it bred worms
and stank. Ex. 16:20, NKJV.

In the culinary arts, fresh is paramount. Same-day freshness in fruits and vegetables, bread, and pasta is crucial. For a really special occasion, don't even
think of making a spinach lasagna using those old, hard, dry noodles out of
a box, frozen spinach, hard dry cheeses, and out-of-the-can sauce. Instead, pick
up just-made lasagna noodles and use fresh-picked spinach from the garden. Put
that together with fresh bite-size mozzarella balls packed in water, fresh ricotta
cheese, and freshly grated Parmesan cheese and a sauce made with fresh tomatoes,
just-picked shallots, bay leaves, basil leaves, and parsley. OK, maybe you have to
use some dried thyme, marjoram, and oregano and maybe a can or two of tomato
paste, but fresh is the name of the game when you are cooking for royalty.

Try a stir-fry of really fresh veggies and mushrooms. Then compare the taste
of the same stir-fry using veggies and mushrooms that have passed their prime,
meaning a few age spots here and there and smelling just a bit off. The difference is
remarkable. Even with modern refrigeration, produce starts going bad the moment
it is picked. So for those with a discriminating palate, the rule is always go with the
freshest ingredients you can possibly get.

Now, don't get me wrong. When eating to live, I am a great lover of leftovers.
They vividly demonstrate God's abundance. And for some food items, freshness
is not an option. Aging or cooking might be important processing steps to chemically change the food, making it more palatable or more nutritious. But for most
items, fresh is best.

Imagine the logistics of feeding and watering more than a million or so people
and all their livestock while camped or wandering in the Sinai desert. Only God
could pull that off. One of the miraculous solutions was the daily manna. It taught
lessons of daily dependence on God and of the Sabbath as a holy and special day.
And with my obsessive fixation on freshness, I can relate to the disappointment of
stinking, wormy manna the next day. But read in Deuteronomy 8:7-9 about what
the Lord had in mind for His chosen: "For the Lord your God is bringing you into
a good land . . . in which you will lack nothing" (NKJV).

*Gracious and loving Lord, make me just as passionate about getting into Your
word of life fresh every day. Teach me the lesson that it will not keep overnight. Teach
me morning by morning to feast on Your living Word.*

December 25

The Gift

Do not be afraid, for behold, I bring you good tidings of great joy which will be to all people. For there is born to you this day in the city of David a Savior, who is Christ the Lord. Luke 2:10, 11, NKJV.

We simply don't comprehend the mystery of how He, the God of the universe, became a zygote in Mary's womb, then spent the normal growing time tucked in a fetal position, organ systems developing, listening to her praying, singing, discussing. Oh, there was plenty to discuss. Being pregnant out of wedlock was a big stress back then. Then to become a new wife just added more stress. Learning to live as Joseph's wife—yes, there must have been many discussions. Then, when the time came, she rode on a donkey for at least 80 miles, bouncing along the rocky road to Bethlehem. On their arrival they found no room in the inn. She was exhausted. What to do? The baby was coming. The animal stall it was, then.

Having babies is rarely easy. That's why it is called labor. It's hard work, and painful, too. But with the whole universe focused on this delivery, I like to think that there must have been specially trained angels in attendance. Perhaps they stepped in to assist. Pressing on the uterus here, guiding the baby's head there, regulating her output of oxytocin to strengthen the contractions. It is OK to wonder, isn't it? By the time Joseph got back with the water, Mary and Jesus were both ready for a good cleanup. Washing with water, then a light rubdown with salt followed by a tight wrap in swaddling clothes and laying Him in the manger.

Meanwhile out in the pasture, shepherds tended their sheep under the stars. Suddenly the darkness was brighter than a thousand floodlights. An angel stood in front of them, the glory of the Lord was all around them. They were terrified. I would have been too. But listen. "Do not be afraid, for behold, I bring you good tidings of great joy which will be to all people." O angel, are you talking to me this Christmas morning? Great joy to all people? Oh, I hear you. Then the light grows even brighter as the angelic choir sings. What a concert of good news.

Jesus, my Lord, thank You for the gift of Your life, ministry, and sacrifice. With humble heart I accept Your saving grace.

December 26
The Jewish Wedding

I go to prepare a place for you. John 14:2, NKJV.

The wedding in the little village of Cana of Galilee must have started out like most other weddings. At first, love may not have been a factor. You see, from what we can gather about those times, this may have been what happened. About a year before the actual wedding, it is likely that the young man's father picked a bride for him (let's call him Ben and the teenage bride-to-be Esther). Following the local custom, Ben and his father would then have gone to speak with Esther's father at her house. If Ben passed muster with Esther's father, Ben would have made out a contract with Esther and offered her a cup of wine. If she drank with him, then the contract was binding, and he would finalize the arrangement by paying the father the bride price—a hefty sum to reimburse the father for all the expenses he had incurred by raising Esther. That done, Ben would make a little speech to Esther, including the phrase "I go to prepare a place for you." Afterward Ben would have returned to his father's house to build a bridal chamber. When completed, it would have to be provisioned with food and drink and everything else needed for the weeklong festivity. Ben's father would have to approve of the chamber. It had to be just right. When people asked Ben when he was getting married, his stock answer would have been: "I don't know—only my father knows."

Meanwhile Esther waited, preparing for marriage, wearing her veil whenever she went outside, a sign that she was conse-

"I don't know—only my father knows."

crated, set apart, bought with a price. As the potential time approached, her bridesmaids waited with her day and night. They kept extra oil for their lamps, because bridegrooms often came at night. Nobody knew when Ben would return for her. Then it happened. Ben and his party came with a shout and a blast on the ram's horn that signaled the marriage as good as done. Esther's father and brothers allowed Esther to be "abducted" and taken to the bridal chamber, with lots of celebrating and merriment along the way. Ben and Esther went right to the bridal chamber, where the marriage was consummated. Friends and family celebrated outside. Sometime during all that eating and drinking the unthinkable happened. They ran out of wine.

Mary, mother of Jesus and friend of Ben's family, was probably assisting with the food and drink preparation and making the guests comfortable. What? No wine? (To be continued.)

My dearest Bridegroom, I know You are preparing Your bridal chamber. I am longing for Your return. I will wait with my lamp trimmed and burning.

Water to Wine

Jesus said to them, "Fill the waterpots with water." And they filled them up to the brim. John 2:7, NKJV.

Running out of wine at a Jewish wedding celebration was a serious problem. As one of the hosts, Mary must have borne some of the responsibility. Fortunately, her Son, Jesus, and His disciples had been invited to the wedding. Just when they arrived, the story doesn't say. But they were there when the wineskins gave up their last drops. Mary doesn't appear worried or flustered. She knew that Jesus was the long-awaited Messiah. Taking matters into her own hands, she told Him: "They have no more wine" (John 2:3, NIV). A simple statement of fact. What would He do?

His response in modern terminology would have sounded like "Mom, why Me? It's not My time." Prefacing His question with the respectful term "Woman," the same term used when He addressed her while hanging on the cross, Jesus asked the question: "What does your concern have to do with Me? My hour has not yet come" (verse 4, NKJV). Sounds to me as if He had slammed the door on her hoped-for solution to the wine problem. I like it that she had no response to Him. Instead, her next words were an order to the servants standing around with their trays of empty glasses waiting to be refilled. Ignoring Jesus' last statement of fact, Mary nods toward Him while instructing the servants: "Whatever He says to you, do it" (verse 5, NKJV).

In hushed tones, not attracting any attention to Himself, Jesus pointed toward six unusually large stone jars and said: "Fill the waterpots with water" (verse 7, NJKV). That is a very normal and unsurprising thing to request when it comes to waterpots. Each held 20 to 30 gallons of water, and they were used for ceremonial washing. Fill the waterpots with water. No big deal. Right? What happened next was surprising and quite unusual. But servants are programmed to act, not ask questions. So when Jesus said, "Draw some out now, and take it to the master of the feast" (verse 8, NKJV), they probably thought, *Oh, boy, this won't be pretty.* But they did it anyway and filled them to the brim. And it was the best wine ever, because freshly made juice is always best.

Is the Creator of all that exists limited to photosynthesis as His only way of producing juice? His daily routine is making miracles happen.

Lord of everyday miracles, I long for a face-to-face relationship with You just as Your mother had with You. Do I dare trust You as she did? O Lord, build that trust in me.

December 28

Letters

You are our epistle written in our hearts, known and read by all men; clearly you are an epistle of Christ, ministered by us, written not with ink but by the Spirit of the living God, not on tablets of stone but on tablets of flesh, that is, of the heart. 2 Cor. 3:2, 3, NKJV.

I wasn't expecting a letter from them, actually. But I recognized the return address. Our past several letter exchanges had all been about one topic of great concern to both of us, so I expected this to be a follow-up. But on reading the letter, it was, instead, a gracious thank-you note for some help I had given so long ago that I had totally forgotten about it. Whether the contents of the envelope is a thank-you note, a letter of acceptance, or one of rejection, introduction, resignation, or recommendation, letters are a way to communicate clearly and formally an important idea.

We do it so much by e-mail now that many people are losing their ability to write beautiful cursive letters. It is still a good idea to take out a nice sheet of quality notepaper and your best fountain pen that feels good in your hand and paints a beautiful line as you brush its nib across the paper. There is something timeless about getting a carefully composed and inscribed handwritten note. For some things, e-mail just doesn't measure up.

I wonder what kind of letter King David wrote, sealed, and then handed to Uriah the Hittite, asking him to deliver it to Joab. Perhaps it was written on coarse paper, probably with a reed brush. Whatever the case, Uriah was delivering his own death sentence. That just has to be the worst kind of letter to be carrying to your commander.

Most letters are addressed to just one individual. They may in fact be marked "confidential" to warn others away. The open letter, on the other hand, has a message of interest to all, or it has information that all need to know.

The letter being described by Paul above opens by asking if he needs a letter of recommendation and then follows by letting the reader know that he or she is in fact the letter of recommendation. That would be me and you. Paul declares, "You are a letter from Christ, known and read by all." He goes on to add that it is not written in ink, nor on slabs of stone, but on "tablets of flesh." I am still trying to get my mind around this. I am a letter of recommendation for God. He has personally written His law on my heart and declares that He will be my God and I will be His person.

Lord, You mean that I am an open letter, known and read by all? Father, without the fruit of the Spirit in my heart, I am sure to blow it. Help me now.

Microsaccades

Fixing our eyes on Jesus, the pioneer and perfecter of faith. Heb. 12:2, NIV.

I t takes two to do this experiment. Get in good light and move close so that you can carefully watch the eyes of your research partner. Then ask them to look intently at a stationary object. If you're a careful observer, you will see their eyes constantly jerking around in tiny movements. These tiny involuntary eye movements called microsaccades have been the focus of a great deal of research. Why can't the eyes hold perfectly still, locked in on a fine target? What is the cause of microsaccades and for what purpose? One conclusion is that the fine movement gives slightly different areas of the retina the chance to detect, which provides for superior image processing by the brain. Another is that this type of movement allows us to spot a new object in the visual field quicker. Something new in the picture gets instant attention. Yet another conclusion is that if the eye didn't move, what we look at would fade from view as the visual cells fatigue. By constantly moving the image, it uses different cells.

The injunction of Hebrews 12 is to look to Jesus, the "author and finisher" of our faith (verse 2, NKJV). How often I have looked to Jesus, then back at myself again, feeling confidently that "my faith is strong." But if Jesus is both the author and finisher, then all the faith I have comes from Him. I need to keep my eyes on Him.

Listen to these sentiments. "I have a strong grip on Christ. My joy is in Christ. I want to serve God in marriage ministry. I think that the church should get involved in more inner-city work. I am going to bring three (or 30) people to Christ this year." Notice that the focus is on self rather than on Christ. Remember that Satan's efforts focus on getting us to look at ourselves rather than Christ. The Holy Spirit's work is to pull my gaze off of self and lock it on Christ.

It is in looking to Jesus that I have hope (cf. Job 8:13). Jesus is the one that holds me in His grasp, in His strong arm that will not let me go (Ps. 18:35; 139:10). Nor is it my joy in Christ that saves me, I am not here to do my work but that of my Father. My prayers have no power except that it is Christ's will. Oh, how often I look away from Jesus.

My Jesus, watch my eyes; remind me when I take them off of You and say to others around me, "Look at me! Look at what I have done." Lord, let me not be wise in my own eyes.

Static Charge

Behold, God is exalted by His power; who teaches like Him?
Job 36:22, NKJV.

Have you learned two or three new wonders of our Creator-God in reading these pages this year? If so, I praise God, because that was part of the plan. No doubt, you already knew much of what you read here, but it never hurts to refresh the memory and pick up yet another opportunity to praise and worship our awesome God. As you can guess, there is so much more territory left to explore, so much more information to discover about the beauty and complexity of God's creation, and so many more connections to make between understanding the natural world and what we can learn about the character of our Creator. My guess is that we will be spending at least a year or two of eternity in a study of this type—maybe more.

That we have so much more to learn was illustrated this morning when I discovered a new theory about static electricity. Now, you would think that static electricity is rather mundane. We have probably learned all about how it works. Rub a balloon on your hair or scrape your shoes across a carpet, and an electrical charge builds up. The balloon will probably stick to the ceiling or to your clothes, your hair stands on end, and you can pass the charge to an unsuspecting classmate's earlobe and get a good laugh out of it. What we have taught for decades is that rubbing nonconductive stuff together causes ions or electrons to transfer from one of the items to the other, thus building up a charge.

Bartosz Grzybowski used a powerful Kelvin force probe microscope to study the surface of nonconductive polymers that had been rubbed together in order to generate a charge. What he learned is that at the nanoscale level, an actual transfer of material occurred from one surface to the other. Thus, instead of just transferring electrons and some negative ions to one and building a positive charge on the other, he discovered patches of both negative and positive charges on both pieces. Indeed, he found wholesale transfer of material from one to the other and vice versa, leaving little fragments of charged material attached. The net charge of all the fragments is what counts.

Isn't every human interaction somewhat like that? I know some who tend to draw my energy, leaving me feeling drained. Others energize and renew me. Does every human interaction involve more than the exchange of pleasantries?

Lord, how do I interact with others? Do I build them up or tear them down? Help me to realize that every encounter is a divine appointment and that I represent You, the Lord of power and light.

December 31

No More

And God will wipe away every tear from their eyes; there shall be no more death, nor sorrow, nor crying. There shall be no more pain, for the former things have passed away. Rev. 21:4, NKJV.

What we have not experienced, we simply cannot comprehend. Thus describing the bliss and beauty of heaven is all well and good, but it is an exercise in futility, because we cannot imagine it (1 Cor. 2:9). Perhaps that is why the Scriptures portray heaven in terms of what we can understand. In heaven, with Jesus, there will be no more tears, no more pain, no more cuts and bruises or skinned knees, no more pain of death, no more goodbyes, no more loneliness, no more broken relationships, no more arguments, no more fighting, no more separation, no more divorce, no more abortion, no more abandonment, no more spousal or child or employee abuse, no more slavery, no more coercion of any kind. That means there will be no more fear, no more sickness, no more cancer, no more disease, no more broken bones, hearts, windows, or homes. No more hunger or starvation, no more thirst, no more shortness of breath or asphyxiation. No more predation, no more parasites. There will be no more killing oneself slowly with alcohol, tobacco, or drugs, and no more killing oneself quickly by jumping off a bridge or a building or pulling the trigger. No more guns, no more bombs, no more terrorism. Nothing will hurt or destroy. Heaven will contain nothing that causes pain, sorrow, or tears.

Are you noticing that these are things so common in our sin-sick world that we hardly take notice anymore? We accept them as the reality of life. How sad. But in heaven there will be no more sin or selfishness, no more deceit, no more cheating, no more lying, no more greed, no more looking for love in all the wrong places, no more philandering, no more sorcery or witchcraft, no killing, no war. Heaven will have no more backstabbing, no more scheming how to get ahead, no more gossip, no more cunning, no more guile, no more defamation of character. No more empty entertainment or gambling. People will cease chasing after other gods, breaking the Sabbath, dishonoring parents, and committing murder or adultery. No one will steal or lie against their neighbor. And there won't be any wishing for anything more because, at last, our joy will be full. Even so, come, Lord Jesus.

My Lord and my God, my alpha and omega, all praise and honor is Yours in heaven and on earth for ever and ever. My heart is filled with joy indescribable just thinking about it.

TEACH Services, Inc.

P U B L I S H I N G

We invite you to view the complete
selection of titles we publish at:
www.TEACHServices.com

We encourage you to write us
with your thoughts about this,
or any other book we publish at:
info@TEACHServices.com

TEACH Services' titles may be purchased in
bulk quantities for educational, fund-raising,
business, or promotional use.
bulksales@TEACHServices.com

Finally, if you are interested in seeing
your own book in print, please contact us at:
publishing@TEACHServices.com

We are happy to review your manuscript at no charge.